Yale Agrarian Studies Series

James C. Scott, series editor

The Agrarian Studies Series at Yale University Press seeks to publish outstanding and original interdisciplinary work on agriculture and rural society—for any period, in any location. Works of daring that question existing paradigms and fill abstract categories with the lived-experience of rural people are especially encouraged.

—JAMES C. SCOTT, *SERIES EDITOR*

James C. Scott, *Seeing Like a State: How Certain Schemes to Improve the Human Condition Have Failed*

Brian Donahue, *The Great Meadow: Farmers and the Land in Colonial Concord*

J. Gary Taylor and Patricia J. Scharlin, *Smart Alliance: How a Global Corporation and Environmental Activists Transformed a Tarnished Brand*

Michael Goldman, *Imperial Nature: The World Bank and Struggles for Social Justice in the Age of Globalization*

Arvid Nelson, *Cold War Ecology: Forests, Farms, and People in the East German Landscape, 1945–1989*

Steve Striffler, *Chicken: The Dangerous Transformation of America's Favorite Food*

Parker Shipton, *The Nature of Entrustment: Intimacy, Exchange, and the Sacred in Africa*

Alissa Hamilton, *Squeezed: What You Don't Know About Orange Juice*

Parker Shipton, *Mortgaging the Ancestors: Ideologies of Attachment in Africa*

Bill Winders, *The Politics of Food Supply: U.S. Agricultural Policy in the World Economy*

James C. Scott, *The Art of Not Being Governed: An Anarchist History of Upland Southeast Asia*

Stephen K. Wegren, *Land Reform in Russia: Institutional Design and Behavioral Responses*

Benjamin R. Cohen, *Notes from the Ground: Science, Soil, and Society in the American Countryside*

Parker Shipton, *Credit Between Cultures: Farmers, Financiers, and Misunderstanding in Africa*

Paul Sillitoe, *From Land to Mouth: The Agricultural "Economy" of the Wola of the New Guinea Highlands*

Sara M. Gregg, *Managing the Mountains: Land Use Planning, the New Deal, and the Creation of a Federal Landscape in Appalachia*

Michael Dove, *The Banana Tree at the Gate: A History of Marginal Peoples and Global Markets in Borneo*

Patrick Barron, Rachael Diprose, and Michael Woolcock, *Contesting Development: Participatory Projects and Local Conflict Dynamics in Indonesia*

For a complete list of titles in the Yale Agrarian Studies Series, visit www.yalebooks.com.

Contesting Development

Participatory Projects and Local
Conflict Dynamics in Indonesia

Patrick Barron

Rachael Diprose

Michael Woolcock

Yale UNIVERSITY PRESS
NEW HAVEN & LONDON

Yale University Press books may be purchased in quantity for educational, business, or promotional use. For information, please e-mail sales.press@yale.edu (U.S. office) or sales@yaleup.co.uk (U.K. office).

Set in Ehrhardt Roman type by IDS Infotech Ltd., Chandigarh, India.
Printed in the United States of America.

Library of Congress Cataloging-in-Publication Data

Barron, Patrick, 1977–
    Contesting development : participatory projects and local conflict dynamics in Indonesia / Patrick Barron, Rachael Diprose, Michael Woolcock.
        p. cm. — (Yale agrarian studies series)
    Includes bibliographical references and index.
    ISBN 978-0-300-12631-0 (hardcover : alk. paper) 1. Social conflict—Indonesia. 2. Conflict management—Indonesia. 3. Community development—Indonesia. 4. Economic development projects—Indonesia—Citizen participation. 5. Economic development projects—Political aspects—Indonesia. 6. Economic development—Political aspects—Indonesia. I. Diprose, Rachael. II. Woolcock, Michael J. V., 1964—III. Title.
    HN710.Z9S6233 2010
    307.1'409598091734—dc22

                                                                                    2010025125

A catalogue record for this book is available from the British Library.

This paper meets the requirements of ANSI/NISO Z39.48–1992 (Permanence of Paper).

10 9 8 7 6 5 4 3 2 1

This book is dedicated to the extraordinary team of field researchers who conducted the qualitative components of this study.

In East Java:	In East Nusa Tenggara:
Endro Crentantoro	Adam Satu
Imron Rasyid	Agus Mahur
Luthfi Ashari	Don dela Santo
Mohammed Said	Olin Monteiro
Novia Cici Anggraini	Peter Manggut
Saifullah Barnawi	Stanis Didakus
	Yan Ghewa

Each demonstrated patience and perseverance far beyond the call of duty and in the process generated a wealth of valuable knowledge and afforded us a unique glimpse into the dynamics of social and political change in rural Indonesia. It has been a pleasure and a privilege to learn from them and to have them as our guides on this journey. We hope that the quality and usefulness of the findings reported here (and their implications) do justice to their efforts and talents and those of the broader community of scholars, activists, public officials, journalists, development practitioners, and (most important) everyday citizens committed to making democracy work in Indonesia.

Nothing short of great political genius can save a sovereign who undertakes to relieve his subjects after a long period of oppression. The evils which were endured with patience so long as they were inevitable seem intolerable as soon as a hope can be entertained of escaping from them. The abuses which are removed seem to lay bare those which remain, and to render the sense of them more acute; the evil has decreased, it is true, but the perception of the evil is more keen.

—ALEXIS DE TOCQUEVILLE, *THE OLD REGIME AND THE FRENCH REVOLUTION*

It is not, after all, standing outside the social order in some excited state of self-regard that makes a political leader numinous but a deep, intimate involvement—affirming or abhorring, defensive or destructive—in the master fictions by which that order lives.

—CLIFFORD GEERTZ, *LOCAL KNOWLEDGE*

One might well ask: Why are we here, in a village of no particular significance, examining the struggle of a handful of history's losers? For there is little doubt on this last score. The poor of Sedeka are almost certainly, to use Barrington Moore's phrase, members of "a class over whom the wave of progress is about to roll." . . . The justification for such an enterprise must lie precisely in its banality—in the fact that these circumstances are the normal context in which class conflict has historically occurred. By examining these circumstances closely, it may be possible to say something meaningful about normal class consciousness, about everyday resistance, about commonplace class consciousness where, as is most often the case, neither outright collective defiance nor rebellion is likely or possible.

—JAMES C. SCOTT, *WEAPONS OF THE WEAK:*
EVERYDAY FORMS OF PEASANT RESISTANCE

Contents

Preface

C*ontesting Development* examines three pressing issues at the nexus of social change and development policy in low-income countries, namely (1) the nature and extent of local-level conflict that accompanies institutional transitions, (2) the role of development projects in shaping those institutional transitions and conflict dynamics, and (3) strategies for designing, implementing, and assessing project responses in transitional institutional environments. It examines these issues on the basis of a detailed empirical assessment of the way a large-scale participatory development project in rural Indonesia—the government of Indonesia's World Bank–supported Kecamatan Development Program (KDP)—interacts with local contexts and conflict dynamics and of the way it influences participants' capacity to respond to them. By *local conflict* we mean disputes—violent and nonviolent—that play out at the local level, within and between villages.

The project operates at the *kecamatan,* or subdistrict, level, below the central, provincial, and district levels, the units at which formal government authority and bureaucratic power are primarily exercised in Indonesia. Although KDP was not designed to reduce local violent conflict, it provides a particularly interesting lens through which to examine the relation between development processes (including projects, programs, and policy reforms) and local conflict. At a cumulative cost of almost three billion dollars, and having evolved since the late 1990s to become a nationwide program, KDP is the largest social development project in Asia and one of the World Bank's flagship "community-driven development" (CDD)

programs. As the community-driven banner implies, KDP is a decentralized project that affords significant opportunities for use of discretion
by local-level staff and substantive input by village communities at every
stage in the design, selection, and implementation process; its primary
objective is to help participants secure small sub-projects (roads, bridges,
water pipes) that accord with their particular needs, priorities, and values.
That is, KDP has an overarching implementation framework for all participating villages, but its design explicitly allows for flexibility in the way
different local environments and peoples are accommodated.

The program attempts to realize the objective of ensuring that funds
match with local needs by applying the design principles of participation,
transparency, accountability, and harnessing of local knowledge to a competitive bidding process. In so doing it aims to help poor villagers (with a
particular focus on members of the most marginalized groups) acquire new
civic skills, decision-making opportunities, and monitoring responsibilities
in order to realize their aspirations. Such skills and opportunities are also
vital for mediating in constructive ways the conflicts that KDP itself inevitably produces, such as those generated by competition over finite resources,
the issuance of challenges to elite power, and instances of malfeasance and
implementation failure. When and where it works well, does KDP in fact
achieve the indirect goal of increasing villagers' capacity to mediate the
conflict that KDP has generated? Does any such ability spill over into a
heightened capacity to manage *non*project disputes? How does KDP compare to other development projects and the conflicts that they generate?
How significant are the characteristics of the local context in shaping project efficacy? More generally, to what extent do development responses that
emphasize change at the local level constitute a new and effective way for
the international community and for governments (national, regional, and
local alike) to manage civil conflict?

Indonesia provides an interesting, important, and instructive case
study of the new forms of intra-country conflict that have been increasingly prominent since the cold war. Following the East Asian financial crisis,
the fall of Suharto's authoritarian New Order government in 1998 led to a
rapid but uneven democratization and decentralization of the Indonesian
state, a transition that was accompanied by an upsurge in violent conflict,
with major outbreaks in at least six provinces and widespread local conflict
across the archipelago. If the development process is understood as one of
managing in constructive ways the conflicts inherent in social and political

change, then it is vital to verify empirically which response strategies work (and which do not), and why. Indonesia's very visible local-level political transitions and the policies and projects enacted to support and respond to them can provide many useful insights into the suitability and sustainability of different conflict management and state-building interventions in other contexts in the developing world. They also enable us to learn more about how a broad array of theories and methods from across the social sciences can be harnessed to assess their efficacy and about the processes by which different types of impact obtain.

Contesting Development is structured as follows. After an introductory chapter outlining the core arguments, evidence, and implications, Part I introduces the major substantive issues to be explored, the specific case study under investigation, and its political and organizational context. Part II attempts to answer questions pertaining to KDP's impact on the basis of extensive empirical evidence that combines qualitative and quantitative methods and data. This evidence is used to frame a comparative assessment of the direct and indirect ways in which KDP (vis-à-vis other development projects) influences local conflict trajectories in a variety of contexts. In Part III, this evidence is then used to inform a broader discussion about the potential role of social theory and research in development policy and practice and, in particular, to provide a framework for understanding the micropolitics of institutional transitions. This body of theory about social change, we contend, is at the heart of the design and implementation of KDP and should explicitly underpin many more development projects (of all kinds), especially those seeking to empower the poor and enhance the demand side of governance reform.

Most important, perhaps, it is not KDP per se that should be replicated—in matters pertaining to governance and legal reform, we argue, institutional isomorphism is bad history, bad theory, and bad practice—but instead the intensive research process that preceded and produced it. This research process helped KDP's founders elucidate key details pertaining to the workings of local societies and of governments and how knowledge of both could be incorporated into development programs seeking to introduce new concepts, principles, and practices. KDP attempted to do so in ways that would not trigger violence but would support the development of legitimate and effective mechanisms for the allocation of resources, while also encouraging broader processes of proto-democratic institutional reform (enhancing civic capacity). Furthermore, vigilant oversight—through ongoing research and evaluation at every stage—allowed for constant program refinement and ensured that the process remained flexible so that social change could be managed over time. Doing all of this requires a strong understanding of the local context beyond the program and a deep appreciation of widespread subnational variation in cultures, histories, and institutions as well as the influence of the state.

A number of people helped with the analysis presented and helped write sections of particular chapters. Michael Woolcock, Claire Smith, and Patrick Barron developed the initial hypotheses and research questions. Claire Smith co-managed the project in the preparation and data collection stages; Patrick Barron managed or co-managed the study from inception to completion. Claire Smith, Rachael Diprose, and Patrick Barron designed and wrote all of the field guides, survey instruments, and data collection methods, conducting many iterations of training and feedback workshops with the research team. Scott Guggenheim, Sri Kuntari, and Michael Woolcock provided guidance and support throughout the study. Qualitative data and analysis are taken largely from provincial reports on East Java (written by Rachael Diprose) and on Nusa Tenggara Timur (NTT) (written by Adam Satu and Patrick Barron). Suzan Piper, Joanne Sharpe, Jessica Gillmore, and Kristen Stokes translated much of the material from Indonesian to English. Samuel Clark and Ambar Mawardi collated the key informant survey data used throughout the book and conducted some of the analysis. Joanne Sharpe supervised the collection and collation of the newspaper dataset and was deeply involved in the analysis. Karrie McLaughlin, with the support of Ambar Mawardi, led the quantitative analysis presented in Chapter 4, which looks at the relative incidence of conflict in KDP and non-KDP areas. Samuel Clark helped write parts of Chapter 7. The maps were designed by Margaret Stewart.

The field researchers were Endro Crentantoro, Imron Rasyid, Luthfi Ashari, Mohammed Said, Novia Cici Anggraini, Saifullah Barnawi, Agus Mahur, Don dela Santo, Olin Monteiro, Peter Manggut, Stanis Didakus, and Yan Ghewa. They were supervised in the field by Rachael Diprose (East Java) and by Adam Satu and Jessica Gillmore (NTT), who worked closely with the researchers to collect data, construct detailed case studies, and conduct preliminary qualitative data analysis. Ambar Mawardi, Budi Santoso, Don dela Santo, Elisabeth Dua Soru, Getrudis Erni, Hafez, Mirnawati Ladongga, Mohammed Said, and Susan Mety were involved in creating and cleaning the newspaper datasets. Representatives of the Indonesian government and of the KDP program also provided support and useful input. Thanks in particular to Suprayoga Hadi of the National Development Planning Agency. Others who contributed at various stages of the research included Vivi Alatas, Anton Baare, Victor Bottini, Juana Brachet, Linda Ayu Citra, Jozefina Cutura, Muslahuddin Daud, Leni Dharmawan, Christopher Gibson, Suprayoga Hadi, Ela Hasanah, Alexa Hergesell, Sidney Jones, Kai Kaiser, Yatrin Kaniu, David Madden, Olivia Melissa, Zeyd Muhammad, Melina Nathan, Ben Olken, Junko Onishi, Menno Pradhan, Arie Purwanti, Taufik Rinaldi, Michael Roston, Sentot Satria, Bambang Soetono, Matthew Stephens, Yuhki Tajima, Inge Tan, Peter Uvin, Katherine Whiteside, Ewa Wojkowska, Susan Wong, and Andrea Woodhouse. Ongoing conversations with Daniel Adler, Xavier de Souza Briggs, Scott Guggenheim, Lant Pritchett, Caroline Sage, and Ashutosh Varshney were instrumental in shaping the broader theoretical framework for understanding the dynamics of institutional change at the local level and strategies for crafting interim institutions that foster both civic capacity and organizational learning.

This book is part of an ongoing research project on local-level conflict and participatory development projects in Indonesia that is overseen by the Conflict and Development Program within the Social Development Department of the World Bank, Jakarta. (The various scholarly and policy outputs of this larger project are available online at www.conflictanddevelopment.org.) For generous financial assistance for the project as a whole and for funding this study in particular we are grateful to DfID, AusAID, the Norwegian Trust Fund (Measuring Empowerment Study, coordinated by Ruth Alsop), and three units of the World Bank: the Conflict Prevention and Reconstruction Unit (led at the time by Ian Bannon), the Social Development Department, and the Development Economics Vice Presidency (especially the Research Support Budget–funded study of Community-Driven Development Projects, led by Ghazala Mansuri). Michael Woolcock extends his thanks to the Brooks World Poverty Institute at the University of Manchester, where he was based in 2007–9 as the final stages of this book were completed. Rachael Diprose extends her thanks to her DPhil supervisors Frances Stewart and Raufu Mustapha at the Department of International Development, the University of Oxford, where she was based in 2005–10, for their patience and support during the completion of the manuscript. Patrick Barron thanks Nuffield College, the University of Oxford, where he was based during the final stages of the project. For helpful and detailed comments on earlier drafts, we extend particular thanks to Junaid Ahmad, Michael Dove,

Scott Guggenheim, Rick Messick, David Mosse, Susan Wong, and Yongmei Zhou, and, of course, to the field research team and our anonymous peer reviewers.

Timely comments were also provided by seminar participants at George Mason University, Johns Hopkins University (SAIS), Harvard University, the University of Manchester, MIT, the University of Oxford, Princeton University, Universitas Indonesia, the World Bank (Jakarta and Washington), and Yale University, as well as at the Southeast Asia Conflict Studies Network conference in Penang, the American Political Science Association annual meeting in Philadelphia, the European Association for Southeast Asian Studies conference in Paris, and the MOST-LIPI/UNESCO conference on Conflict in the Asia-Pacific Region in Jakarta.

Jean Thomson Black, our editor at Yale University Press, has been both admirably patient and encouraging as we have found our collective voice. Thanks in particular to Jack Borrebach and all the production team at the press for their help. We have done our best to respond to the constructive suggestions from these very different quarters, but inevitably could not do justice to them all.

Our respective partners, families, and friends have had to endure our many long absences in the quest to bring this large study to completion; a final and very special thanks to them for their forbearance and active support over the course of many years.

Contesting Development

CHAPTER 1

Institutional Change, Development Projects, and Local Conflict Dynamics

To most observers, the village of Wates in the district of Ponorogo, East Java, appears much like hundreds of thousands of others in the developing world. In many respects, to echo James Scott, Wates is "a village of no particular significance." It is not in the crossfire of a raging civil war or sectarian violence; it is not besieged by HIV/AIDS; it is not suffering from drought, pestilence, or floods—it is, rather, the quintessential rural village in a steadily growing developing country. Absent such major problems, "doing development" in Wates should be relatively straightforward.[1] It is regularly selected to receive development projects because its residents are poor (though not, for the most part, extremely or chronically so); East Java, as Indonesian provinces go, is quite prosperous, and Ponorogo, by all informed accounts, is reasonably well governed (in that it is free from large-scale violence) compared with other districts in the country. Accordingly, one might expect development projects in Wates to be appropriately designed and dutifully implemented and to have, in due course, a positive impact. The logic of international development assistance is predicated on being able to identify villages such as Wates and provide them with resources in the form of projects—primary schools, health clinics, credit schemes, irrigation systems—that enhance their residents' welfare and to verify that such enhancement has in fact taken place. Both the problem (poverty) and the solution (projects) seem sufficiently clear and measurable; with appropriate human and financial resources and adequate managerial oversight, it is not unreasonable to presume that the residents of places like Wates will, indeed, become the beneficiaries of development and to infer that the projects bringing this about can be expanded and replicated elsewhere.

For all the books about development that open with horror stories of private graft and public corruption, the hubris, extravagance, and recalcitrance (or worse) of development agencies, the unspeakable crimes committed against innocent women and children, or graphic accounts of the extraordinary survival strategies of slum dwellers, it is unfortunately the case that one much less frequently encounters discussions of the circumstances that more plausibly characterize, at least at one level, the lives of most poor people in most poor places most of the time. These circumstances, viewed historically (Fogel 2004) and at the aggregate level in South Asia and East Asia (where most of the world's poor people live), are ones displaying steady, if highly uneven, material improvement.[2] We chose to begin with Wates precisely because of its seeming "banality," to cite Scott again, because it provides an eminently normal context within which to explore the sweeping dynamics of institutional change taking place across the developing world in the early twenty-first century. This is an age characterized by rising integration and exclusion, prosperity and inequality, hope and frustration, heightened awareness of diversity and similarity, and—most important for our purposes—a pervasive belief that external agents (of any kind, national or international) have the ethical obligation, political mandate, and necessary knowledge to intervene for the better in the lives of the less fortunate.

Banality may be a less than compelling premise on which to secure funding for development projects or research programs, but it need not mean that something is uneventful, uninteresting, or uninstructive. On the contrary, we hope to show that villages such as Wates are in fact high-energy environments for exploring and understanding the fundamental questions pertaining to processes of institutional change, the conflicts to which they inherently give rise, and the role that development projects play in helping or hindering them.[3] Greater understanding of the dynamics and complexities of development in normal contexts, especially in places not encumbered by the large-scale civic strife that makes development even more complex, might also enhance the efficacy of policy initiatives undertaken in more difficult circumstances, where the challenges of good governance and institution-building are yet more pressing.

Wates is interesting to us because it was selected to participate in the Kecamatan Development Program (KDP), a large, decentralized participatory development project unveiled by the Government of Indonesia and the World Bank in the final years (as it turned out) of the Suharto regime. It was rapidly scaled up in 1998 and beyond following the departure of the New Order government in the wake of the East Asian financial crisis. Indonesia was hit especially hard by the crisis, enduring a collapse in economic activity on a scale close to that of the Great Depression (Krugman 2000). At the time, it was vital for the ongoing credibility of both the new government and the World Bank to respond promptly and effectively to the crisis but to do so in ways that marked a clear departure from policies that only a few years earlier had been hailed (or excused) for their capacity to yield spectacular rates of economic growth and thus poverty reduction (Guggenheim 2006).[4]

The program, designed by social scientists on the basis of a national study conducted in the mid-1990s on local-level institutions, spoke to these needs and imperatives: it promised to deliver resources to hard-hit communities at a scale and speed large enough to make a discernable economic impact but in ways that were qualitatively different from those of the past. In this sense, as Mosse (2005b) and Mosse and Lewis (2005) observe, KDP was also part of a broader change in development assistance in the late 1990s that saw many international agencies shifting attention away from large-scale technical assistance initiatives to governance reform based on bottom-up participation and institution-building, a process facilitated by "the failings of ruling regimes (including corruption within them) [that were] no longer censured as internal matters but . . . [became] central to the concerns of external donors" (Mosse 2005b, 4). Beyond the politics of national-level or development agency agendas, KDP's emphasis on participation, institution-building, and governance reform meant that it fell within (indeed, embodied) this "new architecture" (Mosse 2005b) of development assistance.

Participants in KDP would be active contributors to, not passive recipients of, decisions pertaining to the type and location of development projects in their villages.[5] Using a competitive bidding model, groups of villagers would be encouraged (by means of ongoing collaboration with trained facilitators) to prepare proposals for funding and to present them to a meeting at the village and then the *kecamatan* (subdistrict) level, where their peers—not government officials or development experts—would decide by means of deliberation and discussion (and in the event of disagreement, via a public vote) which proposals best met the criteria of poverty reduction, cost effectiveness, immediate need, and sustainability. Some proposals would be accepted and receive funding, and others would not. Decisions reached, and the bases for them, would then be posted on community bulletin boards for all to see; after funds had been dispersed, accountability meetings would be held to ensure that resources were spent as intended. Government officials from the village level upward would be involved in the process, but—in a marked change from the past—would not determine needs or make decisions about funding priorities. Journalists would be welcome to monitor the project at every stage and free to report on what they observed. In this sense, the designers of KDP hoped that it would achieve more than simply the large-scale dispersal of resources to poor communities in the aftermath of a financial crisis; they also hoped that, by changing the very processes and procedures by which decisions affecting everyday village life were made, they could cultivate long-suppressed civic skills and instill new precedents regarding resource allocation mechanisms that, in time, would become a defining feature of transparent and accountable local government in Indonesia. In short, KDP would be a democracy project disguised as—or at least as well as—a development project.

Not long after KDP's inception, the subdistrict where Wates was situated was selected to take part in the program, which meant that it would conduct three rounds of decision making about the allocation of development resources in as many years. With each round, villagers became increasingly familiar with project rules and procedures, and those who had yet to have their proposals accepted became correspondingly confident that their turn would soon come, particularly if their needs were at one point in time more pressing than those in other villages nearby. In the third year, however, two hamlets in Wates—Bedog and Joso—both proposed the paving of roads, and it soon became apparent that only one of them would be funded. When the proposal from Bedog lost out at the KDP decision meeting, participants "were locked in argument," observed a community leader. Bedog had submitted its proposal twice before but had never received funding because the amount of money needed was relatively large. Determined to win funding this time, group members had spent three months performing community service (*kerja bakti*) to widen the road in the hope that this would make funding more likely. Problems intensified when the proposal verification team who examined the technical viability of the proposal said the road was still not wide enough. Further, the village head was worried that there would be complications because the road to be paved passed though state forestry land, and there was no permit to allow paving. When they lost for the third time, "the Bedog community felt very disappointed with the competition results," said a local teacher. "How else would they feel?"

Unhappily for the Bedog team, the Joso proposal won. The village head was from Joso, and villagers started to suspect him of bias; it did not help matters that one of the village-level KDP facilitators was the village head's younger sibling. As the news sunk in, residents of Bedog became increasingly upset and felt that this latest setback was a continuation of an ongoing trend which had resulted in their exclusion from the development of Wates. Disappointment and suspicion fed into other problems in the village, in particular, the polarization with regard to two different candidates in the upcoming local village head elections. No explicit violence resulted, but relations in the village worsened. In the same subdistrict, competition at the intervillage level also led to tensions: certain villages that had not had their proposals funded accused the KDP subdistrict facilitator of receiving bribes, although no evidence was produced. In retaliation, some of the villages that lost refused to pay the land and building tax to the subdistrict authorities.

The program may have elicited these kinds of tensions, but in the years before the project began Wates was hardly an oasis of harmony or a village untouched by development efforts. In 2001 an international NGO was evicted from the village after local leaders spread rumors that the NGO, funded by countries with majority Christian populations, was proselytizing for Christianity. (Wates is predominantly Muslim.) Furthermore, many youth in the village were members of *silat* (martial arts) groups, and tensions led to violence when members of the Winongo silat group were beaten by members of the rival Terate group.[6] Local political ruptures helped intensify conflict. The 1999 village elections saw the displacement of the incumbent elite. Traditionally, losing candidates tend to assume other political roles in the village; for example, they become members of the Village Development Council (LKMD).[7] But when the council was reconfigured following the shift to regional autonomy, some members lost their jobs. Such challenges to traditional power structures also led to widening sociopolitical divisions in the community, increasing the likelihood that local conflicts would escalate. No one in Wates had been killed in violent conflict in recent memory. Yet tensions disrupted social life.

This is a snippet of everyday life in a normal village in Indonesia. In its very ordinariness, we suggest, life in Wates exemplifies the processes of social change encountered by millions of people in low- and middle-income countries today and shows the ways in which such change is contested. Change and contestation are driven by forces far larger than particular development projects, but as initiatives explicitly mounted to intensify the pace of change, development projects enable us to examine change itself, the dynamics of contention surrounding it, and the ways in which both of these can be affected by the introduction of external resources and rules. In this sense our study seeks to build on research that has shown how development actors bring their own cultural heritage, agendas, politics, and interests to the development process and how this shapes their understanding and adoption of a program's (institutional) rules, which may result in a reality very different from the one envisioned by development policy makers (Mosse 2005a, 2005b; Mosse and Lewis 2005; Cornwall and Coelho 2007). We focus on the experiences of participants in and observers of KDP over time and the mechanisms by which they manage the contests that it generates.

For our purposes, it is important to note that change and contention may be products of development failure (for example, corruption or malfeasance) but that they also accompany "success."[8] In Indonesia, a crippling financial crisis has passed, democratic government has replaced a repressive dictatorship, a secessionist war has ended, absolute poverty is falling, and health indicators, education levels, and foreign investment are all improving ("Democracy in South-East Asia" 2009; Mietzner 2008). Indonesia's seemingly "quiet revolution" (Rieffel 2004) has been hailed as a resounding success. Development projects, widely defined, have contributed to such material progress; billions of dollars in investment from the public and private sectors have generated more and better roads, provided ubiquitous mobile phone coverage, and expanded irrigation systems; policy changes have lowered transaction costs, raised productivity, facilitated internal and overseas migration, and enhanced access to markets and services. Indonesia is on track to meet Millennium Development Goals such as achieving universal primary education, promoting gender equality, and reducing child mortality.[9] And yet, far from the attention of the global media or most international observers, local conflict, some of it violent, is prevalent across Indonesia (Varshney 2008; Barron et al. 2009b).[10]

This is hardly Indonesia's problem alone. Conflict is widespread in democratic, increasingly prosperous India (Brass 2003; Varshney 2002; Wilkinson 2004),[11] and the biggest contemporary developmental success of all, socialist China, is experiencing similar regional convulsions in conjunction with its economic boom (Perry and Seldon 2003; Unger 2002), to the extent that one knowledgeable observer calls it a "ticking time bomb" (Muldavin 2006). Such countries, like today's rich and middle-income countries before them, are in the midst of a "great transformation" (Polanyi 1944)[12] that is fundamentally remaking and realigning their institutions, power structures, and class relations. Development, whether driven by capitalism or by socialism, reconfigures prevailing social structures, rules systems, and political arrangements by altering (among other things) social identities, intergroup relations, the bases of collective action, and the distribution of power.[13] If social revolutions are in fact more likely as material conditions *improve* than as they deteriorate, as an influential strand of social theory has long maintained,[14] the policy challenge for all developing countries, but especially increasingly prosperous ones, is to build institutions that can adapt to changing economic and political conditions and that can manage in constructive ways the ongoing tensions, conflicts, and reconfigurations that such change elicits. Left unchecked, these processes have the potential to undo many of the hard-won accomplishments achieved to date or create openings for resurgent populist dictators. If "nothing short of great political genius" is required to manage transitions "after long periods of oppression," as de Tocqueville astutely observed during the years following the French Revolution, how can the development community today, both international and domestic, anticipate and respond to this challenge in ways that are equitable and legitimate and that limit violence? More generally, if prosperity and violence tend to go hand in hand (Bates 2000), what are the implications for development theory, policy, and practice?

For all the millions of dollars spent trying to unlock the "mystery" of economic growth,[15] considerably less attention and fewer resources have been given to understanding the precise mechanisms underpinning the Schumpeterian forces of "creative destruction" that such growth unleashes on underlying social, legal, and political institutions, reconstituted versions of which are crucial for igniting the growth process in the first instance and sustaining it into the future (Rodrik 1999; Easterly, Ritzen, and Woolcock 2006).[16] Economic growth may be a necessary condition for poverty reduction (Kraay 2006), but we have barely begun the study of its microinstitutional foundations, the manner in which growth itself transforms institutions over different time horizons in different places, and how the conflicts emanating from such transformations can be equitably managed.[17] We contend that unpacking the dynamics of everyday conflict in "normal" villages such as Wates, where conditions are improving with and without the aid of development projects, provides one fruitful entry point into these key deliberations. Making sense of this conflict, however, and responding constructively to it require the deployment of disciplines too often marginalized in development policy debates. Important as it is, the discipline of economics "was not created to explain the process of economic change. . . . Standard theories are of little help in this context. Attempting to understand economic, political and social change (and one cannot grasp change in only one without the others) requires a fundamental recasting of the way we think" (North 2005, vii).

In this instance, unlike more orthodox technical challenges, the development problem (conflict) is hard to define and measure, and the putative solution (good governance) has no clear theoretical foundation, maps onto no coherent policy instrument, unfolds on no predictable trajectory, and falls into the jurisdiction of no single professional constituency or academic discipline. Put most bluntly, no one knows how to do this, at least not in way we know how to do other complex tasks such as removing tumors from the pre-frontal cortex ("brain surgery") or putting spaceships on Mars ("rocket science").[18] The lack of a tool kit for building institutions is not for want of adequate interest, commitment, resources, or intelligence; it is, rather, an endemic feature of this particular *type* of development challenge, one that confronted the ancient Greeks, a long line of Chinese rulers, the founders of the United States, the postcolonial governments of Africa and Asia, the architects of post-Soviet Eastern Europe, and today's developing nations and that will confront tomorrow's citizens everywhere. It is never solved once and for all; it is, instead, an ongoing political project requiring vigilant attention and renewal from each generation, in its own way, in each context. The challenge of building institutions to maintain order, facilitate exchange, constructively manage conflict, and constrain elite power has no one right answer and never will; as such, it should not be assumed that strategies deemed successful in one place will work in another (Haggard, MacIntyre, and Tiede 2008). For this kind of problem, the wheel does literally need to be reinvented each time, in each place; not from scratch, to be sure, since mixings of ideas and innovations from various sources have long been elements of institution-building processes (Bayly 2004), but reinvented nonetheless. Insofar as the high-modernist organizational imperatives of development agencies predispose them to construe this challenge in ways they understand—that is, to "see" it in ways that "render it legible" (Scott 1998) to familiar policy modalities, discourses, and assumptions (Mitchell 2002), to regard it as a mere variation on other development challenges—they close the very avenues through which effective, legitimate, context-specific responses may emerge and evolve. Indeed, for such development challenges, omnipresent belief in the desirability or possibility of *a* solution is itself a major part of the problem.[19]

This type of development problem may be distinctive, vexed, and deeply consequential, but social science is not silent with respect to identifying possible ways forward. In matters of institution-building, for example, social theory argues for, among other things, focusing attention on processes of deliberation rather than importing organizational blueprints deemed to be "best practice" elsewhere (Evans 2004).[20] These processes include creating spaces for equitable contestation between contending stakeholders, in and through which the form, content, and legitimacy of institutions is forged (Fung and Wright 2003). Because such contests are frequently very inequitable, it is often necessary to enhance the capacities of constituent groups to engage meaningfully in them (Gibson and Woolcock 2008), and no matter what form they take, it is important to provide adequate feedback mechanisms (checks and balances) to ensure that disappointments, grievances, and violations (real or perceived) are addressed in a timely manner. Social theory also warns of the dangers of perpetuating "isomorphism" (DiMaggio and Powell 1983), of beginning the reform process with a predetermined institutional end state in mind, stressing instead the importance of working iteratively from what is to the next feasible and supportable step, wherever it may lead. In this sense, institution-building and the reform of political and legal systems more generally can be said to be an ongoing process of waging "good struggles" (Adler, Sage, and Woolcock 2009, 16). Put differently, institutional forms and functions emerge historically through political contestation, and it is the task of external development agents to try to help make those contests just a little more equitable and less violent than they might otherwise be. It is in and through equitable processes of contestation that the content, legitimacy, and effectiveness of institutions emerge.

Institutional Transitions in Indonesia Since 1998

In the late 1990s and the decade following, Indonesia found itself in the midst of a period characterized by multiple seismic institutional transitions. In political terms Indonesia changed from a consolidated centralized autocracy to a fledgling decentralized democracy; in economic terms it moved abruptly from boom-and-bust to steady recovery, from crony capitalism to chaos to (the beginnings of) democratic capitalism; in social terms an "imagined community" (Anderson 1991) forcibly uniting more than two hundred major linguistic groups across six thousand of Indonesia's nineteen thousand islands now found itself listening to a vast assortment of claims, aspirations, and concerns, expressed ever more confidently and loudly.[21] Expanding opportunities to communicate and interact—whether in trade, marriage, or violence—heightened awareness of these differences (and similarities), rendered individual and group identities more malleable and complex, and made different aspects of those identities more or less politically salient at different times in different ways. Ten years has been a long time in Indonesia.

The Kecamatan Development Program is an attempt, albeit an inherently imperfect one, to embody principles from social and economic theory in a huge development project enacted in response to these swirling institutional transitions, one overseen by large, powerful development bureaucracies: the World Bank and, most important, the Indonesian government's Ministry of Home Affairs. A major function of both bodies is to build roads, bridges, schools, and irrigation systems; this remains a core business, but in the post-Suharto era they found themselves also confronting a bewildering array of new and complex local governance issues. This reality simultaneously presented, and continues to present, paradoxes and contradictions, yet also hope and fascination. Whether development agencies established to assist governments or to directly implement the "hardware" of physical infrastructure can also effectively implement the "software" of governance reform remains to be seen, but in any event this is the challenge they now confront, and one to which this study speaks.

If all of these contending forces of change were in evidence, however, and if one could show that KDP was unambiguously successful as a development and democracy project in Indonesia, it categorically would not, in and of itself, be *the* solution to local governance problems in the developing world; it is, rather, one context-specific response to a context-specific manifestation of a general problem. Our aim is not to determine whether KDP was a success or a failure but, rather, to understand how, and under what conditions, change is managed peacefully when development projects are introduced. This project is an idiosyncratic response but one founded on solid social theory and careful social research. If there are broader lessons from the KDP experience, they stem less from its operational design than the principles that underpin it and the way in which its design was arrived at and implemented. If nothing else, perhaps a key lesson is that, with sufficient external force and internal pressure, seemingly immovable objects like large, powerful high-modern development bureaucracies can be moved, at least a short distance for a short time.[22]

Thus KDP emerged in a period of great flux and accompanying contention in Indonesia. The fall of Suharto resulted in a "critical juncture" (Bertrand 2004, 10), with new opportunities for accessing political power resulting in accentuated competition between different ethnic and religious groups and their leaders. The result was at least nineteen thousand deaths from large-scale ethno-religious violent conflict in Sulawesi, the Malukus, and Indonesian Borneo (van Klinken 2007) and the displacement of more than 1.4 million people (Hedman 2008).[23] Long-running separatist tensions at either end of the archipelago reignited. In other provinces, local conflicts—previously managed through the coercion and, at times, oppression of the state apparatus—took violent form in some cases (Tajima 2009) and were managed peacefully in others (Diprose 2009b), with 2002 alone seeing almost five thousand deaths spread across each and every Indonesian province (Barron, Kaiser, and Pradhan 2009). "Routine" forms of violence such as vigilante lynchings, land conflicts, and local political struggles were prevalent (Tadjoeddin and Murshed 2007; Varshney 2008; Welsh 2008). Structural change to Indonesia's political and governance framework through decentralization may have brought governance closer to the people and begun the process of accommodating long-standing demands for greater autonomy, but it has also created a new arena for the contestation of power in Indonesia's districts, triggering ethno-religious tensions and violence in some cases while helping to ameliorate them in others.[24]

Within this environment, KDP continued to operate and, indeed, expand. In Aceh, where a civil war raged until the signing of a peace agreement in mid-2005, the project has operated continually since 1998, one of the very few development projects to maintain a continuous presence in the troubled province (Barron, Clark, and Daud 2005). Soon after the Indian Ocean tsunami devastated the province in December 2004, KDP was expanded to cover every rural subdistrict as the conflict continued. After the Helsinki peace settlement was reached, it was used to provide reintegration assistance to conflict victims (Morel, Watanabe, and Wrobel 2009). In

Maluku province, project activities had to be suspended between 1999 and 2000 at the height of the conflict, but they resumed without significant problems the following year (Government of Indonesia 2002). At times, KDP staff also played a conflict mediation role. In Central Kalimantan, where at least 150,000 ethnic Madurese fled the province, project facilitators helped negotiate safe passage to avoid further slaughter (Smith 2005).

The variation in the form, prevalence, intensity, and duration of conflicts across Indonesia, and the presence of such projects as KDP in their midst, provides a potentially fruitful venue for examining local conflict and dispute-resolution mechanisms, processes of conflict escalation, the formal and informal institutions that underpin and drive the conflicts, and the ways in which development projects affect (accentuate, limit, transform) them. By exploring carefully selected instances of this commingling of institutional change, development projects, and conflict dynamics, we hope to shed light on all three elements. Such an analysis can become, we contend, the basis for building a richer storehouse of evidence and for crafting stronger theory with which to better understand complex processes of social change at the local level. This in turn can help in the enactment of more effective context-specific strategies in response to them.

So understood, the dynamics of development in Wates and villages like it are anything but banal; they are a window through which to examine early twenty-first-century manifestations of the achievements (democracy, human rights, improved nutrition) and especially the discontents (conflict) that accompany the historical process of transforming social, political, and legal institutions. At present, however, the consensus among scholars, policy makers, and practitioners regarding the importance of building effective institutions for development is matched only by the limited theory and evidence on which to base a coherent response.[25] At worst, development experts and national political leaders impute a theory of change and justify policies after the fact, but too often these theories and actions are part of the problem.

Overview

This study was undertaken in an attempt to assess whether and how KDP was fulfilling its lofty ambitions of facilitating institutional and governance reform from below. To what extent does the project influence, for better or worse, proto-democratic decision-making processes and institution-building at the local level? Through what mechanisms are any such impacts realized? How do contextual factors shape these processes and outcomes? We sought to address these questions by exploring how KDP interacted with prevailing social tensions and the management of local conflict during the six years that followed the fall of the New Order government, a period of wholesale transformation in the institutions governing everyday life in Indonesia. By *local conflict* we mean disputes (both violent and nonviolent) that play out at the local level—that is, at the subdistrict level and below, within and between villages. Such conflicts tend not to result in large-scale devastation, although, as we will see, their impacts can individually and collectively be great; their importance as an object of study lies in part in their role in defining the ways in which local societies and institutions function and, as such, in shaping the nature of the progress that occurs.

The Kecamatan Development Program was not designed as a conflict-reduction or conflict-management program. Nevertheless, it provides a particularly interesting venue for examining the relation between development (programs) and local conflict, precisely because it is implemented below and outside the primary purview of the state apparatus—the district, provincial, and central governments where top-down decision making and patronage have traditionally defined governance in Indonesia. At the time our study was undertaken, KDP was already one of the World Bank's flagship community-driven development (or CDD) programs, having channeled more than one billion dollars to more than twenty-eight thousand villages, or 40 percent of the total, in Indonesia. Since then, the program has expanded further. The Indonesian government, impressed with early successes, decided to roll out the project to every village in the country and to put significant amounts of its own revenue into the program. Rebranded in 2006 as the National Community Empowerment Program (or PNPM, to use its Indonesian acronym), the cumulative budget of the program was projected to be US$3 billion by 2011, by which time it would cover every village across the country.[26]

Many claims and counterclaims have been made regarding the efficacy of CDD projects (Mansuri and Rao 2004; 2011). The evidence base is steadily increasing, but studies to date have focused more on discerning economic impacts (such as income generation) than social or political outcomes.[27] Little systematic attention has been given to exploring, over time, the means by which these latter outcomes materialize (or not). Even fewer of these studies have been able to marshal extensive qualitative and quantitative evidence.

The project (now PNPM) operates in a country in the midst of multiple, ongoing and uneven transitions that have, at times, been accompanied by violence. In addition to outbreaks of large-scale and violent communal conflict in a number of locations and ongoing secessionist conflict in two provinces, widespread (and often violent) *local* conflict has occurred across the country (Barron, Kaiser, and Pradhan 2009). What are the strengths, constraints, and limitations of projects such as KDP in an unstable social and political environment where identities, rules systems, and group relations are being reconfigured, where long-standing grievances now have the space to surface with less fear of government reprisal, and where access to power—indeed, the very basis of political decision making and conflict resolution—is being renegotiated? Can interventions such as KDP support progressive, nonviolent social change in such a dynamic environment? Or might they make matters worse? In short, are they part of the problem or part of a solution?

If these are the broad issues being explored, there are two primary empirical questions we seek to answer in this book. First, does KDP generate fewer conflicts, or at least less serious conflicts, than other development projects? Second, does participation in KDP help villagers find more constructive solutions to local-level conflict in general, and, if so, does it help resolve certain types of local conflict more effectively than others? These questions give rise to a related set of secondary questions. Through what mechanisms are any such positive outcomes achieved and potentially negative outcomes avoided or minimized? That is, how exactly do these outcomes materialize? Given that KDP endeavors to accommodate local contextual realities, are certain elements of these contexts more important than others in determining the program's effects? What factors—internal to the program or in the local environment—influence the extent and manner of the program's impact?

Assessing the efficacy of social development projects such as KDP is difficult because a defining feature of many such projects is the nonstandardized ways in which they seek to adapt to idiosyncratic local circumstances and, in the process, generate outcomes (such as enhanced participation and inclusion) that do not have an established or clear metric. For this reason, our strategy has followed from a canonical, though too often ignored, research principle which states that the nature of the problem should determine the choice of methods used, not vice versa (Mills 1959).

Given the diversity of contexts that characterizes Indonesia and the nonstandardized nature of KDP, a methodological strategy was developed that employed an integrated range of different data sources and types of research tools. Research was conducted in matched areas consisting of places that had taken part in the program and those that had not. As discussed in greater depth below, a team of twelve researchers and supervisors conducted nine months of qualitative fieldwork in forty-one villages in two very different provinces.[28] During this time they developed sixty-eight case studies of conflict pathways; these cases explored the evolution of specific local conflicts, some of which were violent. The cases ranged from disputes about land and natural resources, cases of vigilante justice, gang fights, political disputes, and conflict over development resources, to domestic and sexual violence. The researchers also collected rich ethnographic material on fourteen topics, ranging from how local governments function to local socioeconomic conditions to the role of traditional and religious leaders, in order to allow for cross-village comparison. In all, more than eight hundred interviews and one hundred focus group discussions were conducted.

A key informant survey was also implemented in the subject villages in order to gather responses to questions relating to perceptions of KDP, its effect on conflict, and processes of social change. The full survey was conducted in areas that had participated in the project; a shorter version was used in comparison sites (because we obviously could not ask questions about the impact of KDP in areas where it was not implemented). In order to assess patterns and forms of conflict (a notoriously difficult concept to measure)[29] and variations between different areas, a dataset of conflicts as reported in local newspapers in the research areas and surrounding districts was constructed (Barron and Sharpe 2008). Two other "larger-N" quantitative surveys were analyzed as part of the study: the government's Potensi Desa (PODES) survey, which provides information about conflict for the more than sixty-nine thousand villages in Indonesia (Barron, Kaiser, and Pradhan 2009) and the World Bank's Governance and Decentralization Survey, GDS (McLaughlin and Perdana 2009).

From the outset we were conscious of the serious endogeneity concerns stalking our enterprise; KDP was not randomly assigned (indeed, it was overtly targeted to poorer subdistricts), and all manner of observable and unobservable factors were likely to have shaped both its placement and any impacts to which it gave rise at the local level. Perhaps more peaceful subdistricts and villages were selected to participate in KDP. In response to these concerns, we drew on two national-level household surveys (PODES and the National Socioeconomic Survey, SUSENAS) to help identify plausibly comparable subdistricts—those that had and those that had not taken part in the project but which were otherwise as similar as possible—and made refinements to these decisions on the basis of distinctive insights from our qualitative research team. Village-level process tracing also helped us separate cause from effect.

Together, these data sources provide the basis for a comparative analytical framework; utilizing the different data sources can help us account for variation in conflict outcomes, in conflict mechanisms (for example, attempts at resolution and common escalation patterns), and in contexts. At different points, as will become apparent, we use different units— subdistrict, village, and conflict case—for comparative analysis.

The qualitative research and key informant survey were conducted in sixteen subdistricts in four districts in two Indonesian provinces: East Java and East Nusa Tenggara (or NTT, to use its Indonesian acronym). The provinces most affected by violent conflict were excluded on the assumption that, in areas of high conflict, where violence levels are affected significantly by external actors and exogenous factors (such as military action), it would be much harder to separate the potential impacts of a local-level project from other causal variables in the research sites. Both provinces are thus medium-level conflict sites with significant levels of *local* conflict. The provinces vary in terms of population size and density (high in East Java, low in NTT), ethnicity (more homogenous in East Java, more heterogeneous in NTT), dominant religious group (Muslim and Catholic, respectively), and provincial development (East Java is relatively rich, NTT extremely poor). The rationale for selecting such different provinces was that if we found similar patterns in very different contexts, it was more likely that those findings reflected broader trends across other locations.

Within each province, two districts were selected on the basis of varying local capacity, defined as the ability of communities and the state to collectively solve or manage conflicts when they arise. In high-capacity areas, emergent problems are usually handled early and effectively (by formal actors, informal actors, or a combination of both) so that they do not escalate and become violent. In low-capacity areas, conflicts tend to emerge more easily and escalate and become violent. We chose high- and low-capacity districts in order to assess the way KDP interacts with conflicts in a range of institutional environments. Our high-capacity districts were Ponorogo (East Java) and Sikka (NTT); our low-capacity districts were Pamekasan (East Java) and Manggarai (NTT). Districts were chosen on the basis of interviews with a range of stakeholders at the national and provincial levels. The newspaper mapping was conducted in the same four districts plus surrounding districts (for a total of twelve districts across the two provinces) in order to determine variation in conflict levels at the district level and to see how representative our districts were in terms of violence and conflict management capacity compared with their neighbors.

Fieldwork was conducted in a total of sixteen subdistricts. Within each district, four subdistricts (kecamatan) were selected: three were program sites (they had taken part in KDP for at least three years), and one was a "matched comparison" site (it had not taken part but was otherwise similar to it). For the first phase of the study we matched KDP locations—using both propensity scoring techniques (measuring observable variables such as demographic and geographical characteristics) and qualitative verification (incorporating unobservable variables such as political culture, motivation levels, and patronage networks)—with demographically and socioeconomically identical non-KDP comparison locations. We later expanded the sample to include a larger range of KDP locations that had participated for varying lengths of time. Villages were selected on the basis of the location of interesting conflict cases identified in the qualitative research, using detailed criteria aimed at making it easier to control for nonprogram effects.

The program may have positive and/or negative impacts on local conflict and conflict management capacity in ways that are direct and/or indirect. The introduction of new resources into poor areas, for example, may directly lead to or exacerbate intergroup tensions; KDP's competitive bidding mechanism and its focus on empowering marginalized groups (such as women) introduce new rules and norms about decision-making procedures, and, in doing so, may indirectly influence local power balances and social structures. Resistance from elites to such changes is a potential basis for conflict, as is discontent from villagers who suspect elites of having violated program rules (for example, by steering resources to themselves or to groups they favor). In cases where elites completely capture the participatory process or where power is so firmly entrenched, however, no conflict may emerge because villagers are not aware of the program's aims or rules;

if they are, violations of procedures may be successfully kept from them (see, for example Gaventa, 1980, 2005).

Conversely, programs such as KDP may have positive impacts on local conflict and conflict management; these, too, may be direct or indirect. Direct impacts relate to the introduction of facilitators and forums. How effective are they in managing conflicts that the project may generate? Are these people and spaces used for managing conflict unrelated to the program? KDP might influence local conflicts indirectly by changing the underlying conflict environment, the structures and norms that make conflicts more or less likely to arise or escalate. It may do so by introducing new collective decision-making processes that include, for example, involvement of different groups that in turn may change intergroup relations. The program encourages participation by marginalized groups and collective decision making; this may lead to behavioral changes and, in doing so, may reshape the relations between citizens and the state and between ordinary villagers and elites. The project may also change norms, attitudes, and expectations regarding the way disputes should be resolved.

By introducing new resources and services into poor communities, development programs inevitably shape local conflict dynamics, not only in areas that have experienced high levels of violent conflict but elsewhere, too. Our evidence suggests that KDP and other development projects frequently trigger conflict or interact with existing disputes and tensions, which can lead to conflict escalation. A key finding of this study, however, is that KDP-related conflicts are far less likely to escalate and turn violent than those relating to other development programs.

Our research found three forms of development-related disputes. First, KDP, by design, introduces competition within and between villages over which proposals should be funded; this can and does lead to tensions, in particular, when groups feel that the decision-making process was not transparent or fair. Over time, however, groups tend to accept the validity of the competition process and, as a result, the outcomes it generates, whether it personally benefits them or not. Only where the program does not function as intended—for example, where one group has captured the process and villagers are aware that this is the case—do larger problems emerge. The second form of conflict stems from these and other program malfunctions, which can be problems of omission or commission. The former is a result of the provision of limited information or of poor implementation; the latter occurs where there has been deliberate and active malfeasance by program staff or local elites (for example, in cases of corruption). The latter is more serious than the former, with cases of corruption providing a basis for larger community unrest. The third form, interaction conflict, occurs when development projects (KDP or others) interact with preexisting local tensions, power structures, or conflicts, triggering conflict escalation and, in some cases, violence. Projects operate in contexts in which power relations are constantly being negotiated; development projects constitute a vital resource that can be utilized in this process. In certain cases, interaction conflicts involve actors using the project for patronage, raising tensions between competing local elites; in others, elites attempt to capture the project for self-enrichment. Other cases concern the resistance of elites to the norms of widespread access to decision making, transparency, and accountability that KDP brings. Where resistance is greater, there is more potential for conflict.

Despite the numerous ways in which projects can trigger conflict, we found that KDP-related conflicts almost never become violent. There was only one minor violent dispute relating to KDP in the research areas during our three years of study, and this stemmed from retribution against a villager who had (correctly) reported an instance of corruption; in contrast, there were thirty-six violent disputes related to other government development programs and the provision of government services. We argue that this was largely because KDP projects, by virtue of emerging from a consultative process whereby communities define their needs, are imbued with a sense of legitimacy and equity, meaning that they are less likely to clash with local priorities and hence reduce conflict. KDP also has a battery of in-built mechanisms (both people and procedures) that allow tensions to be addressed as they arise. The constant presence of facilitators in villages, for example, makes quick response to problems at the onset all the more likely and encourages accountability for doing so. Resolution success rates of KDP-related problems are very high. This is in marked contrast to many other development projects, which lack such mechanisms and, as a result, conflicts are far more likely to turn violent and remain unresolved.

Although KDP forums, facilitators, and complaints mechanisms are used frequently and effectively to deal with conflict related to the program, we find little evidence that KDP per se has a positive impact on conflict at an aggregate level in our research areas or a *direct* positive impact on non-project-related conflict at the local level. In East Java and NTT, the direct impacts of the project on conflict management are minimal in the first three years of the program. Moreover, the forums and facilitators are rarely used for addressing conflicts unrelated to the program; where they are so used, it tends to be in an ad hoc manner. In none of our research locations had KDP forums been institutionalized as a regular (or more general) conflict resolution device.

There are four major reasons for this. First, other institutions exist at the village level to deal with conflicts that are not related to the program, so, in most cases, KDP is not seen as the appropriate mechanism for addressing them—facilitators or other program staff are not seen as having jurisdiction over these issues. Where conflict management institutions do not exist (for example, in areas with lower conflict management capacity and for certain forms of conflict such as that relating to other development projects), KDP forums and facilitators are sometimes used. This suggests that the project can complement existing conflict mediation mechanisms. It may be that in the parts of Indonesia with the highest levels of violent conflict, where many local institutions have collapsed, KDP can play a role in resolving certain kinds of disputes, such as those relating to administrative procedures and resource allocation.

Second, in some cases facilitators are not perceived as having the personal legitimacy to handle disputes. In particular, where they are seen as corrupt or to have unfairly favored one group over another, it is unlikely that they will be called on to mediate contentious issues. In order for program facilitators to be effective, they need to be seen to be honest, independent, and neutral. Indeed, the perceived and actual (political) neutrality of most KDP facilitators is a defining virtue of the program in the eyes of participants. In some cases, however, particularly where the power of the traditional elites is entrenched, it is precisely because facilitators are independent and follow program rules that they are depicted as illegitimate. In such environments, legitimacy is earned by adhering to rather than challenging patronage networks. Under such conditions, facilitators are depicted negatively (as biased, culturally insensitive, and having their own agendas) by elites who influence public discourse, and therefore they would not be the first port of call when arbitrating disputes.

Third, in many cases facilitators are unwilling to address conflicts and problems brought to them that are not related to the program. In large part, this is because they are (not unreasonably) risk-averse. Many facilitators are conscious of the sanctions that might follow—for them and for the communities in which they work—if they deviate from the project manual and operational guidelines. Our findings suggest that more flexibility needs to be built into these guidelines to allow for "altruistic deviance" by facilitators.

Fourth, in some cases KDP facilitators are not called on to mediate disputes because of gaps in their capacity. These gaps differ by the position of the facilitator. Subdistrict facilitators tend to have the technical skills needed to help mediate issues, but often they do not have adequate time or the local knowledge necessary to understand the positions of the disputants and to win their trust. Village facilitators, on the other hand, tend to have time, local expertise, and legitimacy, but they often do not have the needed technical training or education.

As it stands, KDP is thus not an effective mechanism for working directly on nonprogram conflict. In some ways, this is a good thing—it allows KDP to remain a politically neutral space wherein communities can work out their needs and priorities. Yet at the same time, there is scope for modifying the program to allow it to more effectively manage local conflict. On the relatively infrequent occasions when nonproject conflicts are addressed through the program, they tend to be resolved successfully. This shows that there is potential for KDP to play a larger mediation role, in particular for development-related disputes. Improved training for facilitators (especially at the village level) and increasing the scope for discretion of those implementing the program (in particular at the subdistrict level) would enhance this aspect of the program. At the same time, it may be necessary to have complementary programs in place to directly address conflict.

If the direct impacts of KDP on conflict management are small, the program nevertheless has notable (and positive) *indirect* impacts on the local institutional environment in the areas in which it operates. The project is helping improve intergroup and state-society relations, and this is helping make areas more immune to violent conflict. We found that across a range of different identity cleavages, KDP had helped contribute to improvements in intergroup relations: ethnic, religious, and class relations in NTT have improved since the project was introduced, and these changes are greater in program areas than in comparison areas. There is also some evidence that relationships between those affiliated with competing martial arts (*silat*) groups have improved in East Java. Further, the improvements in group relations grow larger over time: villages that have taken part in KDP for four years show, in general, greater improvements than those that have participated for shorter periods. We contend that these results obtain because KDP provides a space for different groups to come together to collectively discuss their needs and priorities, an opportunity that is rarely afforded them elsewhere (especially at the intervillage level). Improving transportation networks may be another (more prosaic) means by which the project facilitates group interaction.

The program also appears to contribute positively to the reconfiguration of citizen-state relations at the local level in many cases. Many different social and political factors at numerous levels have contributed to democratization in Indonesia in recent years, but our comparative analysis of program and comparison areas suggests that KDP is helping drive and consolidate this process. Marginalized groups (in particular, women) are far more likely to take part in KDP meetings than in other village government meetings. Moreover, increased participation in the program appears to be spilling over into other domains of village life: 50 percent more villagers reported that more marginalized groups were coming to village meetings in KDP areas than in the matched comparison sites, and three-quarters of all villagers in areas that had taken part in KDP for the longest time (four years) reported that more groups came to village meetings than in the past. Decision making in village meetings has also become more democratic, and this effect is greater in KDP areas than in the comparison sites. There is mixed evidence that KDP has helped improve problem-solving and conflict resolution. The survey results show similar perceived improvements in program and comparison sites; the qualitative fieldwork, however, shows clear linkages between the program and such normative changes, with KDP (when it functions well) creating a positive precedent, in the process helping stimulate demand for changes in the ways in which local decision making and conflict resolution operate.

The strength and direction of each of the different forms of direct and indirect impact are contingent on the extent to which the program functions well and the contexts in which it works. The capacity of the local environment is crucial for determining overall project impact.[30] In low-capacity environments, where KDP is poorly implemented (as a result of, say, inadequate socialization of participants or weak enforcement of program rules, or where patronage systems are yet to be circumvented by the program despite the efforts of facilitators), the program can exacerbate local conflict by providing a new resource over which elites (and subordinate villagers) compete. A well-implemented program in a low-capacity environment can, however, produce positive outcomes. Capacity operates at multiple levels and can work in multiple (sometimes opposing) directions, depending on the form of impact being assessed. The success of KDP mechanisms for addressing conflicts stemming from the program, for example, varies considerably depending on specific interactions between implementation effectiveness and district and village capacity, with district capacity often playing the most important role. Where conflict stems from KDP malfunction, lower district capacity increases the use of KDP forums and facilitators, whereas lower village capacity decreases it; conversely, local capacity has little effect on the use of KDP forums for in-built issues.

Whether KDP is working well or not is more important than the context in which it operates in determining the level and direction of impact. Where program functionality is poor, few positive spillover effects are observed, with only marginal positive impacts on group relations and decision making. In low- and high-capacity areas, getting the program working properly greatly enhances the positive impacts the program can have. Where the program does not work as intended, not only are positive effects limited, but there is also a chance that the program will have negative impacts. Local capacity, at the village or district level, seems to have little effect on whether KDP forums are used to address in-built conflict and little effect on the likelihood that KDP processes will successfully resolve either in-built or malfunction-based conflicts when they are used. However, local capacity does appear to have an impact on the likelihood of KDP processes (forums or facilitators) being used to address conflicts arising from KDP malfunction.

Finally, KDP does not displace existing forums for local dispute resolution; indeed, in high-capacity environments it can serve as a valuable complement, strengthening well-functioning institutions already in place, while in low-capacity environments it can provide a positive alternative to (or substitute for) absent, captured, or dysfunctional forums. The marginal impacts of a well-functioning KDP are higher in low-capacity areas because KDP forums need to take on a wider range of tasks, though a minimal level of capacity is needed to provide a basic foundation on which to build. On the other hand, indirect impacts are greater in high-capacity areas, where KDP can facilitate and act as a catalyst for processes of political and social change.

These results and the mechanisms that bring them about suggest a number of broad implications and specific recommendations pertinent to the design of development projects, especially those predicated on notions of enhancing governance and taking context seriously. These relate to how we understand the complex relation between development (projects) and conflict, minimizing the negative impact of development projects on local conflict, enhancing the positive roles that projects can play in addressing conflict and the capacity to manage it, and how we evaluate the efficacy of such projects. More generally, our findings speak to the analytical basis on which policy makers engage the particular challenges posed by political and legal reform, concerning which there is at once both a broad consensus for action—everyone agrees that "good governance" and "building the rule of law" are essential for development—and yet insufficiently grounded theory and solid evidence informing how (and by whom) it might actually be undertaken.

Since the end of the cold war, and especially since the beginning of this century, conflict has emerged as a major issue for development scholars, activists, and practitioners. How and why it became so, what lessons can be discerned from the emerging literature on the conflict-development nexus, and how various forces combine to frame the way we tend to think about these problems and enact solutions, form the point of departure for our exploration.

PART I

Issues, Contexts, Methods

The Conflict-Development
Nexus Revisited

In recent years, understanding violent conflict and identifying ways to prevent it have become major preoccupations of the international development enterprise. Even so, the ways in which the conflict-development nexus has been conceptualized in development theory and practice tend to obfuscate a more complete understanding of how policies, projects, and practices—and the types of contexts within which they occur—affect the onset and trajectory of violence and the ways that (violent) conflict, in turn, influences development outcomes.

The increasing interest of the international development community in the issue of conflict has been apparent in its engagement with this issue as a subject of both empirical study and policy concern.[1] Much of this stems from the recognition of a number of truths that had previously received scant attention but which early failures of the postcolonial and, more recently, the postsocialist development effort exposed all too clearly. The first of these was the identification of the deleterious impacts of war on growth and poverty reduction. The second half of the twentieth century was marked by a steady but rapid rise in the number of wars taking place around the world. At mid-century most of these could be understood as wars of independence; the old European empires were weakened by two devastating world wars, and changes in the organization of the global economy lessened the importance of controlling far-flung territories from which the inputs that had driven industrialization could be extracted. As the cold war intensified, multifold civil wars emerged, with competing groups (organized along ethnic or loosely ideological lines) battling for access to the state and the control of often immense natural resource wealth that this conferred. With regimes and rebel groups equipped and financed by their respective Great Power sponsors, the number of such conflicts intensified until it reached its nadir in the early 1990s. Even after this point, civil wars were widespread: 127 took place between 1945 and 2003, resulting in an estimated 16.2 million deaths (Fearon and Laitin 2003).

As the severity and longevity of such wars became clear, violent conflict became increasingly identified as a major barrier to development. The vast majority of these wars and civil conflicts took place in the very same states into which developed countries were pumping billions of dollars in development assistance. The immediate impacts of violence were obvious, with scholars demonstrating that the onset of civil war negated gains made in the pre-war period. As part of this research effort, a number of economists have sought to determine the costs of wars to economies by creating models that generate plausible counterfactual levels of growth that might have been achieved if war had not occurred. Estimates of impacts differ depending on the data used and the specifications of the model, but in general they point to annual decreases in GDP of around 2 to 2.2 percent (Collier 1999; Hoeffler and Reynal-Querol 2003; Restrepo et al. 2008). A regular civil war is estimated to cost between US$60 billion and $250 billion, with economic costs averaging US$123 billion per year for the past four decades (Chauvet, Collier, and Hegre 2008). Incomes are reduced by around 15 percent, and the proportion of people living in absolute poverty increases by almost a third (Moser 2006). The World Bank's World Development Indicators list five countries with single-year losses of more than 40 percent of GDP: Liberia in 1990, Rwanda in 1994, Georgia in 1992, Armenia in 1992, and Iraq in 2003. In each, large-scale violence was a major contributing factor (World Bank 2009). Practitioners' interest in conflict also increased with the rising awareness of its impact on displacement and migration, and the consequences for regional political instability: in large part because of armed violence, there are about twenty-six million internally displaced people around the world and another sixteen million refugees.[2]

The impacts of violence on growth, poverty, and development are not restricted to war zones. Recent work has shown that of the 740,000 deaths from armed violence each year, 490,000 deaths—or nearly two of every three—occur outside war zones (Geneva Declaration Secretariat 2008, 1). A sizable proportion of these occur in "postconflict" countries where wars have formally ended (Muggah 2009b). In El Salvador, Guatemala, and Nicaragua, the number of homicides in the postconflict period was greater than wartime death rates (Waiselfisz 2008, 4). In 2006, violence in Central America was estimated to have cost approximately US$6.5 billion, 7.7 percent of GDP (Dominguez 2008, 13–14). Violence is also present in states that have not recently experienced war. In Rio de Janeiro, for example, gang violence resulted in 4,534 homicides between May and December 2002 alone (Cramer 2006, 219). The cost of lost productivity from criminal violence alone is estimated at US$95–$163 billion per year, or about 0.14 percent of global GDP (Geneva Declaration Secretariat 2008, 1).

The recognition that destructive conflict could seriously disrupt hard-won social and economic development gains made the consideration of violence and its impacts central concerns of those supporting international development initiatives. The conclusions seemed depressingly self-evident: What use was there in channeling budget support to governments who would all too likely be overthrown by coup or rebellion? What use was there in building a road, renovating a hospital, or opening a school if the resulting infrastructure was burned down in a violent protest, if doctors would not show up at work because of security concerns, or if children were too frightened by local militia groups to pay much attention to their homework? Violence and war were increasingly conceptualized as "development in reverse" (Collier et al. 2003, 13–32). In certain quarters, underdevelopment and thwarted economic opportunities were cast as fertile conditions for encouraging radicalism, fundamentalism, and suicide bombings. In the aftermath of 9/11, development was from many quarters construed as an antidote to terrorism.

From the recognition that violence was all too often a major barrier to development, it was but a short conceptual jump to the notion that development agencies should try to prevent violent wars and conflict in the developing world. Such tendencies were reinforced by a steadily increasing body of analytical work by governments, within multilaterals and NGOs, and in think tanks and universities purporting to show that development agencies had the tools to mitigate the risk of war and large-scale violence.

A Brief Intellectual History of the Conflict-Development Nexus

Early twentieth-century studies of conflict were primordialist or essentialist in emphasizing that violence was natural and inevitable, in particular in societies that were "primitive" and ethnically divided.[3] Because cultures are different, the argument went, and because ethnic affiliation remains *the* attachment over which people will shed blood, culturally plural societies where different ethnic groups live side by side are bound to have higher levels of conflict. Even at the end of the twentieth century, this was the explicit claim of Huntington (1993) and his controversial "clash of civilizations" thesis.[4] Others used similar reasoning to highlight religious diversity as a source of violence and war (Hobsbawm 1998; Goody 2001). Such arguments created little space for external agents to influence conflict except through force (military interventions) or large-scale social engineering (as was attempted in the Great Lakes region in Africa; see Chretien 2003). The scope for the development industry to influence conflict seemed limited, even as it raised awareness of the issue and offered an explanation for it.

Increasingly, however, primordialist conceptions of violence began to be discredited in the conflict studies literature (Horowitz 2000). Such approaches were accused of reifying cultural identities and resulting group formations as static and given, with little consideration of the ways identities wax and wane and the ways group boundaries become more or less porous in response to endogenous and exogenous forces, whether historical, geographical, political, or in combination (Sen 2006; North, Wallis, and Weingast 2009). Further, as an explanatory tool for examining the incidence, severity, and longevity of violent conflict, the primordial view was very limited in its ability to predict variation over time and space. The theory said little about why some ethnic groups live together for centuries and then rise up against each other or about why in some cases ethnic groups can live peacefully side by side, while in others they cannot (Varshney 2007).[5]

In reply to the essentialism and determinism of the primordialists, a literature emanating from political sociology emerged that highlighted the socially constructed nature of ethnicity and the extent to which conflict often has an instrumental basis, thereby becoming a mechanism for individuals or groups to advance their interests (see, for example, Eriksen 1993; Rothchild 1997). Ethnic affiliation, from this standpoint, is neither static nor given: seeking membership in identity groups may be a natural human trait, but people have multiple layers and forms of identity and may choose to emphasize certain ones in different ways in different times and places. Ethnicity does not need to be the defining narrative of group formation when other identities (gender, class, place of origin, occupation, and so on) are often equally important or can become so. The question then becomes: Why do particular identities (ethnic or otherwise) get emphasized at different points in time, and under what conditions—and via what mechanisms—does this translate into intergroup conflict and violence?

The political sociology literature has proffered two strands of responses to this question. The first emphasizes the role that intellectual and political elites play in creating and sustaining conceptions of the self and the group. Wolf (1964, 1999), for example, argues that cultures are, in part, derivative of the power relations that prevail within a community and that cultural formations and the dynamics that underpin them can, with proper study, be understood by examining how power is structured and deployed. Brass (1997, 16) extends the point to show how these cultures, created and sustained by leaders (or "fire tenderers") for reasons of power, are then used as resources to be mobilized for the acquisition of further political power, economic benefits, and social status. The extent to which they can do this is in part a function of the way institutions shape ethnic identities and how important these ethnic identities are to their political context (Posner 2005). The empirical bases of many of the instrumentalist assertions rest on the close examination of particular conflicts in particular situations, and as such have sought to deduce (or impute) rational motivations to the actions of certain actors. Whether the analysis is structural or relational, ethnicity and group identity gain saliency through the rational pursuit of interests (individual or collective).[6] More recently, Stathis Kalyvas (2006), in his investigation of the logic of civil war, has shown how participation in and experience of violence vary within a conflict, with local patterns of engagement driven by local incentives for participation. Kalyvas and Kocher (2007) further add to studies that examine the level of risk in joining violent insurgencies or rebellions by demonstrating that it may be equally risky *not* to join such action, because noncombatants are likely to be singled out, pressured, or targeted for violence by the insurgents.

The second strand stresses the importance of understanding the characteristics of the civic institutions within which conflicts are embedded. In his study of ethnic conflict in India, Varshney (2002) criticized the focus on formal institutions, arguing that it is the strength of underlying informal civic associational structures and, to a lesser extent, informal networks that helps explain the likelihood of violence between ethnic groups. Where the members of such structures and networks are socially diverse and intertwined, Varshney argues, citizens have frequent, sustained, and personal interactions with those who are demographically different from them, thereby making it harder for opportunist elites to ignite or fan conflicts along communal lines. Through their overlapping membership in social, political, and business associations, citizens find their interests and aspirations conjoined; in contrast, within more balkanized social environments, erstwhile potential triggers for group-based conflict are less effectively reduced, anticipated, and mitigated.[7] Rumors, innuendo, and accusations circulate unchecked and more quickly metastasize into drivers of larger and more serious contestation (compare with Roy 1994). The focus of such work on the nature of social relations at the local level has been particularly influential on the development arena, with analytic work and practice focusing on how social capital can be built and harnessed to prevent violent conflict (Colletta and Cullen 2000).

A third body of research on conflict turns its focus to questions of political economy, looking at the economic, political, and institutional factors that can help explain violence. Johan Galtung (1969, 183), one of the grandfathers of the conflict studies and peace science movements, posited that where a society is characterized by underlying conditions of domination and exploitation, there exists a form of structural violence within which true "positive peace," which redresses such inequality, can never take hold. The basic implication is that attempts at managing conflict must address fundamental (primarily class) inequalities. The contributors to Stewart (2008) extend this line of work, arguing that durable, deepening, and overlapping horizontal inequalities between groups are more likely to lead to violence. Diprose (2008, 2009a, 2009b; Diprose and Ukiwo 2008) in turn finds that this is especially the case where such horizontal inequalities are perpetuated by a state that favors particular groups and excludes others, most notably with regard to controlling access to elite positions within the state. Related research includes the work of John Burton (1990), who has argued that conflict flows from the denial of the provision and assurance of basic needs by government institutions or the market; levels of conflict are thus determined by the extent to which basic needs are met. Similarly, Charles Tilly (1998) emphasizes the economic basis of conflict but argues that "durable inequality" between different cohorts is what matters in explaining conflict.

Other scholars have sought to explain variations in violence levels by emphasizing the presence (or absence) of different types of bureaucratic institutions. Arend Lijphart (1977, 2008) has focused on the ways different institutional arrangements that ensure participation by various groups can help ameliorate potential or actual conflict. Gurr, Marshall, and Khosla (2001) attempt to show the types of regimes—on a scale ranging from democracy to totalitarian states—that make countries more or less likely to experience civil war. Ted Gurr and his collaborators have argued that states are less likely to experience turmoil if they are fully fledged democracies or autocracies. States with political systems that lie in between, however, or that are in transition between the two end poles, are more likely to undergo civil unrest (see also Bates 2008).

A wide range of hypotheses and theories about the causes of violence have thus been identified. A literature that grew substantially in the late twentieth century has sought to test such ideas econometrically. Large-n, multicountry datasets have been established that compile information about conflict incidence and impact, along with a range of independent explanatory variables. The Correlates of War datasets housed at the University of Michigan and Pennsylvania State University (Singer and Diehl 1990), the Conflict Data project at the University of Uppsala and the International Peace Research Institute in Oslo (Harbom and Wallensteen 2007, 2008), and the Minorities at Risk dataset at the University of Maryland (Gurr 2000; Toft 2005; Hewitt 2008) have all been used to model the risk of conflict of different countries and as a basis for assessing the efficacy of different approaches to violence reduction. These datasets, however, only include conflict involving the state and ignore many of the large-scale "horizontal" conflicts involving warring groups such as those experienced in India and Indonesia.[8] The work of Paul Collier, Anke Hoeffler, and their colleagues at the World Bank and the University of Oxford has sought to empirically demonstrate why countries disintegrated into civil war (for example, Collier and Hoeffler 2002) and what can be done to prevent or end conflicts or stop them from restarting (Collier, Hoeffler, and Soderbom 2008).[9] Such studies tend to use national-level data from multiple countries.[10] Over time, more and more scholars have sought to investigate sources of intra-country variation econometrically.[11]

The policy recommendations of this growing body of work, often implicit, are diverse; they emphasize everything from absolute and relative poverty to formal institutional structures and colonial legacies to stocks of local social capital as factors that influence conflict or its absence. At times, different studies point in different directions. Yet many of the factors identified as causes of conflict and many of the suggested ways to mitigate violence lie in areas in which the development industry could have some influence. Development, traditionally conceived, deals with economic issues such as growth, poverty, and the financing of infrastructure. If slow growth, endemic poverty, and spatial isolation cause (or strongly correlate with) violence, then aid agencies are potentially well placed to put in place programs that could help prevent it. In addition to providing loans for infrastructure and economic development, development agencies could also affect formal institutions by means of capacity-enhancing technical assistance or by the provision of advice to developing nations about appropriate policies to foster economic growth.[12] If aid agencies could help reshape the underlying structures that gave rise to violence, then development could be used as a tool for preventing violence.

Preventing Violence Through Aid

Once the research literature began to converge on some of the causes and sustaining factors in civil wars and collective violence, the door was wide open for, in Duffield's (2001) terms, a merging of security and development. Aid agencies started to develop operational approaches aimed at reducing the incidence and impacts of violence. Just as previous generations of development planners sought to deal with barriers to growth such as inefficient trade policies or use of the state budget, preventing violence became an integral concern of the development enterprise (Uvin 2002).

Three areas where concerns about violence have affected development policy and practice are particularly notable. First, there has been a rapid move to providing reconstruction and peace-building support to countries emerging from war. Such efforts stem from a growing recognition that many peace processes fail and bring a return to widespread violence. Collier et al. (2003) showed that there was a significant chance of violent conflict reemerging within ten years in areas where civil wars had ended. Supporting the (often nascent) institutions of the postwar state, delivering services to those affected by conflict, and rebuilding the physical and economic infrastructure that allows growth to take hold became development priorities (Ghani and Lockhart 2008). The World Bank increased lending to postconflict countries by 800 percent between 1980 and 1998 (World Bank 1998, 1), and "securing development" (Zoellick 2008) became a fundamental concern of the Bank. The Peacebuilding Commission was established within the UN system in December 2005 in recognition of the increased role of "soft" peace-building activities that go beyond traditional ("hard") peacekeeping duties.

Such aid continues to be used for a wide range of purposes, from demobilizing and disarming rebel groups and supporting the reintegration of former combatants through reinsertion benefits, job creation, and livelihoods assistance[13] to establishing or providing support to transitional justice programs including truth and reconciliation commissions, supporting security-sector reform, building civil capacity, supporting human rights awareness, community development, rebuilding infrastructure destroyed in the conflict, planning and monitoring elections, and building government capacity (see Forman and Patrick 2000).[14] The means by which aid is delivered has received increased emphasis. Community-driven development approaches, where villagers collectively decided on their development priorities and what projects they would like, have become increasingly common in postconflict areas (Cliffe, Guggenheim, and Kostner 2003; Barron, Humphreys, et al. 2009).

Violence prevention and mitigation efforts have not been confined to states emerging from protracted violent conflict. Increasingly, bilateral and multilateral donors have funded programs such as conflict resolution training, peace journalism, and other local peace-building initiatives in a host of developing countries. There has been a growing focus on new issues such as urban and criminal violence, in particular in Latin America (Ayres 1998; Moser and McIlwaine 2006). Most of the major aid agencies now have conflict units, which finance and advise about such activities. International NGOs have also become increasingly involved, such that conflict has become a major business line.[15] As greater emphasis is placed on violence prevention, donor and NGO conflict programs increasingly operate in areas where violence has yet to occur on a large scale but where there is reason to believe that it could.

As an extension of this work, donors and aid agencies have also started to integrate conflict concerns into their strategies for delivering assistance. A variety of agencies employ conflict analysis frameworks as part of the preparation of poverty reduction strategies and other plans.[16] The literature about the causes of violent conflict has given rise to an early warning literature (with a related industry) that seeks to help donors and aid agencies identify times when particular countries or areas are at risk of conflict. At the national level, early warning systems and the academic research focused on identifying variables correlated with violent conflict have begun to feed into the macro-policymaking of development agencies. Some country assistance strategies, for example, now focus on shaping the social and economic structures that seemed to underpin unrest (such as poverty, inter- and intragroup inequality, and unemployment). Identification of subnational conflict patterns can highlight regions, demographic groups, or sectoral areas to which resources should be channeled in order to prevent escalated violence or enhance the likelihood that fledging peace agreements will be consolidated.

Aid and the Production of Violence

If the larger body of research into the causes and impact of violent conflict provided a rationale for development agencies to expand their engagement in high-conflict settings, a smaller but growing literature argues that though aid may at times help reduce violence, it can also worsen it. As the reach of the development enterprise expanded, it became increasingly clear that not only were development interventions at times ineffectual in the face of violent conflict, in some cases they triggered violence (Anderson 1999; Uvin 2002). In short, far from being a solution to conflict, this literature argues, under certain conditions development projects can be part of the problem.

Researchers working in this tradition have given attention to particular areas of development activity. One of the first was the role that big infrastructure projects could play in driving violence. Large-scale involuntary resettlement as a result of the construction of dams, for example, could clearly have a negative impact on traditional livelihoods and kinship structures, creating new needs and breaking down local institutional structures that were previously used to handle such issues (Cernea and Guggenheim 1993). One prominent case was the Chixoy dam in Guatemala, which was built with World Bank funds between 1978 and 1982. Seventy-five thousand indigenous people were asked to move. After many decided not to do so, an intimidation campaign began, with some reports stating that death squads killed four hundred who refused to move.[17] Increasing worries about adverse impacts (an estimated forty to sixty million people around the world have been displaced by dam construction) led to the formation of the World Commission on Dams in May 1998. The commission's final report adopted a rights and risks approach to assessing the suitability of future dams, arguing that affected communities should be active stakeholders in making decisions about whether planned dams should go ahead and how compensation and relocation should be carried out (World Commission on Dams 2000). One result has been a large decrease in the number of new dams built with support from the World Bank, the international agency which had previously been the largest funder of such ventures.[18]

In parallel, critiques of World Bank– and IMF-driven structural adjustment strategies, a cornerstone of the main development paradigm in the 1980s, and the Washington Consensus (Williamson 1989, 1994), which shaped the approaches of the 1990s, grew from the newly emerging global civil society. Such critiques tended to be concerned with either ideology (for example, what role the state should play in managing a given country's economy— Duffield 2001) or sovereignty (to what extent agencies such as the IMF or World Bank should tell countries how to spend their resources—Caufield 1998). Yet from a conflict prevention perspective, the biggest problem with the dominant models and modalities was that, in their desire to rapidly reform seemingly inefficient institutional arrangements and resource allocations, they ignored the *processes* underpinning such changes and how they could be managed peacefully (Paris 2004). The development of the West has shown how such progress requires ongoing bargains between different interests and class groups and the development of new or adapted institutions to manage the competition inherent in that process (Bates 2000; Blanning 2007; North, Wallis, and Weingast 2009). Far too often, tensions associated with these "great transformations" (Polanyi 1944) become violent.[19] If such drawn-out changes are conflictual, aid that aims to accelerate such processes—that aims to promote "history in a hurry"[20]—is likely to be even more so. It is hardly surprising that in some places such efforts result in violent resistance.[21]

If structural conditions such as inequality increase the likelihood of violence, in some cases program conditionality might have increased the risk of conflict. Cramer (2006, 235–36) cites the examples of Sierra Leone and Yugoslavia, where structural adjustment made environments more prone to violence. Such critiques can be overdone. Cramer (2006, 235), following his examples, cites the "slightly tiresome trend" of blaming all ills on the structural adjustment programs of the IMF and the World Bank, overstating the importance of such programs and the agency of international financial institutions, and finds no evidence that structural adjustment causes wars (Cramer and Weeks 2002). Even so, the observation that foreign policy advice can shape environments in ways that potentially make them more prone to violence is a sound one.

At a lower unit of analysis, Peter Uvin (1998) makes an important point in his examination of the role of the development industry in the period leading up to the 1994 genocide in Rwanda. Agencies were complicit in these atrocities, he contends, not because they deliberately supported future *genocidaires* but, rather, because, in remaining deliberately apolitical, they failed to realize that they were supporting certain structural conditions that were associated with, if not the sole cause of, the genocide. These conditions include the lack of demands to get rid of the ethnic identity cards that all Rwandans had to carry and that reinforced social and political divides.[22] Drawing from Ferguson's (1990) critique of the aid industry, he argues that most of those working on development projects had economic or technical training but little understanding of social, political, and historical factors. This led to a lack of attention to the way aid was reinforcing structures that could give rise to acute violence (Uvin 1998, 156).

Attention to the inadvertent political role NGOs often play has also increased in the humanitarian field. Groups such as International Committee of the Red Cross and Medicins Sans Frontieres have traditionally prided themselves on their capacity to remain neutral when implementing emergency relief programs in conflict and postconflict zones (Tirman 2003). Yet over time a debate has emerged about whether such groups can in fact remain neutral (Rieff 2002; Leader 2000). In the "new wars" of the late twentieth century (Kaldor 2006), belligerents increasingly finance themselves by plundering aid.[23] Food aid can also be used to "lure civilian populations into areas controlled by government or rebel forces" (MacRae and Zwi 1994, 20). After the Rwandan genocide, 150 organizations were providing assistance to refugees in camps in Congo and Tanzania, many of which were controlled by people who had helped lead the genocide (Medecins Sans Frontieres 1994). Over time, 145 groups withdrew, believing it was morally indefensible to be supporting populations such as these, especially as further armed raids were originating in the camps. In arenas as diverse as Darfur (Young et al. 2005) and Serbia (Rieff 2002), aid agencies have been accused of exacerbating tensions and increasing human insecurity. If aid can function as a tool of war, questions must be asked about the costs and benefits of humanitarian interventions (Terry 2002). In part as a result of such concerns, a "new humanitarianism" has emerged (Fox 2001) supported primarily by British and American aid agencies; it assumes that relief groups should play a larger role in promoting human rights (Rieff 2002). Other groups remain convinced that taking sides can be dangerous because it may be ineffective and encourage violence (Duffield 2001; Stockton 1998) or because it may lead to the targeting of aid agencies. Such agencies can also weaken states. If they provide services that the state used to provide, they may inadvertently encourage them to move their resources and energies to fighting wars (Prendergast 1996).

It is not at all clear that these debates have led to wholesale changes in development and humanitarian practice. Rieff (2003) notes, for example, that most agencies stayed in Afghanistan while the Taliban were in control despite egregious human rights abuses. The flow of nongovernmental groups to postconflict situations where (some) aid will almost inevitably have (some) negative unintended consequences continues. Yet it is true that the rhetoric of doing no harm (Anderson 1999) has become something of a mantra within the development enterprise and that increased attention is now paid to the ways projects can have negative impacts on conflicts (see, for example, Nyheim, Leonhardt, and Gaigals 2001). Upholding Anderson's Hippocratic Oath may be unrealistic at times: projects, by design, change things, and as such these changes often give rise to conflict. But debates about the problematic and multidirectional relationships between aid, development, conflict, and violence are now becoming more mainstream, and projects and approaches have benefited from this shift.

Understanding the Conflict-Development Nexus: Enduring Gaps

Understanding of the links between development and violence has thus grown considerably in recent years and has increasingly informed the way development interventions have been designed and implemented. This is, by and large, for the good. Yet serious gaps remain in our collective approaches to understanding, theoretically and empirically, the conflict-development nexus, especially at the local level.

Local Conflict

One weakness has been the lack of attention to local conflicts and the ways in which they sometimes escalate into broader violence. The literature about conflict and development that we have outlined has focused mainly on large-scale violence and the ways development interventions can minimize the risk of civil wars and rebellions. This is understandable, given the obvious negative impacts of such forms of violence. It is unsurprising that the arenas of widespread destruction have received more attention from scholars and practitioners than areas where persistent low-level violence occurs. Yet consideration of everyday or local violence is also vital for an understanding of how development processes (and the projects and policies that help drive them) bring about change, for better and sometimes for worse, in poor communities.

Local violent conflict is worthy of consideration for a number of reasons. Small-scale but frequent violence can exact a large toll. As we have noted, on a global scale most conflict deaths occur outside of war zones. In the tourist mecca of Rio de Janeiro, gang violence resulted in almost five thousand deaths in a six-month period in late 2002 (Cramer 2006, 219). In "nonconflict" parts of Indonesia, too, local violence results in thousands of deaths (Barron and Madden 2004; Barron, Kaiser, and Pradhan 2009). Local incidents of violence can also initiate processes that lead to larger conflagrations of violence (Barron et al. 2009b; Diprose 2010). Continued recourse to violence as a means to solve small, local problems can deaden popular sensibilities about the role of other institutions in managing conflicts, potentially leading to greater acceptance of large-scale violence later on.

Understanding how everyday violence is produced, sustained, and utilized can also provide an important lens for interpreting broader processes of development, change, and violence. If development can be characterized as the continuing (re)negotiation of power, institutions, and resource allocation, then *local* violent conflicts are all too often the means by which such change is negotiated. Communities face continuing struggles to maintain order in the context of perennial human conflicts related to property (ownership, boundaries, use), common resources (water, land), leadership (selection criteria, scope, and limits of authority), and family dynamics (inheritance procedures, domestic disputes, sexual relations).[24] In many respects the mechanisms by which such problems are managed are as varied as humanity itself. Yet if the general historical arrow points in the direction of greater codification of systems of rules and increasing professionalization of their adjudication and enforcement, then it is also the case that the road itself is littered with overlapping and competing ontological understandings of what "the rules" are, which ones apply in which areas under which circumstances, and what procedures constitute a fair and reasonable approach to upholding and enforcing them. Even in putatively developed countries, simultaneously navigating within and between different normative systems for governing behavior is a major individual and collective challenge (see Ellickson 1991). In the developing world, where the state often has a more limited reach, capacity, and legitimacy, such challenges are greater. If projects are to be effective, understanding such dynamic processes across multiple units of analysis is vitally important.

Transitions, Development, and the Necessity of Conflict

Differences also remain between the way conflict and violence have been conceptualized in academic work on social change and how they are generally understood by development agencies and the practitioners who design and implement programs. The latter have primarily viewed conflict and violence as problems that can be prevented or mitigated. Accordingly, it is believed that policies and projects can help prevent conflict by changing the underlying structures that give rise to violence. The prevailing policy wisdom continues to assert that conflict in low-income countries is primarily a product of the absence of development or of development that is not conflict-sensitive. Violent conflict is deemed to be a result of ethnic diversity, acts of greed or grievance, weak institutions, inequality, low social cohesion, or simply poverty itself—all characteristics often associated with the developing world. Prescribed policy solutions come from a menu of structural fixes ranging from pro-poor economic growth, building the rule of law, and redressing inequalities between groups to enhancing the security sector, enforcing property rights, promoting judicial reform, improving the quality of service delivery, and delivering more conflict-sensitive development. It is deemed possible to establish a virtuous cycle wherein more or better (conflict-sensitive) development will reduce violent unrest, which in turn will bolster growth, reduce poverty, and enhance prosperity. This is the logic that underlies efforts to "break the conflict trap" (Collier et al. 2003).

We are in favor of all these efforts and recognize the problems they are trying to address. Yet there is a certain ahistoricism to such views. Historians of social and economic change in the West have emphasized that progress was contested at every point, with violence a major force for change (Bayly 2004; Blanning 2007). As Cramer (2006, 279) notes, "in retrospect, many changes that came to be seen as progressive have their origins in social conflicts that have taken a violent turn. This is a paradox of violence and war: violence destroys but is often associated with social creativity." Development by its very nature means change, and change almost always threatens existing interests. Indeed, the very idea of human and societal progress is predicated on the idea of conflict. This creates a serious dilemma for development actors: they can hardly be promoters of violence, yet the conflict that stems from development *processes* and development *projects* may be necessary in the short run for progressive change to occur once violence has abated.

Such insights are not new: a long-standing branch of social and political theory contends that economic progress and social conflict are closely intertwined, indeed, that the latter is often a constituent element of the former (Polanyi 1944; Moore 1967; Skocpol 1979). Conflict, with its potential for violence, and prosperity essentially go hand in hand (Bates 2000). This is particularly true in developing countries, where poverty and lack of opportunity underscore the need for change and where, conversely, otherwise desirable periods of economic growth themselves become forces for realigning class structures and (potentially) reimagining the bases of group identity. Economic progress is built in part on Schumpeterian processes of creative destruction, and the development process more broadly is inherently one of multiple uneven and contested transitions in social structures, rule systems, and power relations. Therefore, where development projects successfully lead to change, they will inevitably generate new conflict, which, all too often, results in violence. Conflict, then, is a constant companion on the road of both economic crisis and opportunity because it involves changing configurations of power and resource allocation, as well as challenges to existing interests, aspirations, perceptions, and expectations. Conflict, it would seem, is a necessary catalyst and an inevitable by-product of development. So understood, the development challenge thus becomes one not of limiting conflict per se but of managing it in constructive ways.

Evaluating the Impacts of Projects and Programs on Conflict and Violence

Finally, there are far too few rigorous assessments showing *how* development projects influence patterns of local conflict and violence. The historical literature cited above has made important points about how processes of accumulation and state expansion drive change and contestation. The development literature contains numerous papers and reports purporting to show (most often) how projects have built peace or (rather more infrequently) how they have triggered unrest. But very few have sought to isolate *specific* program or project impacts and the *specific* mechanisms by which violence is produced or averted.

This is true for projects that are explicitly designed to build peace. Disarmament, demobilization, and reintegration programs for former combatants, for example, have become "compulsory" for international postconflict responses (Kingma 2001, 1), accounting for more than US$600 million in donor funds per year (Muggah 2009a). Yet very few of these have been evaluated in ways that allow for assessments of project impacts on areas such as social cohesion and security (Humphreys and Weinstein 2007).[25] The literature about the impact on conflict of programs that do not have a specific peace-building purpose is even thinner.

This chapter has explored the analytical underpinnings of concerns that are at the heart of the conflict-development nexus. If the dominant trend in the literature, and the primary basis on which policy deliberations have been conducted, has been to focus on large-scale conflicts (civil wars), cross-national comparisons and aggregate predictors (or drivers) of violence, a large space remains for investigating everyday conflicts using local-level comparisons and exploring the combinations of factors that shape the trajectories these conflicts take over time. Filling such a space is interesting in its own right, but it also provides a potentially complementary set of insights that might contribute to a richer general theory of conflict escalation and resolution. An alternative lens through which to view the conflict-development nexus is needed in order to craft interventions that are attuned to the complex dynamics of conflicts and the contexts in which they play out. If violent conflict can have positive or negative effects on progress, then new analytic models are needed to comprehend the problem of local violence in the developing world and to evaluate the barriers to more peaceful progress. And such models need to inform the development of approaches to assessing the impacts of projects on conflict and violence.

Assessing the Impacts of the Kecamatan Development Program on Local Conflict

This book presents our attempts to grapple with such issues. In doing so, we chose to focus on the Kecamatan Development Program, a massive community development project that operates in extremely different provinces across Indonesia. The program covered every rural village in Indonesia by 2010; the cumulative program budget to 2011 will be almost US$3 billion. We move in Chapter 3 to a discussion of the contextual details of the areas we studied and the bases on which we made key methodological decisions to help us discern the various ways in which KDP was engaging with those contexts, especially as it pertained to the management of local conflict.

Basic analysis of the KDP structure presents a number of hypotheses about how the program could shape the nature of local conflict in the areas where it functions. The program may have impacts on local conflict and the capacity to manage it in a number of ways, direct and indirect; these effects, in turn, may be negative or positive.

Direct Effects

Direct impacts may be observable along two dimensions. First, KDP introduces decision-making forums at the hamlet, village, and subdistrict (kecamatan) levels. In these forums, villagers and village representatives meet to prioritize and then vote on which proposals should be funded. These forums could have either positive or negative impacts on local conflict and the way it is managed. Program documentation showed that in some cases KDP forums were used to address conflicts that are not related to the program (Government of Indonesia 2002). Given the extent to which the legitimacy and authority of traditional forums were eroded during the Suharto period, we hypothesized at the study's outset that KDP forums may create a space wherein problems not related to KDP could be addressed and, we hoped, solved.[26]

Conversely, the introduction of such forums could trigger destructive conflict. The KDP model explicitly introduces competition and thus contestation over resources into the development planning process. Poor villagers have all given valuable time to preparing their proposals, but there is never enough money to fund all projects. This could lead to conflicts in the KDP forums, which, if not handled adequately, could become violent.

Second, KDP introduces facilitators at the village and kecamatan levels. These individuals are tasked with helping villagers understand the process, helping them identify and prioritize their needs, and ensuring that the project process (from the formation of proposals to decisions about their funding and implementation) runs smoothly. They also play an important role in monitoring the program once implementation is under way. If these project facilitators are trusted and viewed as impartial, they may also play a role in mediating non-project-related conflicts. Prior to the study's beginning, some anecdotal evidence—for example, from Lampung province in southern Sumatra—showed that KDP facilitators at times play an important role in helping calm tensions. According to one report, tensions had escalated between the migrant Javanese population and local ethnic Lampungese after a conflict involving the burning of Jepara village (Government of Indonesia 2002). Facilitators could play such a positive role as trusted and respected insiders or impartial outsiders.[27] They could also, however, play a negative role. Where they fail to fulfill their role as program monitors, to resolve issues arising within their jurisdiction, or to report or take action against corruption, or if they steal money from the project, they may trigger new conflicts or allow existing ones to escalate.

Indirect Effects

Development projects shape the contexts—the social, political, and economic structures—in which they operate.[28] The resources and rules that programs introduce and the incentives that these produce help shape the structural and relational contexts in which conflict becomes more or less likely to arise or to escalate. There are a number of different ways in which KDP may shape such contexts.

First, the program may influence the relations between different groups. In our villages, identity cleavages exist along a number of dimensions, with ethnicity, religion, class, and political affiliation being the most prominent. Involvement at various stages of the program may improve the relations between groups, demystify "the other," and promote forms of collective action that operate across groups. Conversely, the program may reduce social cohesiveness or trust between groups, particularly if the groups who make proposals tend to be formed by people with similar attributes (ethnicity and so on).

Second, the program may lead to behavioral changes and, in doing so, could reshape intragroup and state-community relations. An explicit aim of KDP is to build the participation of villagers in political and civic life, an important dimension of empowerment (Gibson and Woolcock 2008). Participation in KDP meetings may help shape norms in ways that encourage other forms of local-level participation, for example, village government meetings. This may have a positive impact on building the democratic decision-making skills of villagers and may spill over into an improved ability to manage conflict.[29] On the other hand, the very processes of social and political empowerment that these initiatives involve may be met with resistance from elites. Raising people's aspirations and rights-consciousness (a key element of democratization) without making remedies available to right perceived wrongs may also make increased tensions more likely. (Whether such change is negative in the long run is another matter.) KDP could also conceivably alter access to decision making by legitimizing informal leaders and improving interaction between them and the state by allowing for the incorporation of local skills and expertise.[30] Conversely, in doing so, the program may undermine the authority of formal actors, hence weakening conflict management capacity.

Third, the program may lead to changes in norms. Violence is not only a symptom of conflict but can also be a response to it. Where norms exist that legitimize violence as a course of action and redress, conflict can easily escalate, fueling cycles of violence.[31] The program emphasizes a collective and inclusive process of decision making and problem solving. Does the program help people understand how to solve problems in nondestructive ways and build an environment where collective and peaceful problem-solving is the norm? Alternatively, the program could also result in negative changes in local norms. If the program repeatedly triggers conflicts, they may compound existing norms of retribution (for example, resorting to violence to solve problems).[32]

The Role of Context: What Influences the Ways in Which KDP Shapes Local Conflict?

The degree to which these effects occur is likely to be in part a function of the context in which the program is operating and of the ways in which it is functioning. The impacts of KDP on conflict and the extent to which these various processes take place are likely to depend on context-specific factors.[33] These variable factors will be both endogenous and exogenous to the program. Endogenous factors include the performance of program facilitators and staff and elite involvement in the program.[34] Collectively, these factors determine program functionality, that is, the degree to which the program is functioning as intended. Exogenous factors include those related to the general preexisting capacity in the area (the quality of local governance)[35] as well as those that originate outside the local area (such as interventions by national politicians and population flows). We call such factors "context capacity." We posit that together these programmatic and contextual factors help determine the extent to which KDP has positive or negative impacts on conflict and the capacity to manage it.

A Framework for Analyzing Process and Impact

We identify five different types of potential impact, each of which constitutes a causal process through which KDP may have an effect on conflict and its management. The effect, if it is present, may be positive or negative; in some cases, it may be both. Chapters 5 and 6 examine in depth the extent to which the hypotheses regarding the different mechanisms of potential impact hold up. Chapter 7 considers variation in impacts—in type and direction—by examining how different elements of context, whether external or internal to the program, matter in determining the type and strength of its impact.

CHAPTER 3

Methods, Contexts, and Project Characteristics

Assessing the efficacy of social development projects is a complex undertaking, not least because a defining feature of many such projects is the nonstandardized way in which they seek to adapt to idiosyncratic local circumstances and, in the process, generate outcomes (such as enhanced participation and inclusion) that do not have an established metric or emerge on a known trajectory over time (Woolcock 2009c). As such, it is extremely difficult—in analytical and empirical terms—to isolate the effects of a program from other contextual factors in the community and beyond. These include aspects of governance and local power structures, and the influence of the selection mechanisms that shape both program placement (such as the political economy of deciding where the program is, and is not, located) and the participation of villagers (including the choices or circumstances leading some individuals, but not others, to be involved).

For these reasons, we developed a methodological strategy that employs a number of different data sources and types of research (see figure 3.1). Each source illuminates part of the bigger picture: large-sample (national) quantitative surveys at one extreme, ethnographic case studies at the other. The overall strategy driving the analysis is that of comparative case analysis.[1] Comparative analysis of the data sources, combined with a careful sampling strategy that seeks to account for exogenous sources of difference (see below), allows us to reach stronger conclusions about impact than would be possible if a single data source were used alone. In short, we

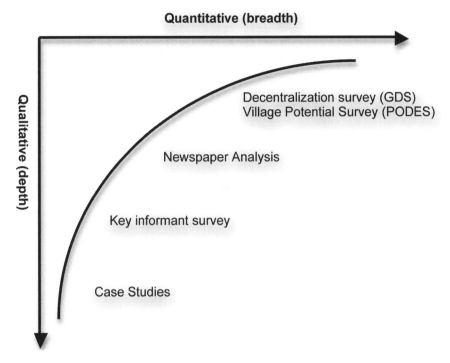

Figure 3.1   Different data sources

deployed a large-scale mixed-methods study seeking to meet, in effect, a legal (as opposed to econometric) standard of causal inference. That is, given the inherent complexity of both the project and the context, we sought to establish what the "preponderance of the evidence," in all its diverse forms, suggested was a reasonable conclusion to draw regarding KDP's impact on local conflict dynamics in Indonesia.

On the qualitative side, a team of twelve researchers and supervisors conducted fieldwork for nine months in forty-one villages. They developed sixty-eight *case studies* of conflict pathways that explored the evolution of specific local conflicts. Some cases were violent, others not.[2] The primary reason for following nonviolent cases was to allow for comparative analysis to determine why only some cases turned violent. The researchers covered a wide range of disputes including land and natural resource conflicts (from large ethnic conflicts to private disputes over inheritance claims), cases of vigilante justice (against, for example, thieves and witch doctors), gang fights, political disputes (relating to local elections and administrative boundaries, among other things), conflict over development resources, and domestic and sexual violence. Throughout the book, we use these case studies to illustrate particular dynamics of conflict, of conflict management, and of the functioning of KDP. The researchers also collected rich *ethnographic material* in fourteen topic areas ranging from how local governments function to local socioeconomic conditions to the role of traditional and religious leaders and so on to allow for cross-village comparison. In all, they conducted more than eight hundred interviews and one hundred focus group discussions.

A *key informant survey* was also conducted in the research villages in order to gather comparable responses to perception questions relating to KDP, its effect on conflict, and processes of social change. The full survey was conducted in areas that had participated in the program; a shorter version was implemented in matched comparison sites (see below).

In order to assess patterns and forms of conflict, as well as variations between areas, we also used local newspapers to create a dataset of all reported conflicts in the research areas and surrounding districts for a three-year period (the *KDP and Community Conflict Negotiation dataset*) (Barron and Sharpe 2008). This allowed us to broadly map conflict in our research areas, estimate aggregate levels of violence, and see the characteristics of the incidents (conflict type, actors involved, impacts, and so on). It also helped us determine how representative our qualitative case studies were.

Two other larger-n quantitative surveys were analyzed as part of the study: the central government's 2003 *Village Potential* (PODES) survey, which provides information about conflict for all of the more than sixty-nine thousand villages in Indonesia, and the World Bank's 2006 *Governance and Decentralization Survey* (*GDS*).[3] Background papers gathering together secondary data and summarizing the relevant literature were written about a number of issues relating to KDP, local conflict, and the areas where the study took place.

Together, these data sources provide the basis for a comparative framework; utilizing the different data sources can help us account for differences in conflict outcomes, mechanisms (such as resolution attempts and common escalation patterns), and contexts.[4] In Part II we draw on quantitative and qualitative sources; at certain points we also use different units of analysis (subdistrict, village, and conflict cases) for comparative analysis.

Selecting Areas

Province Selection

Our two research provinces were East Java and East Nusa Tenggara (NTT). Both qualitative and quantitative data were collected in four districts and sixteen subdistricts within these provinces (see map 3.1). Selecting a relatively small number of locations allowed us to examine our research areas in depth. We chose East Java and NTT for a number of reasons. First, although neither province had experienced unrest to the extent of, say, Aceh, Central Sulawesi, or Maluku provinces, both had significant levels of (often violent) conflict. When we chose our sites, no datasets existed to show this condition, but discussions with experts in Jakarta, occasional news reports, and news from project facilitators all suggested that violence was not uncommon. As the research proceeded, we found that conflicts over land and natural resources or development money, fights between gangs and martial arts groups, domestic violence, and battles over political authority were all common. Most academic and policy attention to violence in Indonesia experienced during the transition focused on areas that saw major episodes of violent conflict; broader patterns in the forms of violence elsewhere in the archipelago during the same period were underexplored. Previous research related to this study posited that there were links between local conflict and larger outbreaks of violence in the less conflict-ridden provinces of Indonesia.[5] Examining conflict and conflict

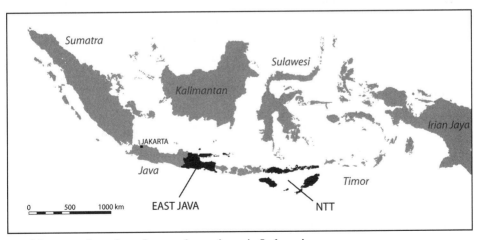

Map 3.1   Location of research provinces in Indonesia

management strategies in areas that experienced low-intensity but still pervasive conflict may help us understand how and why conflict escalated as it did in higher-conflict areas, as well as the links between the forms of conflict across Indonesia and the specific forms that occur in particular areas.

Second, we deliberately chose to exclude the provinces with the most violent conflict on the assumption that development projects are most likely to have a measurable effect (positive or negative) at the level at which they are operational. The program functions mainly at the subdistrict level and below; if it does produce any positive externalities that help communities constructively manage conflict, it is thus most likely to be in aiding the management of conflicts that exist at those levels. Given the nature of conflict in many of the high-conflict provinces, where tensions eventually subsumed the district and in some cases the province following significant contagion of violence as it spread from village to village, the selection of such places would have biased our research against observing any project impact. Further, in areas of high conflict, where levels of violence are likely to have been affected significantly by external actors and exogenous factors (such as military action), it would be much harder to separate the impacts of a local-level project from other causal variables in the research sites. Ethical considerations (including the likely physical dangers to which researchers would be exposed) also led us to conclude that it would be unwise to place numerous researchers in high-conflict areas for extended periods of time.[6]

These reasons suggested selecting medium-conflict sites for the research, which left much of Indonesia. The PODES survey shows that in 2002 violent conflict was present in every province in the nation (Barron, Kaiser, and Pradhan 2009). Given that violence exists everywhere, we decided to pick two provinces that were as different from one another as possible, on the assumption that we would find interesting conflicts to study wherever we went. These criteria—moderate conflict and maximum diversity—led us to select provinces that vary considerably in terms of population size and density (high in East Java, low in NTT), ethnicity (more homogenous in East Java, more heterogeneous in NTT), dominant religion (Islam and Catholicism, respectively), and level of development (East Java is relatively rich, NTT extremely poor). The rationale for this was that if we found similar patterns in very diverse contexts, it was more likely that these findings would hold true across other locations.

District Selection: High and Low Capacity

Given the extent to which we relied on in-depth fieldwork, with long periods of time spent in each location, it was clearly infeasible to conduct research in all districts in our selected provinces.[7] We hypothesized that the impact of KDP would depend, in part, on the external environment and thus picked districts that had distinctly different characteristics. One key element of the environment is local capacity, which we define as the ability of communities or the state to collectively solve or manage conflicts when they arise. In high-capacity areas, emergent problems are usually handled early and effectively (by formal actors, informal actors, or a combination of both) so that they do not escalate or become violent. In low-capacity areas, weak mechanisms for mediating conflict or fragile local-level institutions likely mean that conflicts will more easily emerge, escalate, and sometimes become violent.[8]

Since decentralization, Indonesia's districts have become extremely important (and to some extent autonomous) in political and economic terms. As such, the district seemed like a sensible place to start in terms of ensuring diversity in capacity levels in the sample. We chose high- and low-capacity districts in order to see how KDP works and interacts with conflicts in a range of environments. Our high-capacity districts were Ponorogo, East Java, and Sikka, NTT; our low-capacity districts were Pamekasan, East Java, and Manggarai, NTT. Districts were chosen on the basis of interviews with a range of stakeholders at the national and provincial levels.

The newspaper mapping was conducted in the same four districts where the qualitative fieldwork and key informant survey were implemented. We also included surrounding districts (in all, twelve districts were covered across the two provinces) in order to determine variation in conflict levels at the district level and to see how representative our districts were compared to their neighbors.[9]

Local-Level Sampling

Fieldwork was conducted in a total of sixteen subdistricts.[10] Within each district, four subdistricts (kecamatan) were selected. Three were project recipient sites and one was a matched comparison site. For the first phase of the study we selected locations that had participated in KDP for at least three years and matched them with demographically and socioeconomically similar non–KDP locations. We later expanded the sample to include a larger range of KDP locations that had been in the program for varying lengths of time.[11] A full key informant survey was implemented in the twelve project recipient subdistricts; a short survey focusing on processes of social change was implemented in the matched comparison locations.[12] Villages were selected on the basis of the location of interesting conflict cases identified in the qualitative research, using detailed criteria aimed at making it easier to control for nonprogram effects.[13]

For the qualitative fieldwork, selection of informants was driven by two aims. First, we wanted to talk with a wide cross-section of the population within each district, subdistrict, and village. Second, special emphasis was placed on talking to persons who were not authority figures and to women for two reasons: these voices are sometimes absent from development-focused research because they require special strategies for access, and KDP specifically aims to ensure that such groups participate substantively in program decision-making processes. Researchers used snowball sampling techniques in order to find respondents who would be able to provide insights into the cases being followed and issues in the village more generally. Focus group discussions were conducted with more vulnerable or marginalized population groups: poor women, educated or elite women, young men, and poor men. For the key informant survey, eight respondents were interviewed within each village and an additional three at the kecamatan level.

Engaging with Contexts

Understanding local context—geographic conditions, local social structures, power dynamics, livelihood and religious identity formation patterns, kinship systems, settlement patterns, group stereotypes, dominant decision-making patterns, and the history of local customs and traditions— is essential for understanding how conflict plays out. Because the importance of understanding context is a key message of this book, it is only appropriate that we provide an overview of the history, culture, and demographic characteristics of East Java and NTT and of the four research districts within them and how Indonesia's transition was playing out in these specific locations at the time the research was conducted. We then discuss the forms of conflict prevalent in each area and the frequencies and impacts of these conflicts across each province. This includes an examination of the types of conflicts that involved development programs with a poverty reduction, service delivery, and governance-building agenda such as KDP. Finally, we take a sample of cases to ascertain the factors that shaped the differing pathways of various conflicts and that helped determine whether and how they escalated. In this process we seek to identify the factors that influence the trajectories of local conflicts; that is, we seek to show why some everyday disputes are resolved quickly and amicably whereas others that are seemingly identical escalate and become violent.

East Java

East Java has a mainly Muslim population made up of two dominant ethnic groups, the Javanese and the Madurese. Though relatively homogeneous in terms of ethnicity and religion, East Java is incredibly diverse in terms of its affiliative identity groups.[14] These include affiliations to martial arts groups, Islamic boarding schools with affiliations with different Muslim clerics, groups living in different locations within and across village boundaries, criminal organizations, and groups with political ties to different parties and different village and regional elites, as well as the rich and the poor, prayer groups, work groups, and occupational affiliations. Many of the identity groups overlap and diverge, creating complex human networks and social cleavages that emerge and dissipate across space and time, particularly during conflicts (box 3.1).

BOX 3.1   A PORTRAIT OF EAST JAVA

East Java is the most densely populated province in Indonesia, with a population of roughly thirty-five million and an average of 720 people per square kilometer. The region includes the island of Madura. Low-level mountainous terrain makes up two-thirds of the province's area; this results in an uneven population distribution. Based on 2002 data, the major ethnic groups in the province are the Javanese and the Madurese (78 percent and 22 percent, respectively).

At the time the research was conducted, East Java had twenty-nine rural districts and eight urban municipalities. East Java is one of the most highly developed provinces in terms of infrastructure, public services, employment, and accessibility in Indonesia. Its capital, Surabaya, has a population of 2.4 million people and is the second-largest city in Indonesia behind the national capital Jakarta (Badan Pusat Statistik 2002a).

East Java is often considered one of the heartlands of Islam in Indonesia; the majority of the province's people identify themselves as Muslims. The north and northeastern parts of the province are the stronghold of many of the Muslim parties in Indonesia, with the National Awakening Party (PKB) and the United Development Party (PPP) dominating in the 2004 legislative election. The performance of parties with Muslim associations in East Java is often used as a barometer of how these parties will perform in national elections.

Provision of education in East Java is split between state and private schools, both of which can be either secular or religious. More than any other province, it is recognized for its plethora of private Islamic boarding schools, known as *pondok pesantren*. Although many pesantren also offer the national curriculum, many devout Muslim students (*santri*) attend secular schools in the mornings and religious schools in the afternoon. The number of pesantren decreases and the political climate changes somewhat as one moves further southwest toward Central Java, where the nationalist and secular parties such as PDI-P and Golkar have greater influence. These nationalist parties do, however, have significant support in some parts of the northeast.

Employment in the province is divided between the agricultural sector (46 percent), industry (22 percent), trade (19 percent), and services (13 percent). The number of unemployed was slightly more than 17.5 million in 1999, increasing to almost 19 million in 2000. Prior to 1990 agriculture was the main source of income for the province; however, since that time the income generated from industry has also become important. East Java produces rice, sugar, coffee, rubber, wood, tobacco, and other agricultural goods. It is also a major producer of shipping products, cement, steel, petroleum fertilizers, electronic goods, pharmaceutical goods, and equipment.

Many East Javanese leave to become migrant workers (*tenaga kerja Indonesia*); poorer workers (mainly women) seek employment abroad as servants and factory workers in order to acquire the capital necessary to build houses and start small businesses back home. In the year 2000, 38,465 East Javanese workers traveled to Saudi Arabia, the United Arab Emirates, Korea, Taiwan, Hong Kong, Malaysia, and Singapore.

Throughout Indonesia's history, East Java has had extensive political, strategic, administrative, and economic influence. Its wealth and proximity to the center of national government on the island of Java have ensured that it has one of the highest levels of development and infrastructure (albeit unequally distributed) in the country. Hindu-Buddhist kingdoms (the

Kediri, the Singosari, and the Majapahit) predominated in East Java from the tenth to thirteenth centuries. Islam began to spread in the region in the thirteenth century and was dominant in East Java by the end of the sixteenth century; it also provided religious and political links between East Java and many surrounding islands. As Islam began to be integrated into East Javanese society during the end of the Majapahit era, tensions between the rituals of Javanese mysticism and the practices of devout Islam emerged.[15] The northeastern part of the province, known as the horseshoe area (*daerah tapal kuda*), eventually embraced Islam, providing one of the bases of support for the national Muslim organizations and parties.[16] It is here, on the island of Madura, that we selected our first research site, Pamekasan, which has lower conflict management capacity.

The prominent political force in the province is the National Awakening Party (PKB), which is closely affiliated with Nahdlatul Ulama (or NU), a mass religious organization representing forty million Indonesians nationwide. Nahdlatul Ulama has a network of religious, educational, entrepreneurial, trade union, and other bodies. It is often but not exclusively associated with syncretic expressions of Islam, which involve traditional Javanese practices. Such syncretic beliefs still dominate other parts of the province, in particular the more secular nationalist areas in the southwest, where we selected our second research site, Ponorogo. Of course, people in these areas still identify themselves as Muslims. Many of those we interviewed referred to themselves as "Identity Card (KTP) Muslims" and they continue to believe in the spirit life, carrying out rituals to worship their ancestors and celebrate key days in the Javanese calendar.

Ponorogo and Pamekasan, the districts in East Java selected for this study, with their varying poverty rates and population sizes, exemplify the province's diversity. The research was conducted in eight subdistricts within these two districts. The population and poverty rate of each are shown in table 3.1.

Pamekasan

Islam forms a part of daily life in Pamekasan; affiliations with Islamic political parties, religious leaders, and boarding schools are the norm. There are two major groups: the *santri* (the pious) and the *banne' santri* (the nonpious). Those who are educated in Islamic boarding schools or who have strong allegiances to local Muslim clerics are often defined as santri and granted elite standing by the community. In many cases they go

TABLE 3.1   POPULATION AND POVERTY RATES IN EAST JAVA RESEARCH DISTRICTS
AND SUBDISTRICTS

	Population	Poverty rate (%)
Pamekasan	696,932	41
Pademawu	66,867	24
Palengaan	65,790	54
Pasaen	48,619	38
Proppo	67,619	64
Ponorogo	842,211	44
Badegan	30,307	64
Jenangan	54,094	33
Sampung	39,888	52
Slahung	53,080	47

Sources: Poverty data are from the SMERU (2004) poverty map, which uses data from the 1999 SUSENAS and PODES surveys; population data are those reported by the local offices of the Bureau of Statistics (Badan Pusat Statistik 2002a, 2002b).

on to occupy both formal and informal leadership positions in the village and the wider region, in government and nongovernment institutions. Other cultural groupings exist along class lines, with peasants or commoners, bureaucrats, and people of noble descent distinguished by the different levels of language used in everyday conversation.

The island's soil surface is dominated by limestone and lime precipitate; despite high rainfall, these geological factors make it difficult for the soil to absorb and store water, leaving a harsh, dry, and infertile terrain (Kuntowijoyo 2002, 26). Such an environment is conducive to growing tobacco, the mainstay of Madurese agriculture, which is the primary source of income for the region. Water is fiercely sought after by the island's peasant farmers, who account for 70–80 percent of the population (De Jonge 1998). The lack of water also affects the livelihoods of other occupation groups in the region such as fishermen and traders, whose sales depend on a successful agricultural harvest. During the dry season, informants told us, tempers flare, and conflict, particularly over access to scarce agricultural resources, becomes more prevalent. The difficult agricultural conditions may play a role in creating the picture, portrayed by some of our respondents, of the Madurese as harsh, hot-blooded, and frank individuals who are likely to use violence to solve problems (see map 3.2).

Map 3.2   Location of Pamekasan research subdistricts

Legends from Madura trace violence back to the year 929.[17] There is a long history of *nyikep,* the custom of carrying weapons, which, many respondents stated, was inherited from their Madurese ancestors and is necessary for their daily agricultural practices. De Jonge (1998) writes in detail of the violent culture that developed following the rebellion of the Madurese and their separation from the Mataram sultanate around 1700, during the Dutch colonial era. When poor and repressed citizens no longer saw the institutions in the kingdom as legitimate centers of power, crime rates spiked and the community began to develop modalities of problem-solving that did not involve government interference (Wiyata 2002, 67–68). The best-known custom in this vein is *carok.*

Carok, which is unique to the Madurese, involves defending one's honor in a violent duel. The custom usually involves challenging one's opponent, most often using a sickle, the main tool of agricultural practice in the region. These duels occur between individuals as well as between groups. Traditionally, duels, more often than not, are carried through to the death, even if this contravenes state law and local regulations. Although carok may have its origins in the harsh environment and feudal politics of Madura (Wiyata 2002, 70), over time the custom has become intertwined with changing local values. Since religious beliefs began to dominate the social landscape, defending slurs against Islam has become one of the key reasons for engaging in carok. The patriarchal nature of Madurese society, often reinforced by local interpretations of Islam, has resulted in women being considered a part of "man's being." Hence, slurs against the name of a wife, sister, or loved one, as well as extramarital affairs, are considered slurs against the husband, brother, or father, for which a just response can entail the honor killing of the perpetrator. For example, as one young man explained in a focus group discussion late one night in a poorer, more isolated village:

Q: What sort of problems does the community here normally face?
A: Problems with women and also *santet* [black magic]. It's dangerous if you have an affair and then are found out; for example, if my wife were to sleep with someone else, she could not be forgiven. Basically she would have to die or she would have to go somewhere far away . . . and never come back. If the woman is still single, she can be seen in the street with whomever she wants! [the respondent laughs to indicate that he is just joking].

Carok is also used to defend property, settle heated arguments between men, and to secure political and economic gain in a calculated way. Villagers told us that the custom is dying out in the more urban areas in Madura, in part because of education and modernization, but it remains strong in some of the more rural villages.[18] Values instilled from birth continue to promote a sense of courage in the Madurese people, best captured by the local expression "*ango'a pote tolang etembang pote mata*" (better white bones than white eyes). This saying expresses the value that it is better to die than to live haunted by feelings of shame. Interviewees in one of the subdistricts where the study was conducted gave an example of how carok plays out in more modern times:

The few meetings between Mahmud and Hayani made her fiancé Musdari wild with anger. It seems he was suspicious all this time.

—SUBDISTRICT MILITARY COMMANDER

At the time, Musdari deliberately went in search of Mahmud. He was carrying a sickle . . . and wanted to kill Mahmud. As it happened, they met on the broken bridge and Musdari stopped Mahmud immediately. After berating him for a moment, Musdari got out his sickle, intending to kill Mahmud. Mahmud immediately ran away into the rice fields. . . . Because Musdari could not kill Mahmud, he vandalized Mahmud's motorcycle until it was irreparable.

—RAHMAH, HAYANI'S NEIGHBOR

Carok in Madura is a tradition which has been passed down from our ancestors; therefore, we have to preserve the tradition. If there is some-one who isn't brave enough to engage in carok, they will be considered not to be true Madurese. But, you also have to take the type of problem into account; if it's about principles, you have to be brave enough to engage in carok. For this reason, it is better for a Madurese person to die rather than have to live with the shame. Also, it will have a mental impact on my descendants; if I am wronged and then I am not brave enough to engage in carok, my children will later be made fools of or belittled because their father was considered a coward. My poor children.

—YOUNG MAN, PALENGAAN LAOK

Madurese culture differs from Javanese culture, which dominates mainland Java. Whereas Javanese farmers cultivate wet fields, the Madurese use a variety of local practices to cultivate the dry fields. Such practices have led to a specific housing pattern that clusters houses together across villages, often along kinship lines. Such a settlement pattern builds strong internal family solidarity in which insults to individuals are regarded as insults to the extended family. Wiyata (2002), however, argues that this residential pattern weakens the sense of community of the whole village—particularly in the more isolated villages, which do not frequently engage with newcomers, traders, and people from other parts of the village—in part explaining how divisions emerge within villages as well as between them.

Pamekasan district has three regions, and different groups of people have come to occupy each. The first is the area in the north, where many peasant farmers, fishermen, and traders live.[19] Muslim clerics (kyai) and those boarding at Koranic studies schools (pondok pesantren) occupy the areas in the west of the district, where the community possesses higher levels of religious education.[20] The area in the southwest is where many of the members of the government administration and parliament live. Many members of the elite or aristocratic classes live in this region.[21] This historical and geographic division of the community has affected social structures. For example, the north and the west have higher levels of crime than the areas to the southeast where the elites reside. Furthermore, mafia-like crime networks led by local thugs (known as bajingan) dominate the north and parts of the religious areas of Pamekasan.[22] To summarize, the following contextual features of the province play out in the kinds of social conflicts that dominate the district and more frequently result in violence: access to natural resources, clashes between bajingan, revenge-seeking through carok (or in areas where this is a fading custom, vigilante responses to unsolved crimes), and political power battles along the major divides and groupings in society described above (see box 3.2).

BOX 3.2   SOCIAL JUSTICE AND RETRIBUTION-SEEKING IN BANYUPELLE

One day two youths from different families were cajoling each other while watching a soccer match. They originally were from different villages, although they currently resided in the same village. On several occasions following a soccer match, the older members of the boys' families had had heated arguments as they sought to defend the boys' and their families' honor. Tensions between the two parties became increasingly heated and rumors of carok spread.

One market day, a mass carok broke out between the two families in the Aengnyonok market in the rural Banyupelle village. After fifteen minutes, three lives had been lost, and countless people were wounded. There was no time to alert the police so that they could intervene. Several participants in the clash surrendered themselves at the Palengaan subdistrict police station after the incident. All but two of the other actors were arrested by the police at their respective homes.

Understanding these local contexts, the social cleavages, the existing power dynamics, and the leading forms of existing conflict can help us distinguish between new conflicts generated by development projects and preexisting conflicts that projects exacerbate. In Pamekasan as with the other districts, the nature of development programs and their provision of resources meant that they were more likely to inflame existing tensions related to resource allocation and management, particularly along the lines of existing cleavages in the villages, than other sources of tension. Yet development projects in Pamekasan also interacted with other preexisting conflict in villages, especially those that were in various ways linked to battles for power, such as village elections. Rarely did development programs interact with cases of vigilantism, except where extended retributive cycles of justice-seeking escalated into broader power battles in the region between groups and their leaders: in this case, programs such as KDP could become arenas of contestation. In particular, when KDP was poorly implemented and monitored, it became an avenue for waging power battles between incumbent and new elites or the groups associated with these elites, often the same groups involved in other conflicts that were less directly related to resources. In such cases, these elites could use their support groups, including the bajingan, to pressure facilitators or other villagers into approving particular proposals; in other programs where monitoring and facilitation were less prevalent, incumbent elites tended to dominate the entire process, often to their own benefit.

Ponorogo

Ponorogo, the third-poorest district in East Java (Badan Pusat Statistik 2000), is situated at the far end of the province, bordering Central Java province (see map 3.3). In contrast to Madura, the dominant ethnic group is Javanese. Geertz's classification of Javanese society provides a useful means of understanding social identity groups in Ponorogo in the current era: the *priyayi* tend to be associated with the bureaucrats and gatekeepers of Javanese morality, the *abangan* are loosely associated with the grassroots non-Muslims (or nondevout Muslims), and the *santri* are perceived to be the devout followers of Islam.[23]

As in Pamekasan, the introduction of Islam in Ponorogo was not smooth; there were challenges from both the grassroots and local leaders to the spread of Islam during the demise of the Hindu-Buddhist kingdom of Majapahit. In protest against the growing dominance of Islam, one local leader, Ki Ageng Kutu (a Buddhist chief during the declining years of the Majapahit kingdom), exiled himself to Kutu village and founded the Surukebeng Martial Arts School. Schools of this nature often house students and teach the broader ideology as well as the physical skills of the martial arts (such as wrestling, stick fighting, and sword fighting) and more mystical skills such as *kebal* (magical powers that prevent sharp weapons from penetrating the body during a fight). They are known in Javanese as *padepokan* (Fauzanafi 2002, 204). Ki Ageng Kutu used the youth in his padepokan as a support base for

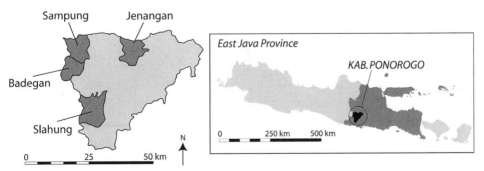

Map 3.3   Location of Ponorogo research subdistricts

his ideology and broader pursuits. The school provided training in *gamelan* (Javanese orchestra) music, a tradition that continues today.

Performances of these martial arts are exemplified in *reyog*, traditional Javanese dance performed to gamelan music. They were traditionally used by Ki Ageng Kutu and his followers and later generations as public satire against the infiltration of Islam in the region (Fauzanafi 2002; Simatupang 2002). By the time of the reign of the Islamic kingdom of Demak in the sixteenth century, reyog was used to weave Islamic teachings with traditional Javanese spiritual teachings (*kejawen*), which were allowed to remain in cultural consciousness as long as they were altered to encompass the teachings of Islam.[24] Reyog performances continue to be very popular in Ponorogo today. They are organized to celebrate special days of the Javanese calendar as well as births, weddings, and other ceremonies; they are scheduled throughout the year, and all local citizens, young and old, attend these performances en masse.

Martial arts groups and practices (known as *silat*) are influential across the region. There are two dominant martial arts groups, each of which has its headquarters in the neighboring Madiun district: SH Terate and SH Winongo. The SH stands for *setia hati*, which means "loyal"; the two groups grew from one organization, Setia Hati, which was formed in Surabaya in 1903 (Ponorogo Manunggal Terate Cooperative n.d., 4). With tens of thousands of members and a hierarchical organizational structure, these groups provide a key source of identity for many male (and sometimes female) youth in Ponorogo, and encounters between them—often at reyog and other cultural performances—can have violent consequences as each group defends its honor in the face of perceived or actual slurs.

These cultural groups are also closely linked to the terrain of Ponorogo, which is divided into two areas: the highlands and the lowlands.[25] The district has fourteen rivers, which irrigate the rice-growing areas in the lowlands; the mountainous areas are used for agriculture as well (Badan Pusat Statistik 2002b, xxxvi). The majority of people work as farmers, farmhands, and laborers, although in the more urban areas employment in government and other service providers is more common.[26] The use of stereotypes is prevalent in the rural communities, and one reference point is the Sekayu River. Respondents from the *wong wetan kali* community (who live to the east of the river) view the *wong kulon kali* community (those to the west of the river) as rough, lawless and kejawen—as people who mix Javanese cultural practices with those of Islam.[27] Meanwhile the wong kulon kali community views the wong wetan kali as newcomers who do not fully understand Ponorogo culture. These stereotypes reflect deep-rooted worldviews that also find expression in daily practices. The district government at the time of the study, for example, sought to paint the kejawan and reyog groups as criminal elements.[28] For those involved in reyog, however, they are traditional heroes who walk the fine line between being warriors and outlaws, with the *warok* (Ponorogo's experts in martial arts and mysticism) as their leaders (Simatupang 2002, 40).

District politics is not removed from the cultural groups and practice. The district head in power when our research was conducted was from the Golkar Party. During the race for district head, which occurred in 2000, prior to our research, he lobbied the reyog leaders to pressure the PDI-P's preferred candidate for the position to withdraw his candidacy.[29] In addition, he lobbied the Islamic leaders in the community and other reyog leaders to pressure the Islamic and opposition PDI-P members of the parliament to support his candidacy. As in Pamekasan, these contextual features help shape the conflicts that are most frequent in Ponorogo and those that are more likely to result in violence: clashes between martial arts groups, battles for political power, and competition for different types of resources valued by local people.

Three major kinds of conflicts were identified in the case research in East Java. The first involved retributive cycles of justice-seeking, for breaking the state law or moral codes in the communities. The second consisted of conflicts over competition for control of state offices especially during district and village head elections. The third involved conflicts over the ownership and use of natural and manmade resources, as well as how these were managed by private companies or the state. Most of the conflicts pertaining to development processes and the implementation of development projects and programs fall into the final category. As with Pamekasan, development processes tended to interact with conflicts over resource allocation and procedural justice-seeking regarding how these resources were managed, as well as local battles for power between incumbent and new elites. But the prevalence of state enterprises in the district (many more than in Pamekasan) meant that there was often an overlap between disputes triggered by development programs and those involving state enterprises, particularly where state land or the same actors were involved. In one case, the tensions between silat groups played out to a minor extent through the KDP forums, demonstrating the need to understand the forms of conflict and social cleavages in local contexts in order to avoid their affecting development programs. Box 3.3 illustrates one example of the kinds of local conflicts taking place in Ponorogo.

BOX 3.3   TENSIONS BETWEEN MARTIAL ARTS SCHOOLS

This conflict took place between members of the SH Terate and SH Winongo martial arts groups at a performance of *campursari* (traditional Javanese songs accompanied by pentatonic music and traditional performance art) in Sampung village.

> There was a fight during a campursari performance to the west of Sampung market . . . ; many people from the west of the market came en masse to Ponorogo, drunk and making trouble with the Terate kids from Medang, who were also watching the event.
>
> —SH TERATE PONOROGO BRANCH COORDINATOR

The group of young SH Terate people from Medang hamlet attacked the SH Winongo youth. In a show of force the Terate supporters sought out more Winongo youth but failed. The SH Terate youth vandalized homes, to the extent that one home was almost burned down near the performance site.

> The house next to mine was vandalized. Those kids came from everywhere. Their motorcycles were roaring away, it was very noisy. . . . The house to the east of mine was going to be burned. . . . If it had spread to here it would have been a disaster—they were carrying bottles of petrol.
>
> —COMMUNITY FIGURE, SAMPUNG

East Nusa Tenggara

The second province selected for the study is East Nusa Tenggara (or NTT). As we have noted, NTT differs in almost every respect from East Java. It is one of Indonesia's poorest provinces, with a regional per capita GDP of only Rp. 2,201,100, or a little more than US$200 (Badan Pusat Statistik 2002c). Seventy percent of its people make their living from the soil, often through subsistence agriculture. The province is located far from the center of national government and, in contrast to East Java, has extraordinary ethnic and geographic diversity. One survey estimated that there are sixty-one linguistic groups in the province alone (Grimes et al. 1997), the result not only of migration over the centuries but also of the continuing strength of clan and kinship systems that result in ethnic differentiation taking place at a very localized level. In the 2003 census, 29.5 percent of people in the province reported themselves as being of an ethnicity with less than 109 persons in the province.[30] Throughout the past century and during the state-endorsed 1980s transmigration program, a small number of immigrants—mainly Savunese,

Bimanese, Buginese, Javanese, and Makasarese—from elsewhere in Indonesia settled on the island of Flores. In contrast to East Java, NTT is also more mixed in terms of religion, with large populations of Catholics and Protestants and a smaller proportion of Muslims.

The province faces extensive problems of poor infrastructure provision, low population density, underdevelopment, and high poverty levels, which make it all the more challenging to implement development programs. Most islands in NTT—there are 556 in all, although only 42 are inhabited—face physical limitations of geography such as low rainfall, lack of irrigation and drinking water, and susceptibility to natural disasters (Sayogo 1994, 4). This is particularly true of Flores, home of both our NTT research districts.

Flores offers an interesting window though which to examine questions about the nature of conflict and conflict resolution in Indonesia (see box 3.4). The island may not be a hotbed of unrest to the extent of, say, Central Sulawesi or Maluku, but conflict is a major part of life in Flores, and it is having a serious and often detrimental effect on the way local communities function.[31] There is large enough variation within Flores to help us gain a better understanding of the role of local factors—and their interaction with provincial, national, and global processes—in determining the forms of conflict and its outcomes (violent or nonviolent). The fact that the area has not yet experienced a major outbreak of violent conflict allows us to examine the kinds of conflict that affect the vast majority of Indonesians and that probably affect those who live in the high-conflict areas, too.[32]

Box 3.4   ADAT IN FLORES

With a population of a little more than 1.5 million at the time of our research, the island of Flores is the largest and most populous island in NTT. Located between the famous Komodo island (to the west), Alor (to the east), Sulawesi (to the north), and Timor (to the south), the island takes its name from how its eastern cape was known to the colonial Portuguese: *Cabo de Flores*, or the Cape of Flowers. The majority of the Florenese are Catholic (84 percent), with only 13 percent adhering to Muslim beliefs, thus almost inverting the Indonesian average. Flores has primarily a subsistence economy that contributes little to Indonesia's GDP; the island has received little attention from analysts of the Indonesian state or economy. Because it is eclipsed by events on Timor, neither academics nor policy makers concerned about conflict have shown much interest in Flores. The island is particularly diverse; the Flores–Lembata region is home to twenty-eight different ethno-linguistic groups. Some of our informants put the number of distinct languages on Flores at more than fifty.

Customs and traditions (*adat*) define many elements of life in Flores. Adat deals with all domains of human life: the social, the political, the economic, and the spiritual. It is simultaneously a customary legal system, a form of social and political hierarchy (with adat leaders at the top), and a set of traditional values. Indeed, when villagers are asked why they do something, it is not unusual for them to answer, "Just because of adat." These habits have been passed down from one generation to another. Despite encroaching modernization, adat values and norms remain strong throughout Flores and adat leaders continue to play an important role as *tokoh masyarakat* (community leaders) in decision making and dispute resolution, especially at the village level. Adat is of great importance in Flores as a rhetorical term that frames local discourse, as a guide for living, and as a means for solving problems.

Adat also provides norms for which kinds of attitudes and forms of behavior are seen as acceptable and which are not. The aim is to preserve balance and harmony among people and to mend broken relationships.[a] These norms include respecting orders and advice from parents.[b] Adat norms govern people's lives and help them, as a local saying goes, "walk on the paved road and cross on the good hill." The breaking of adat norms means disrupting the flow, thus affecting others' lives; these relations and ties need to be restored in a special ceremony. In settling a problem, adat leaders might invite the village elders, the local government, and the neighboring adat leaders to meet. At the start, an adat leader asks both sides to provide details of the case. If both sides recognize and agree about what has happened, then an appropriate sanction is applied. With the mediation of the adat leader or leaders, the parties negotiate the sanction and the way to retie both sides again with a peace ceremony. Adat authorities have responsibility not only for giving a verdict but also for investigating the case and for implementing and enforcing the sanction. Although adat laws and actors remain strong, the means by which adat is enacted are changing. Whereas before it was passed down orally, in recent years (and especially in Sikka district) there have been attempts to write down adat law.[c]

Notes

a. See Tule (2000) on the role of the adat house in creating and sustaining social harmony in Flores.

b. In Manggarai, a common expression that encapsulates this is "*Pede dise ende, mbate dise ame*," which means, "Orders [advice] from your mother and an inheritance from your father." Indeed this advice helps perpetuate adat; instructions for adat living are passed down through the generations.

c. Informants told us that the village apparatus, adat elders, and the BPD (village council) had produced a *hera tada* (written adat law) so that each hamlet would have the same norms and sanctions.

Manggarai

We chose two districts, Sikka and Manggarai, for the research. As with district selection in East Java, Manggarai was chosen for having lower capacity to manage conflict than does Sikka (that is, violence is more likely in the former). Table 3.2 outlines the population and poverty rates in each district.

Manggarai is relatively densely populated in comparison with other districts in Flores (Badan Pusat Statistik 2002c) and is located on the opposite end of the island from Sikka. Despite the higher rate of poverty in Manggarai, it arguably has greater development potential than Flores's other districts. It is by far NTT's largest district. In June 2003, the district was split in two with the formation of West Manggarai.[33] It has good soil, and its economy is based on wet rice irrigation, coffee plants, vanilla, pearls, gas power, and tourism. A range of cultural and lineage groups inhabit Manggarai. A large proportion of its land is held communally and governed according to the adat system. Boundaries are not formally titled or codified but are usually defined by geographic features such as field boundaries, rivers, roads, avenues of trees, and other (often malleable) features. These

TABLE 3.2   POPULATION AND POVERTY RATES IN NTT RESEARCH DISTRICTS AND SUBDISTRICTS

	Population	Poverty rate (%)
Manggarai	591,222	68
Cibal	33,715	72
Kota Komba	38,491	72
Lamba Leda	26,158	77
Ruteng	60,045	72
Sikka	264,560	61
Maumere	23,163	56
Nita	29,090	74
Paga	12,759	73
Talibura	23,474	63

Sources: Poverty data is from the SMERU (2004) poverty map, which uses data from the 1999 SUSENAS and PODES surveys; population data is that reported by the provincial offices of the Bureau of Statistics (Badan Pusat Statistik 2002c).

boundaries can be altered over the years in response to changing needs and power balances.[34]

Manggarai (map 3.4) is the only district in Flores that was influenced and colonized by the Goa kingdom of South Sulawesi as well as the Bima kingdom of the island of Sumbawa. Verheijen (1991) reports that the Goa influence in Manggarai was felt much earlier, before Goa became an Islamic kingdom. The Bima kingdom spread Muslim influence, and Islam remains strong in the western part of Manggarai, as well as on the northern coast of Flores. Manggarai adopted Bima's modes of government (the *kedaluan* system), which continues to influence everyday life and leadership. The *adak* (kingdom) of Manggarai was made up of thirty-eight kedaluan, which were used by the Dutch as the main unit of administration for the area. The *dalu,* the head of the kedaluan, governed the different *gelarang* (intervillage governments) below the kedaluan level. These intervillage governments, in turn, governed the villages (*beo* or *golo*) within their area, each administered by a *tua beo* or a *tua golo* (Toda 1999, 248). The Dutch appointed the dalu as king of Manggarai. This system of government was practiced until Indonesian independence was achieved, although the Bima system formally left Manggarai in 1929 (Erb 1999). During the precolonial and colonial periods, the kedaluan were often at war with each other.

Verheijen (1991, 16–21) has reported that Manggarai encompasses five cultural groups: the Komodo, the Waerana, the Rajong/Razong, the Rembong, and a group in Ngada district (on the northern coast). In practice, however, group identity still has its roots in the old colonial system

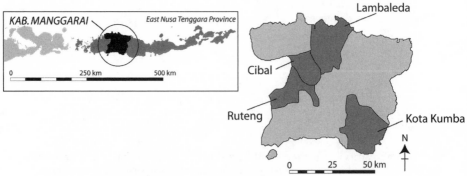

Map 3.4   Location of Manggarai research subdistricts

outlined above. The kedaluan in Manggarai still form the primary basis for group identity and (in some cases) the markers for intergroup tensions. The fact that the subdistricts that formally divide Manggarai today were built on the historical borders of the kedaluan (with one or more kedaluan absorbed into each subdistrict) has only served to reinforce the system as a basis of identity to the present day.

At the micro level, group identity is based on *panga* or *mbaru* (lineage) and the beo or golo (village). Generally, these fit well together because people of the same lineage form one unit—sharing risk and creating wealth—and live together in a village. Lineage and village identities can be extended through marriage, as well as through alliances between lineages formed because of common interests. Several lineages with the same historical background may join together to fight against other groups. At the same time, there is also a unity between the golo and the *lingko* (the traditional round garden). A golo has its own communal garden as a center for the farming system; this garden is meant to unite all the different lineages in a village. Because of this, problems regarding land will usually involve the whole lineage or several lineages and villages.

Traditionally, adat elders were the repositories of knowledge about traditional land boundaries. *Kar,* or a map, showing the borders, name, and measurements of each piece of communal land was held by the king of Tamur in the early twentieth century. During District Head Gaspar Ehok's rule, however, this map was burned; some allege that it was an act of arson. Therefore, no written record exists for much of the land in Manggarai. The knowledge and authority of adat systems have been under attack since the Dutch era, and traditional methods of intervention and conflict resolution have also been undermined. As the state and accompanying ideas of modernity have penetrated to the level of the village, an ontologically diverse marketplace has developed wherein different groups make appeals based on different normative systems of justice (Bowen 2003). This can result in competing claims for land, leading to conflict (Prior 2003, 2004; Clark 2004).

Furthermore, in many cases people in Flores do not try to negotiate their problems by themselves, for a number of reasons. First, norms of group and adat identity are very strong, so individual disputes tend to get elevated into matters for group concern. Thus, most land-related problems in Manggarai are not considered to be between individuals but between groups. As a result, group leaders are often utilized to deal with problems on behalf of the disputants. Second, in many situations the problem is deeply entrenched, particularly when it relates to land, as land is very closely identified with the cultural heritage and cosmology of the different linguistic groups. As such, resolution is often considered beyond the capacity of the disputants, who, knowing this, do not even try to resolve it themselves and instead seek the assistance of adat elders.

These cultural and contextual factors shape the problems that result in conflicts in Manggarai, particularly those concerning land, access to land, unclear boundaries, and encroachment by the state or other groups on communal land. Unlike East Java, where there is a much clearer division between disputes over, say, land and contraventions of social norms such as those involving offended pride, Manggarai has a propensity for greater overlap, particularly regarding ownership of land. The likelihood that development programs will be contested and that these struggles will have more deadly consequences is therefore greater. This is because many of these programs, including KDP, require access to particular parcels of land in order to implement the activities that villagers chose to fund.

One such problem is illustrated in box 3.5. The issue emerged when the state decided to prohibit the cultivation of protected forests (state-owned land) by the adat communities who traditionally cultivated such land. The land in question had been designated as protected forest on the basis of a declaration by the Dutch authorities in 1937. In 1972, a six-person team from the provincial government redrew the forest borders. In October 1984, the borders of the protected Kuwus Forest were extended, encroaching on land already cultivated by the adat community in question. On January 21, 1986, these extended borders were confirmed by the Minister of Forestry in Jakarta. The question was whether the adat community was involved in determining the borders between the adat land and the protected land. The documents state that the borders were made with the agreement of the local population but do not name names; the only fingerprints on the document are those of the administrative village head, who represented the state. According to the government, the village head signed on behalf of the villagers; according to the adat community, the village head had no right to sign on their behalf because only the traditional village head and the land guardian have the customary right and community-given moral authority to do so. The case remains unresolved.

Box 3.5   Conflict Between the Police and the Colol People

Ninety percent of conflict in Manggarai is over land.
—MILITARY DISTRICT COMMANDER, MANGGARAI

One day people from the villages of Colol, Biting, and Cangkul (approximately 120 people in all) boarded three trucks and made the two-hour drive to the district capital, Ruteng. There they planned to negotiate with the police for the release of seven villagers arrested, the day before. The seven had been arrested because they were suspected of working on land that was deemed protected forest. The district government had been destroying crops—coffee, bananas, taro—and huts within the protected forest and had tried to arrest those working in those areas. The protesting villagers wanted to negotiate with the police to release the seven arrestees, as well as to change the status of the land. In the protest they claimed that they worked on their own land.

When the villagers arrived, however, matters took a violent turn. According to the police, the villagers tried to attack the police and the police station with stones, knives, and wooden bats. The police took what they called protective action. A violent clash ensued between the police and the Colol people. The police fired on the crowd, which was massed around the station. Six people died, more than forty were severely injured, and another thirty villagers incurred minor injuries. Three policemen were injured.

An internal investigation found some junior officers guilty of misconduct and suspended them from going on training courses for a period of time.

Sikka

Sikka consists of two main ethnic groups: Sikka Krowe and Lio. The former is the largest cultural group, but in the past it was divided into three *swapraja*, or kingdoms: Sikka, Nita, and Kangae. Sikka was traditionally the most powerful group in the government bureaucracy, largely because the Dutch viewed the group's leadership as the easiest to work with. During the Dutch administration, many different areas were combined to form the Sikka region, under the control of a member of the Sikka ethnic group. The Dutch implemented a strategy aimed at having the Sikka-dominated region as the center of government, the economy, and the development of religion. Such a strategy led to jealousy among the indigenous groups, with many feeling colonized by the Sikka people. Some consider that the Sikka people continue to be favored in the postcolonial environment, and it has been argued that in the past the Catholic Church has provided greater support for the indigenous Sikka people.[35] The relative dominance of the ethnic Sikka group has declined, however, as education levels—and with them access to political positions—have increased for other ethnic groups in the district. This has resulted in greater competition between groups, contributing to local conflicts.

At the micro level, group identity in Sikka can be formed through kinship or lineage, through the unit area (the village or hamlet administrative area), or through common interests. Those who are not from the same village or lineage group are generally considered to be *orang luar* (outsiders). Group identity is often a gateway for nepotism and corruption. In Manggarai, communal land forms a basis for group identity, but in Sikka most land is held individually, with the exception of some land belonging to the ethnic Lio group. Sikka is also smaller than Manggarai, and this geographic difference affects the transportation and information network. It is easier to get to villages in Sikka than in Manggarai; the transportation infrastructure is better in the former, and villages are in general better connected to local markets. Improved transportation links in Sikka are undoubtedly contributing to growing modernization within the district (see map 3.5).[36]

Sikka also has some potential for development, including tourism. Crops grown include copra, cacao, and corn, but many areas face water shortages and very dry land. Maumere and Nita, two of the subdistricts where the research took place, have serious water problems. During the dry season, people have to buy water for family needs or they have to compete in order to get the limited public water that is available. The price of cash crops is very low, making life difficult for many peasants.

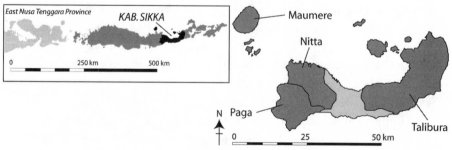

Map 3.5   Location of Sikka research subdistricts

A serious and widespread problem in Sikka is domestic violence (which is also common in Manggarai). Across Flores, respondents outlined that, given the patriarchal nature of their society, women are to serve and obey their husbands. Domestic chores are the responsibility of local women, and failing in these duties or disobeying the demands of men often triggers incidents of domestic violence. Often such cases relate to *belis*, the local dowry system. Belis ties the wife's family to that of her husband; it is also meant to convey respect for the bride. The amount of the belis is often negotiated, and payment is analogous to the groom's owning the bride and treating her as he pleases. The families of women with higher social status can command higher sums in the form of belis. Other sources of frequent conflict in Sikka are similar to those found in Manggarai: land ownership, battles for political power and positions, access to other resources, and the management and allocation of these resources.

A Project Among Many

Into these culturally, demographically, politically, and economically diverse contexts a variety of development projects have been placed. In the years following the fall of the New Order government, among the largest of these has been the Kecamatan Development Program. Some of its core elements and signature characteristics were alluded to in Chapter 1; before reviewing in detail the range of empirical evidence assembled to try to disentangle different kinds of project effects and context effects, we reprise some of KDP's key features.

KDP aims to introduce transparent, accountable, and participatory development planning at the local level. This approach stands in stark contrast to the practices of the Suharto regime, in which development decision making was mainly delivered top-down from the central government to the provinces, districts, subdistricts, and villages. During the New Order, village governments, in particular village heads, sought development funding primarily by forming allegiances with and lobbying for funding from higher-level bureaucrats in the governance hierarchy. This gave them control over both spending and policy at the village level. As Antlov (2003a, 74–79) stresses,

> New Order politics was based on ideological monopoly, forced allegiances, and political mobilization ahead of elections. A closing down

of politics was introduced in 1971 with the "floating mass" policy (formalized in law in 1975), whereby political activities were banned below the *kabupaten/kota* (district/city) level. . . . Along with the legacy of anti-politics, depoliticization has had the effect of depriving ordinary citizens and prospective leaders alike of critical knowledge about how to engage in politics. For decades, people learnt that the only way to resolve conflicts was through violence; that the only way to reach decisions was by monopolizing power; that the only way to gain promotion was by manipulating connections; and that the only way to conduct politics was through patronage. . . . Previously, under Law No. 5/1979, village governments had to conform to a standardized pattern and traditional governance structures were not recognized. Villages had no autonomy and were under the direct authority of the sub-district government—they could take no decision without prior approval of a higher authority. In exchange for their subordination and loyalty, village heads, as "clients of the state," were invested with almost unlimited powers; they were the "sole power" in the village. As the *ex officio* chair of the now discontinued Village Consultative Assembly (LMD) and the Village Community Resilience Board (LKMD), the village head was in firm control of village-level government.

It is into this governance environment—one defined by the hegemony of, and patrimonial ties between, village elites and higher-level bureaucrats—that KDP, with its contrasting principles of local participation, transparency, and accountability, was introduced. The program's defining element entails the provision of block grants to subdistrict committees, which are comprised primarily of nongovernmental representatives from constituent villages, who together decide how the grant in each subdistrict will be spent. Initially, groups of villagers brainstorm and then prioritize ideas for small things they would like to see funded in their village—for example, the paving of a road, the building of a bridge over a stream, a community center, or a savings and loan fund.

Supported by input from technical experts such as engineers, they then submit proposals for funding to the committee at the subdistrict level. Each village sends a group to participate in the selection committee at the subdistrict level. Those villagers then set about the task of evaluating the merits of the proposals, assessing their technical and financial feasibility, the level of voluntary contribution from the village, and their likely impact and sustainability; the most important criterion for selection, however, is the extent to which the project benefits the poor. All deliberation is conducted in public, and all outcomes are posted on community bulletin boards, with journalists encouraged to report any abuses in local newspapers; NGOs are also trained and contracted to monitor any problems.

The program thus introduces, or tries to introduce, rules-based, transparent, and accountable competition into village life. In the process it creates winners and losers—some proposals are funded, some are not—and thus the potential for conflict. But it also creates new spaces for public deliberation, new avenues for participation by marginalized groups, and new opportunities for the cultivation of civic skills: debating difference, assessing claims, managing meetings, and keeping records. It also challenges the prevailing hierarchy of top-down elite-centered decision making.

In the vein of Cornwall and Coelho's (2004) arguments about "new democratic spaces"—the hybrid institutions at the interface between state and society evolving from governance reforms that provide greater space for the inclusion of civil society in governance—KDP in this sense represents a "participatory sphere institution." Cornwall and Coelho (2007) identify such institutions as creating spaces wherein more marginalized groups can be included in governance and create change in policy and practice.[37] As they argue, substantive participation and ultimately policy change are contingent on closing the gap between the legal and technical apparatus created to institutionalize participation for poorer, more marginalized citizens—such as that provided through KDP rules and processes—and substantive inclusion (ibid.). Does the program manage to increase real participation, and if so, does this generate tensions or conflict? If not, do disillusioned villagers protest when KDP does not generate change in practice, or do they suffer from the problem of quiescence, so that tacit domination prevents their voice from ever emerging to question hegemonic power structures (Gaventa 1980, 2005)?

Cornwall and Coelho (2007) contend that power dynamics course through every dimension of participatory sphere institutions. They also assert that these new institutions are infused with the power relations and cultures of interaction of other spaces (the contexts from which participants originate). As such, they emphasize the importance of understanding the context in which such institutions are introduced as a basis for understanding whether and how they become an avenue for change (albeit contested) or simply a new means by which old elites reassert their dominance. Furthermore,

Cornwall (2002) argues that where institutions do not give attention to design features that help mediate conflict, secure particular configurations of roles and forms of representation, and address the tensions and trade-offs between inclusiveness and effectiveness, it is easy enough for old ways and forms of exclusion and domination to persist in new spaces. Introducing new institutions is inherently conflictual and is likely to generate tensions as the power, decision making, and resource allocation mechanisms of the old guard are challenged. We return to this theme at various points in this book, for it underpins our main research question: What is the relation between context, KDP, and conflict?

Specifically, do the new spaces, avenues, and civic skills introduced by KDP help villagers find constructive resolutions to disputes, project-related or not? Or does the program worsen tensions and make conflicts more likely? The project also introduces rules relating to procurement and implementation aimed at minimizing corruption, while building expectations among villagers of transparency and accountability (Woodhouse 2005). Does increased transparency make program-related conflict less likely because corruption is harder to get away with? Or does bringing such program malfunctions to the surface and creating expectations of community oversight of other village development programs trigger fresh conflict? In short, can such projects as KDP be part of a solution to managing local conflict, or (like too many other development initiatives) is it part of the problem?

The program consists of a rather straightforward system of decision making and administration. Block grants of between US$60,000 and $110,000 are provided directly to subdistricts. These grants can be used for almost anything that villagers feel is a development priority for their village (some items are off limits: houses of worship, for example, cannot be built with KDP funds). Though primarily justified on instrumental grounds— KDP can deliver high volumes of well-targeted material resources to poor communities—its broader and more ambitious aim is to encourage and institutionalize community participation in decision making and priority-setting. It seeks to do this via a series of carefully facilitated meetings held at the hamlet, village, and kecamatan levels. In many areas, these forums, though part of Indonesia's cultural heritage, were largely defunct prior to the introduction of KDP; they were revitalized and now form an integral part of the program. Suggestions for proposals originate at facilitated brainstorming meetings (*penggalian gaggasan*) at the hamlet level. The process of brainstorming is run by village facilitators. They travel to each hamlet in the village, advertise the brainstorming sessions through formal channels as well as outreach to villagers less likely to hear about the process through the more formal top-down processes, and assist villagers in writing their proposals. A special meeting is then held for women from all hamlets, with the aim of assisting them to further develop their ideas and build their skills for participation in the village-level meeting. In so doing, KDP seeks to include the voices of those likely to be marginalized—in particular, poor women and people in isolated hamlets—and better incorporate them into the decision-making process. Such efforts serve to decrease the gap between the technical rules and substantive participation that is important in such participatory sphere institutions.

After proposals ideas are developed they are taken to a village meeting, (Musyawarah Desa, or MD) where the community democratically decides which two proposals are most worthy to be discussed at the subdistrict intervillage meeting (Musyawarah Antar Desa, or MAD). At that subdistrict meeting, village delegations (which in the first three-year iteration of KDP consisted of the head of the technical implementation team, the village head, and four other community members, generally elected, at least three of whom had to be women) present their proposals and together decide which will be funded. This forum produces vigorous negotiations and horse-trading because the project intentionally does not fund all proposals.

The KDP process is facilitated at various stages by a network of local project facilitators who help socialize the program, organize the meetings, link the community with outside assistance (if necessary), and ensure that project implementation runs smoothly. In each KDP village, two village facilitators (FDs) are selected (one man and one woman) to introduce the project to villagers. At the subdistrict level, two subdistrict facilitators (FKs) are appointed, one focusing on social issues and the other on technical matters. The subdistrict facilitators have institutional backing but are relatively independent of local power structures, which means that they should be well placed to troubleshoot problems that may arise.

Proposal selection usually takes six to eight months, after which each successful village forms a Village Project Implementation Team; the villages together form a Financial Management Unit for the entire subdistrict. These are elected positions held by locals. The community then carries out its project, with the majority of labor and material acquired locally. Most projects are finished within six months, bringing the total program time to approximately one year. In order to encourage the incorporation of KDP practices into village life and to ensure that new groups of villagers get an opportunity to apply for funding, KDP works on a three-year cycle (the whole year-long process is repeated two more times). The program went through three iterations as a project funded primarily by the World Bank (with the operational guidelines fine-tuned as the project went along) before becoming a fully national project (renamed PNPM) in September 2006 with significant government co-financing.

In a strictly organizational sense, KDP has clearly been deemed successful by the entity that has a democratic mandate to allocate public resources as it sees fit, namely, the Indonesian government. A series of evaluations has shown the project has had significant economic impacts (Alatas 2005; Voss 2008). From an empirical standpoint, however, what can one say about whether KDP is realizing its larger goal of building the credibility and effectiveness of local governance? If the inevitable summary answer is that "it depends," can we specify more precisely the conditions under which the program is helping or hindering these processes? Is there a discrete "KDP effect," or does its impact, for better or worse, turn on particular elements of the program or the ways in which it interacts with specific aspects of the local context, particularly in terms of generating and mitigating conflicts? What are the implications of any such findings for broader development theory, research, and policy? It is to a detailed consideration of these questions that we now turn.

PART II

Arguments, Evidence, Interpretations

CHAPTER 4

When Do Development Projects Generate Conflict?

Development projects introduce new resources into communities. In the absence of effective rules and procedures for managing these resources, projects may trigger new conflicts or feed existing ones. The Kecamatan Development Program specifically aims to empower marginalized individuals and groups within villages, thus changing local power balances and hierarchical structures. This in turn may cause conflicts as elites and their support bases resist these changes. This chapter assesses the nature and extent of conflicts triggered or caused by KDP. In so doing, it seeks to answer the following questions: Does KDP trigger or cause new conflict or worsen existing conflicts? If so, what forms do these conflicts take, and what are their impacts? How does the program compare with other development projects—both governmental and nongovernmental—in terms of its effect on local conflict dynamics?

We start by outlining the prevalence and impacts of KDP-related disputes and conflicts. We find that small-scale conflicts related to KDP are common, but that these rarely escalate into broader conflicts or have significant negative impacts. We then examine three different forms of project-related conflict: in-built, program malfunction, and interaction conflict (the latter two are more serious than the first). Then we discuss why KDP-related disputes and conflicts tend not to escalate and argue that the program's very design features—its forums, facilitators, and complaint procedures—mean that tensions tend to be addressed before they grow larger. Only where these means do not work effectively, and in environments where prevailing tensions and political competition are already high, is there a significant risk of conflict escalation. Finally, we compare the presence of KDP-related conflicts with those that stem from other development projects. We find that in general KDP tends to produce less violent conflicts than do other development programs (even though KDP is, in many cases, much larger) and that this is a function of other programs' tending to have weak conflict management mechanisms as well as a lack of transparency, accountability, and opportunities for community participation in decision making.

The Prevalence and Impact of KDP-Related Conflicts

Small-scale (micro) conflicts related to KDP are common. The program does lead to tensions between villages, between groups within villages, and within different groups; however, these tensions very rarely escalate into larger conflicts, and they almost never become violent. The key informant survey, for example, asked whether the program had caused "community problems/conflicts" in the respondent's village or subdistrict.[1] Nearly half of respondents at the village level indicated that problems had occurred as a result of village-level KDP meetings: 46 percent of respondents reported problems/conflicts in East Java and 19 percent in Flores.[2] In subdistrict-level forums, significantly higher levels of problems/conflicts were reported: 85 percent reported them in East Java and 57 percent did so in Flores.[3]

Rates of reported conflict are higher at the subdistrict level for a number of reasons. First, competition is generally more pronounced between villages than within them (see below). There is more pressure on village representatives to deliver resources and services back to their villages than there is for groups within villages to have their proposals forwarded to the subdistrict level. Second, intervillage meetings are more likely to comprise social equals than are intravillage meetings, where the process of empowering poorer or more marginalized citizens is still in progress, sometimes tempered by more elite-centered village development councils (which are often made up of village heads, elders, and other authority figures). Within villages, KDP attempts to avoid elite domination of decision making, as described below. Furthermore, in the cases where hegemonic decision-making power structures are deeply rooted in local norms and practice and KDP is unable to override existing mechanisms of top-down decision making, then it is also possible that survey results showing fewer grievances in the village-level forums may indicate the lack of voice, or the powerlessness of individuals or groups at the village level. As Gaventa (1980) has argued, in situations where groups are extremely marginalized and in situations of entrenched inequality, their lack of political response can itself be a function of power relationships, with elite power serving to maintain the quiescence of the non-elite. Similarly, Lukes (1974, 23) argues that "the most effective insidious use of power is to prevent such conflict arising in the first place." That is, power can also be exercised to shape what people think they want and need so that grievances do not emerge.

For example, one KDP village facilitator described the nature of attendance and decision making in KDP meetings in an isolated village in Pamekasan, our low-capacity district. She stated that the village elites, particularly those with allegiance to the village head, were the only ones who attended KDP meetings and often were the only ones who were invited to meetings, leaving little space for contestation of decision making from program beneficiaries who were completely excluded from the process. Facilitators are responsible for reaching out to marginalized groups to help enhance their ability to participate. In this case, the male KDP village facilitator resigned because he felt existing power structures limited the ability to do this. Contestation tended only to emerge in informal meetings among program facilitators, not in those involving villagers. One respondent explained how this happened in practice:

Q: Who attends the meetings?
A: It was precisely the people who were invited by the village head who would come to the KDP village meeting. If they hadn't been invited they wouldn't come. . . . Mainly representatives from the LKMD [Village Development Council], PKK [Family Welfare Organization—often the main women's organization in the village], BPD [Village Representative Council] and religious figures were often invited. The people who would normally not attend the forums were people who didn't agree with some of the village head's decisions, or the village head's political rivals . . . it is as if they knew that their opinions wouldn't be heard even though they had been invited to attend the forum. . . .

The village head makes all the decisions relating to development problems because he is responsible for all the development which

takes place in the village . . . both KDP and non-KDP . . .; the villagers agree because it is indeed the village head's responsibility to
oversee construction and village developments. . . . Subu used to
be the KDP village facilitator in the village, but then he resigned
because he felt reluctant to reproach or take action against someone
of a higher status [in conversation about the village head] . . .

. . . the KDP village facilitator from Lada [another village]
always gets in arguments with the other KDP village facilitators,
although only at the informal forums, not at the formal meetings.
The subdistrict head (*camat*) always asks that people [not be]
ridiculed in public in the formal forums. . . . For this reason there
aren't any hot debates like there are in the informal meetings with
the village facilitators.

—FEMALE VILLAGE FACILITATOR, PAMEKASAN, MADURA

In other villages in the same subdistrict, special attention was given by
village facilitators to seeking out people less likely to attend meetings via direct
visits to their houses. This was in part because of the role of the village head
in the process. Such instances exemplify the importance of committed "street-
level bureaucrats" (Lipsky 1983) in encouraging participation and supporting
participatory arenas if the gap between the institutional rules of the game and
change in practice is to be achieved (Cornwall and Coelho 2007). In the example below, change by means of participation was beginning to take place.

There were approximately 70 women at the KDP village forum. This is
quite a lot for a meeting at the village level. Normally, the women don't
go to the meetings. . . . Actually, it isn't such a problem, but they are generally too shy to attend. Perhaps it's because that is what they are used to
here [in Madura]. . . . Just to get women to attend the KDP village meetings they had to be given invitations first. The village head invited us by
going around each of the hamlets. The KDP village facilitator also told us
about the meetings in the Koran recital groups. . . . After the KDP meetings, which were attended by a large number of women, the women in
this village experienced a transformation. Those who used to say nothing
at meetings suddenly started to put forward their ideas. We could say that
after the implementation of KDP the women started to gain more confidence. For example, before the implementation of KDP there was only
one woman who would read the *Yasin* [part of the Koran] at the Koran
recital groups, but after KDP, a lot more women started offering to read

it. There used to be one woman who would always chair the meetings, but now the women are taking it in turns.

—FEMALE MEMBER OF A KORAN RECITAL GROUP,

SANA DAYA VILLAGE, PAMEKASAN, MADURA

In this way, frequent but nonviolent conflicts in KDP forums, in particular at the subdistrict level, may be as much a sign of healthy contestation and proto-democratic decision making as they are problems with program processes (see, for example, Diprose and Rianom 2010; Diprose, Abdul Cader, and Thalayasingam 2010).[4] Because the KDP intervillage meetings are held with representatives of similar status from each village, power imbalances are less likely and grievances are more likely to be expressed. But where there are major imbalances in the terms of recognition of different groups—that is, where there are major status differentials and political power imbalances—outcomes that are perceived to be unfair are more likely to generate responses that entail violent conflict.[5] As one subdistrict official in Ponorogo deftly put it, the success of development programs should not be judged "by whether only a few problems emerged, but how many problems came up and how many were successfully resolved. If a kecamatan says that they came across three problems but they were only able to resolve one of them, and another kecamatan had ten problems but they resolved six . . . the kecamatan able to resolve six problems was more successful."

In spite of the high levels of reported conflict, particularly at the subdistrict level, very few of these conflicts escalated into violence. No survey informants in East Java reported violence in village-level meetings; in NTT, only one noted violent conflict (and this was a result of retribution meted out to a program participant who alerted officials to an instance of corruption).[6] At the subdistrict level, one respondent in sixty-eight reported violence in East Java and two in forty-seven did so in NTT.[7] Even so, these incidents of violence were not considered serious enough to be reported in local newspapers.[8]

Indeed, the findings are supported by both the qualitative fieldwork and the newspaper survey of conflict and violence in East Java and NTT. The qualitative field team in East Java found eleven cases of KDP-related conflict in the six KDP subdistricts where the research was conducted. In all eleven cases, there were no deaths or injuries; the only violent impact was the damaging of a water pump in one location. In NTT, the team found five conflicts, none with physical impacts. Across the fourteen districts covered in the newspaper survey, forty-two KDP-related conflicts were picked up

TABLE 4.1   REPORTED KDP CONFLICTS AND THEIR IMPACTS, 2001–3

KDP conflicts	Conflicts	Violent conflicts	Persons killed	Persons injured	Cases of property damage
Total	42	1	0	2	0
East Java	10	0	0	0	0
NTT	32	1	0	2	0

Source: KDP and CCN newspaper dataset.

between 2001 and 2003. Of these, only one became violent; it resulted in two injuries (see table 4.1).[9] As we discuss below, these rates are extremely low when compared with other development programs, policies, and projects; thirty-seven violent and newsworthy non-KDP development conflicts took place in the research areas (see below).

Why are micro-conflicts within KDP so common? Why do they so rarely escalate into broader problems? And why do they almost never become violent? Answering these questions requires consideration of the types of conflicts and problems caused by KDP and of the ways in which they are resolved or prevented from escalating.

Forms of KDP-Related Conflict

The program can cause or heighten conflict in direct or indirect ways.[10] It *directly* leads to conflict where a particular element or procedure of the program results in tensions. This includes situations where individuals or groups feel dissatisfied with program processes or outcomes, for example, with the way funding decisions were made or with the role a particular facilitator played. Two basic types of conflict are directly related to KDP: in-built conflict and program malfunction conflict. The first relates to the processes of contestation (of deliberation, advocacy, and debate) purposely included in the KDP model. The second concerns what happens when the program does not function as intended, for example, when corruption occurs or when implementation is poor.

At other times the impact is *indirect*. In such cases, the program interacts with existing social tensions and power structures, leading to the escalation of existing conflicts or generating new ones. Here the introduction of the program was not a cause of the conflict per se; rather, the program contributed to conflict by creating a structural opportunity for the realignment of power relations, resources, interests, and values. As we discuss below, in many cases in-built, program malfunction, and interaction-related conflict overlap. Separating them provides a useful framework, however, for thinking about program-generated conflict because, as we explore in more detail below, each has different impacts.

Competition in KDP: A Source of Local Conflict?

At the village level . . . there were some feelings of jealousy which emerged between hamlets because some of them had their proposals accepted while others did not. Those which were unsuccessful asked, "Why did they receive savings and loans funds from KDP and we did not?"

—HEAD OF THE KDP FINANCIAL MANAGEMENT UNIT,
WAE BELANG, RUTENG, MANGGARAI

The competition principle is actually very good; it encourages people to think.

—KEMIRI, A MIDWIFE, JENANGAN, PONOROGO

When you compare them, I think that KDP is better than P3DT [a government development project]. The competitive system can reduce the possibility of *ngamlopi* [providing money in envelopes] to officials who carry out monitoring visits to the field, . . . P3DT always used to provide envelopes to officials who came to the site, but there is none in this KDP [because] the community understands the process.

—SUBDISTRICT HEAD, SLAHUNG, PONOROGO

The program's model of decision making is based on the principle of open competition; this is a potential source of conflict. Groups within villages put forward proposals for things they want funded.[11] They decide which ideas should be taken to the village-level meeting and then to the subdistrict level for consideration. In the subdistrict forum, different villages need to collectively decide which proposals deserve funding against a criteria of need, village contribution to the project (mainly through voluntary labor or land provision), and technical viability. Project resources are not enough to fund all proposals. In essence then, villages and groups battle among themselves for access to resources. Groups use the traditional tools of coalition-building (the powers of rhetoric, appeals to reason, bargaining, and deal-making) to win support for their proposals.

A review of the project cycle shows a number of points at which such competition is explicit and hence tensions emerge:

- Brainstorming meetings at the hamlet level.
- Decisions about which proposals to promote. Only two proposals are allowed from each village, one of which must come from a women's group. Given that proposals normally come from geographically concentrated groups (for example, villagers from one hamlet), the decision may cause tensions between groups in the village, particularly at the second village-level meeting (MD II).
- Decisions about which proposals should be funded in the subdistrict forum. Given that not every proposal can normally be funded, intervillage conflict may arise over which villages' proposals are funded, particularly at the third intervillage meeting (MD III).
- Determining who will implement the projects. This may cause tensions at the third village meeting, where village implementation teams are formed, and during implementation.

These types of tensions are deliberately designed into KDP. Indeed, the program explicitly aims to *create* nonviolent contestation by stimulating competition at these stages. Such managed conflict, it is hoped, can lead to better proposals, better prioritizing of local development needs, can increase incentives for participation, and can lead to an exchange whereby different villagers (and villages) learn from each other how to design and present effective projects that are likely to win funding, and, concomitantly, learn to deal with disappointment. Further, it is hoped that the competitive process—conducted as it is within a rules-based system that is simple, transparent, and accountable—will help villagers acquire organizational and civic skills that carry over to the successful management of local conflicts.

Yet there are also considerable risks with this strategy. In areas where tensions were already high, some informants argued that stimulating competition between villages led to more conflict, particularly since it challenged the existing alignment of power and interests accompanying the more top-down decision-making hierarchies. For example, in Pamekasan, Madura, East Java, village leaders and local facilitators circumvented KDP processes and pursued a deliberate strategy of avoiding competition in the allocation of funds, although some informants argued that this was as much a means of maintaining their own power base as a strategy for reducing tensions in the community (see box 4.1). In some cases in our low-capacity areas, KDP at first fell victim to the sociocultural predispositions and existing power structures of participants. Old patterns of power and hegemonic decision making prevailed at the expense of the needs of intended beneficiaries, the poor, which should have been prioritized in the funding process, and to some extent a gap remained between rules and effective participatory practice.[12]

BOX 4.1   CONFLICT AVOIDANCE IN MADURA: DIVIDING THE FUNDS

In a number of subdistricts in Pamekasan, East Java, efforts were made to limit competition between villages in the KDP process. For the first year of KDP-I in Pademawu subdistrict, it was decided at the subdistrict level that only five villages (of the twenty-two in the subdistrict) would be eligible for funding in that year.[a] Funds were then divided almost exactly equally among the five villages. In the second and third years, again, the funds were divided equally among all eligible villages. Competition was absent (see Probo 2003a). A member of the village council in one of the villages that received money in year two (again without competition) described the motivations behind splitting the money equally:

> The impacts can be great if [funds] aren't divided equally between all the villages, for instance if Village A gets [funds] while Village B alongside it doesn't. This can turn into a "boomerang" for the village head because he will be seen as incompetent in attracting the program [to the village].
> —MEMBER OF THE VILLAGE REPRESENTATIVE COUNCIL, PADELLEGAN, PADEMAWU, PAMEKASAN

The quashing of competition was less about limiting community conflict than about village heads' cementing their own power. They viewed the potential for attracting development programs to the village as a means of consolidating their power and status; they thus spared no effort to ensure they received a project. The easiest way to do this was to agree with other village heads to split the money.

Note
      a. This decision was not in line with KDP-I regulations. For year one of KDP-I, program rules stipulated that if a subdistrict (kecamatan) had more than ten villages, half should be eligible for the program, with the remaining 50 percent eligible in year two, and all villages eligible in year three. Thus eleven villages should have participated in year one. The limit on the number of eligible villages in the first two years was not instituted to limit competition. Rather, the number was limited in order to ensure that all newly competing villages could receive adequate facilitation (see Wong 2003).

The research in all four districts in the two provinces found that the competition inherent in KDP process did sometimes cause tensions. In East Java, 61 percent of survey respondents reported that competition over proposals in village-level meetings had led to tensions or conflict; 19 percent of respondents in NTT reported the same.[13] The qualitative fieldwork supported this finding, with a number of informants reporting cases of tensions related to KDP competition:

> It is normal for people who feel disappointed because they didn't get a loan to make threats, ordering the people who did receive loans to pay their money back immediately. They will say: "seize their processions." If they don't repay their loans we surely won't get any more loans. Someone even suggested that they be sent to the police or to jail.
>
> —RESPECTED COMMUNITY FIGURE, NEBE, TALIBURA, SIKKA

> Feelings of dissatisfaction with KDP mechanisms can be seen on a micro-scale with the onset of conflict in the KDP forums. The community likes to make a lot of noise in the KDP forums. At the subdistrict level, they speak loudly and assertively because they feel dissatisfied with the competition process. In fact, there have even been people who have walked out because they didn't agree with the decisions made at the MAD (Intervillage Forum).
>
> —SUBDISTRICT HEAD, RUTENG, MANGGARAI

> In the Intervillage Forum in Year Three of KDP, the [atmosphere] was tense. [Q: In what way was the atmosphere tense?] Well, each hamlet put forward their proposals and each hoped that their proposal would be prioritized. This was the cause of the tension because the community knows that the KDP process begins at the bottom. So each hamlet hoped to win.
>
> —VILLAGER, SUMEDANGAN, PADEMAWU, PAMEKASAN

In the village of Wates, in Slahung, Ponorogo, East Java, competition had fueled tensions between different hamlets (discussed at length in Chapter 1). Yet in general, though competition within or between villages led to disappointment for unsuccessful groups, rarely did this lead to prolonged tensions. In the case in Wates, the research team felt it unlikely that the conflict would reemerge in a destructive form. Indeed, as we explore in more depth, *in no cases did tensions related to competition escalate into more serious conflict.* Competition causes meeting participants to argue, but very rarely do tensions within KDP forums spill over into everyday life.[14] We did not find any cases in the research where tensions relating directly to competition fueled anything more than small-scale disputes. Indeed, as we explore in Chapter 7, it was actually lack of competition that was more likely to cause tensions.

Tensions Due to Competition Within and Between Villages: Changes Over Time

In the short run, tensions related to competition were more likely to take place within villages. As the amount of time KDP had been in a subdistrict increased, these tensions tended to ebb, while, conversely, the potential for intervillage tensions related to competition increased (see figure 4.1).

In our research sites, *intravillage tensions* related to competition increased gradually in the first couple of years of the program but then started to tail off as more of the proposals were funded. In the early years, tensions were often relatively high. This is because in many cases the

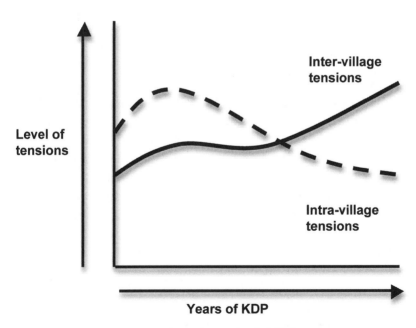

Figure 4.1   Tensions generated by competition in KDP

principles that KDP embodies differ from those normally applied in development-related decision making at the village level. Although forms of consensual and deliberative decision making (such as *musyawarah*) have a long history in many villages, these principles were rarely applied to decisions about village budgets. Top-down decision making over development resources was the norm. In contrast, KDP brings with it processes that encourage participation across the village and a meritocratic basis for distributing resources.

Tensions within villages over competition were more likely in Year Two of KDP than in Year One. This is the case for two reasons. First, socialization of KDP principles is a process rather than an event; in areas where democratization was less advanced, it would often take more than one year for villagers to realize that they could truly put forward proposals of their choosing. In Year Two villagers undertook the competition process with vigor, compared to the first year, when village elites were more able to dominate the process. Hence, tensions within villages tended to be higher in Year Two.[15] Yet these tensions did not continue to escalate. As program processes were better understood, villagers generally understood that the primary basis of competition was need; the emphasis was not on equal distribution of money across hamlets over time. This concept made intuitive sense to most of the villagers we spoke with. As understanding of KDP increased and the decision-making cycle was repeated, tensions *within* villages declined (see figure 4.1). A villager in Pamekasan reflected on these patterns when he commented that

> the tensions which emerged in the village meetings in KDP Year 1 were not like those in the third year. . . . In the first year, it was more certain which proposals would get funding; while there were proposals from different hamlets, the community did not feel there was competition. . . . Later, when each proposal was discussed in the forum, it appeared that several individuals forced the proposals from their hamlet to be put forward [to the intervillage meeting]. However, after the session, there were only two proposals left. These two proposals caused tensions. Each supporter wanted their proposal to be prioritized. This was to such an extent that there were exchanges of foul words. Then there was agreement from the forum to determine the priority by taking a vote, and in the end all the attendees agreed. . . . Outside of the forum there were still tensions, but, yeah, these were limited to

complaints and grumblings. . . . But the village officials [and the community leaders] and I immediately approached them. We went directly to their houses.

In contrast, *intervillage tensions* related to KDP were low in Year One but tended to increase over time, with tensions highest in Year Three as the gap between the rules and substantive participation began to close. One reason is that in Year One true competition was absent in many areas. In Manggarai and Pamekasan districts, where capacity to implement the program and manage tensions was lower, village heads and the program's subdistrict facilitator illegally decided ahead of time which villages would get projects (see box 4.1). When rules were adhered to, the program dictated that some villages would be eligible in Year One and others in Year Two. In Year Two, tensions were higher as villages, and their representatives, gained a better understanding of program rules and as the hold of traditional elites over the decision-making process began to wane. In contrast to intravillage tensions, intervillage tensions continued to rise in later years of the program, particularly when the same villages or specific proposals repeatedly missed out on funding. This can take place within villages, as demonstrated in the Wates village case. But it is more likely to take place between villages, in large part because the same ethos of solidarity and support does not, in general, exist across villages as it does across hamlets within the same village. A perception emerged in some circles that certain villages (and in some cases certain hamlets) were constantly being prioritized at the expense of others. In the intervillage forums in the early years, there was always the hope that if a proposal was not funded in a particular year, it could be forwarded again in the following year. This became less likely as the program came to a close and the same villages (for varied technical, needs-based, and even political reasons) missed out.

It is an open question whether tensions between villages would continue to increase if the program stayed in subdistricts for more than three years. Our sample of four-year subdistricts (two) is too low to allow general conclusions, especially because these subdistricts were given "reward" status—that is, they received an extra year of the program for good performance.[16] In principle, with more rounds of program participation, villages should acquire a better understanding of the basis of competition; it is also more likely that each village would receive funding at some point, especially following the adoption of KDP nationwide. Such processes would work toward limiting intervillage tensions relating to competition within the program. On the other hand, if certain villages manage to capture the process, as happened in some of our research subdistricts, it is likely that tensions would continue to grow as villagers became aware of their right to participate in the process.

This substantiates the basic point made above, namely, that competition related to KDP does not in and of itself cause significant problems. Villagers generally learn the program rules and, over time, tend to accept them and even like and appeal to them. Program forums and facilitators are almost always able to address directly (and effectively) any tensions relating to individuals or villages not having their proposals funded. But where the program malfunctions, or where large power differences and processes of explicit political contestation over development resources remain, competition does in certain instances spark larger disputes.

When Things Go Wrong: Program Malfunction

Where efforts to reach out to marginalized groups succeed and where participatory decision making, implementation, and follow-up go as planned, competition for funds does not result in serious conflict. The in-built conflict management mechanisms work well in limiting conflict related to competition by providing a space for managed contestation. When the program does not operate as it is meant to, however, it can lead to larger conflicts. That said, as noted above, we found only one such case that turned violent.

Program malfunction stemmed from problems of omission or commission.[17] The first concerns instances when the program did not function properly because of inadequate socialization or a lack of transparency regarding program rules and processes. This was either intentional (where rumors or misinformation spread or information was deliberately withheld) or unintentional (where mistakes occurred owing to human error). Either way, when individuals or groups did not properly understand how the program works and why certain decisions were made, the likelihood of conflict increased. The second involved deliberate malfeasance, most commonly corruption on the part of program staff, local government, or other actors. In these cases, too, the program was more likely to lead to conflict. In some instances, deviations were not noticed at the time, stimulating grievances that later escalated; in others, intentional program deviations were observed at the time, and the responses (of communities or program staff) to these acts often triggered conflict. This was a common problem for development programs across the board in our research sites.

Problems of Omission: Poor Socialization and Implementation

Our evidence suggests that poor socialization and implementation can lead to disputes about the allocation of resources or the implementation of the program. In such cases, no deliberate act of wrongdoing occurs. Yet poor performance on the part of facilitators or program staff—what we deem a problem of omission—results not only in substandard program performance but also in negative spillovers in terms of increased local tensions. In many cases, poor socialization allows for rumors and the spread of misinformation, even when the program is being implemented by the book. These are typically minor disputes, but in some instances they escalated into more widespread conflicts. In such cases, if there had been better socialization, the problems would most likely have been solved early on. Such cases demonstrate that following the rules is not enough for KDP facilitators. Villagers often lack direct experience in democratic decision making, and entrenched interests often work against the forces of transparency and participation that KDP promotes. Indeed, people need more than just an invitation to participate if democratic spaces are to be expanded (Cornwall and Coelho 2007). In addition, they need to first recognize themselves as citizens, not merely as beneficiaries or clients, and this requires popular education and mobilization that can enhance the skills and confidence of marginalized groups and thereby enable them to enter such participatory arenas on a more equal footing (see Mahmud 2007; Mohanty 2007; Williams 2007; von Lieres 2007; von Lieres and Kahane 2007). This affirms the importance of KDP's focus on socialization as it highlights the need for facilitators to work intensely and creatively to ensure that target communities understand properly the program's aims and procedures.

Consider, for example, a case from Madura, East Java. One village facilitator thought he had been fired by the village head (referred to in Madura as the *klebun*). His term had actually come to an end in the KDP cycle, but lack of information regarding program rules meant that this was not clear to the facilitator. Consequently, he shifted his allegiance to the klebun's opponent, and this played out in later conflicts in the village.

I was only the village facilitator for five months. . . . I was terminated by the klebun without clear reason. Without saying thank you. . . . I was pushed aside because the klebun was afraid I would straighten out the road [criticize the klebun's flaws]. I was considered to know a lot about the matter of the assistance, so I had to be pushed aside. Perhaps the klebun was worried that later I would make trouble over the matter of the way the money was used.

—FORMER VILLAGE FACILITATOR, PANAGGUAN, PROPPO, PAMEKASAN

In the example above, there was no deviation from program rules, but poor socialization led to confusion, misperceptions, and misinformation that later fueled other village conflicts. A similar process occurred in another village in Pamekasan:

Rumors appeared that the Lawangan Daya savings and loans funds had been used for the personal interests of the TPK [KDP Village Project Implementation Team], Lurah [village head] and the Village Development Council organizers. In fact, people said that the program money was used to build the Village Development Council chairperson's house, whereas I know myself that Pak Jamat [the chairperson] built the house from the proceeds of selling his own car. . . . These are just the wrong views of people who are envious of the success of Lawangan Daya in implementing the saving-borrowing enterprise. . . . The program money has now reached Rp. 97 million from Rp. 60 million.

—KDP VILLAGE PROJECT IMPLEMENTATION TEAM CHAIRPERSON,
LAWANGAN DAYA, PADEMAWU, PAMEKASAN

Poor explanation of program rules was a common cause of tension. For instance, in Satar Punda village, Manggarai, Flores, the village facilitator's explanation of KDP mechanisms differed from those applied in the field. At first the facilitator made a list of about fifty households in Pering hamlet from two different groups and explained that both would receive funding. Only twenty-two households in the kelompok Bawang Merah (Red Onion group)[18] received funding, however, and none of the members of the kelompok Mangga Udang (Mango Shrimp group) received money. This, again, resulted in tensions within the village.

Disputes relating to poor implementation emerged not only during the competition process (where the funds are allocated) but also during the implementation phase in the field. They often resulted from poor socialization in the initial project cycle. Four examples from three of the different research districts demonstrate that these conflicts emerged because of poor socialization and implementation and also demonstrate the potential broader consequences.

Water Pipes in Sikka

The first case pertains to a clean water project in Magepanda village, Sikka. The work that took place in the field was not consistent with that planned for in the draft budget. As a result, not all of the pipes were laid and tensions among the village elite mounted.

> There was a tug-of-war going on between the government and the project manager. This was because they should have used steel pipes, but they used PVC pipes instead. Apparently, there weren't enough pipes. They have started to ask for contributions from the community, but the community is still asking for the report from the project manager, the head of the Village Development Council. The villagers are willing to contribute, but first the report must be clear.
>
> —FORMER VILLAGE HEAD AND CURRENT MEMBER OF THE VILLAGE
> REPRESENTATIVE COUNCIL, MAGEPANDA, NITA, SIKKA

In addition, there was a large discrepancy between the length of the pipes described in the draft budget and the length of the pipes that had already been laid in the field. According to the approved funding proposal, 3.5 km of pipe had to be laid in order to complete the project. But in reality, 5.8 km of pipe was needed to cover the distance. These problems stemmed in part from poor technical planning. Another contributing factor, however, was that the initial proposal was not particularly clear. Therefore, the project manager, the village head, the head of the Village Representative Council, and the head of the KDP Village Project Implementation Team all interpreted the proposal in different ways. This led to tensions as each accused the others of corruption or deception.

> The clean water project in Magepanda has yet to be finished. There are still parties who are blaming each other and trying to obstruct the construction process. The KDP implementers in the village have already been selected, but they have no function.
>
> —FORMER VILLAGE HEAD, MAGEPANDA, NITA, SIKKA

Road Construction in Manggarai

The second case concerns a dispute over a 2.5-km stretch of the Bea Mese–Lando road. Tensions erupted when the proposal from Lando village for KDP to resurface the road was accepted. The resurfacing began as planned, and the first 150 meters were completed, but 500 meters of the remaining road to be resurfaced lay within Bea Mese village's administrative jurisdiction. The community there, spurred on by their leaders, started to sabotage the stretch already completed, pushing the stones to the side of the road. They complained that their labor should be involved in the laying of the stones on the road in their area, not labor from Lando village. Meanwhile, the villagers from Lando did not agree because they had already followed the correct proposal submission procedures, including those used at the meetings at the subdistrict level. Why had the villagers from Bea Mese not objected to the project at the intervillage meeting in which they participated?

Again, the primary reason for the problem was poor socialization of program rules, this time at the subdistrict level. With tensions mounting, conflict was only avoided after the intervention of the subdistrict head, the head of KDP's Subdistrict Financial Management Unit (UPK), and the police. The subdistrict head invited the village heads, the head of the Village Development Council, respected community figures, and the KDP staff from the two villages to a meeting to discuss the problem. After the discussion, they agreed that the Bea Mese community would be given Rp. 12 million to resurface the 500-meter stretch of road located within their village.

Bridge-Building in Ponorogo

The third case, from Slahung, Ponorogo, differs from the above two in that the dispute was the result of effective socialization processes that ensured that villagers understood when a facilitator had deviated from program rules. Although this triggered tensions, the resulting dispute nonetheless demonstrated villagers' desire for accountability and adherence to program rules. Slahung received funds to build a new bridge connecting two hamlets after a proper competitive process. The project became controversial, however, when the district consultant who managed the program viewed the site and decided that the proposed design should be slightly altered for technical reasons. The design was changed and a foundation was quickly built without consulting the community, which had already had the design approved. Moreover, the change in design meant that a small section of the riverbank cultivated by a local farmer would be lost to the bridge and the road leading to it. This farmer's son was offended because his family was not consulted and because their permission was not sought for access to or use of the land; the community was also angered by the lack of consultation.

> The conflict over the bridge arose due to a shift in the bridge location, so while the proposal was designed so that the bridge went straight ahead, it was shifted to the south a little . . .; the changes were not a result of consultation with the community. . . . The community then started questioning why the bridge was shifted, thinking that the result would not be good, let alone the fact that there was land owned by one citizen that would be negatively affected.
> —FORMER KDP VILLAGE PROJECT IMPLEMENTATION TEAM CHAIR,
> SLAHUNG, SLAHUNG, PONOROGO

The newly formed Village Representative Council initially became involved by advocating for the land user, supporting his appeals to the district parliament, and attracting media attention to the case. The council also assisted in resolving community tension concerning the design change by facilitating a meeting where implementers of the program spoke about the reasons for the change and explained elements of the KDP procedure, while the community was able to air their grievances. The issue was put to a vote, and it was decided that the planned bridge would revert to its original design. Members of the district parliament and executive, the security forces, KDP facilitators, and the media all attended the meeting. While the community was satisfied, the labor and materials that had gone into the construction of the foundation were wasted, and villagers were required to make up the shortfall themselves.

Microcredit in Ponorogo

A final example shows how poor socialization and implementation of KDP led to an ongoing conflict, program failure, and wasted resources. Members of a KDP savings and loan group in Panjeng, Ponorogo, had borrowed money from the program for a cattle-fattening initiative and failed to pay back the funds. Deviations from program rules, poor socialization, and poor verification of the proposals put forward by the groups had occurred. Most of the verification team did not live in the subdistrict and had no local knowledge of the relative success or failure of local cattle-fattening initiatives and market trends. Hence, the money was not always used for its intended purpose.

Locals wanted to borrow money for cattle-fattening initiatives. The subdistrict official would first check the site [to verify] whether the borrower really had cattle and had a cattle stall. When the site was checked there was indeed a stall and cattle. Perhaps the official considered that the inhabitants had experience in raising cattle, so the funds flowed. But in fact the cattle were not his, and nor was the stall. They were just his neighbor's cattle that he claimed to own, and the cattle stall too belonged to someone else. . . . The subdistrict official came to the village—the term is "to check the reality in the field." In fact, he was tricked by the community [laughing].

—CHAIR OF FARMERS' GROUP MARGO MAKMUR,
PANJENG, JENANGAN, PONOROGO

There was always someone who owed money. . . . Sometimes they didn't understand that the money really had to be returned, that it hadn't just been given [to them]. . . . The worse debts at the time were those of that cattle farmers' group. . . . Actually profits were made from the first sale. Then when the second cattle auction came round, what do you know, the prices had dropped. They were only enough to cover the buying price and costs of cattle feed, but the costs of rearing the livestock, well, they were not covered. After that the prices dropped even further and the farmers couldn't return their loans.

—TREASURER OF THE SAVING AND LOANS GROUP, PANJENG,
JENANGAN, PONOROGO

Actually the three monthly repayments would not have been that burdensome if they were just interest repayments, but it was really difficult because the principal also had to be repaid. . . . In my experience every three months the cattle had to be sold because there was no money to pay off the principal. There was no guarantee that within that three-month period we'd make a profit because cattle prices weren't stable. In fact after a while my capital was used up because I hadn't made any profit over three months. . . . What I did was to buy cattle, sell them after three months to make the interest and loan principal repayments, and use the remaining money to buy more cattle. That's how I used up my capital through this method.

—FORMER KDP VILLAGE PROJECT IMPLEMENTATION TEAM CHAIR,
SLAHUNG, PONOROGO

As members of the savings and loan groups stopped making repayments, it also emerged that the repayment system being implemented in Panjeng was not in accordance with program rules and was costing the group members more in interest payments. Villagers made comparisons with neighboring villages' loan systems and began to distrust program facilitators, particularly in the Financial Management Unit, and instead asked the male village facilitator to intervene. Various parties tried to get the group members to make their repayments, but they simply had no money to do so. To this day, tensions still exist between program beneficiaries and five group members who have yet to pay back their loans.

In this case, the drop in cattle prices was not the cause of the conflict; it merely triggered the dispute about failed repayments. Poor socialization and implementation of the program stimulated grievances that then surfaced when the match was thrown into the kindling.

Problems of Commission: Intentional Deviations and Corruption-Related Disputes

These cases show the consequences of unintended poor socialization and implementation. Facilitators or other program staff did not deliberately set out to subvert the program. Other cases of conflict due to program malfunction occurred as a result of intentional deviations from program procedures. Program malfunction cases are more serious than those described above, none of which resulted in violence or escalated beyond the level of a small dispute (with the partial exception of the bridge case). In particular, malfunction cases related to corruption, which are by no means rare, can sow seeds that in the right conditions grow into fully formed conflicts. This can have negative outcomes if perpetrators are caught but there is no means of recourse. They can also have positive outcomes, however, in terms of increasing demands for accountability and transparency, thus increasing the likelihood that the needs of beneficiaries will be met.

Corruption and KDP

In both provinces, numerous cases of corruption led to tensions that were significantly larger than those relating to competition within the program. Often corruption works hand in hand with elite capture of program processes (as we saw with the events in Wates that opened this book). Such cases were by no means rare in the villages we visited, particularly in Manggarai and Pamekasan, our two low-capacity districts.[19] In Lamba Leda subdistrict, Manggarai, KDP was suspended after large-scale embezzlement by the subdistrict facilitator. It was discovered that 10 percent of the budget (Rp. 59,897,200, or roughly US$6,000) had not been distributed. The subdistrict facilitator claimed that he would distribute the funds at a later date, but this never happened, and the funds were never seen again. In total, he is believed to have embezzled approximately Rp. 80 million (approximately US$8,000) in KDP funds across the projects. Although he and the program have been suspended, as this book was written he had not yet been punished by the courts, and the funds had not been returned.

Similarly, in Pamekasan there was evidence of corruption (see box 4.2). The village head from Panagguan argued that corruption is "natural" and that it often indirectly benefits the community. Neither point is valid. Indeed, we had many more informants who were outraged by corruption than the number who thought it helped the poor. For our purposes, however, it is most important to note how such instances can lead to conflicts. In some cases, where corrupters are exposed, the long-term effects may be positive; in others, corruption emerges only later, resulting in grievances that can spill over into broader conflicts (see box 4.3). In this case, despite threats of violence, no one was physically hurt. However, in a case in Flores Timur district—the only violent KDP case in the areas covered by the newspaper survey—corruption resulted in injuries to two people (see box 4.4).

BOX 4.2 EXAMPLES OF VILLAGE-LEVEL CORRUPTION IN PAMEKASAN, EAST JAVA

The proposal was determined by the village head in the village-level KDP forum. Beforehand each hamlet had been asked to submit their proposal, but we spread the word that the proposals would not necessarily be agreed to. And, if they weren't agreed to, the hamlets shouldn't be disappointed. . . . There was a fierce debate in the forum, and then

subsequently each hamlet submitted their final decision to the village head. Procedurally there is no difference in decision making between KDP and what is usually done by village communities; all the processes are decided through deliberations although the final decision rests in the hands of the village head. . . . What's confusing was that these people asked for *dana siluman* [a term used when the destination of outgoing funds is unclear, in this context meaning that the funds were being used as illegal fees for the subdistrict staff] of 3–5 percent of the total assistance received by the villages. This was the case for all the villages in Pademawu, according to instructions from the district government. But when I wrote down the allocation of money that I give to the subdistrict people as a fee for district government staff who came to the village, they were angry and asked me to change it, to charge it to the purchase of materials with a price slightly higher that the actual price.
—FORMER KDP VILLAGE FACILITATOR, PADELLEGAN, PADEMAWU, PAMEKASAN

Don't be surprised if the village head gets involved in minor acts of corruption of development program money which enters the village. Frankly, I've also been involved because, if you're not like that, how is the village head meant to get enough money to pay for all their activities? In my opinion, minor acts of corruption are natural—some of the money is used to help the community anyway. . . . The officials at the top are involved in corruption, let alone those at the bottom.
—VILLAGE HEAD, PANAGGUAN VILLAGE, PROPPO, PAMEKASAN

Box 4.3   Power Takes Precedence: Four Million Rupiah Vanishes

The program arrived in Satar Punda village, Manggarai, in 1998. Local facilitators were elected and trained, and the KDP Village Project Implementation Team was formed. Rafael Hommo was selected as its head, Alexius Djomnag, the village secretary, took the role of Implementation Team secretary, and Simplisius Derry was chosen as treasurer. Things proceeded smoothly, and funds were distributed for productive economic activities.

One day, however, Rafael arrived at Simplisius's house and asked to borrow KDP funds so that he could start a honey business in Java. Simplisius turned him down, but after constant pressure from Rafael, who argued that as the head of the Implementation Team he had authority to allocate KDP funds, he gave in. Simplisius agreed to lend Rp. 4,000,000, and Rafael signed a receipt dated October 30, 1999. Simplisius wanted to go to the nearest town to obtain an official stamp for the transaction, but Rafael refused, arguing that he was not a child and would return the money one month later. Feeling guilty about lending program money, Simplisius reported what had happened to the KDP subdistrict facilitator.

In late January 2000, Rafael returned from his business trip to Java. Angry that Simplisius had reported the loan to the subdistrict facilitator, he started abusing him, shouting, "*La'e Acume*" ["dog's penis" in the local language]. Simplisius returned to his house, feeling offended. Events took a turn for the worse when the Itwilkab [district investigations office] arrived to carry out an investigation. But their focus was on Simplisius rather than Rafael; they insulted the treasurer, saying that he should make sure his children got a good education so they didn't end up as stupid as he, while they were polite to Rafael. Simplisius became extremely angry and went home to fetch his machete: "I want to kill them both [Rafael and the head of the investigations team]." Only his wife's intervention made him back down. Rafael moved to Java with his wife and children and has yet to return or pay the money back.

BOX 4.4   CORRUPTION AND REVENGE IN FLORES TIMUR

Latonliwo village, Tanjung Bunga, Flores Timur. The head of the Village Development Council (LKMD) stole KDP funds. The village had been awarded Rp. 49,834,150 (around US$5,000) for an 850 meter long drainage system. The construction went ahead. But after only 413 meters were built, and only Rp. 10,150,000 (US$1,000) was spent, the money ran out. Most of the remaining money had been kept by the head of the Village Development Council, except for Rp. 1 million (US$100) that he had lent to a friend. This was not the first time money had gone missing from a village project in Tanjung Bunga. Previously funds to build twelve rainwater collection tanks went missing with only 44 percent of the money awarded being spent on the tanks. The KDP district technical consultant knew what had been going on and decided to take action and bring the case to the attention of the public. One night, the head of the Village Development Council brought three friends— a hamlet head, the head of the KDP Village Project Implementation Team, and his son—to visit the district consultant and his friend, a local community leader. On arriving, they beat them in revenge for their temerity in exposing their corruption, and in order to cover up the accusations. Escaping with just some bruises, the district consultant reported the case to the police.

Source: Adapted from *Dian*, 7 February 2002.

The Importance of Socialization and Links to Conflict

Analysis of the cases above shows the intrinsic and complex relation between socialization and conflict. In general, the relation is positive: increased knowledge of the rules, processes, and aims of KDP tends to limit the number of program malfunction conflicts, although it may stimulate smaller in-built conflicts that can be managed. The latter are as much a sign that the program is working well as that there are problems with implementation, because people have enough knowledge to contest deviations from the program. Socialization is particularly important for a number of reasons.

First, effective socialization ensures that program participants and beneficiaries understand the intentions of the program and how it will be conducted and implemented. Where the aims or decision-making mechanisms for development projects are not clear, individuals or groups will not see the project processes or outcomes as fair. This, as we explore in more depth below, can provide multiple bases for conflict. Rumors, misinformation, political maneuvering, and exclusion of groups with mandated rights are all, in themselves, triggers and sources of conflict. Indeed, this is particularly important for participatory programs, in which the number of people involved in decision making and implementation is much higher than in more centralized or predetermined projects.

Second, socialization, both for program facilitators and beneficiaries, is intrinsically linked to good program implementation. Of course, poor implementation can be purely the result of human error; however, in many of the cases discussed above (and more often than not) poor implementation was a result of a lack of understanding or a lack of capacity on the part of facilitators to deliver the program or challenge incumbent power structures seeking to co-opt the program. Poor socialization can thus lead to conflicts at the competition or implementation stage.

Third, socialization, in improving accountability and transparency, can allow for ongoing bottom-up monitoring, which can prevent program malfunctions from occurring and grievances from building. With adequate socialization, when deviations occur, official monitors and program beneficiaries are aware of the channels for recourse and upholding accountability and transparency. In this sense it generates smaller conflicts, because participants have enough knowledge to contest any deviations or mistakes they see as they occur. Misperceptions can be handled quickly, and mistakes are dealt with before they potentially escalate into more serious program malfunction conflicts.

Effective socialization thus can prevent many conflicts that emerge from problems of either omission or commission. Good socialization can result in the early discovery of program malfunctions (intentional or unintentional), thereby preventing grievances from forming. Yet the cases also show that effective socialization can trigger conflicts. In particular, in many of the corruption cases, knowledge of how processes should work is what led to tensions. Indeed, this was so in the sole violent KDP example in this study (box 4.4): the exposure of corruption led to injuries to two people. Development actors, in seeking to uphold the program rules, challenged incumbent power structures at their own personal risk. Empowering villagers by building countervailing forces (Gibson and Woolcock 2008)—for example, requiring a minimum level of participation by women, posting decisions in public places, giving villagers a genuine voice in how resources are allocated—may lead to conflict in the short run. Yet over the longer run, such conflicts can be positive. The corruption case (box 4.4) went to court, and, arguably, future cases of corruption are less likely. Thus KDP (and development projects more generally) should not aim to prevent all conflict from arising; rather, programs should ensure that where conflict related to program malfunction does occur, it stimulates future improvements in the program.

The Link Between KDP and Existing Tensions: Interaction Conflict

Development programs can do harm not only by directly triggering conflicts but also by feeding into existing ones. Projects operate in social contexts in which power relations are constantly being negotiated, and development projects constitute a vital resource that can be utilized by different actors in this process, as Cornwall and Coelho (2007), Gaventa (2005), and others have noted. Interaction conflicts occur when development projects interact with preexisting local tensions and conflicts and challenge incumbent power structures when opposition to traditional power structures is emerging and solidifying (box 4.6 below). Programs may provide a vehicle for these power struggles to surface, triggering conflict escalation and, in some cases, violence.

This can happen in a number of ways. First, influential positions, such as those of village program facilitator and implementation team member, can be subject to political competition, particularly where there are marked political blocs in a village. In such cases, KDP becomes a resource, material or symbolic, that is fought over. Second, the money associated with projects, which is often vast compared to existing village budgets, can be tapped by an individual or for the benefit of a person's family, kinship group, or political party. Third, involvement in the program can provide a basis for the strengthening or extension of systems of patronage, with elites seeking to build their power by using development resources to buy the support of particular individuals or groups. Fourth, capturing KDP processes (by, for example, threatening facilitators to ensure their compliance with elite-level decision making) can also be a means of maintaining hegemony over knowledge and power and so, in the vein of Gaventa (1980), assuring the quiescence of the populace by limiting their knowledge.

Individuals in our research villages often used the financial resources, legitimacy, and access to other forms of power that come with having won a development project as a means for strengthening their position and building their support base. The data revealed a number of conflicts that involved the interaction of KDP with preexisting forms of competition. In such conflicts, the program cannot be said to have been the primary cause; however, the program contributed to the escalation of tensions. In order to ensure that programs such as KDP do not have negative impacts on local conflict, it is necessary to consider the ways in which the program interacts with the existing sets of power relations in the villages in which it operates.

Several of different forms of interaction conflict can be identified in our data: (a) battles for political power among elites (for example, village head elections); (b) control of development resources; and (c) elite resistance to democratization.

Power Battles Between Elites and KDP

Using KDP as an instrument in power struggles is the most common form of interaction conflict. In almost every village in our sample, development projects had become ensnared in local power battles between different elites within the village. In one subdistrict in Pamekasan, Rp. 1 million (approximately US$100) was taken from the budget for all the villages that were successful in obtaining KDP funding. The money was put toward the campaign budget of one of the dominant political parties for use in the upcoming legislative elections.

In Panagguan village in Pamekasan, a KDP proposal to provide water facilities was used as a political tool. The village head dominated the KDP proposal process to ensure that one of the hamlets where he was seeking support in the election (but which at the time supported his opponent) gained access to a water pipeline and hence gave him their patronage.

> At the time, much of the Danglebar hamlet community did not support the klebun (village head). . . . Leading up to the village head election, the klebun turned the water in Danglebar back on [through a KDP-funded project] by connecting PVC pipes there to channel water. In this way, the klebun obtained the support of the people of Danglebar in the village head election.
>
> —VILLAGER, PANAGGUAN, PROPPO, PAMEKASAN

> I prioritized the clean water project in Danglebar hamlet so that their [electoral] support would come to me. I had already calculated it many days beforehand. Many villagers of the hamlet tended to support my opponent.
>
> —VILLAGE HEAD, PANAGGUAN, PROPPO, PAMEKASAN

This action led to a heated conflict between election candidates and the eventual damaging of the water pump storage facility by those who were frustrated with such political maneuvering. Implementation of the project was delayed by the village head until after the election to ensure that the hamlet in question voted for him. Such elite capture resulted in a swing in the vote in the target hamlet in the village head's favor, as well as the creation of a new policy by the village head that the beneficiaries had to pay for access to the water, which should have been freely provided as a part of the KDP proposal. The village ultimately suffered sanctions from the program for the delay in implementation and was not able to compete for funds the following year. This case provides another prime example of the incentives for elites to capture KDP and the kinds of conflicts generated by doing so.

In a similar case (box 4.5), while the village head initially influenced the program by selecting the head of the project implementation team in a way that contravened KDP rules, the villagers knew enough about program rules and processes that they were able to contest any diversions. Good socialization (meaning that people knew of and were able to contest processes at points in the project cycle) assured that the conflicts came to a head fairly quickly; with the help of local leaders (both formal and informal), the problems were efficiently and effectively resolved.

Box 4.5   Road Surfacing Project in Tattangoh

Conflict and social tension arose in Tattangoh village in Pamekasan concerning three related issues during the third year of KDP. Each was colored by the rivalry between two different power blocs within Tattangoh, one led by the village head and the other by the Village Representative Council (BPD).

The first problem arose when the village head appointed the KDP Village Project Implementation Team (TPK) without going through the required selection process. One villager in particular was disappointed by being passed over for a position on the team. The second problem occurred between the disappointed villager and the appointed head of the Project Implementation Team, both of whom managed rival crews working on the KDP road surfacing project. The team head declared a certain day to be a holiday, but on that day his crew began work as usual whereas the rival crew stayed home. The disappointed villager was so incensed at the team head's deceit, which deprived him and his men of payment for a day's work, that he threatened carok (ritual revenge dueling) on two separate occasions. He was prevented from carrying out his threats in both instances by local leaders and the village head.

The third matter concerned the acquisition of stones used in the road surfacing. Accusations that the stones were not being bought fairly from local quarrymen led to a blockade of the work site, organized by someone linked to the disappointed villager and identified as a member of the opposition to the village government. Negotiations between parties mediated by the village head and other community leaders successfully resolved the confrontation.

Development Resources and KDP

The cases above show how groups seek to capture development resources in order to bolster their position within the community. Access to development resources sustains, and in cases expands, systems of patronage. However, in other examples the motivation for elites to capture development resources is simpler: they want the resources themselves. Take, for example, a case from Tengku Leda village in Manggarai (box 4.6).

In poor areas of Indonesia, where resources are extremely limited, many people seek access to the state (by holding political positions or as civil servants) for self-enrichment. The salaries for these positions are extremely low, in some cases not much higher than those for laborers or successful farmers. Instead of remuneration, the motivation for seeking state positions is often related to the potential for bribes, kickbacks, or the chance to bring projects back to the person's village or kinship group.[20] In Flores, competition for civil service positions has been so high that in certain instances riots have occurred when people have not been accepted in the annual round of recruitment. In 2004 the central government decided to take back responsibility for recruitment decisions from the local administrations in Flores because the system was perceived as being too corrupt. Large-scale protests were held by candidates who had paid bribes to local officials for a "guaranteed" job. Development projects offer opportunities for corruption and for resources to be directed in inequitable ways.

BOX 4.6   VILLAGE ELECTION IN TENGKU LEDA

The program helped fuel tensions between the village head and others in Tengku Leda, Manggarai. One Martinus Rudung, who had been a strong supporter of his friend the village head during the election campaign, was appointed to a position in the KDP Village Project Implementation team, as were other friends.

Initially tensions emerged between those who supported the winning candidate in the elections and those who supported his opponents. For example, when the village held a party to celebrate his success, there was some debate about whether the supporters of the opponents should be invited. Furthermore, local leader Laurens Guntur, who had supported one of the losing candidates, thought that he would at least be elected as the head of the Village Development Council and as a technical consultant for KDP, and was upset when he won neither position.

After a while, the nature of tensions within the village changed. Having won the election, the village head took control of KDP finances. At first his friends, who now constituted the Implementation Team, accepted this. Yet it soon became clear that the village head was not sharing information about the project finances with others on the team; neither the treasurer (Domi Abraham) nor the KDP field manager (Martinus Rudung) knew anything about KDP finances. Feelings arose that the village head was trying to capture the program for himself. Tensions worsened when the money left over at the end of the KDP financial year was not divided up evenly (in the form of cement, sand, and cash), as has been agreed. This triggered the feelings of antipathy toward the village head.

—RELIGIOUS AND COMMUNITY LEADERS, TENGKU LEDA, LAMBA LEDA, MANGGARAI

Resistance by Elites to Democratization

The third form of interaction conflict relates to resistance by elites to the normative frameworks that projects such as KDP bring with them. KDP is a democratization project; it aims to promote transparency and widespread participation in decision making. As such it is not surprising that it is often met with resistance by incumbent elites who want to maintain the power balance in their favor. The control of decisions about development resources is one of the ways in which elites maintain positions of power, and hence elites are often extremely reluctant to cede this task to others.

Many Indonesian villages are still quasi-feudal "mini kingdoms." In such cases village heads and traditional leaders see themselves as playing the role of benign dictators who look after the welfare of the people and ensure their security. As Antlov (2003a, 2003b) points out, elites were traditionally loyal to their patrons in the higher levels of the Indonesian bureaucracy in return for sole authority and carte blanche power over village affairs. Leaving aside the question of whether this is really in the best interests of subjects in the village, it is clear that KDP (and indeed the *reformasi* movement more broadly) envisions a different model of social structure and control. The democratization process that began in 1998 and the administrative decentralization that followed created an environment of flux. In many parts of rural Indonesia, this has led to tensions between the way things were done in the past—when local village and subdistrict elites held the purse strings and were not held accountable by villagers—and new normative systems that emphasize widespread autonomy and checks and balances on forms of political power. Local culture and custom, as well as appeals to tradition (adat), have been utilized by elites seeking to cling to power.[21]

In some of our research areas, development and political decision making were, prior to the introduction of KDP, the purview of a few elite villagers. This was especially true in our low-capacity areas, but this was by no means evenly spread or limited to these districts. In areas where such power structures are deeply entrenched, the incentives to capture the processes and forums within KDP and to keep them within the realm of a few trusted clients are likely greatest. The program not only challenges their very authority, but it inevitably ends their hegemony over decision making and governance by extending it to many more people. This is likely to expose the elites to criticism of past practices, including corruption;

moreover, they would no longer be able to maintain either their monopoly of power and resources or the quiescence of villagers whose lack of knowledge also likely meant a lack of protest.

Because of the dissemination of information and the opening up of power and knowledge through KDP, conflict is likely, in response to knowledge of mistakes and deviations. It can also take the form of the efforts of elites (through threats, intimidation, slander, and so on) to prevent the program facilitators from reaching alternative voices or of political factions in the village each attempting to use the program for political gain or leverage. We saw examples of this in each of the cases discussed above—villages elites beating the KDP consultant who exposed corruption, extreme and almost violent frustration on the part of the facilitator who was criticized for not maintaining the status quo of corruption, and the case of the village elections where KDP was used for election point scoring.

Programs such as KDP promote transparency and greater attention to community demands, but tensions arise at this juncture of new and old ways of seeing and doing, a common outcome of social change. The clash between two normative worlds and the resistance of elites to change can and do lead to tensions.

Aside from the cases, the key informant survey collected data about levels of elite involvement in KDP and non-KDP development projects. By comparing reported levels of elite involvement in both types, we can get a sense of the extent to which KDP changes elites' roles in these participatory types of projects. As table 4.2 shows, in some areas there is a big difference between the level elite involvement in KDP and other development programs. For example, in Pademawu, East Java, more than twice as many informants reported disproportionate involvement by elites in non-KDP projects (87.6 percent of informants) as did in KDP (37.5 percent). In other subdistricts there was less of a difference, with Badegan (at the other extreme) reporting the same high levels of disproportionate elite involvement in both types of projects. In most cases, the subdistricts in our low-capacity districts (Pamekasan and Manggarai) had the greatest degree of reported difference between disproportionate elite involvement in KDP and in other programs, indicating that there is some change occurring in these areas and that villages perceive that KDP is less likely to be dominated by elites. Conversely, the higher levels of reported disproportionate elite involvement in other development programs shows the perceived pervasiveness of elite capture of the development process in these low-capacity

TABLE 4.2   REPORTED DISPROPORTIONATE ELITE INVOLVEMENT IN KDP
COMPARED WITH INVOLVEMENT IN OTHER DEVELOPMENT PROJECTS

Degree of difference (% change)	Subdistrict (% reported involvement in non-KDP projects – % reported involvement KDP projects) Difference	Province (district)
High (≥ 40%)	Lamba Leda (60.0–20.0) 40.0%	NTT (Manggarai)
	Pademawu (87.6–37.5) 50.1%	East Java (Pamekasan)
Medium (20%–40%)	Nita (54.1–16.7) 37.4%	NTT (Sikka)
	Pasaen (68.8–37.5) 31.3%	East Java (Pamekasan)
	Proppo (100.0–78.2) 21.8%	East Java (Pamekasan)
	Ruteng (62.6–25.0) 37.6%	NTT (Manggarai)
	Slahung (56.3–31.3) 25.0%	East Java (Ponorogo)
Low (0%–20%)	Badegan (66.7–66.7) 0.0%	East Java (Ponorogo)
	Cibal (38.9–27.6) 11.3%	NTT (Manggarai)
	Jenangan (18.8–6.3) 12.5%	East Java (Ponorogo)
	Paga (56.3–43.8) 12.5%	NTT (Sikka)
	Talibura (50.1–31.3) 18.8%	NTT (Manggarai)

Source: Key informant survey (KDP program sites only).

regions; there are likely to be challenges in opening up the participatory process if working in these areas. There is still a question, however, about the likelihood that this will generate conflict.

The fieldwork showed that elites have the autonomy to capture KDP process in the way they do other projects; whether they do so is a partial measure of KDP's efficacy in providing constraints on elite power. If elites' roles differ significantly between KDP and non-KDP projects, we can assume that KDP is creating incentives for *compliance* with more participatory and open decision-making processes. In contrast, if the difference in elite involvement is minimal (and especially if elite involvement is high) we can assume that there is *resistance* at play; that is, that elites develop strategies to maintain disproportionate involvement in development decision making and resource distribution.

How does this relate to the level of conflict triggered by KDP? Is conflict more likely to result from compliance with program rules (where elites' roles change significantly, and hence decision making presumably becomes more uncertain) or from resistance (where elites try to maintain their disproportionate role)? Table 4.3 shows how changes in elite involvement correlate with the reported extent to which conflicts were said to take place in KDP forums. The results show a relatively clear trend for East Java, but one needs to examine both the starting point of reported disproportionate elite involvement in programs and the changes relating to the introduction of KDP.

Overall, in East Java, subdistricts exhibiting little change in elite involvement were considerably more likely to report conflict in KDP forums. This initially suggests that where there is resistance to a changed role among elites, reported conflict is more likely and a probable indicator of a villager's knowledge of such resistance to change. This is only the case, however, where the starting point of reported elite capture was high in absolute terms. One of the areas with the lowest reported change, Jenangan (see table 4.2), also had the lowest level of reported elite capture of all subdistricts in the sample of non-KDP programs (only 19 percent) compared to other places. Therefore the level of change with the introduction of KDP may only be low, because the program was being introduced into an area

TABLE 4.3   CHANGE IN ELITE INVOLVEMENT AND LEVEL OF KDP-TRIGGERED PROBLEMS/CONFLICT

Province	Level of change in elite involvement	Cases in which conflict was triggered (%)
East Java	High	10.5
	Medium	39.9
	Low	70.5
NTT	High	21.4
	Medium	15.3
	Low	22.3

Source: Key informant survey (KDP program sites only).

that was already open to participation and inclusion of a wide range of groups; in this case, then, a low level of change indicates not resistance but compliance. But there was simultaneously a high frequency of reported conflict in KDP forums in Jenangan. This indicates that, in general, it is a healthy space to express views across the board and contest problems, small or large, as they arise, and therefore conflict was more likely.

In other words, the findings from East Java demonstrate that when programs are being implemented in environments where there is resistance to openness and participation, knowledge of this on the part of villagers is likely to generate conflicts related to a program, whereas compliance on the part of elites is less likely to do so. Yet when programs that are likely to generate micro-conflicts, such as KDP with its competition mechanisms, are introduced into areas where such openness and participation are already the norm, then such programs are likely to generate contestation and conflicts concerning knowledge of program problems and mistakes or the competition process itself, rather than conflicts around elite capture and resistance to change. As we have stated, however, the nature of the conflicts which the program generates (interaction conflicts and program malfunction conflicts, especially those stemming from elite capture) is of greater concern than their frequency. The evidence from NTT is less clear.

Thus KDP-related conflict is more likely, at least in East Java, under two sets of conditions: when elites actively resist local democratization in low-capacity areas and when, in areas where there was less elite capture in the first place, people comply with KDP rules, but power is equalized and grievances can be voiced and quickly dealt with. As we explain in later chapters, it is the substantive nature of development-related conflicts that should be of concern, however, particularly those concerning interaction with local contexts and governance capacity. A case from Madura (box 4.7) shows an example of how, prior to the introduction of KDP in an area where elite-centered decision making was the norm, development could still be contested, albeit under fairly extreme conditions. The case shows the intersection between elite interests, conflict, and development programs, as well as the problems that can result from elites seeking to cling to power.

In the case presented in box 4.7, there was little response to community demands to shift an abattoir—the activities of which were disturbing community life and polluting waterways—before it was burned down in frustration, and there was little consultation with the community about its desires and needs during the process of rebuilding the abattoir. This conflict then

Box 4.7   Abattoir Destruction and Violence in Madura

At the end of 1998, an incredible stench once again wafted into the central area of Banyupelle village. Blood, feces, and refuse from the slaughter of animals taking place at the centrally located abattoir festered and rotted, eventually draining into the river nearby. The river was used by the local people to bathe and wash and as a source of *air wudhu* (water for ritual ablutions) for *sholat* (ritual prayers).

> The problem of the abattoir waste had been reported countless times by the community. . . . Because there was no follow-up and because *reformasi* (the reform era) was in full swing . . . the people were brave enough to destroy the abattoir.
> —VETERINARIAN, BANYUPELLE, PALENGAAN, PAMEKASAN

The community's long-standing frustration with the impact of the slaughtering activities eventually intensified when a kyai commented in a sermon that the river water was *najis* (unclean) and so it could not be used to purify oneself for daily prayers. The district government made little effort to resolve the problem and ignored the complaints of the villagers.

In the final days of the fasting month in 1998, a mob of about five hundred people destroyed the abattoir, toppling the walls, prying up the floor, and completely burning the roof. Only about 10 percent of the abattoir floor remained. This incident resulted in the destruction of public property and significant levels of community tension, and it triggered a series of disputes among elites.

Lacking an alternative site, the slaughterers continued killing their cattle in the ruins of the roofless abattoir, as much for practical reasons as to make a political statement. The village head (klebun), renowned for his links to criminal groups, politically opposed the head of the slaughterers' group. Discussions about building a new abattoir began, but no one could agree on a location. The klebun made a nonconsultative executive decision on the new site: it was not far from his home but a long way from the public services required by the slaughterers. Land was purchased by the klebun at a low price and sold to the district government for a profit. Construction of the new abattoir began, corners were cut, and rumors circulated about the embezzlement of funds. Uncertainty about the construction process annoyed the slaughterers, who felt excluded from the decision-making process.

In the year 2000, the community again expressed its discontent by destroying the remaining floor of the old abattoir. The head of the slaughterers' group eventually built an abattoir on his property. While the community was finally satisfied, the new public abattoir went unoccupied and tensions among the elites increased. Meetings were held to try to resolve the problem, but the elites continued with their own agendas.

> The first meeting discussed plans to occupy the new abattoir, the second was held after the slaughterers' demanded that the abattoir floor be widened and that electricity be supplied to the site, whereas the last meeting was held to plan the occupation [of the abattoir] after the demands for a roof were met. But even after that, they didn't occupy it because they had further demands for security. They asked for police to be on guard from six until the morning, after they had finished cutting up meat.
> —VILLAGE HEAD, BANYUPELLE, PALENGAAN, PAMEKASAN

> Intrigue and blunders continued to occur in elite government and nongovernment circles. The district office followed its own agenda, and the klebun followed his. All the while, the slaughterers were carrying out their activities on private land, resulting in a loss of tax income and a waste of public resources on an empty abattoir. A final agreement was reached to occupy the public abattoir at a meeting hosted by a kyai. Security forces, government staff, and the village elite were present. However, following the meeting, the kyai stated that "the slaughterers don't want to occupy it. They say a kyai was robbed [there]." Despite assurances from the klebun that he would guarantee the security of the abattoir (for a small price, of course), the building remains unoccupied to this day. Extensive public resources were wasted and the issue remains contentious in the community.

became a power battle between elites to monopolize and benefit from the spoils of development funding from the district government coffers: the use of development funds was unclear, certain contractors were favored (with no transparent materials acquisition process), and much political maneuvering went on behind closed doors. The result was that the new abattoir was not used, the conflict had not (at the time of writing) been resolved, and public resources were wasted. This is a common story of the interaction between development programs and conflict, particularly in periods of democratization as villagers become more vocal, make more demands, and learn from introduced projects that promote transparency.

Limiting Interaction Conflict

In the field, we found that almost all development projects, including KDP, helped trigger interaction conflict. Yet they did not *always* do so.

Analysis of the cases above, as well as other examples we found, provides some lessons as to when interaction conflicts are most likely to occur.

First, and most simply, interaction conflicts are most likely when conflict or social tensions of the types noted above (and in Chapter 3) are already present. Where tensions between different elites within a village, for example, are already high, there is an accentuated risk that projects such as KDP will get pulled into the conflict. Where there are already issues related to land ownership or use, development projects can easily make things worse. The basic implication is clear: before a program enters an area, it is necessary to understand which forms of *local* social tensions/conflicts are present, so that program staff can ensure that the program does not fuel latent tensions.

Second, KDP interaction conflict was more likely in areas where existing value systems and cultural norms ran contrary to the principles embodied in the program. If different sets of rules and norms clashed, conflict was more likely.[22] In particular, where elites did not buy into the principles of grassroots participation, transparency and accountability, there was a greater likelihood that they would try to subvert the program. The program, in turn, would interact with other tensions on the ground. For example, in Proppo subdistrict in Pamekasan, KDP rules do not fit easily alongside local norms.[23] The village heads in this region exert considerable dominance over many areas of decision making about village administration, planning, and development (Barnawi 2003). Patronage systems operate by buying the loyalty of villagers. This system of social organization does not sit easily alongside the principles of democratization and equitable participation endorsed by KDP. It is not surprising that there are more problems with the program in places such as this than in areas where there is less resistance to the principles and practices KDP espouses.

Third, where there was weak socialization, monitoring, and implementation of the program, or where responses to program deviations were inadequate, there was an enhanced risk that the program could interact with existing issues. Poor program functioning, as discussed above, allows for grievances to build, which over time can erupt into conflict. Program malfunction conflict is serious enough, but when it interacts with existing tensions, there is potential for more serious unrest. Ensuring that the program functions as intended is the best defense against interaction conflict.

Why Do KDP Conflicts Not Escalate?

As we have outlined above, a number of different forms of conflict are related, directly or indirectly, to KDP. Yet in most cases tensions related to the program, even when they are frequent, do not escalate into full-fledged conflicts. Why is this so? There are two major reasons why conflicts do not tend to grow in size or become violent. First, KDP has in-built forums, facilitators, and other complaints mechanisms that provide an outlet for tensions and opportunities for redress. Second, the principles the program embodies make it less likely that misunderstandings will occur whenever socialization is well implemented. Conflicts escalate only where the program does not function well.

Problem Solving in KDP Forums

One of the major reasons that KDP conflicts do not tend to escalate is the availability of forums, in which people and procedures are available for dealing with problems before they grow in size. The program does trigger conflict, but in general the tensions it creates are constrained by the same forums and processes from which they emerged. Box 4.8 provides an overview of the type and number of meetings.

Indeed, KDP forums are commonly used for dealing with KDP-related conflicts/problems: 92 percent of survey respondents in East Java reported using them to address KDP-related problems, and 96 percent did so in NTT.[24] Forums at the subdistrict level were more likely to be used for solving KDP conflicts than those at the village level (95 percent compared to 85 percent), reflecting the fact that more conflicts emerge at this level.[25] Further, respondents reported very high success rates for the forums in solving KDP-related conflicts: 84 percent of informants in East Java, and 72 percent in NTT.[26]

In-built tensions—that is, forms of competition or contention that are part of the KDP design—were more likely to be addressed in forums than were program malfunctions associated with KDP. This was particularly true in East Java, where only 21 percent and 11 percent of informants reported that forums were used to deal with problems relating to KDP staff and to corruption, respectively. The reasons for this are that competition-related tensions are much easier to deal with than those relating to corruption or other malfunctions; there are few avenues of recourse within forums when malfunctions occur, aside from the sanctions

---

Box 4.8   KDP Forums and Meetings

As outlined in previous chapters, the KDP process involves forums or meetings at the hamlet, village, and subdistrict (intervillage) levels: the *Penggalian Gaggasan* (brainstorming ideas sessions), the *Musyawarah Desa* (intravillage meeting), and the *Musyawarah Antar Desa* (intervillage meeting), respectively. These meetings are held to elect staff, brainstorm and decide on proposals, to account for funds, and to deal with specific problems that arise during implementation. Formally speaking, KDP stipulates that approximately twenty meetings be held, depending on the number of hamlets in each village. Often, however, villagers decide that extra meetings are required; if problems occur, in some cases as many as seven extra meetings have been held.

The meetings are open to all. Villagers are encouraged to join the discussion, debate the merits of proposed projects, and participate in decision making. Facilitators endeavor to ensure that more marginalized voices are heard. In some villages a one-person, one-vote system is used, in which each person places a kernel of corn in the envelope of his or her preferred project. Other villages have introduced a weighted voting system in which people can show their preference by spreading their kernels across preferred projects.

Source: From Discussions with KDP Team.

---

that can be enacted at the end of the project cycle. Moreover, forums are held relatively infrequently following the allocation of funding. Other processes and facilitators need to be accessed for problems arising from implementation.

Although village and subdistrict forums were equally likely to address in-built conflicts, the latter were substantially more likely to deal with program malfunction conflicts than were village forums.[27] The qualitative fieldwork demonstrated the reasons for this. Villagers view the subdistrict-level forums and facilitators as having greater authority to deal with problems with the program's functioning. Program staff members in the subdistrict are employees tasked with running the program in a fair and appropriate way. At the village level, in contrast, facilitators are effectively volunteers. Further, as noted above, power imbalances are less prominent in subdistrict meetings than in village meetings. As a result, the likelihood that a particular group will challenge a program process or outcome is higher at the subdistrict level than in the village. Third, those who attend subdistrict meetings are more likely to understand how the program is meant to function, and hence whether there has been a deviation from program rules, than those in the village.

Where forums were used to address KDP-related problems, they were more likely to be successful at addressing in-built conflicts (see table 4.4). As Wong (2003) has rightly noted, issues related to corruption in KDP are generally more difficult to solve than problems relating to the inherent competition in the KDP process.[28] Yet almost 70 percent of informants in East Java and almost 80 percent in NTT still said that these problems were usually resolved successfully, albeit less often.[29]

TABLE 4.4   TYPES OF KDP PROBLEMS DEALT WITH IN KDP FORUMS AND SUCCESS RATES

Source of problem/conflict	Type of tension (in most cases)	Respondents agreeing it was dealt with in forums (%)	Respondents agreeing it was resolved in forums (%)
Problems understanding the project	In-built	88	96
Decisions about which projects to advance to the subdistrict forum	In-built or malfunction	87	98
Decisions made about funding at the subdistrict forum	In-built	72	90
Decisions about procurement or implementation	In-built or malfunction	69	92
Problems with KDP staff or facilitators	Malfunction	39	83
Corruption	Malfunction	33	74

Source: Key informant survey (KDP program sites only).

When combined with insights from the qualitative fieldwork, this suggests that while it may be difficult to resolve protracted problems of this type,
which have already risen through the project bureaucracy, a large proportion
of corruption cases are addressed early in the project cycle (at the village or
subdistrict level), where they are normally able to be resolved satisfactorily. In
East Java and NTT, survey respondents indicated that *in-built* problems were
resolved simply because there was no other place (East Java) or because it was
the appropriate place (NTT). Both these answers demonstrate the extent to
which the forums are perceived to be a natural place to address these types of
problems; it also suggests that KDP's in-built processes (and the authority
and legitimacy the program bestows upon facilitators), in addition to KDP
staff's personal attributes, help contribute to successful resolution.

The pattern is slightly different, and somewhat inconclusive, for KDP
malfunction problems, with the successful resolution of corruption problems (East Java) and other problems (NTT) attributed to the role of KDP
staff. This seems to suggest that these problems required significant
assistance from KDP staff or facilitators in getting forums to address more
difficult and often sensitive problems. It is not hard to imagine that when
forums address these problems, which often implicate key KDP actors, a
little extra facilitation is required to arrive at a successful outcome. In some
cases, outside actors are also required (see below).

When KDP-related problems were not resolved in the forums, it was
largely due to a lack of facilitation in the meetings rather than to expectations that these problems should not be solved in KDP forums. This suggests that whereas the inherent legitimacy afforded the KDP institutions
and processes and the particular characteristics of facilitators are important
in understanding why different types of problems are taken to the KDP
forums, a focus on improving facilitation and socialization more broadly
would help in resolving KDP-related problems.[30]

Generally, then, various types of KDP-related problems can be
successfully addressed by the forums. The program explicitly aims to introduce conflict in the form of competition for resources; therefore, some
conflict is inevitable but not necessarily negative. Conflict that is channeled
through appropriate institutions and mechanisms that prevent it from
taking violent form can be an engine for progressive social change, helping
build the social and civic skills associated with identifying collective needs
and enhancing democratic decision making. Even conflict over KDP malfunction—for example, in cases of corruption—can have positive effects if

it is addressed, including increasing citizens' consciousness of rights and demands for transparency. The data shows that in a wide range of locations (with varying governance and conflict management capacity), KDP is able to effectively channel conflict related to the program and, in doing so, is able to resolve the problems it inevitably creates.[31]

The Role of Facilitators

Another internal mechanism by which KDP conflicts are controlled at an early stage is the program's facilitation network (see box 4.9). Program facilitators are used outside KDP forums to deal with conflicts related to the program, although to a lesser extent, and with less success, than was the case for forums.

In East Java, 52 percent of respondents reported that KDP-related problems/conflicts were resolved by KDP facilitators outside the forums;

BOX 4.9   THE NETWORK OF KDP FACILITATORS

A network of KDP facilitators seeks to ensure that the project runs smoothly and that problems are promptly addressed. At the village level, two facilitators (FD) are elected. One must be a woman and one a man. Their major roles are to introduce the project to villagers and local leaders, to help to organize hamlet and village meetings where project ideas and priorities are brainstormed, and to provide technical assistance in writing proposals when villagers lack the skills. Also at this level is the KDP Village Project Implementation Team (TPK), the members of which are elected by villagers. The team takes responsibility for coordinating the project, including tasks such as buying material and organizing labor.

At the subdistrict level, two facilitators (FK) are appointed, one responsible for social participation and one for technical concerns. Together they try to ensure that the project in the subdistrict as a whole runs smoothly. Subdistrict facilitators usually come from outside the local area but live locally and spend a lot of their time traveling between the villages taking part in KDP. They also work closely with the local subdistrict head (camat) and his staff.

At the district level, the district consultant (KMKab), who is appointed, provides general coordination with little direct involvement in village-level activities.

Sources: Discussions with KDP staff; Government of Indonesia (2002).

in NTT, 60 percent of respondents reported the same.[32] These rates, though lower than those for forums, are high. Outside the forums, subdistrict facilitators and village facilitators were the most actively involved in resolving KDP-related conflicts whenever they were not involved as one of the parties to the conflict. The extent to which results were similar across subdistricts suggests that it is the institutional role of the KDP facilitators, rather than their personal qualities alone, that explains their ability to resolve disputes outside KDP forums, although in East Java there was also a role for informal or formal leaders outside the KDP process.[33] The main reasons why KDP facilitators were reported to have been used to address conflicts outside the forums, and the reasons for their success, were that they were believed to possess the resources and authority to solve the matter at hand and, to a lesser extent, because the facilitators offered assistance when the problem emerged. Despite (or because of) the fact that most subdistrict facilitators come from outside the subdistrict to which they are assigned, they seem to have little trouble establishing authority to resolve KDP-related conflicts.[34] In both provinces, and especially in East Java, a large proportion of respondents reported that non-KDP staff ("others") helped resolve KDP-related problems and conflicts (see figure 4.2).

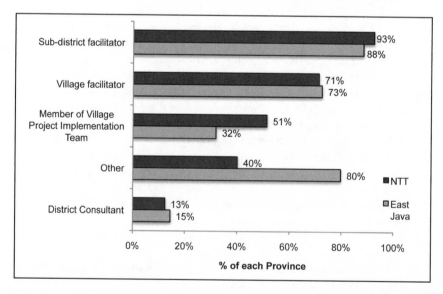

Figure 4.2   People who helped resolve KDP-related problems/conflicts outside KDP forums.

Source: Key informant survey (KDP program sites only).

Educating villagers about the role of facilitators is important. The program has facilitators at the village, subdistrict, and district levels; they are obvious points of contact for the community when program-related problems arise, as well as targets for elites seeking to avoid participatory mechanisms and to control decision-making processes. At the village level, the facilitators are local people with whom the community is usually familiar. In three of the six KDP-related cases followed in Pamekasan, East Java, program facilitators or consultants initially attempted to address the grievances of beneficiaries and the broader community involved in the conflicts. In some cases, forums were held to address the problems. In Ponorogo, in all six cases, program facilitators and forums were involved in attempting to resolve problems at their onset. This is not to say that they were successful in all instances, because they were not in most of the large conflicts we followed. Even at a minimal level, however, the disputants could identify authorities and places to express their grievances, or, in some cases, these authorities recognized that there was a problem and sought to resolve it before it escalated.

Consider, for example, one of the largest drawn-out conflicts in Ponorogo. The case, which involved KDP and actors from all groups in the village in Slahung, related to the district consultant's decision to change the technical drawings and design of the KDP-funded bridge without consulting the community (see above). In this case, on identifying the grievances of the landowner and other project beneficiaries, the village and subdistrict facilitators approached the aggrieved persons to try to resolve the key issues. Although these efforts failed, they did signify the beginning of a number of institutionalized initiatives to resolve the dispute. Follow-up by leaders and other institutions outside of the KDP process, in collaboration with KDP facilitators, was also instrumental in resolving the dispute.

Other Complaint Mechanisms

Many conflicts triggered by development programs result from program malfunctions and frustrations with processes, with weak avenues of recourse or none at all. The program has internal mechanisms to deal with these early on, making the escalation of the problems less likely.

As we have seen, development projects inevitably trigger tensions since they involve the allocation of finite resources. In places such as

Indonesian villages, where there are problems with corruption, decision-making processes, and elite capture, these tensions are likely to be prominent. It would thus appear to be obvious that programs and projects must plan for ways to deal with the grievances and problems that arise. The field-work in East Java and NTT, however, encountered no other development programs with complaints units or clear, institutionalized mechanisms for dealing with routine problems arising from implementation.

The lack of such planning for the grievances that arise can lead to programs having destructive consequences. For example, if we examine further the case of the burning of the abattoir (see box 4.7), there were no avenues of recourse for frustrated villagers, and when they did try to complain early on to district officials in the Office of Animal Husbandry, there was no response to their request to relocate the abattoir. The villagers also complained several times to the village head, but he argued that the issue was outside his authority. Eventually the abattoir was burned down by aggrieved villagers. When plans were made to rebuild the abattoir in a different location, there was no point of contact readily available to allow villagers to communicate with the district office. The result was that the remainder of the initial abattoir was burned down. When contact was made, no action was publicly taken, or, if it was, the results were never reported back to the community. The problems continued to escalate and more and more people, each with their own interests, became involved.

In a number of cases in Flores, conflict emerged because of government corruption related to development resources. Some of these cases escalated because of a lack of complaints mechanisms to deal with the resulting tensions. Box 4.10 outlines two conflicts in Sikka, Flores, related to the government's Rice for the Poor (OPK/Raskin) program, which escalated for this reason, among others.[35] Indeed, in such cases there are few in-built mechanisms for containing conflict. Given the extent to which participation is discouraged and to which courts are unlikely to convict local politicians of corruption, communities often have few available outlets for dissent. Thus demonstrations in many cases turn violent as frustrations rise.

The Importance of Complaint Mechanisms

In contrast, KDP has a dedicated unit to handle complaints, with points of contact at the provincial level (through the Regional Management Unit, or RMU), as well as facilitators who can be approached in person or

BOX 4.10   RICE FOR THE POOR? TWO CASES OF CONFLICT OVER RICE
DISTRIBUTION IN SIKKA

The government's OPK (Special Market Operation) and Raskin (Rice for
the Poor) programs, which are aimed at helping poor communities, have
resulted in corruption in some villages. A key component of the safety net
constructed in 1998 after the Asian financial crisis, the OPK program provided subsidized rice to poor households. In 2002, OPK was replaced
by a similar program known as Raskin. Corruption has taken place not
only at the village level, where the poor have to struggle to collect the
funds required to buy Raskin, but also at the district level. Similarly, at the
provincial level, the involvement of Dolog (the government warehouse for
foodstuffs) in the transportation of rice throughout NTT has resulted
in other irregularities. Two cases in Sikka, Flores, show how corruption in
the program can trigger broader conflicts:

December 15, 2000, Nele Wutung village, Sikka: The village and hamlet
heads made their way to the Dolog office in Maumere, the district capital,
to collect the village's 2,940 kg of rice. During their trip home, they stopped
to unload 200 kg (four sacks) of rice at the house of the head of Kode hamlet. The remaining 2,740 kg was finally unloaded at the Nele Wutung village government office. The villagers who had been waiting at the meeting
hall heard the news that four sacks of rice had been unloaded earlier. They
suspected that the rice had been stolen. When they questioned the hamlet
head he said that he was ordered by the village head to unload the rice at his
house. Meanwhile, the head of another hamlet, Delang, said that the village head had used her own money to purchase the rice directly from the
Dolog. The villagers became frustrated, not only with the contradictory
answers but also with the fact that the village head was not in her office.
They waited at the village hall; by nightfall approximately sixty-two households had still not received any rice. The community soon became restless
and staged a protest in front of the village office. That night the village
head arrived and tried to clarify the situation. The village secretary, however, had no record of the apparent purchase of the 200 kg of rice by the
village head. The atmosphere that night was tense and fiery. Two groups
formed in the village: those who supported the village head, and those who
were in opposition. At about 2 A.M. flames could be seen rising from the
village office. The village head's supporters said that the opposition had
committed the arson in frustration; others said that the village head's supporters had done it to hide the receipts for money "borrowed" from the
village budget. The case is still unsolved.

July 5, 2002, Watu Gong village, Sikka: The community was waiting
for discounted rice to be delivered from the Dolog. Several hours passed

without any sign that the rice was on its way. The rice eventually arrived at 2 P.M. The village government, which had been assigned the task of distributing the rice, believed that using a scoop was the most accurate means of distribution. The villagers, however, preferred that scales be used to ensure that everyone received their fair amount. They were worried that the village head would try to skim off some rice for himself if a scoop was used. The two parties could not agree. By 4:30 P.M. the rice had still not been distributed, and tensions were rising. Six disappointed villagers decided to storm the village office, each taking a sack of rice. Seeing this, many other villagers followed suit: before long, the atmosphere was chaotic with widespread looting of rice. Police on their way home from a neighboring hamlet happened to be passing by. Seeing the developing chaos, they fired shots into the sky. Slowly the situation was brought under control.

---

forums where problems can be openly discussed. Complaints to the Regional Management Unit can be submitted in person or anonymously by post. Although the role and function of this unit have evolved with the program, it primarily handles large cases that are outside the capacity of local facilitators, somewhat diffusing tensions. Many of these cases relate to corruption within the program. Between August 1999 and May 2005, the Handling Complaints Unit in NTT addressed 74 corruption cases, 8 of which took place in Manggarai and 4 in Sikka. In East Java, between September 2001 and May 2005, the unit addressed 131 such cases, 3 in Pamekasan and 13 in Ponorogo.[36]

In many instances, follow-up of reported cases had a positive impact in diffusing tensions. None of the cases reported to the complaints unit in East Java became violent, and many were resolved. For example, the RMU had followed through on one case in Pasean, Pamekasan, where program staff members were accused of misappropriating funds. When the staff members in question were caught, they gave the funds back to the project. The RMU also followed up on cases of damaged water pipes and a case in which villagers were facing sanctions from the program for not meeting the implementation targets. The villagers spoke openly of the positive role the RMU had played in resolving the problems and of their frequent visits to the field. In the interviews, however, villagers also demanded more feedback about the outcome of cases forwarded to the complaints unit.

These complaint mechanisms are extremely important. Where they were absent, where there was a complaints unit but it took no action, or where there was no feedback mechanism for reporting the outcomes of complaints, then conflicts involving non-KDP programs were more likely to escalate. All programs, especially those dealing specifically with conflict resolution and postconflict reconstruction, require internal complaints handling mechanisms, action processes, and systems for reporting back. KDP has these mechanisms, although the fieldwork shows that they could be improved. More resources need to be provided for the complaints units to visit villages (those experiencing and those not experiencing problems) on a regular basis to provide the opportunity for communities to air grievances at a publicized time.

In general, *all* development programs, projects, and other initiatives should have clear complaints mechanisms in place that (a) are accessible to beneficiaries, (b) take responsibility for program decisions and communicate these and complaints outcomes to villagers, (c) are willing and able to listen to villagers and hear their complaints, and (d) clearly publicize their availability and functions.

The Role of Outside Actors in Solving KDP-Related Conflicts

In some cases it is necessary for outside actors to get involved in KDP-related problems. This is the case both for problems relating to competition within the program (see box 4.11) and for program malfunction problems. At the same time, the qualitative fieldwork highlighted the fact that facilitators alone often could not solve problems related to KDP malfunctions. Although facilitators and program structures are essential for access and for preventing violent conflict in the first instance, they are not always successful at dealing with significant program malfunctions such as deviations in processes, corruption, problems with facilitators, or the kinds of problems that sit outside everyday KDP interactions and processes. Not only are facilitators often intimidated or threatened, but they may be a part of the problem if they are implicated in program malfunctions.

Often it is necessary for other actors (informal leaders or the state) to get involved. In Pamekasan, all the large conflict cases required intervention from an outside actor: one case involved the district head reaching an informal agreement with the village head; the other involved the village head and community and religious leaders intervening in the dispute. In the

---

BOX 4.11   COMPETITION AND KDP: DISPUTES IN MANGGARAI, FLORES

August 2003, Bangka Lelak village, Ruteng subdistrict: Three proposals were submitted by three different hamlets: a proposal for clean drinking water (Tongger) and two proposals for a village road (from Mbohang and from Manu). A conflict emerged about which should be put forward to the KDP intervillage meeting. At the meeting, Tongger and Mbohang hamlets agreed that the Mbohang proposal should go forward. The group from Manu hamlet disagreed, however. A heated debated ensued; agreement was impossible.

> The group from Manu expressed their disappointment by tearing down the KDP information board. The next day, the residents of Manu carried the board to the subdistrict head's office to register their objections. There, the subdistrict head explained KDP mechanisms, procedures and regulations. After they had the regulations and process explained, the Manu residents understood and were satisfied with the explanation.
> —KDP SUBDISTRICT FACILITATOR, BANGKA LELAK, RUTENG, MANGGARAI

> Two people from Pagal subdistrict were not satisfied because their proposals were rejected by the verification team. Consequently, they reported their complaints to the district head, who in turn ordered the subdistrict head to handle the case. The subdistrict head, a representative from the district-level PMD (the Village Community Empowerment body within the Ministry of Home Affairs), the village head, and the Village Development Council (LKMD) solved the problem in the subdistrict office by accepting their proposals.
> —HEAD OF THE VILLAGE DEVELOPMENT COUNCIL, PAGAL, CIBAL, MANGGARAI

---

bridge-building case in Slahung, Ponorogo, outlined above, the media, local leaders, and government officials were all involved in the resolution process. In two villages in Sikka, Flores, parties external to the program stepped in when repayments by KDP borrowers dried up.

At the KDP forums at the hamlet level, the village head and several respected community figures from Hobuai hamlet had to step in and take action when it came time to collect the repayments. They wrote a letter to the KDP Financial Management Unit in Talibura as well as to the KDP subdistrict facilitator and the subdistrict head to indicate their regrets . . . they also requested that all of the parties reconsider their proposal.

—PRIMARY SCHOOL SPOKESPERSON, WERANG,

TALIBURA, SIKKA

We once formed a Team for the Collection of Delinquent Loans. The team included members of the police and military. We went to all the villages and after two weeks we had collected Rp. 60 million [US$6,000]. I think the team was very effective, but we didn't have enough operational funds to pay the large lump sum requested by the team. That's why we have only done it once until now.

—SUBDISTRICT HEAD, PAGA, PAGA, SIKKA

The surprising thing is that when we went out with the police, military, subdistrict head, village head, Village Representative Council and KDP Village Project Implementation Team, they actually wanted to repay their loans!

—SECRETARY OF THE KDP FINANCIAL MANAGEMENT UNITY,

PAGA, PAGA, SIKKA

In Cibal subdistrict in Manggarai, a *Tim Sukses* (Success Team) made up of members of various formal and informal institutions was formed to overcome problems with delinquent loans. The cases demonstrate that although facilitators and forums can deal with many problems by themselves, resolution of problems is often easier where there are strong links between the program, informal leaders, and the state.

In East Java, the most successfully resolved KDP-related cases involved program facilitators working together with outside formal and informal leaders. In one such case in Ponorogo, the village facilitator (FD) used creative means to find ways for the saving and loan group to pay back their funds. He employed the program principles while adapting the repayment system to the local conditions and seasonal nature of the livelihood of local people, and he worked with the local group leader to reach agreement; his local knowledge and the technical resources provided by the program were central to the success of his initiative. In the other successfully resolved case (the Slahung bridge case), outside actors—the district parliament, the village representative council, the media, members of the district executive, and the security forces—all sat down with program facilitators and beneficiaries to seek an agreement and then to enforce it.

Eventually a meeting was held in the district hall. The district administration, district parliamentarians and the district consultant all attended. At the time, the village technical assistant couldn't say much. The KDP subdistrict facilitator supported him, but he wasn't particularly strong. Then the district consultant supported the technical assistant. But the community wanted the bridge construction to return to the original proposed design. After this was agreed, it was over.

—FORMER KDP VILLAGE PROJECT IMPLEMENTATION TEAM CHAIR,
SLAHUNG, SLAHUNG, PONOROGO

The same theme emerges in both KDP and non-KDP conflict cases that have escalated. Often both formal (state) and informal (nonstate) actors are needed for the problem to be successfully resolved. Where there is synergy between the state, informal leaders, and program staff, development conflicts are much more likely to be resolved.

Comparing KDP Conflicts and Other Development-Related Conflicts

In Padellegan village, the chair of the Village Representative Council responded this way when asked to comment on the difference between KDP and other projects:

There is a huge difference. With KDP the community can be directly involved, through putting forward proposals, planning, and implementation. . . . In putting forward proposals, they can be involved and give their opinion, starting from the hamlet level to the village level. Then, in the planning they can also get involved . . . and in implementation they can be involved as labor, which adds to their income. . . . In other projects, only certain people are involved in the meetings, it's enough with just the village head and his officials . . . even then not everyone attends. . . . The saying goes, "It's enough to only have four people at a meeting." . . . Yes, at most the village head, the secretary, the head of the Village Development Council . . . and in the implementation of the project it is usually only outsiders.

For all villages, the evidence is mixed as to whether true participation was taking place at the start of KDP or whether people adhered to the rules on paper. The comments of the council chair could be equally indicative of change in the nature of participation, or of village heads knowing how to "report" increased participation from people outside of elite circles (such as the poor) even though in practice it was still dominated by the old guard who reigned under the New Order government. Countless villagers stated that the traditional women's organization, the Family Welfare Organisation (PKK), often associated with the village head's wife and daughters or female kin, dominated the women's participation and proposal writing process. On the other hand, the road project in Bedog, Wates, introduced in Chapter 1, was a case of the most isolated hamlet being prioritized, at least at the village level.

As we have seen, KDP-related conflicts are generally solved or at least dealt with before they escalate. Almost without exception, they do not become violent. How does this compare with conflicts related to other development projects in Flores and East Java?

As table 4.5 shows, KDP conflicts are less likely to result in violence than those related to government administration and service provision or other donors' programs. Whereas only one of forty-two KDP conflicts reported in local newspapers between 2001 and 2003 became violent, thirty-six government-related conflicts (5 percent of the total) had violent impacts. The newspaper data only included one violent conflict related to other donors' programs, but this is also proportionally a greater share (5 percent, compared with 2 percent for KDP).

If we look at all the development case studies collected in the field, it is clear why KDP conflicts tend to be less violent than non-KDP development conflicts. As discussed above, KDP has forums, facilitators, and other internal complaints mechanisms to handle conflicts as they arise. When it works well, KDP also provides space for nonprogram actors (such as local government officials) to play a role in resolving program-related problems; other programs, which often have more rigid hierarchies and less room for creative implementation strategies, provide fewer opportunities for benign intervention when things go wrong (see box 4.12). Comparative analysis of the cases shows one other reason why KDP conflicts are less likely to turn violent: because KDP provides opportunities for communities to define their needs, programs are less likely to clash with local priorities.

The research followed a number of other non-KDP development conflicts, in particular, in East Java. These included conflict over forest development policies in Dayakan, problems related to mining refuse in

TABLE 4.5　DEVELOPMENT CONFLICTS AND THEIR IMPACTS

Type of program	Conflicts	Violent conflicts	% Violent	Persons killed	Persons injured	Cases of property damage
KDP	42	1	2	0	2	0
East Java	10	0	0	0	0	0
NTT	32	1	3	0	2	0
Non–KDP public sector	713	36	5	4	38	11
East Java	619	20	3	2	23	6
NTT	94	16	17	2	15	5
Non-government and international programs	19	1	5	0	1	0
East Java	17	0	0	0	0	0
NTT	2	1	50	0	1	0
Total	774	38	5	4	41	11

Source: KDP and CCN dataset.

Sampung, and the abattoir case in Banyupelle, Pamekasan, discussed above. In these cases, there was no facilitator proximate to the villagers who could assist with problem resolution, nor were there forums available to discuss the problem. In all three cases, transparent and accountable processes were missing. Those at higher levels did not respond adequately (if at all) to the complaints and grievances of the beneficiaries, after repeated attempts. Acts of civil disobedience and violent property destruction resulted, as seen in the burning down of the forest in Dayakan, the blocking of the culverts that diverted the mining wastewater in Sampung, and the burning down of the abattoir in Banyupelle.[37] Similar outcomes resulted from failed attempts to resolve disputes surrounding the distribution of aid to internally displaced people fleeing to Madura from other areas experiencing conflict (box 4.12).

BOX 4.12   AID AND CONFLICT IN MADURA

Three violent development-related conflicts took place in East Java related to aid promised to internally displaced Madurese fleeing from the conflict in Central Kalimantan. The cases show that when beneficiaries of aid are left out of decision making and needs identification processes, things can get out of hand.

May 10, 2001: Hundreds of internally displaced people (IDPs) from Central Kalimantan rioted over the distribution of food aid in Truman village in Sampang subdistrict. Officials had promised each refugee Rp. 10,000 (approximately US$1), to be distributed at the village head's house. But they underestimated the number of displaced persons likely to appear, and when funds ran out the IDPs rioted and vandalized the house. They were angry because officials were using figures submitted by the village head rather than those calculated by the IDPs themselves. They also accused the village head of corruption, stating that they only received Rp. 19 million (US$1,900) of the Rp. 25 million (US$2,500) allocated for food aid that day.

September 10, 2002: "At least 1,000" students and IDPs clashed with police when a demonstration against the Bangkalan district government got out of hand. Demonstrators were demanding an explanation about the distribution of food aid to refugees and requested that an official address the crowd directly. The government offered demonstrators the opportunity to send representatives to meet with the government, which they refused. Police were called and a clash ensued. Eighteen students and IDPs were injured during the clash; two were hospitalized.

July 10, 2003: Fifty IDPs from Central Kalimantan who were staying in Ketapang Barat village, Sampang, vandalized temporary accommodation funded by aid from Kuwait that was channeled through the local government. The construction was 80 percent complete but was put on hold following the vandalism. Following this, representatives of the IDPs met with subdistrict and district officials and demanded that no further barracks be built because they limited options for IDPs hoping to return to Kalimantan and because existing accommodations were sufficient (and in many cases unused). Rather, they argued, aid funds should be used to provide food staples and education for their children.

Source: Newspaper articles from the KDP and CCN dataset.

In contrast, in most of the KDP cases followed in this study, mechanisms were in place to address the issues as and where they arose. For example, in the case in Jenangan, Ponorogo, the community protested plans to change a bridge design (made unilaterally by a KDP district consultant), and meetings were held to help resolve the problem. This resulted in quick action from higher-level program officers, informal leaders, and the media. There was state, program, nonstate, and community participation in the resolution process, and the case was resolved peacefully. Similarly, informal leaders in Proppo were important actors in resolving a case in which KDP project workers protested against nepotism on the part of one of the technical team leaders by blockading the road.[38] In another case in Pasean where there were problems with disbursing funds, KDP facilitators quickly intervened and the problems did not escalate.

The comparative analysis thus makes it clear why KDP, when it works as intended, causes less, and less serious, violent conflict than many other development programs. When it does not work as intended, KDP is less successful at managing the tensions it generates.[39] The program has a clear structure of forums and facilitators (with secondary functions such as acting as points of contact for discussion of problems), it aims to promote transparency and inclusion through socializing program processes and results, and it has systems in place for ensuring accountability and effective handling of complaints. It also provides mechanisms for communities to define and prioritize their needs, hence making it less likely that development projects will be resisted by community members. Cumulatively, all of these factors contribute to limiting KDP-related conflicts by minimizing the potential for conflict and providing opportunities for redress when problems do occur.

Summary

This chapter has shown that development and conflict inevitably go hand in hand. Development projects and programs introduce resources into poor areas, and intergroup competition over such resources can lead to tensions. Programs such as KDP, which explicitly aim to empower marginalized groups, also introduce new rules and norms about how decisions should be made, thus influencing local power balances and structures. Resistance of elites to such changes is another basis for conflict; in cases where they completely circumvent the KDP process, they may prevent any conflict from arising because villagers are unaware that there is anything to be contested. Accordingly, those designing and implementing development projects must be aware of the ways in which projects can trigger conflicts or interact with existing ones, and must develop strategies and mechanisms for dealing with development-related conflicts as they arise.

The research team found that micro-conflicts related to KDP are common but that these rarely escalate and almost never turn violent. There are three forms of development-related disputes. First, KDP introduces competition within and between villages over which proposals should be funded. This can lead to tensions, in particular when groups feel that the decision-making process was not transparent or fair. However, the research found that, over time, groups tend to accept the validity of the competition process and, as a result, its outcomes. Only where the program does not function as intended (for example, where one group has captured the process) do larger problems emerge. The second form of conflict relates to these and other program malfunctions. Malfunctions can be problems of omission or commission. The first is a result of poor socialization or implementation; the second concerns deliberate and active malfeasance by program staff or local elites. The latter is more serious than the former, with cases of corruption providing a basis for larger community unrest.

The third form, interaction conflict, occurs when development projects (KDP or others) interact with preexisting local tensions, power structures, or conflicts, triggering conflict escalation and, in some cases, violence. Projects operate in theaters in which power relations are constantly being negotiated; development projects constitute a vital resource that can be utilized in this process. In some cases, interaction conflicts involve actors using the project for patronage, raising tensions between competing local elites; in others, elites attempt to capture the project for self-enrichment. Other cases relate to the resistance of elites to the norms of widespread access to decision making, transparency, and accountability that KDP brings. Where resistance is greater, there is potential for more serious conflicts to arise, particularly in areas where decision making has been traditionally elite-centered. In areas where there is more compliance with KDP rules, but where democratic processes were already under way, the kinds of conflicts that KDP generates are more frequent because of open contestation, but likely more manageable via KDP mechanisms.

Despite the numerous ways in which projects can cause conflict, we found that KDP-related conflicts almost never escalate or turn violent. This is in large part because the program has effective in-built conflict resolution mechanisms. Project forums, facilitators, and other complaints-handling mechanisms mean that tensions can be addressed before they grow in size and severity. Resolution success rates of KDP-related problems are very high. This is in marked contrast to many other development projects, which do not have such mechanisms. As a result, conflicts relating to other governmental and nongovernmental projects are far more likely to turn violent.

If development projects can, under certain conditions, enhance the resolution of local conflicts—existing ones and those generated by projects— might they also be able, under different conditions, to help reduce overall levels of violence? It is to this question that we now turn.

CHAPTER 5

Can Development Projects Be Part of a Solution?

We have shown that KDP is very good at solving program-related problems. Like any development project, KDP causes tensions and on occasion triggers conflict, but almost all of these conflicts are dealt with through the program's in-built conflict resolution mechanisms. In this respect, KDP often works better than other development projects. Is there any evidence of increased conflict management capacity in KDP areas in terms of *nonprogram* conflicts? Are the KDP mechanisms used to deal with nonprogram conflicts? Are there other social spillovers that result in improved conflict management capacity? If so, in what ways has the program made a difference? And for what types of conflicts, in what contexts?

The next three chapters seek to answer these questions through comparative analysis of levels and outcomes of conflict, conflict management processes, and different elements of social relations in areas that have taken part in the program and otherwise similar areas that have not. In this chapter we look at *conflict levels* and *outcomes at the macro level* using the newspaper dataset, which records all reported incidents of conflict in twelve districts in the two provinces between 2001 and 2003.[1] Merging this with data about where and when KDP was operating allows us to compare conflict trends in subdistricts that received the program and matched comparison sites that did not, as well as in program areas before and after KDP implementation. Conflict levels and outcomes are but two indicators of conflict management capacity. Underlying structural factors and exogenous forces may lead to different levels of conflict in areas that have similar conflict management capacity. Comparative examination does, however, provide insight into the strengths and limitations of the program in changing local conflict dynamics. In particular, we examine in more depth the processes, both direct and indirect, by which such change is effected.

Forms of Conflict in East Java and NTT

Before we examine the impact of KDP on conflict and its outcomes, it is necessary to provide a brief sketch of the forms and impacts of conflict in our research areas. We recorded 1,840 discrete incidents of conflict in the three-year period in the twelve districts we studied, 591 of which were violent.[2] Conflict in our research areas resulted in 275 deaths in this period, 158 of which were in East Java and 117 in NTT. The death total was highest in the first year (120 deaths), and declined to 91 in the second year and 64 in the third. Totals ranged from four deaths in Ponorogo district (East Java) to 52 deaths in Manggarai (NTT) (see table 5.1).[3] While violence is relatively common, and its cumulative impacts are significant, most of the violent

TABLE 5.1   CONFLICT-RELATED DEATHS, 2001–3

District	2001	2002	2003	Total
Bangkalan	20	13	12	45
Madiun	6	3	2	11
Magetan	3	3	3	9
Pamekasan	11	5	1	17
Ponorogo	0	4	0	4
Sampang	14	15	9	38
Sumenep	17	12	5	34
East Java	*71*	*55*	*32*	*158*
Ende	1	11	3	15
Flores Timur	2	15	5	22
Manggarai	41	2	9	52
Ngada	2	1	4	7
Sikka	3	7	11	21
NTT	*49*	*36*	*32*	*117*

Source: KDP and CCN dataset.

conflicts remained relatively small-scale; 47 percent of conflict-related deaths in East Java and 38 percent in NTT were the result of conflicts between individuals.[4]

There are four major types of conflict in the research areas, plus a number of other conflicts that do not easily fit into any of the broad categories. First, there are conflicts about *physical resources*, which include disputes over the ownership of, access to, or use of either natural or manmade resources. By far the largest proportion of these conflicts is over land—private land, state-owned land, or communally held (adat) land. In the three years of our study, 218 conflicts of this type took place in the research areas, 70 of which were violent. These resulted in 73 deaths, 109 injuries, and 13 cases of property damage.[5]

The second category is *administrative conflicts*. These include disputes about procedures or the management of service provision, for example, government development projects and other forms of government-funded goods and services. It also includes disputes over donor projects, KDP, and the management of companies. (We analyzed many of these disputes in Chapter 4.) Another form of administrative conflict is disputes about jurisdictions within government. In the three-year period of our study, 932 administrative conflicts took place in the research areas, 53 of which were violent. These resulted in five deaths, 81 injuries, and 16 cases of property damage.

The third form of conflict is that relating to competition for *political positions and influence*. This includes contestation over state or nonstate positions, primarily at the village or district level, as well as disputes within and between political parties for influence over decision making. Over the three-year period of our study, 102 conflicts of this type took place in the research areas, 8 of which were violent. These resulted in 2 deaths, 7 injuries, and 9 instances of property damage.

Fourth, and most common, is *vigilantism and retribution, including* revenge attacks and lynchings relating to a diverse range of phenomena: theft, witchcraft, sanctioning of social deviants, sexual indiscretion, murder, broader identity clashes, damage to property, accidents, humiliation, and the like. These could be carried out by and targeted at individuals or groups (and their property). During the three years of study, 549 conflicts of this type took place in the research areas, 430 of which were violent. These resulted in 178 deaths, 443 injuries, and 289 cases of property damage.

Finally, a range of *other conflicts* were found in the field, the most common being those related to domestic violence and other intrafamily arguments. Over the three years of our study, 39 such conflicts took place in the research areas, 30 of which were violent. These resulted in 17 deaths, 27 injuries, and 10 cases of property damage.

Although conflict is common in both provinces, the forms it takes—in terms of how actors organize themselves, where they live, whom they target, and preferred modes of violence—differ greatly between areas. As figure 5.1 shows, vigilante conflicts are far more frequent in East Java than in NTT, whereas resource conflicts, primarily over land, occur much more frequently in NTT than in East Java.

Institutional, economic, and cultural factors all contribute to this variation. Within each area, serious disputes tend to concern a given issue (such as land), and there are also commonalities within areas in how such conflicts are expressed—the ways in which actors participate in conflict, the symbols and strategies they employ, and so on. In Ponorogo, East Java, many conflicts concerned the management of or access to state-managed resources, including those managed by state-owned enterprises. Such conflicts were less prevalent in Pamekasan, where there are few state-owned enterprises. Access to water and irrigation facilities was a more common source of conflict in Pamekasan, where water is scarce. In Flores, land disputes were more common than in East Java. In Flores, strong cultural value systems associated

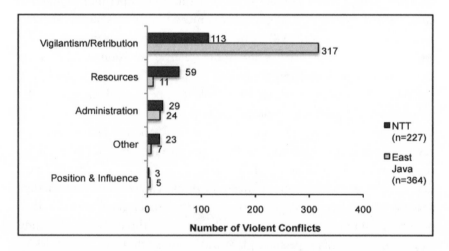

Figure 5.1   Number of violent conflicts by type in East Java and NTT (2001–3). Source: KDP and CCN dataset.

with landownership and identity formation play an important role in social life, whereas the importance of land in East Java tends to be primarily a function of its economic value, and it is less strongly associated with local cultural value systems. In both East Java and Flores, some of the more violent forms of conflict are those prescribed and seemingly driven by local cultural behaviors and norms: the history and development of rival martial arts groups in the Ponorogo research area, a Madurese cultural practice of condoning and even insisting on bloody retribution over matters of honor in areas where this tradition is still prevalent, the communal battles over traditional landownership and usage rights in parts of Flores, where actors split along lines of ethnicity and lineage. Yet local leaders play a large role in helping shape the specific cultural realm that regulates conflict. Further, effective intervention by local leaders (formal and informal) and state institutions (including the security sector) can prevent culturally legitimized forms of violence from escalating (Barron and Sharpe 2008; Diprose 2004).

Conflict in KDP and Non-KDP Areas

Are subdistricts that have participated in KDP more or less likely to experience violent conflict than those that have not? And are there any differences in the forms of conflict that occur in KDP and non-KDP areas? Using the data on conflict incidence in our twelve districts, we find little evidence of any systematic differences in conflict and its impacts between program areas and nonprogram areas. Whereas levels of conflict and violence are lower in KDP areas in East Java, the opposite holds for NTT. For some forms of violence, the presence of KDP is correlated with lower rates; for others, the opposite is true. Collectively, the macro evidence does not point toward a significant programmatic impact on levels of conflict and violence.

Average Levels of Violent Conflict in KDP and Non-KDP Areas

Figure 5.2 shows comparative levels of violent conflict in KDP and non-KDP areas for East Java and NTT. The "KDP" bar shows the mean annual number of violent incidents that took place in subdistricts in the years in which they took part in the program; the "non-KDP" bar shows the mean number of violent incidents in years in which the subdistricts were not in the program.[6]

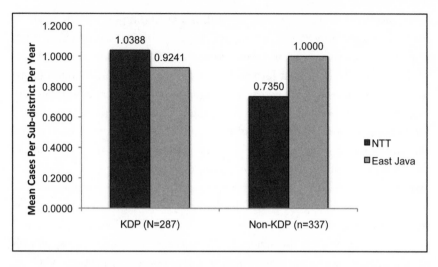

Figure 5.2   Mean number of violent conflict incidents per year per subdistrict in East Java and NTT (2001–3), KDP and non-KDP.

Source: KDP and CCN dataset.

In East Java, marginally more violent conflict took place in non-KDP areas than in areas with the program, with a mean of 1 violent conflict in the former and 0.92 in the latter. In NTT, areas with KDP reported higher levels of violent conflict (1.04 versus 0.74).[7] If we take all conflict, violent and nonviolent, findings are similar, with lower rates in KDP areas in East Java, and lower rates in NTT in non-KDP areas (see table 5.2). The big and statistically significant exception is that there is a higher probability of an area having a case that results in a death in KDP areas than in non-KDP areas in East Java.

Changes over Time

We can disaggregate the data further to examine comparative levels of violent conflict in areas that have been in the program for different lengths of time. As figure 5.3 shows, in East Java there are similar levels of violent conflict in subdistricts that have not participated in KDP and those that have taken part for one or two years.[8] Only in areas in their third year of the program are rates of violent conflict noticeably lower. There is a less clear pattern for NTT.

TABLE 5.2   MEAN NUMBER OF CASES OF CONFLICT WITH IMPACT PER YEAR PER
SUBDISTRICT IN EAST JAVA AND NTT, 2001–3

	East Java		NTT	
Impact	Mean KDP	Mean non-KDP	Mean KDP	Mean non-KDP
Injury	0.47	0.60[b]	0.72[b]	0.56
Property damage	0.12[a]	0.23[b]	0.20[b]	0.16
Death	0.33[a, b]	0.24	0.35[a, b]	0.19

Source: KDP and CCN dataset.

[a] Statistically significant at the 3 percent level.
[b] Denotes higher probability of a given impact (compared to the other group).

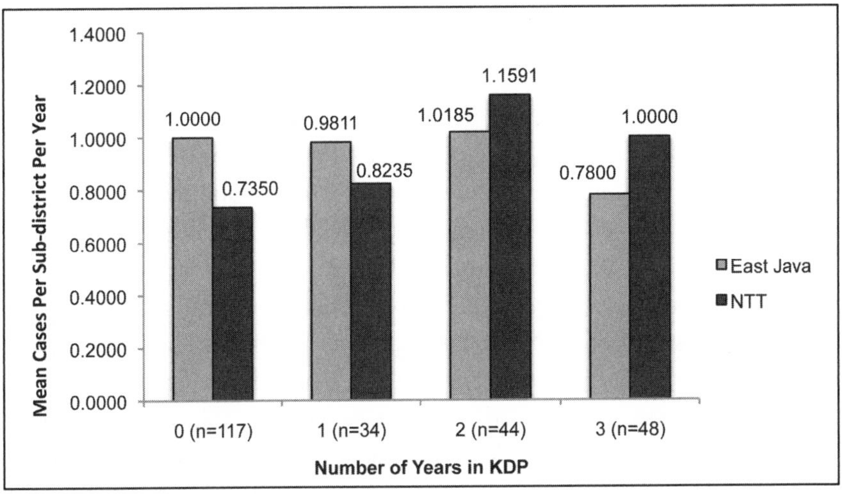

Figure 5.3   Mean number of violent conflict incidents per subdistrict per year in
East Java and NTT (2001–3), by year of KDP.

Source: KDP and CCN dataset.

What do these results tell us? First, it is clear that KDP, in and of itself,
does not have a significant positive impact in reducing levels of violent conflict at an aggregate level. Indeed, if anything the evidence points in the
other direction. Violent conflicts are more likely in areas that take part in
KDP in NTT, though not in East Java, and conflicts resulting in a death are

more likely in KDP areas in both provinces. Can we say that KDP is leading to higher levels of violent and destructive conflict?

The short answer is: not really. Many factors determine an area's conflict profile. Violent conflict is a rare event. The research has shown that there needs to be a confluence of a range of different phenomena in order for a dispute or social tension to escalate into violence. Existing social, political, and economic structures and historical legacies all help explain why some areas are violent and others are not. The program, with its rules and norms, is but one factor in determining an area's conflict environment.[9] The reason most of the results are not statistically significant is because there is large variation between subdistricts in terms of the prevalence and impact of violence. This is true in both KDP and non-KDP areas, and it points toward other local factors' playing a large role in determining levels of conflict.

Indeed, we would also expect a bias against finding lower aggregate levels of conflict in areas with KDP. This is so because KDP was targeted at the poorest areas of Indonesia, with the subdistricts that received the program first being among the poorest.[10] Previous research on conflict in Indonesia has shown links, albeit complex ones, between forms of poverty and incidence of conflict. For example, the PODES survey shows that in rural areas, a higher fraction of poor people residing in a village is associated with a significantly higher likelihood of violent conflict, as is an increase in the proportion of poor people (Barron, Kaiser, and Pradhan 2009, 709). The international literature to some extent supports this finding, although the causal relationship is strongly contested;[11] other studies demonstrate that it is not always the poorer areas that have the highest levels of conflict.[12] Given that KDP was not randomly assigned and that we are not formally controlling for other structural factors in the community, we might expect a bias toward higher conflict in KDP areas.

The lack of evidence that KDP, in and of itself, positively influences *aggregate* levels of conflict, however, should not be interpreted as meaning that KDP has no influence at smaller units of analysis. It does mean that development agencies should resist temptations to believe that CDD projects can, ipso facto, be expected to deliver peace in moderate-conflict environments. As previously noted, however, KDP's key organizational and decision-making innovations occur at the community level, where it is designed to provide a flexible structure that can be adapted to the specific features of local contexts. As such, we would be more likely to find its impacts on local conflict trajectories and conflict management capacity at the community level and for those impacts to be highly contingent on the nature and extent of its interactions with those contexts.

A range of forms of conflict exist in East Java and Flores, and local patterns of conflict vary with local conditions. A large number of such local factors help dictate the incidence and form of conflict. In order to understand more precisely the impact of the program, it is necessary to examine in greater depth how particular cases of conflict play out in areas with and without the program, and specifically whether and how KDP interacts with key aspects of the social context within which the program is embedded. We explore these issues in the rest of this chapter and the two that follow.

The Direct Impacts of KDP on Conflict Management: Forums and Facilitators

In order to ascertain KDP's impact on conflict management capacities at the community level, it is necessary to examine in more depth the ways in which the program is utilized (or not) for conflict management, as well as the impact of the program on a range of variables that help shape the likelihood of conflict emerging or escalating.

The remainder of this chapter does the former: it looks at the ways in which KDP may directly impact conflict and conflict management capacity. The two potential direct effects that KDP could have are illustrated in figure 5.4. The first is that it introduces *spaces for discussion and debate*. The KDP forums at the hamlet, village, and subdistrict levels may be used for conflict resolution or for directly addressing the underlying social tensions that could escalate into conflict. In most cases, effective conflict mediation requires a dialogue between disputing parties. This needs to happen in a place that is perceived to be neutral—hence the fact that many long-standing protracted disputes are mediated in places far away from the homes and power bases of the disputants.[13] The same is necessary for local conflict resolution; disputants need to feel they are in a safe place that putatively favors neither party. In particular, in resolving disputes with no technical "divide the pie" solution, and hence where creative, adaptive agreements are necessary, there is a need for what Heifetz (1994) calls a "holding environment" to contain the stresses each party faces in compromising. Do KDP forums provide such a space?

Figure 5.4   Potential direct impacts of KDP on conflict

Second, as detailed in Chapters 3 and 4, KDP introduces *people* who may play a role in conflict mediation. To reiterate, the program places facilitators at the subdistrict level and requires the election of village-level facilitators. Other key staff members include the district consultant and the Village Project Implementation Team. The subdistrict facilitator and district consultant are usually not from the areas in which they are stationed. Are they able, then, to effectively play the role of neutral outsider in arbitrating disputes between villagers and villages, including nonprogram matters? Village facilitators, in contrast, are generally from the village in which they serve. Their position has authority, yet they are not salaried program staff or official government employees. Does this give them sufficient credibility and legitimacy to mediate disputes that are unrelated to the program or disputes that others (with clearer linkages to the state) may not be willing or able to effectively mediate?

Supervision missions and reports from field staff prior to the study seemed to suggest that KDP forums and facilitators were in many cases playing these roles. In North Maluku, for example, an area that has experienced high levels of conflict and violence, KDP subdistrict facilitators supported the reconciliation process in southern Ibu.[14] The program supported a football competition between villages, for example, and KDP forums were used to promote relations between villages that previously had little interaction (World Bank 2002). The provincial KDP team formed a Reconciliation Team composed of Christian and Muslim community leaders, customary leaders, youth, university students, and KDP subdistrict facilitators. In Lampung province in the south of Sumatra, a series of thefts led to a vigilante response in which Javanese villagers burned down sixty houses in a Lampungese hamlet (Barron and Madden 2004). As part of the reconciliation efforts, an intervillage meeting was held that resulted in the use of KDP funds to rebuild the destroyed houses, a measure that was seen as promoting reconciliation between groups within the village and with other villages.[15] In Central Kalimantan province on Borneo, KDP staff played a role in trying to prevent the massacre of Madurese by Dayaks from escalating (Smith 2005). Indeed, an internal review of KDP in high-conflict areas of Indonesia concluded that "KDP provides a useful framework for negotiations and consensus-building. The meetings and procedures provide open fora for communications and discussion. In locations such as Aceh and the Malukus, communities are able to come together despite the conflict situation and reach common ground. KDP provides a nonviolent forum to mediate differing interests and reach a broad consensus (through 'musyarawah') on what is in the best interests of the community" (Government of Indonesia 2002, 3).

The research in East Java and NTT found, however, that there was little aggregate evidence that KDP forums or facilitators were playing a direct role in the management of conflict unrelated to the program. Program forums were not often used for dealing with nonproject conflicts, although when they were they tended to be successful. More markedly, KDP facilitators almost never addressed non-KDP conflicts outside the forums. In East Java and NTT, the program played only a very small *direct* role in local conflict management and resolution; as we shall see, however, its *indirect* impacts were significant.

The Use of KDP Forums for Managing Nonproject Conflict

The program introduces planning and decision-making forums at a number of levels. Are these forums used in East Java and NTT to address conflicts that are not related to the program?

The key informant survey found that KDP forums are used occasionally, but not regularly, for addressing conflicts unrelated to the program. This use is higher in subdistrict project forums. The results, when combined with evidence from the qualitative fieldwork, show that on occasions KDP forums are ad hoc venues for conflict resolution but that their use for dealing with nonproject conflict has not been institutionalized.

Thirteen percent of village informants surveyed in East Java and 20 percent in NTT reported that KDP forums had been used in their area to solve conflicts not related to the program.[16] In both provinces, reported use for non-KDP problems was higher at the *subdistrict* level, where 20 percent of informants reported use in East Java, and 47 percent did so in NTT.[17] Yet this may be because subdistrict-level key informants would be more likely to know about how KDP is functioning in the wide range of villages within that subdistrict, whereas village informants may only know about their village. Indeed, where forums are used for dealing with non-KDP issues, evidence from the fieldwork shows that this is more likely to be at the village level.

The fact that KDP forums are not used regularly for dealing with nonprogram conflicts is confirmed by the qualitative research. In almost every village, respondents were clear when asked about the extent to which issues not related to KDP were discussed in KDP forums:

> They only talk about KDP during the KDP meetings.
>
> —FARMER, MAGEPANDA, NITA, SIKKA

> The KDP forums aren't used to discuss other issues outside of KDP.
>
> —VILLAGE SECRETARY, TENGKU LEDA, LAMBA LEDA, MANGGARAI

> In the KDP forums in Cumbi village, we have never raised any other issues besides issues or conflicts involving KDP.
>
> —VILLAGE FACILITATOR, CUMBI, RUTENG, MANGGARAI

> In the KDP forums—both the village-level, and the intervillage subdistrict meeting—only KDP problems are discussed. However, there was a case where the subdistrict meeting was used to discuss the problem of village development . . . but, problems outside of KDP have not been resolved in KDP forums, because there would definitely be interruptions from the participants because they would consider it irrelevant.
>
> —GOLKAR MEMBER, PADELLEGAN, PADEMAWU, PAMEKASAN

Although the majority of informants made such claims, KDP forums are on occasion used for conflict mediation. Especially in East Java, conflicts related to other development projects sometimes make their way into KDP forums. In NTT, other conflicts between villagers are discussed on occasion (see figure 5.5).[18]

Nonetheless, when KDP forums are used for dealing with non-KDP problems, they are usually successful. In East Java, 63 percent of informants reported success in such cases; in NTT, 61 percent did so.[19] This is a lower success rate than for KDP-related problems.[20]

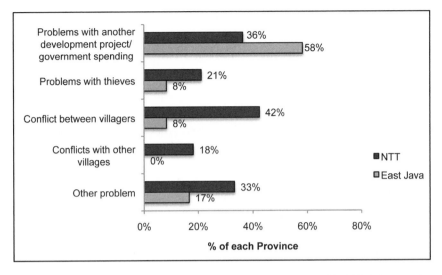

Figure 5.5 Types of non-KDP problems/conflict addressed in KDP forums, by province.

Source: Key informant survey (KDP program sites only).

Note: The percentages show those who said that KDP forums were used for a given type of problem/conflict, of those who reported that KDP forums were used for non-KDP issues. Hence the small sample sizes.

Why were KDP forums used so infrequently? And why, when they were used, was it for these types of problems? Answering such questions requires an understanding of people's perceptions of the forums, of conflict resolution norms, and of the roles of local elites and program staff.

Problems and Jurisdictions

The primary reason why KDP forums are not generally used for solving most kinds of conflict that are not related to KDP is simple: villagers have other institutions and actors that they deem more suitable for these purposes. In almost all villages, people know where they should take a given type of problem or dispute. Particular people are seen as having the legitimate jurisdiction for addressing specific types of conflict.[21] Take, for example, intervillage land conflicts in Manggarai district in Flores. Disputants know that conflicts should be taken to the subdistrict head, who normally tries to deal with the problem in an adat manner involving traditional leaders.

If this is not successful—as is often the case—the dispute will rise to the district-level government or move into the formal court system. In contrast, domestic violence cases are usually addressed within the family or, if a homicide is involved or the case is a repeat offense, by the police (normally at the subdistrict level). In Ponorogo, East Java, conflicts between martial arts groups are usually dealt with by the police, in consultation with the group leaders. Program forums are not seen as having legitimate jurisdiction over these types of problems.

> Resolution [between martial arts groups] is carried out only by the leader of the group with the problem; it can also be mediated by a third party. I was once a mediator when there was a problem between SH Terate and BS [Bintang Surya]. . . . Problems [between inhabitants] are usually settled in routine hamlet meetings. . . . When there's an urgent problem, a special meeting will be held.
>
> —VILLAGE REPRESENTATIVE COUNCIL CHAIR,
> WATES, SLAHUNG, PONOROGO

A range of actors and institutions are seen as having a legitimate role in mediating disputes. In the research areas, the government (at the district, subdistrict, village, and hamlet levels), the security sector (both police and military), the judicial system, traditional adat and other community leaders, the church, *kyai* (Muslim clerics), and others all play a role in mediating different forms of disputes. Given the extent to which perceptions of the correct place to deal with problems are bound up in social norms—which have in most cases developed over long periods of time—it is unsurprising that forums introduced relatively recently would not be seen as the appropriate place to handle most kinds of disputes. When survey respondents were asked for the reasons why KDP-related conflicts were solved in KDP forums, the top two responses were that there was nowhere else to turn or that KDP forums were the most appropriate place for them to be addressed. In contrast, only in one subdistrict (Cibal, Manggarai) was either of these reasons given.

Of non-KDP conflicts, those relating to other development projects are the most likely to be addressed. This is the case for two reasons. As we noted in Chapters 3 and 4, often few avenues of recourse are available for problems that emerge from government or donor development projects. In the past, local leaders and officials had hegemonic control over development resources. With the recent democratization of life at the village level, which has led to a stronger system of checks and balances, conflicts over development projects are arising in ways not encountered in the past.[22] Many government and donor projects do not have effective in-built complaints and conflict management mechanisms, leaving an institutional void as to where these problems can be discussed. In some cases, KDP forums fill this vacuum.

Program forums are primarily designed to deal with the kinds of problems that tend to emerge from development projects: complaints about processes of resource allocation, jealousy on the part of those who do not receive projects, and so on. Given that these types of problems are similar to those that emerge from KDP—the program malfunction conflicts we identified above—it is hardly surprising that KDP resolution mechanisms can in some cases play a role in dealing with them.

In NTT, a number of respondents also said that KDP forums were used to deal with conflicts between villages. There were a number of examples of KDP forums being used to discuss theft, problems relating to the control of livestock, and other matters. In these cases, the absence of other opportunities to bring people together was cited as the reason why KDP forums were used. Given the declining frequency with which *musyawarah* (meetings for group decision making through deliberation) are held in many villages, KDP forums are seen as a comparatively rare opportunity to bring the whole community together in one place:

> Problems relating to village development were raised in the KDP forums in Wairterang and Egon. These were problems that were not related to KDP, but were raised in the KDP forums. As KDP staff members, we normally give the village head an opportunity to chair the forum if there are any problems that were not related to KDP [which needed to be discussed]. We only give suggestions. Or, if we don't feel brave enough, we just keep quiet. We just let them resolve their problems themselves in the KDP forums.
>
> —HEAD, KDP FINANCIAL MANAGEMENT UNIT,
> TALIBURA, TALIBURA, SIKKA

The evidence supports the thesis that people will only bring conflicts to KDP forums that they think can be effectively addressed there. Reported successful resolution rates for conflicts brought to KDP forums are high: 86 percent for development-related problems, 100 percent for problems relating to theft and conflict with other villages, 96 percent for conflict between villagers, and 74 percent for other conflicts.[23]

Thus KDP forums are most likely to be used when there are no other institutions to deal with the problem or when people believe that KDP is able to deal with the particular conflict. In general, institutions exist in East Java and NTT to deal with most types of conflict, although by no means do they always do so effectively, and they are not uniform in their strength and efficacy across villages, nor are they found everywhere. There is no evidence that KDP displaces other problem-solving forums—that is, that where institutions exist, KDP usurps their role or crowds them out. Rather, the places where people take different conflicts are likely to be determined by the institutional history in the area. Within districts, there was little marked difference (by design) between our program (KDP) and matched comparison (non-KDP) subdistricts in terms of their institutional profile. Where there were differences, they were far more likely to be a function of the historical development of local cultures, and the broad processes of socioeconomic change that helped form them, than of any specific outside development intervention.[24]

It is still an open question, however, whether effective institutions still exist to deal with most problems and forms of conflict in the parts of Indonesia that have experienced extremely high levels of violent conflict. The relative lack of use of KDP forums may be due in part to the nature of conflict in East Java, a lower-conflict province where social relations and institutions have not broken down to such an extent that mechanisms such as KDP are used as a last resort for problem-solving (Diprose 2004). We do not have comparative data about the program and conflict management in any of the highest-conflict provinces, but there is evidence that, *at the district level,* areas with lower capacity to manage conflict use KDP more for this purpose.[25] The KDP forums were used more often in areas with low preexisting capacity to manage conflicts (in Manggarai and Pemekasan districts) than in those with higher capacity (Sikka and Ponorogo). As we will see in Chapter 7, there is evidence that where no institutions exist to deal with a particular type of problem, in some cases KDP forums play that role.

Resistance from Local Elites and Facilitators

The second reason why KDP forums are rarely used for managing nonprogram conflicts is resistance from both facilitators and local leaders to using them in this way. In a number of cases, when people brought up problems in the program's forums that were not related to KDP, facilitators or local government officials told attendees that the forums were not the correct place to discuss them. In many instances, program facilitators were reluctant to sanction the use of KDP forums for nonprogram conflict resolution.

There are a number of reasons for this. First, in some areas such as Manggarai, facilitators were averse to taking perceived risks by allowing discussion of non-KDP conflicts. There are explicit sanctions for people who contravene decisions made in KDP meetings; inappropriate behavior can result in the exclusion of a subdistrict or village from participating in the program in the following year. For this reason, KDP officials in Manggarai tended to avoid taking unnecessary risks.[26] Second, facilitators and leaders often did not want to mix KDP and non-KDP issues and were concerned that the forums could fail if they were to discuss complex and sensitive issues not directly related to KDP and involving people participating in the KDP forums (Didakus 2004).

They may have a point. Arguably, one of the reasons KDP has been able to keep operating in many high-conflict areas such as Aceh province during periods of high tension and unrest is its perceived political neutrality. In the case of Aceh, both the government and GAM (the rebel Free Aceh Movement) supported the program because it was seen as benefiting the poor people of the region; if the same forums had been used to talk about conflict-related issues, it is unlikely that they would have been as successful or allowed to operate in the same way.[27] Although conflict issues are certainly not as sensitive in Flores or East Java as in Aceh, if particularly tense cases (such as the intervillage land conflicts in Manggarai) were discussed, there might be a negative impact on the extent to which agreement on other *nonconflictual* issues could be reached in the forum.

Some problems are best dealt with indirectly, and there may be cases in which forums can play a positive role. In particular, conflicts related to development projects or conflicts between individuals (rather than groups), where there are fewer negative consequences arising from an unsuccessful resolution, could potentially be addressed in forums. Given the high success rates achieved when KDP is used, facilitators and local leaders could be encouraged to use KDP forums for discussing other conflict-related problems in cases where other institutions do not exist to deal with them and where it is unlikely to affect the functioning of the program. That they do not do so, as we discuss below, is often a result of a lack of understanding about the positive roles KDP can play in conflict management.

The Role of KDP Facilitators in Conflict Management

As we have seen, the KDP institutional structure places facilitators and staff at a number of levels, from every participating village to a national secretariat in Jakarta. Third-party intervention can take place by choice (if an actor decides to intervene), by circumstance (if an actor happens to be present when a conflict occurs), or because the disputants take the problem to a particular actor. What role do KDP staff and elected facilitators play in helping mediate conflicts that are not related to the program?

Survey respondents were asked about the role played by KDP facilitators and staff in problem-solving and conflict resolution outside KDP forums.[28] The evidence from both the key informant survey and the qualitative fieldwork is that they do play such a role. In East Java, 52 percent of survey respondents said that KDP facilitators had successfully resolved conflicts/problems outside KDP forums; in NTT, 60 percent reported the same.[29] Almost without exception, however, these conflicts relate directly to the program. Whereas KDP forums sometimes address conflicts that are unrelated to KDP, staff and facilitators almost never take the role of conflict mediator in dealing with such issues.[30]

Every respondent in East Java and 96 percent of those in NTT who had said KDP facilitators resolved problems outside of forums said that the problems were related to KDP. In NTT, program facilitators' involvement in non-program conflict was isolated to two subdistricts, Lamba Leda, Manggarai, and Talibura, Sikka.[31] Informants, both KDP staff and villagers, confirmed the findings. Facilitators hardly ever get involved in directly mediating conflicts that are not related to the program. Why is this so? Comparative analysis of the cases followed in the study provides insights into why different actors play different conflict mediation roles and why some attempts are successful but others are not. Effective conflict mediators need to have three qualities— legitimacy, willingness, and capacity—if they are to successfully intervene as third parties in conflict. Examining the extent to which different KDP facilitators have these qualities helps explain why they rarely successfully intervene in conflicts that are not directly related to KDP.[32]

Legitimacy

In order for mediators to be successful, they must be deemed to be legitimate. Two types of legitimacy are relevant. The first is *institutional legitimacy:* the mediator must be seen to have legitimate jurisdiction over the specific problem. In other words, it must be clear to all concerned that it is appropriate for a given dispute to be adjudicated by a particular third party. Where a gap exists between the dispute and the (perceived or actual) jurisdictional mandate of a particular third party, legitimacy is likely to be low. As we noted above, KDP forums are often not seen by disputants and others in the community as being the appropriate places to deal with disputes that are not related to KDP or, to a lesser extent, other development-related problems. The same is yet more true for KDP facilitators. They and other KDP staff are viewed by communities as having a mandate to deal with problems related to the program. In almost all cases, however, the same is not true for other aspects of life and for other forms of conflict. Other actors and institutions—government at its various levels, the security sector, community or traditional leaders—are deemed to have authority to mediate disputes.

Second, in some cases the *personal legitimacy* of KDP staff was a factor limiting their role in conflict mediation. In a number of cases where the facilitators were not viewed as being of high professional and moral repute, villagers were less likely to take problems to them. In some cases KDP officials had lost their credibility and some of their authority because of perceived corruption. In Lamba Leda subdistrict in Manggarai, the subdistrict facilitator, who had been accused of stealing Rp. 80 million (US$9,000) of project funds, was on trial at the time the fieldwork was conducted. When the accusations started, they began to seriously affect his personal standing and authority and hence had a negative impact on the program:

> Repayments began to dwindle after they found that the FK and the Financial Management Unit had corrupted Rp. 80 million of funds. If the community had wanted to pay their installments, where would they have taken them?
>
> —VILLAGE SECRETARY, SATAR PUNDA, LAMBA LEDA, MANGGARAI

It is not surprising that communities will not see such individuals as having the legitimacy to intervene in conflicts that are not related to the program. Another reason for the perceived lack of legitimacy of facilitators and KDP staff was the lack of input that some communities had in determining who their program representative would be. Village facilitators are meant to be elected in an open process; in most cases they were, but in some the process was not seen as legitimate.

> As far as who would be chosen as the village facilitator . . . it all depended
> on who the village head liked; there was no democratic election.
>
> —TEACHER, TENGKU LEDA, LAMBA LEDA, MANGGARAI

This was also true for others involved in the program, for example, local
verification teams.

> The technical staff at the subdistrict confused those of us at the village
> level. . . . Perhaps if the village technical assistant was from the village,
> or members of the community were appointed, the result would have
> been much better. The village technical assistant was taken from the
> subdistrict level even though they had already selected graduates from
> the technical high school from around here.
>
> —VILLAGE IMPLEMENTATION TEAM MEMBER,
> TLONTOHRAJA, PASEAN, PAMEKASAN

In other cases, for example Padellegan in Pamekasan, the community
trusted the village facilitator to the extent that he was also asked to run
other development projects, as well as play a role in village administration.[33]
(We explore this further in Chapter 7.) However, it suffices to say that,
in general, local-level KDP staff are not seen as having the institutional
legitimacy—or, in many cases, the personal legitimacy—to address conflicts
that are not related to the program.

Willingness to Act to Seek a Solution

Effective mediators also need to be willing to act constructively and
proactively to help disputants find solutions. As we noted above, in many
cases facilitators did not feel it was their role to deal with conflicts unrelated
to the program. For example, in Talibura, Sikka, there was an attempt by a
villager to use the KDP village forum to discuss an unresolved land case.
The subdistrict facilitator said, however, that the KDP forum should only
be used for program-related matters. His decision may have been wise: the
facilitator in question argued that KDP was successful in Talibura—both in
its operation and in building inter- and intracommunity relations—because
it remained a relatively neutral, depoliticized forum. If the forum also dealt
with other conflicts or tensions, the shared acceptance of the legitimacy of
the KDP process would have been compromised. The result was that the
problem was not dealt with within the KDP structure, and respondents

reported that they were less likely to ask the facilitator to help with conflicts in the future.

If facilitators are to be expected to play a direct role in resolving non-KDP problems and conflicts, then they must be trained to play such a role. But before such an agenda is adopted, serious thought needs to be given by the KDP design and implementation team (and, by extension, those considering KDP-type programs elsewhere) to the potential trade-off between possible enhanced conflict resolution and the potential impact on the perceived neutrality of the program. No doubt the harshness of this trade-off would be even more pronounced in areas where conflict-related cleavages are more marked and all-encompassing than in our research districts in East Java and NTT.

We should note that in some cases facilitators were themselves part of the problem rather than the solution. Some of the conflicts we followed revolved around distrust of program facilitators, with saving and loan groups refusing to repay their funds to the KDP Financial Management Unit and wishing instead to store the funds in the village. In Ponorogo, when saving and loan groups could not repay their loans, conflicts ensued between program facilitators and beneficiaries. In other examples across all four districts, program facilitators became parties to disputes when they were seen as having been co-opted by elites. Furthermore, in some cases where facilitators sought to reduce tensions between hamlets competing for funds, they were viewed as favoring one party or the other, thereby heightening tensions.[34]

Capacity

The third requirement of effective conflict mediators is that they possess the capacity to solve the problem. Capacity has a number of elements. It involves having the *resources*—human, financial, and administrative—to resolve the matter; it also includes having the *understanding* necessary to be able to effectively arbitrate a conflict in a specific context. This includes both technical understanding (for example, conflict resolution skills) and contextual or local knowledge (Geertz 1983), what James Scott (1998) has called "*metis.*"

Program facilitators are embedded within an institutional structure that is relatively well funded and capably staffed. If they need back-up, they can call on a range of colleagues at every administrative level, from the village to the national capital. In theory, then, they should have the resources to solve the problems they encounter. Yet facilitators at different levels face different constraints, which helps explain their lack of capacity in dealing with non-KDP conflicts. For example, village facilitators are often pressured by village elites to circumvent the participatory process and adhere to elite-centered decision-making norms. We also saw cases, some of which we presented in Chapter 4, in which facilitators at all levels were pressured, intimidated, and even threatened for not maintaining the status quo. Despite the back-up of the KDP structure, both their willingness and capacity to safely intervene are hampered.

Subdistrict Facilitators

At the subdistrict level, time pressures are such that subdistrict facilitators have little time to play an extensive role in issues not related to the project, especially if they cover rural areas where considerable travel is necessary. A more important weakness in some cases is their lack of understanding of the local area. Subdistrict facilitators are deliberately chosen from areas outside where they work. In general, this improves their perceived neutrality, but it does mean that at times they are not sensitive to local conditions. In Tlontohraja village in Pamekasan, for example, the subdistrict facilitator did not understand the local culture well and hence did not coordinate with local community figures. This led to problems in the implementation of the program. In Pasean subdistrict, villagers and KDP staff told us that it was difficult for subdistrict facilitators to perform their tasks well because they were not from Madura and hence could not understand certain aspects of Madurese culture:

> If the subdistrict facilitator came from Pasean the program implementation would certainly be more effective because they could understand the character of the community. Most of the FK come from outside the district so that many don't feel at home living here. Like Sidik, the subdistrict facilitator who only stayed a few days in Pasean and after that said goodbye to go home to Malang and didn't return again.
> —DEVELOPMENT COORDINATOR, SANA DAYA, PASEAN, PAMEKASAN

Being from outside the area was not an absolute barrier to being accepted in the community, however. The new subdistrict facilitator in Pasean (Yuyun, Sidik's replacement) made efforts to integrate herself and to adapt to the local culture by changing her dress style:

> Yuyun has begun to be able to follow the culture of the Madura people. In the beginning she never wore a *jilbab* (head covering) when she came

to the village, but after a while she began to wear a jilbab, too. This is a very effective strategy to approach the village community when carrying out program education and awareness-raising because the community feels that the subdistrict facilitator is not an outsider but has already become a part of their life by wearing clothes similar to those worn by the people [here].

—VILLAGE REPRESENTATIVE COUNCIL CHAIR, SANA DAYA,
PASEAN, PAMEKASAN

Local knowledge is complex, deep, and diffuse. Although Yuyun had made important symbolic efforts to gain the trust of the local community, something that should not be underestimated, in other respects her understanding of the local situation was not as deep.[35] Indeed, others complained that Yuyun had not adapted to local conditions:

What Yuyun intended was to try and implement the procedures in the PTO [the project's technical manual], but she hadn't adjusted them to community conditions. In fact, the impression given was that she was forcing her wishes arbitrarily onto others.

—VILLAGE REPRESENTATIVE COUNCIL CHAIR, TLONTOHRAJA,
PASEAN, PAMEKASAN

This is not to say that outsiders cannot be accepted in the areas in which they work. Facilitators can do a very good job, even when they are from completely different parts of Indonesia. But in terms of sensitive issues such as the resolution of conflicts, those with local understanding have a major advantage (Gibson and Woolcock 2008).

Village Facilitators

At the village level, facilitators have more time and generally have substantial local knowledge. Yet often they do not possess the technical skills to play a productive role in conflict resolution. Training for village facilitators is minimal; they receive little, if any, instruction in conflict management. Many are relatively young; this affects not only the sense of authority they command but also their conflict management wisdom, which is largely learned through life experience. In both provinces, the program contributed to a noted rise in the civic skills of village facilitators because of their experience in the program. In Padellegan, for example, the former village facilitator is now the village head. In Sikka, another former village facilitator said he had learned much from his position:

> Yes, my step into the Village Representative Council was determined when I was still the village facilitator. Before this I was just an ordinary villager, just one of the little people.
>
> —FORMER VILLAGE FACILITATOR AND MEMBER OF THE VILLAGE
> REPRESENTATIVE COUNCIL, LOKE, PAGA, SIKKA

Thus while facilitators may not be seen as legitimate or able to solve non-KDP problems in the short term, their positions can help them build capacity and understanding in the long run. Indeed, targeting former village facilitators may be a good strategy for finding appropriate people to support in building village-level conflict mediation capacity.

Where facilitators were successful in solving problems outside of forums, survey respondents cited the following reasons as being most important: they had the resources to solve the problem (most important reason in NTT, second most important in East Java), they had the knowledge to do so (second most important in NTT, third in East Java), and they had the authority to do so (third in NTT, first in East Java).

Summary

In East Java and NTT, the direct impacts of KDP on conflict management are minimal. Its forums and facilitators are rarely used for addressing conflicts unrelated to the program. Where they are used, it tends to be in an ad hoc manner. In none of our research locations had KDP been institutionalized as a regular conflict resolution device, for a number of reasons.

First, other institutions exist at the village level to deal with conflicts unrelated to the program. Where these institutions do not exist (for example, in lower-capacity areas and for certain forms of conflict such as that relating to other development projects), KDP forums and facilitators are sometimes used. This suggests that KDP can act as a complement to existing conflict mediation mechanisms. It may be that in the parts of Indonesia with the highest levels of violent conflict, where many local institutions have become tainted or have collapsed, KDP can play a role in resolving certain kinds of disputes, such as those relating to administrative procedures and resource allocation. Second, in some cases facilitators are perceived as not having the personal legitimacy to handle disputes. In particular, where they are viewed as being corrupt or as having unfairly favored one group over another, it is unlikely that they will be called on to mediate contentious issues. In order for program facilitators to be effective, they need to be seen to be honest, independent, and neutral.

Third, in many cases facilitators are unwilling to address conflicts and problems brought to them that are not related to the program. In large part, this is because they are risk-averse. Many facilitators are scared of the sanctions that might follow—for them and for the communities in which they work—if they deviate from the project's operational manual. Fourth, in some cases KDP facilitators are not called on to mediate disputes because of gaps in their capacity. These gaps differ by the position of the facilitator. Subdistrict facilitators tend to have the technical skills needed to help mediate issues, but often they do not have adequate time or the local knowledge necessary to understand the positions of the disputants and to win their trust. Village facilitators, on the other hand, tend to have time and local expertise and legitimacy, but they often do not have the needed technical training.

As it stands, KDP is thus not an effective mechanism for working *directly* on nonprogram conflict. In some ways, this is a good thing—it allows it to remain a politically neutral space wherein communities can work out their needs and priorities. As we will see in Chapter 6, however, it is in this space that social and state-society relations can improve, leading *indirectly* to enhanced conflict management capacity. Indirect mechanisms, in short, provide the primary channel through which the program generates positive outcomes. At the same time, there is scope for adapting the program to allow it to more effectively manage local conflict. When nonproject conflicts are addressed through the program, they tend to be resolved successfully. This suggests that it is possible for KDP to play a larger mediation role, in particular for development-related disputes. Nonetheless, it may be necessary to have complementary programs in place to directly address conflict.

CHAPTER 6

Indirect Effects of Development Projects on Local Conflict Dynamics

I n Chapter 5 we found that in most cases KDP had little direct effect on conflict management. There are other ways, however, in which the program may lead to changes in the level and impacts of local conflicts and in how they are managed when they arise. This chapter examines three ways in which KDP may *indirectly* impact conflict management capacity: through changing social structures, forms of behavior, and norms and perceptions in the localities where it works.

Development projects such as KDP aim, albeit implicitly and in often unacknowledged ways, to reshape inter- and intragroup and state-society relations. The program strives to empower villagers and democratize village life, enhance participation in decision making (particularly for marginalized groups), and improve the quality of that decision making by promoting greater transparency and accountability. This necessarily involves attempts to transform local structures and norms, which for our purposes we collectively define as the *conflict environment* of an area (see figure 6.1). If KDP affects the underlying conflict environment, it will likely have indirect impacts (positive or negative) on the likelihood that conflict will arise, the form it will take when it does, the ways in which it is dealt with, and hence the potential for escalation.

In this chapter we examine three possible indirect impacts of KDP on local conflict environments: (a) the program's effect on intergroup relations; (b) its effect on the political and social behavior of individuals and groups (and thence its impact on intragroup and state-society relations);

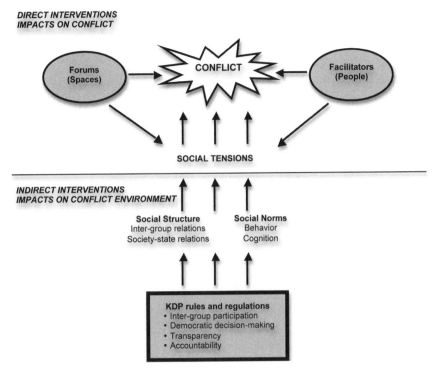

Figure 6.1 Direct and indirect impacts on conflict and conflict environments

and (c) the ways in which it affects people's perceptions and normative frames, including villagers' expectations, understandings, and values with respect to violence, peace, and collective problem solving. We test for the presence and strength of these effects before looking for relationships between these indirect effects and conflict outcomes. We use data from the key informant survey, qualitative fieldwork, and newspaper archives. For the former, we include data from our matched comparison locations.[1]

Group Relations

One factor that may play a role in determining levels of conflict is the nature of social interaction between groups. In his research on conflict and civil society in India, Varshney (2002) argues that it is the extent of interaction between different identity groups—in his case, between

Muslims and Hindus—and in particular the extent to which such inter-action is institutionalized, that determines why some Indian cities are peaceful and others violent, despite having similar proportions of Muslims and Hindus. The assumption is that attitudes and norms of behavior toward other groups change (for the better) with frequent interaction; as groups that previously saw their interests as separate begin to interact, opportuni-ties arise for cooperation and collective action resulting in common rewards. Hence individuals start to emphasize points of similarity as they work together.[2] Varshney's work was conducted in urban India. In places such as rural Flores, where pre-modern kinship systems continue to frame social relations between individuals and between groups, opportunities for enhanced interaction may break down the rigidity of primordial culture, religion, and class structures.

Evidence from our study, as well as previous work on conflict in Indonesia, indicates that a large proportion of violent conflict is group-based. Of all the violent conflicts we found in the newspaper datasets, 51 percent had a group as at least one of the actors; for the most violent conflicts (those that involved two or more deaths), 73 percent involved at least one group.[3] Where conflicts are between individuals—for example, disputes between two people over access to water—group-based identities tended to determine in part whether the conflict would escalate. This is not surprising; humans are social creatures whose lives are embedded in networks—social, political, and economic—from which they deduce their identities. As numerous authors (for example, Horowitz 2000) have noted, group-based identity can be ascriptive (for example, based on race, lan-guage, clan, or caste) or affiliative (for example, political affiliation or membership in a martial arts group). In many cases these overlap. Where different groups emphasize their differences, conflict is more likely.[4]

If KDP provides more opportunities and a regulated institutional framework for interaction between groups that would not have taken place otherwise, it may improve relations between groups, hence making destruc-tive conflict between them less likely. The program seeks to encourage two different types of interaction. The first is *intravillage* interaction in group forums, hamlet-level musyawarah (deliberation meetings), women's forums, and project implementation teams that involve members of the community from different groups. The second is *intervillage* interaction, in which representatives from different villages come together to discuss and priori-tize village development proposals. Does the KDP process help improve relations between different groups? And do these improvements lead to a reduction in levels of violent conflict?

Forms of Difference in East Java and NTT

Before proceeding further, we recap briefly the different groups and group cleavages that exist in East Java and NTT. Individuals in both provinces identify themselves as belonging to a number of different groups. In most of the villages in our study, groups are not completely polarized; in contrast to other conflict-ridden parts of the country, interaction does take place in everyday life between individuals from different identity groups. But identity cleavages are, at times, used as bases for group mobilization, in some cases for purposes of generating conflict.

East Java

In the East Javanese research districts, a number of identity cleavages underlie social tensions and on occasion are utilized when groups are mobilizing for conflict. Where cleavages overlap, problems tend to be bigger. Though East Java (unlike NTT) is for the most part ethnically and religiously homogenous, key cleavages that define identity groups include geographical differentiation (hamlet, natural topography, location in reference to the main road, and martial arts geographical base), martial arts group affiliation, competition between criminal groups (bajingan), support of different Islamic clerics, familial or kinship relations, political allegiances to village and district elites, state-nonstate allegiances (that is, groups in the community versus the state), differentiation between rich and poor hamlets (often along occupational lines), and differentiation between program beneficiaries or between program beneficiaries and program facilitators (for both state and nonstate programs).[5]

Geographic cleavages tend to exist at a low level; thus people feel affiliation with their own hamlet or village. A sense of group identity at the subdistrict or district level, if it exists at all, is not sociologically salient. In some cases, geographic identities relate to topographical rather than administrative boundaries. For example, Slahung, Ponorogo, is divided into two distinct regions: the mountains and the plains. In Pademawu, Pamekasan, there are distinct regional identities, with the district split into a coastal area, a dry field area, and an urban area. In Slahung, geographic location has become an identity marker as a result of gaps in development policy between areas within villages and subdistricts (Anggraini and Rasyid 2004).

Gang cleavages are also important in both districts, although the nature of the gangs differs. In Ponorogo, martial arts groups are extremely important markers of group identity and allegiance. Those in the Ponorogo area have their genesis as organizations of resistance against the Dutch in the early twentieth century. The two dominant groups (SH Terate and SH Winongo) stem from the same organization, Setia Hati, which split in the late 1940s. The groups are driven by strong quasi-mystical ideologies packaged in a way that relates strongly to *kejawen* (syncretic Javanese Islam) spirituality, with which the community is already familiar. Leaders justify the existence and actions of the groups in spiritual terms. The triggers of battles between groups are often cultural in nature, for example, traditional campursari (Javanese dance) performances. The groups are particularly strong in marginalized villages, where locals have unfulfilled hopes and expectations; the martial arts groups and the cultural ideologies they embody provide a social outlet that can free them from the otherwise rather mundane routine of their everyday lives (Probo 2003b). Affiliation with the groups maps on to geographic identities; Winongo has its base in towns, whereas Terate is stronger in more rural areas in outer Ponorogo. In Pamekasan, membership in or relationships with different mafia-like criminal groups (bajingan) provide a strong identity marker. In many villages in Pamekasan, bajingan have gained credibility as problem-solvers and enforcers. They have relationships with village heads and with kyai (Muslim clerics), who need the bajingan to maintain law and order (Ashari 2003).

Political allegiances are also important. They include affiliation with political parties as well as with individuals at the village or district level. As discussed above, village head elections are often extremely tense, in part because candidates have spent large amounts of money on campaigning and in part because they do not want to lose face by suffering defeat, especially in Madura (see box 6.1). At the district level, political allegiances tend to be to figures such as candidates for the district head position rather than to parties (Barron, Nathan, and Welsh 2005; Erb and Sulistiyanto 2009). Differences between the rich and the poor and between rich and poor hamlets are pronounced in some areas. Villagers are readily able to identify the poor and the rich within villages.

BOX 6.1   THE VILLAGE HEAD ELECTION IN PALENGAAN LAOK

The March 2000 village head election in Palengaan Laok was tense. Prior to the election, a rumor circulated that the candidate who went on to win had falsified his educational qualifications. In response, the candidate's campaign team mobilized masses of supporters, including bajingan ("thugs"), to protest at the subdistrict office. They said that if his qualifications were not verified, then someone would be murdered. The situation was so heated that their demands were met.

The votes were counted on election day, and the candidate accused of having false certificates—who also had the backing of one of the senior kyai (Muslim cleric) in the region—won. On the morning of election day, party symbols for the winning candidate had appeared throughout the village. This contravened the election law. As a result, the four losing candidates wrote a letter of complaint to the district head and sent copies to the other government and security agencies and even to the District Court. Receiving no response, the losing candidates mobilized five hundred people to protest at the district government office. When they finally met with the district head, he stated that there were no regulations prohibiting the use of party symbols on election day (though he had signed the regulation which stated the prohibition).

> Indeed, there was already a syndicate agreement between the district head, the parliament, and the kyai [who supported the winning candidate] to resist the complaints. . . . Until Kyai Z [another senior kyai in the region] intervened at the time and appealed to the district head that what was "true should be endorsed and what was wrong should not."
> —VILLAGE REPRESENTATIVE COUNCIL CHAIR, PALENGAAN LAOK, PALENGAAN, PAMEKASAN

Eventually the district head held a meeting with *Muspika* (the committee of district representatives from all the security and government agencies) at which the only person who disagreed with the district head was the representative from the District Court. The losing candidates employed a lawyer and asked the police to investigate, but the investigation was half-hearted, and they had little evidence to take to court, so they did not proceed.

Pamekasan and Ponorogo do not have great ethnic or religious heterogeneity, and hence while both of these are important components of people's identities, they do not constitute significant markers of us-them identification. All the subdistricts in East Java where research was conducted are almost entirely Muslim. In certain areas such as Jenangan subdistrict in Ponorogo, however, affiliations with different religious organizations are important:

> Once there was another Islamic group that came to this village. This mosque [pointing to the mosque in front of his house] was about to be occupied by Islam Jaulah, you know, the ones who have a tradition of going out for a few days each month to spread religion. So one of their groups from somewhere once stayed at the mosque here, but the community here opposed them. This is a public mosque; it's an NU mosque, what's more.[6] How could they want to take it over like that?
>
> —VILLAGE SECRETARY, PANJENG, JENANGAN, PONOROGO

There are other salient identities in East Java that are formed along more affiliative lines. In the analysis below, we address them in the section about relations between other identity groups.

NTT

In Flores, the most noticeable form of group identity is ethnic in nature. Ethnic diversity is extraordinary: one survey estimated that there are twenty-eight different ethnolinguistic groups in Flores, and sixty-one in NTT province (Grimes et al. 1997). Ethnic identity works at a number of levels. Five of the major group identities correspond with the district boundaries of the island: Manggaraian, Endenese, Ngadanese, Sikkanese, and East Florenese. Within each of these, different tribes exist. For example, in Manggarai (our low-capacity district on Flores), subdistrict borders map on to the boundaries of different *suku* (ethnic groups). Yet the continuing strength of clan and kinship systems has meant that ethnic differentiation takes place at a very local (particularistic) level: 29 percent of the people in NTT province report that they are part of an ethnic group that has fewer than 109 other people in the province (Suryadinata, Arifin, and Ananta 2003).

Religious identity is also an important marker. Catholicism is the dominant religion within Flores, but in contrast to East Java, other religious groups make up a considerable share of the population. In villages such as Paga in Sikka, indigenous inhabitants tend to be Catholic, whereas newcomers are more likely to be Muslim, Hindu, or Protestant (Didakus 2004). Local terms have been coined to distinguish Muslims from Catholics.[7]

Class and vocation are also salient identity markers. Groups exist to represent the interests of occupational groups such as fishermen and farmers.

In some of the more remote villages in Manggarai, however, differentials in wealth are smaller. In most areas in Flores, political affiliation is not particularly important in group formation. Even more so than in East Java, parties command little loyalty from villagers. Indeed, many of the candidates for the April 2004 local legislative elections had previously run for different parties. It was not uncommon to see people in Catholic villages donning the t-shirts they had received for free from Islamic parties such as PAN (the National Mandate Party). Indeed, PAN commanded a significant share of the vote in some homogenous Catholic villages. People had voted for the local PAN candidate, we were told, because he was a respected community figure and was seen as having the ability to bring money and projects back to the village. Indeed, patronage politics is strong in Flores, with candidates expected to bring back resources (legally or illegally) to the communities who elect them. This leads to local ethnic politics, in which particular suku clans support "their man" in order to ensure that they have access to district-level decision making and the benefits it confers (Barron, Nathan, and Welsh 2005).[8] When asked why candidates run for election, a senior seminary official replied that candidates "were in the party because there was an opportunity offered by the party. The problem is that the candidates don't know the ideology of the party . . . people are easily mobilized. The primordial criteria are still there—in conflicts between parties, candidates, and in other areas of conflict like land conflict. The parties and candidates manipulate those feelings to get elected."

In contrast to East Java and much of Indonesia, there does not seem to be a strong gang culture. Incidents of fighting between individuals do not tend to escalate into broader intergroup disputes.

They [youths] generally resolve the fights themselves.
—DEPUTY HEAD, VILLAGE DEVELOPMENT COUNCIL,
TANAH RATA, KOTA KOMBA, MANGGARAI

The cases involving youths are generally triggered by drunkenness. They get drunk, they fight and then once they are sober they are reconciled.
—HEAD, CATHOLIC PRAYER GROUP, TANAH RATA,
KOTA KOMBA, MANGGARAI

The fights are generally triggered by alcohol. They will normally hug and make peace once they are sober again. I even saw some of them crying because they regretted their actions.
—FARMER, KOTING A, MAUMERE, SIKKA

The evidence also seems to show that disputes fuelled by the consumption of large amounts of alcohol in Flores are not transmuted into broader conflicts and do not worsen relations between groups.[9] The reason is that the youths tend to come from the same group, they live together in the same area, and they know each other. Small incidents, therefore, do not harden preexisting cleavages, and those who get into drunken fights tend to recognize them for what they are.

The Impact of KDP on Group Relations

How does KDP affect the different forms of constructed group difference we have just outlined? A number of informants claimed that the program had led to improvements in trust between different groups:

> Yes, KDP has had positive effects . . . the community has been able to mature. Also, we can see that since the implementation of KDP a feeling of unity has been cultivated. Perhaps this is because people within the groups help each other. There is a feeling of closeness [between them].
>
> —VILLAGE FACILITATOR, PAGAL, CIBAL, MANGGARAI

> For instance, when we were working together to build this road, people who could afford to gave cigarettes to those without. That can strengthen relationships.
>
> —KRAJAN HAMLET HEAD AND HEAD OF THE KDP PROJECT VILLAGE
> IMPLEMENTATION TEAM, KEMIRI, JENANGAN, PONOROGO

> Problems between martial arts groups did not affect the KDP program; in fact there are members of martial arts groups who participated in the program, for instance in Pintu village and Kemiri village.
>
> —DEVELOPMENT COORDINATOR, KEMIRI, JENANGAN, PONOROGO

Informants noted two different mechanisms by which levels of interaction are increasing. First, musyawarah (the consultative meetings aimed at moving forward by generating consensus) are increasingly rare in many of our research villages. The reasons for their demise vary by region. In Sikka and, to a lesser extent, in Manggarai, Flores, the encroachment of the Indonesian state in rural areas during the Suharto era, accompanied by explicit attempts to normalize and standardize (that is, Javanize) governance structures across the archipelago, has in many ways modernized village life.[10] Accompanied by profound social changes such as urbanization and increased population movement, this has meant that the role that community forums play in day-to-day life has in many cases declined. Although multi-stakeholder forums such as the government's *rakorbang* (Development Coordination Meeting) now exist at the district level, but with varying degrees of success (Ashari 2005), few opportunities exist at the subdistrict level for collective decision making and problem solving.[11] Thus intervillage coordination meetings, in particular, are very rare. In establishing a decision-making forum with authority to allocate resources, KDP fills a vacuum.

> Competition has positive effects . . . the community in a subdistrict can all come together and learn the method and process for obtaining assistance. So they get to know the community out there [the communities in other villages].
>
> —VILLAGE SECRETARY, PANJENG, JENANGAN, PONOROGO

The qualitative findings from East Java showed that many of the interactions in the villages visited were within groups rather than between them; shared interests tended to exist within groups rather than across groups (Diprose 2004). There were three key exceptions in the subdistricts visited: the village-level meetings (musyawarah, although these usually only involve elites), KDP forums and implementation activities at the village and the subdistrict levels, and higher-level ad hoc meetings set up by leaders to resolve problems, which after repetition became institutionalized but which could dissolve with a change of leadership (Diprose 2004; Ashari 2005).

Second, KDP facilitates group interaction by financing improvements in transportation networks. This may seem a tenuous link, but it was brought up time and again by informants, particularly in Manggarai, where the minor road network is almost nonexistent. Indeed, analysis of the non-KDP development projects that are going to our villages and of the APBDes (the village budget), shows that KDP is by far the biggest player in terms of small-scale local road construction.[12] Where transportation networks are poor, the program was cited as having improved interaction:

> KDP has been very helpful for the community, especially in terms of transportation. People never dreamed that they would eventually be able to pass through Lando village in a motorized vehicle. The problem was that the land there is so steep and rocky. But after the

implementation of KDP in 2000, a road which could be used by motor-ized vehicles was built.

—VILLAGER, LANDO, CIBAL, MANGGARAI

KDP has improved transportation. With improved transportation the villagers have become more mobile and, in turn, interaction has increased.

—KDP SUBDISTRICT FACILITATOR, RUTENG, MANGGARAI

KDP has had a positive impact in this subdistrict. Now, the isolated regions can be reached by road. This has allowed the community to market their produce. Also, the people's economy has strengthened. Similarly, it has become a lot easier for the community to interact because they are a lot more mobile.

—KDP FINANCIAL MANAGEMENT UNIT CHAIRPERSON,
PAGAL, CIBAL, MANGGARAI

But can we link increased interaction to improvements in intergroup relations? It could be that encouraging groups with different identities (and interests and value systems) to interact could fuel tensions, particularly if the environment in which such interaction is taking place is a competitive one. Data from the key informant survey, however, supported by cases from the qualitative fieldwork, suggests that relations between groups across a range of identity cleavages are improving. And comparative analysis of our program and comparison locations shows that KDP is playing a role in driving such change.

Ethnic Relations

Ethnicity is an important marker of difference in NTT, less so in East Java. This is not surprising given the heterogeneity of self-reported ethnic groups in the former compared to the latter.[13] In NTT the majority of infor-mants in KDP treatment locations (58 percent) reported improvements in relations between ethnic groups after the program arrived.[14] Survey infor-mants most commonly stated that including more ethnic groups in decision making than in the past had led to improved relations. Nearly 90 percent of the informants who reported improvements said that KDP had played a role.

These are perceptions data, and as such there may be built-in biases, for example in the incentives of KDP staff and elites to favorably report on the program. But if we bring in information from our matched comparison villages in Flores and disaggregate responses by the number of years an area has been in the program, the evidence appears to strongly back the claim that KDP improves relations between ethnic groups over time. The extent of positive change in ethnic relations steadily increases as KDP stays in a location for longer periods. In the one-year KDP villages, 38 percent reported improvements in ethnic relations; in two-year villages, 50 percent reported improvements; in three-year villages, 63 percent did so.[15] In villages that had participated in KDP for four years, 69 percent of informants reported that ethnic relations had improved in that time period. Similarly, the percentage of people reporting that the program had improved ethnic relations "a lot" increased over time.

This suggests three things. First, ethnic relations are improving across all our research locations in Flores. Only six informants (4 percent) reported a worsening of ethnic relations. This correlates with the drop in the number of conflicts with a reported ethnic basis in the three-year period of our research.[16] Second, the program is playing a role in driving such change. Reported rates of improvement are markedly higher in areas that have been in KDP for more than one year. As one subdistrict head put it, "The implementation of KDP, through the coordination of groups, has increased levels of trust between different clan, ethnic, and religious groups as well as between the rich and poor." Third, this improvement increases over time. In short, the longer KDP operates in an area, the greater positive impact on ethnic relations it seems to have.

Relations Between Religious Groups

Similarly, KDP appears to have led to an improvement, albeit a less marked one, in relations between religious groups in NTT.[17] In our research sites, of those who had an opinion, more than half (or 39 percent of all respondents) noted some improvement in religious relations, with the rest citing no change. Of those who reported favorable change in the KDP sites, 89 percent attributed it to KDP. Again, the fact that more groups were involved in decision making than before was the most commonly given reason for improvements in relations between groups.

Bringing in the comparison locations (those in the program for one year) reveals a marked difference between the KDP and comparison locations: only 15 percent of informants in the one-year villages reported an improvement, compared to 39 percent of informants in the villages that had been in KDP for more than one year.[18] The effect of time is, however, less marked. The percentages of people reporting improvements were fairly similar across the villages that had participated in KDP for two, three, and four years.

Class Relations

In both provinces, the majority of respondents with opinions indicated that there had been improvements in levels of trust between the rich and the poor. In East Java, 38 percent stated this, whereas in NTT 55 percent noted some improvement. When asked why relations between rich and poor had improved, informants in East Java most commonly cited the presence of more bridging forums; in NTT the most popular reason was that more groups were involved in decision making than had been earlier. In East Java, 93 percent of respondents who reported a favorable change said that KDP was responsible; in NTT, 95 percent reported the same.

> I think that KDP is indeed prioritized for the poor. Relations between business groups increased; for example the tempe [fermented soya bean cake] maker[s] stored their products at the *warung* [food stalls]. Relations between the rich and poor, and between religions, also improved.
>
> —SUBDISTRICT HEAD, SLAHUNG, PONOROGO

This is an important finding, given that in the research areas rich-poor cleavages existed between occupational groups within villages, between elites and other members of the community, and between hamlets. These three major cleavages were prominent in many of the conflict cases followed in this study. However, whereas in NTT improvements are closely correlated with the length of time the program has been in an area, this is not the case in East Java. In NTT there is a noticeable trend of improving levels of trust the longer a village participates in KDP; in East Java, the pattern is less clear, although there appear to be larger positive changes in non-KDP areas, which would suggest that trust in general is rising in this province.

Political Affiliation

KDP appears to have little impact in our research areas on relations between people affiliated with different political parties. Most informants in

East Java and all in NTT noted that they did not know whether there had been changes in levels of trust between those affiliated with different political parties. This is largely because political parties are neither pervasive at the village level nor connected to the KDP process. One subdistrict head in Ponorogo commented: "There was no influence from the political parties on KDP; nor, on the other hand, did KDP influence relations between political parties. Political parties only appear towards the general elections. Outside they do not appear at all. It seems they only work at the time of the general elections."

Another informant said that relations between parties had improved but that KDP had not influenced this change. In his view, no matter what political party was in power, it would not have a positive influence on the lower levels of society:

> In my opinion there's been an improvement in relations between political parties, but this hasn't been due to KDP; in fact, there has been no relationship between the political parties and KDP. . . . This increase occurred because the community here has become aware that no matter who leads, the common folk remain just that, the common folk. People who say they're going to help the ordinary folk, they forget their promises once they gain a seat. So for the people here it's simple, really. If political parties want to give aid, they're voted for, if not, then not.
>
> —VILLAGE REPRESENTATIVE COUNCIL CHAIR,
> WATES, SLAHUNG, PONOROGO

Relations Between Martial Arts Groups

As we noted above, identities in East Java and NTT are fluid and multifaceted, and become salient under different conditions. A range of other identities are important. In Ponorogo, affiliation with martial arts groups is particularly important. In East Java, seven survey respondents noted that the relations between martial arts groups had changed since KDP had been in operation, with most reporting improvements. KDP has not played a significant role in this area, however; no survey respondent attributed the improvement to the program. The qualitative fieldwork revealed that the primary reason for the decline in violence between the martial arts groups in Ponorogo was the efforts of the district police chief, who in 2001 began holding regular meetings between martial arts group leaders. They agreed to hand over troublemakers to the police for prosecution. This approach was successful because martial arts groups are highly organized and hierarchical, and once senior figures took ownership of the problem they were able to use their influence within the system. Another theory says the district head at the time of this research, himself an honorary member of the SH Terate group, deliberately stirred up martial arts group violence in preparation for the 1999 district head election, in order for him to present himself as the strong man capable of handling the situation. According to this view, martial arts group conflict was "allowed" to die down once he had been elected (Probo 2003b).

Nevertheless there is some evidence that KDP has helped build relationships between *silat* groups, though it did not trigger or primarily drive such processes. In Jenangan, Ponorogo, members of different martial arts groups were involved in implementing KDP projects at the village level. As noted earlier, members of different martial arts groups participated together in KDP in villages such as Pintu and Kemiri in Ponorogo. Cases of conflict between these groups occur frequently throughout Ponorogo, and few bridging forums exist. Yet members of martial arts groups were able to get involved in KDP, albeit on a personal rather than institutional level (Rasyid 2004).

Behavioral Change

The second indirect mechanism by which KDP may effect change is through its impact on people's behavior. The program is in many ways a democratization initiative masquerading as an antipoverty project. It aims to deliver small-scale infrastructure to marginalized communities, but the mechanisms it uses are aimed at empowering communities, socially and politically as well as economically. Indeed, the program is conceived by its auteur as a way to "trigger and support processes in which villagers exercise discretion in solving self-identified development problems" (Guggenheim 2006, 126). Villager participation in project-related decision making, it is hoped, will lead to changes in behavior outside of the project, in the process indirectly strengthening state-society relations and, ultimately, helping transform the local state.[19] Participation in KDP may make other forms of participation (for example, in other areas of village governance and decision making) more likely. Are there, in fact, any spillovers in improving the quality of governance? And is there a link between more democratic decision making and improved conflict management?[20]

At the macro level there appears to be a case for the latter. Cross-country evidence has shown that democracies are less likely to experience civil war than authoritarian states (Hegre et al. 2001). On the other hand, though democracies may be more likely to channel conflict in peaceful ways, *democratizing* countries, that is, those in transition, may not (Gurr 2000, 2001; Snyder 2000). A vast literature has explored the links between conflict and societal transition.[21] But while a rich empirical and theoretical base now exists for understanding national-level transitions and their links to conflict, there is a lot less evidence concerning whether and how these processes play out at the local level.

In the literature about Indonesia, it is now commonplace to link the transition of 1998 to the outburst of violent conflicts that occurred across the archipelago. The New Order era (which ran from Suharto's accession in 1965 until his downfall in 1998) provided development and security during most of its tenure, but they came at the expense of the institutions of civil society (Liddle 1999). Security sector institutions such as the police and military and formal government institutions (at all levels) were eroded by corruption, distorting the ways in which decisions were made and in which material resources and power were allocated, to the point that, over time, the very basis of their legitimacy was undermined. The collapse of the New Order left a vacuum in conflict resolution; formal institutions were not trusted or able to manage problems, and civil society was too weak to take up the slack (Tajima 2009). It also left different groups with a number of grievances and differential access to the state (Bertrand 2004). The result was an institutional environment unable to address the needs of many ordinary Indonesians. In many cases, groups that perceived themselves excluded felt that there were few nonviolent avenues for redress.

To a lesser extent, the political decentralization implemented in 2001 has also been cited as a factor in outbursts of violent conflict.[22] Decentralization provides both new opportunities and threats. It offers opportunities for improving accountability and the delivery of services at the local level; this, in turn, can mean that grievances can be addressed and conflict more effectively managed when it arises. At the same time, decentralization has created an environment of flux, where groups battle for power and resources in a climate of contested and changing rules. With more resources at the district level, there are incentives for local elites to attempt to capture decision-making processes. Too often, corruption in Indonesia has been merely devolved rather than addressed or redressed (Bjork 2003; Aspinall and Fealy 2003; Morishita 2005).

Yet how do these processes play out *locally*? And how do external interventions interact with ongoing processes of change? In the sections that follow, we first briefly outline some of the dynamics of local-level political change in the post-1998 period. We then examine the empirical evidence regarding the extent to which such processes of change have affected the political behavior of villagers in our research sites. Finally, we attempt to ascertain the extent to which such changes are solely a function of changing context or whether we can reasonably attribute some impact to KDP.

The Dynamics of Local-Level Democracy in Indonesia

Much has been written about the impacts of democratization and decentralization on Indonesian political culture and practice. In April 2004 Indonesians voted for individual legislative candidates at the national, provincial, and district levels for the first time. This was followed by the election of the national president in October of that year, and then the first direct election of district heads (*bupati*) in mid-2005. The seeming smoothness with which these processes took place led one prominent observer to remark on "Indonesia's quiet revolution" (Rieffel 2004).

In terms of decentralization, attention has focused largely on changes at the district level. This is understandable: since the decentralization reforms, district spending has accounted for 31 percent of total government expenditures (an increase from 17 percent), and more than 2 million of 3.3 million civil servants have been transferred to the districts. Yet democratization and decentralization have also had a great impact at the village level. Institutional changes have created new opportunities; these, when combined with other factors such as a free and change-oriented press, have led to cultural and behavioral transformations.

Antlov (2001, 2003a) outlines the institutional shifts. Law 22/1999, concerning regional governance, replaced Law 5/1979, concerning village governance. This prompted a vast array of changes. Village heads could now be called by traditional names. The appointed Village Consultative Assembly (LMD) and Village Community Resilience Board (LKMD—which we call the Village Development Council) were replaced by an elected Village Representative Council (BPD), in effect a local legislature separate from the local executive. The Village Representative Council has the power to approve the village budget, previously a task of the district legislature, and they can propose the dismissal of the village head. Villages are allowed to raise funds from local sources.

These developments have vastly altered the dynamics of village political life. There is now a real counterbalance to the village head. Indeed, in many cases there is genuine political competition between the two village-level political power blocs: the village head (and his supporters) and the Village Representative Council (and its supporters). Given that the councils have numerous members (normally nine), ordinary villagers have greater access to points of political leverage. The research found that the Village Representative Council membership includes a wide range of people including defeated village head candidates, traditional leaders, and young activists. Political power is thus diffused among different groups within the village.[23]

Democratization has also led to cultural changes, with villagers far more willing to participate in local political life. The research found that communities are increasingly willing (and able) to protest perceived wrong-doing by their political representatives. The protest culture that has emerged since 1998 has percolated down to the village level; in many villages, mass protests against misuse of funds are now common. In Nele Wutung, in Sikka, Flores, for example, villagers held demonstrations in front of the district parliament and the district head's office in Maumere to protest the alleged corrupt practices of the village head.

> The whole community protested and reported the case to the district head. However he wasn't able to resolve the problem so it was taken to court.
>
> —MALE FOCUS GROUP, NELE WUTONG, MAUMERE, SIKKA

> The villagers went straight to the police. They took the rice with them as proof . . . there were throngs of them.
>
> —FORMER KDP SAVING AND LOAN GROUP CHAIR,
> NELE WUTUNG, MAUMERE, SIKKA

There is also evidence that villagers are getting more politically savvy. A study of the 2004 legislative elections in four provinces found that money politics was still strong (Barron, Nathan, and Welsh 2005). Candidates and parties would give potential voters gifts such as *ikat* (traditional cloth) garments, rice, and generators. Villagers would gratefully take the gifts, yet this did not seem to affect voting choices on election day. "We take what they offer," one villager in Sikka told us, "and then vote for who we want to anyway." It is into this context of flux and uneven instances of political empowerment that KDP and other development programs enter.

Impact of KDP on Local Democracy

How does KDP affect these processes of democratization? We examine two indicators of behavioral change. First, we look at differences in the number of groups that participate in village meetings over time and differences between those participating in KDP meetings compared to other meetings. Second, we examine changes in village-level decision making. Given the changing context outlined above, it is extremely difficult to separate the influence of KDP from other contextual effects. Is an observed change attributable to the program or to the broader constellation of events that have marked Indonesia's transition? The inclusion of matched comparison locations gives us some leeway to disaggregate program effects from the broader processes of social and political change that have been sweeping Indonesia in recent years. We find that, in general, positive changes in local democracy are observable across all our research locations but that they are more marked in KDP areas.

Changes in Participation

Sixty percent of informants in KDP areas in East Java and 81 percent in NTT noted that people come to KDP meetings who do not usually get involved in other village meetings. It is interesting that the most commonly cited change in both provinces was an increase in women's attendance and participation, followed by that of poor people and ordinary villagers (see table 6.1).

> From what I've observed, it seems every year there are more people attending, you see, so it's not just community figures attending but also the number of ordinary village folk and women attending is increasing. . . . Perhaps it's because they've begun to realize that the KDP program is actually for their needs, too.
> —KDP FINANCIAL MANAGEMENT UNIT CHAIRPERSON,
> PASEAN, PAMEKASAN

In NTT substantial increases in participation by minority ethnic and religious groups were also recorded; that this was not the case in East

TABLE 6.1   PEOPLE WHO GO TO KDP MEETINGS WHO DO NOT USUALLY GO TO
VILLAGE MEETINGS

Group	East Java respondents citing increased participation (%)	NTT respondents citing increased participation (%)
Women	54.5	94.6
Poor people	30.3	93.5
Ordinary villagers	40.9	87.1
Minority ethnic groups	—	78.5
Remote hamlets	28.8	77.4
Minority religious groups	1.5	53.8
Opposition to village government	24.2	26.9
Others	24.2	1.1

Source: Key informant survey (KDP program sites only).

Java can again be put down to the province's relative ethnic and religious homogeneity.

Women and Participation

Some men say that women are already given a chance, and they just don't want it. But that is not true. If they were given a chance, women would take it.

—WOMEN'S RIGHTS ACTIVIST, MAUMERE, SIKKA

Participation of women in KDP is only around 5 percent because it is a tradition in Madura that women are not allowed to mix with men in a single forum, so it is not because their awareness is lacking, but rather the tradition.

—VILLAGER, PADELLEGAN, PADEMAWU, PAMEKASAN

After the KDP meetings, where many of the women were invited, the women in Sana Daya experienced many problems. They usually stayed quiet at meetings. Now they've begun to propose things. Perhaps this can be interpreted as indicating that after KDP women have become bolder. For example, there was a women's Koranic recital group reading Yasin [a book of the Koran]. Just one person regularly turned up. But after KDP arrived many of them began to come and offer something.

—FEMALE PROGRAM BENEFICIARY, SANA DAYA,

PASEAN, PAMEKASAN

Women have only just started to come together [in meetings] since KDP. PKK [the government-instituted family welfare organization, which is run by women, usually those in the families of village elites] has been around for a long time, but only a few people would come, the people who came to the saving and loans routine meeting yesterday afternoon, those ones. Women were unwilling because, first, back then it wasn't clear what the Family Welfare Organization's activities were. . . . Aside from that, there was a cynical view of women who attended meetings in the village hall. "Well aren't you like a civil servant, attending meetings at the village hall, how much are you receiving in wages, who wants to be told to come to the village hall anyway?!" That's the way the women would jeer. After being treated like that, women were usually embarrassed and *wegah* [reluctant] to go. But since KDP, women's participation has improved.

—MIDWIFE, KEMIRI, JENANGAN, PONOROGO

Across almost all the research locations, women are represented poorly in the public realm in village life. Women face a number of barriers to participation, both cultural and structural.[24] Enshrined social structures and institutional practices discourage involvement by women because they face restrictions due to their limited resources, time, skills, and numerous familial obligations. Too much work in the house, in the field, and with children leaves women with little time to go to village talks and meetings or to get involved in other elements of village decision making, including conflict resolution:

Usually if the husband is going to the meeting, the wife will stay at home. If a meeting is about social matters, many women will go. But when they are in meetings, they cannot open their mouth.

—MIDWIFE, NELE WUTONG, MAUMERE, SIKKA

Some women speak at village meetings, but it is mostly men. It is difficult for women to speak. They feel that men should be speaking, not them.

—RETIRED FEMALE TEACHER, BLORO, NITA, SIKKA

Women who are active and invited to meetings . . . are mainly teachers.
—HEALTH WORKER, PADELLEGAN, PADEMAWU, PAMEKASAN

Normally only the men get involved in conflict resolution. They will attend [the forum] and eat there. The women don't attend because there are prohibitions. . . . That's just the way it's been since the time of our ancestors.
—WOMAN IN FOCUS GROUP DISCUSSION, BLORO, NITA, SIKKA

When asked why his wife did not attend village meetings, a government official in Bloro, Sikka, said that she had too much work in the house. Most other men gave similar answers in interviews. Numerous women explained their lack of involvement by arguing that they did not have enough time and could not afford to leave their work. While women were being interviewed for the research, children often ran around the house, and women looked after them while also preparing food. At the same time, children rarely interrupted interviews with men, and women usually took care of refreshments. In a sample of villages in Sikka, Flores, women rarely play leadership roles in two important village institutions: the Village Representative Council and adat (traditional) leadership (Cutura 2003). The same is true for the other three districts. For example, across the six research villages in Sampung and Badegan subdistricts in Ponorogo, there was only one female representative in the Village Representative Council (Anggraini 2004).

Yet the qualitative fieldwork supports the survey evidence that, though not in a uniform way across all our research sites, there are signs that things are starting to change with KDP. Numerous informants (both men and women) told us that the participation of women in terms of attendance and active engagement once there was much higher at KDP meetings than at other village meetings. In some sense this likely reflects the extra efforts taken in the design of KDP to encourage participation, the willingness and capacity of facilitators to elicit it in situations where it contravenes local norms (in a sense, the buy-in of the facilitators themselves to the participatory process), and the level of buy-in by elites, all discussed below.

There are a number of reasons why the participation of women is higher in KDP meetings. First, the way in which the program is publicized encourages women and other marginalized groups to take part. The research found that in many cases simply inviting women to come has a large impact (see box 6.2). Women are not invited to most village meetings; in KDP, they are explicitly encouraged to come. The type of meeting largely determines the extent of women's participation. Program meetings are open, so more women take part. Most villagers, especially those who were not invited to restricted gatherings, were aware of the distinction between open and restricted meetings. Most important, women come because they have direct incentives to do so. At least one proposal from every village must come from a women's group; thus women actually have a reasonable chance of seeing their initiatives funded. This makes them more likely to attend KDP meetings than other village meetings, where funding is less likely.

BOX 6.2   THE ROLE OF WOMEN IN KDP IN FLORES

Many women in this village are involved in KDP. They were all invited to meetings and they went because they heard that KDP would give money to the village.
—FEMALE ADAT LEADER, WATUGONG, MAUMERE, SIKKA

Now more women come to KDP meetings. They come because of money, because they think they will see some benefit from it. Otherwise, women would not want to come.
—TEACHER AND VILLAGE REPRESENTATIVE COUNCIL MEMBER,
WATUGONG, MAUMERE, SIKKA

There are more women at KDP meetings than at village meetings because of the socialization process. Women also think that KDP will help them personally.
—KDP OFFICIAL, BLORO, NITA, SIKKA

The women used to not speak, but now they often speak up . . . the women at the *musbangdes* (KDP village meeting) are part of a weaving group, but they have marketing difficulties.
—VILLAGE HEAD, BLORO, NITA, SIKKA

The general level of community participation in the KDP meetings was quite good . . . [at the most recent meeting] there were about 100 people . . . indeed there were more men, but there would have been about 30 women, too.
—KDP VILLAGE FACILITATOR, PAGAL, CIBAL, MANGGARAI

All this is not to say that KDP is a panacea for women. They still participate much less than do men; they are less likely to hold important positions
within the KDP structure than are men, although the requirement that each
village have a female facilitator does help. Where they do attend meetings they
are, in general, less likely to be vocal than are men. Yet the signs are encouraging. To try to promote the equal participation of women is to work against
norms that have developed over centuries. It can hardly be expected that one
program can change this overnight. Even so, KDP is having an impact,

Are There Spillover Effects?

We would hope that participation in KDP would encourage villagers
to participate in other elements of village political life. In order to understand
whether this is the case, we need to disaggregate the democratizing impact of
the program from that of the broader processes of social and political change
after 1998. The survey data show that across all research villages (KDP and
non-KDP) there is evidence of more groups attending village meetings than
in the past. This change appears to be of a greater magnitude in villages that
have taken part in KDP than in those which have not. "KDP forums at the
village and subdistrict levels can increase community interaction. I think that
gradually more and more community groups became involved [in village
meetings not related to the program]," said a village head in Ponorogo.

In East Java, the longer KDP has been in a village, the more different
groups participate in *all village meetings*. In villages without KDP,
42 percent of informants reported that more groups were coming, compared
to 62 percent of informants in villages that had been in KDP.[25] This impact
increases over time: 75 percent of respondents in four-year KDP villages
reported that more groups came to non–project-related village meetings.

In Slahung subdistrict, Ponorogo, East Java, the qualitative fieldwork
found that KDP forums had become vehicles for increasing community
awareness of development programs and increasing their involvement in
program planning and development (Anggraini and Rasyid 2004). Indeed,
there had been calls from community members for similar involvement
in other development projects, with KDP becoming the yardstick for
community participation:

KDP is the only program which openly involves the community. Before
KDP there were intensive work groups from BP3MD [a previous

government development project], but the villagers just participated without receiving any explanation first. KDP is different because it relies on a socialization process first. I am brave enough to bet that KDP is better because the community is satisfied. Even though they haven't all been involved, I am sure that they are satisfied. That is because we did the work ourselves in an effort to better the village. So, we made it really solid. It would be different if other people had made it. They wouldn't have paid any attention to detail.[26]

—HEAD OF KDP VILLAGE PROJECT IMPLEMENTATION TEAM,
TENGKU LEDA, LAMBA LEDA, MANGGARAI

What's even better is that in Crabak, Gombang and Seneop villages, KDP has encouraged high community initiative. After experience with KDP, the community requested that any development project should involve the community like KDP. . . . When the fourth year was proposed recently, there was a village facilitator in Desa Broto who sketched a bridge. He had studied from the KDP subdistrict facilitator and the village technical assistant. The drawing was very, very good, like an architect's sketch.

—DEVELOPMENT COORDINATOR, SLAHUNG, PONOROGO

The differences are less marked in NTT, with similar high levels of reported increases across villages that have had KDP for different periods of time, although there still appear to be greater improvements in KDP areas.

KDP and Local Decision Making

Survey informants were also asked whether decision making was more democratic now than in the past.[27] The evidence shows again that it is becoming more democratic almost everywhere. As figure 6.2 shows, 57 percent and 77 percent of informants in KDP areas in East Java and NTT, respectively, noted that decision making had become more democratic. Less than 5 percent of informants in East Java and less than 3 percent in NTT said that it had become less democratic. These figures show impressive impacts from Indonesia's decentralization and democratization initiatives.

But can any of these changes be attributed to KDP? The data show that in East Java, villages that have taken part in the program report greater changes: 67 percent of informants in four-year villages say decision making

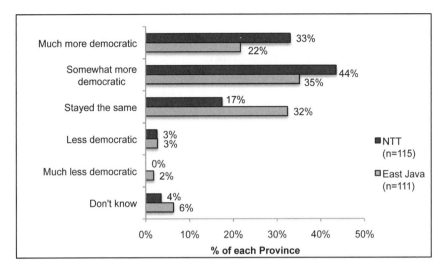

Figure 6.2   Changes in village-level decision making since taking part in KDP in NTT and East Java.

Source: Key informant survey (KDP program sites only).

has become more democratic, compared to 46 percent in nonparticipating villages. In NTT the evidence is more ambiguous, although, again, informants in four-year KDP villages were the most likely to say decision making had become more democratic (94 percent).

We should note that the project does not always lead to such behavioral change. In numerous cases both the reputation and impact of KDP were negatively affected by contra-democratic actions by people involved with the program. Where the program does not operate in the manner it is meant to (and especially where transparency is low), behavioral spillovers do not occur. We explore this in more depth in Chapter 7. Where KDP does work well, however, it positively reinforces the processes of democratization and decentralization, which have resulted in real increased participation by ordinary villagers.

Changes in Norms and Perceptions

The third hypothesis is that KDP improves local conflict management by changing the ways in which people understand problems and the best ways to respond to them. Violence, as we noted above, is not only a symptom of conflict but a learned response to it. When faced with a dispute with another party, individuals or groups can pursue a number of courses of action. They can try to reach agreement directly with the other party or they can take the case to an external third-party mediator. Alternatively, they can take direct action without involving anyone else. Responses may or may not be violent. The way people respond to conflictual situations is determined by a number of different factors. The presence and quality of intermediaries will help determine whether people use them.[28] The extent and contours of the animosity with the adversary, and the extent to which the barrier between "us" and "them" is inflexible, will also determine the form of action.

Perhaps most important, however, are the norms that regulate the appropriateness of responses to a given problem. Rule systems govern people's understandings and behavior in response to events, actions, or choices. Human interactions and exchange are shaped by incentives, which in turn are structured by rules, whether formal laws or informal norms (North 1990, 3). Understanding the rules that exist within a given society is vital if we want to understand the ways in which social, political, and economic relations are structured, and hence the ways in which people and communities interact (Barron, Smith, and Woolcock 2004).

We hypothesized at the study's outset that development programs could help shape norms with regard to how people understand and respond to disagreements and disputes. The program emphasizes a collective and inclusive process of decision making and problem solving. In practice, do the routines and practices that constitute participation in the program help people learn how to address conflicts and problems in nondestructive ways?

Changes in Problem Solving and Conflict Resolution

We showed above how decision making and problem solving are changing in Indonesian villages. More groups take part, including marginalized groups, and the program is seen as more democratic. But is it any better? Are communities and the state able to handle conflicts in better ways than they could in the past? Are peaceful solutions more commonly reached? In this section we ask three related questions: Do people try to solve problems differently than in the past? Are people better or worse at solving problems or conflicts than in the past? If there are differences, can we attribute them to KDP?

Survey informants were asked two perception questions related to changes in the quality and nature of problem solving and conflict resolution. First, they were asked whether they thought the quality of village-level problem solving had changed since KDP's arrival. Second, they were asked whether problem solving and conflict resolution were more violent, more peaceful, or had stayed the same since KDP had arrived. As can be seen in figures 6.3 and 6.4, informants were generally positive about changes. In East Java and NTT, 42 percent and 69 percent, respectively, said that village problem solving had improved. Higher rates of improvement were reported by subdistrict-level informants: 67 percent and 89 percent said it had improved in East Java and NTT, respectively. Respondents also said that problems and conflicts were now solved in more peaceful ways. Of the respondents in NTT, 73 percent said that village-level problem solving was now more peaceful; in East Java, the proportion is lower (35 percent), with a majority saying the nature of problem solving had stayed the same. Nonetheless, fewer than 1 percent said that problem solving was now more violent than it had been. At the subdistrict level, in both provinces a large majority of informants reported that problem solving was more peaceful than before (76 percent in East Java, 79 percent in NTT).

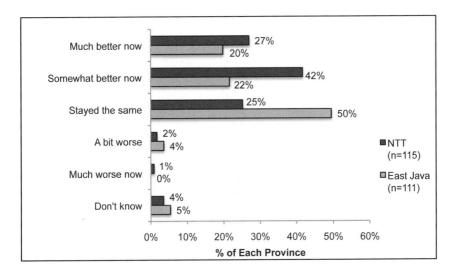

Figure 6.3   "Has village problem solving improved since the start of KDP?"
Source: Key informant survey (KDP program sites only).

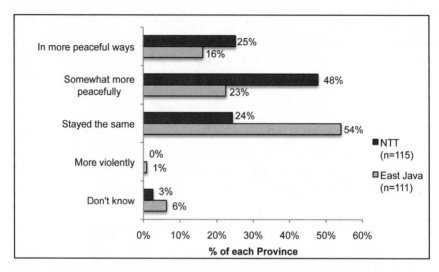

Figure 6.4   Changes in quality of village conflict resolution since the start of KDP.
Source: Key informant survey (KDP program sites only).

That reported improvements in subdistrict-level problem solving and conflict resolution are greater than village-level ones is not surprising. The research found that institutions exist to deal with most problems and conflicts within the village. Both formal structures (the government hierarchy, which extends down to the election of neighborhood heads) and informal ones (community leaders, adat leaders, and so on) exist, and people generally know which institutions and actors are most suitable for dealing with which type of problem. This does not necessarily indicate that these village-level institutions are fairer or that they are not laden with the norms and power structures of villages, but rather that options exist for villagers to seek assistance with their problems, as opposed to other situations and realms where there are no avenues for redress. The same is true to some extent at the district level, where the executive, the legislature, the security sector, and the numerous arms of civil society all play a role in addressing particular types of conflict.

A vacuum exists at the subdistrict level, however. The subdistrict head, an administrator, implements decisions made at the district level. The police, although present, have little autonomy in decision making at this level and are vastly undersupported (Baare 2004; Meliala 2005; Muna 2004). Adat structures are also weak at this level. Even so, a number of problems arise between villages that require mediation or other forms of intervention. The research found that most problems within villages could be successfully handled. Where conflicts cross village boundaries, however, they are more likely to escalate, in large part because few extra-village conflict resolution and mediation mechanisms exist. Especially in places such as Flores, the district capital is much too far away for villagers to seek outside intervention.[29] Conversely, district-level actors are often reluctant to deal with conflicts in remote villages. Interviews revealed that many district government figures feel that if the problem is big enough, it will come to them. Unfortunately, by the time it does, it often has built in intensity, making resolution much more difficult than if it had been addressed early on.

Is KDP Responsible for Changing Norms of Conflict Resolution?

The survey data does not point strongly to KDP areas experiencing larger changes in problem solving norms than non-KDP areas. Indeed, there is no difference in reported rates of positive change between program and matched comparison sites. With regard to changes in conflict resolution, 56 percent of informants in KDP areas and non-KDP areas reported improvements. Similarly, 55 percent of informants in KDP areas reported improvements in problem solving; in non-KDP areas, the rate was 56 percent.[30]

It would thus appear from the survey evidence that norms of problem solving and conflict resolution have changed over time, and for the better, but that this is due to factors other than KDP. Yet the qualitative fieldwork does show concrete links between the program and the building of civic skills that allow for better and more peaceful resolution of problems and conflicts. One example is the program's effect on modes of interaction between elites. As we noted in Chapters 3 and 4, in some places KDP was seen as a resource to be captured by competing power blocs within the village. Sometimes this triggered interaction conflict such that competition over KDP resources led to an escalation of preexisting tensions. But in other cases the forums and rules of the program provided a space where elites could learn how to compete in nonviolent ways:

A positive impact achieved after the implementation of KDP in Pademawu subdistrict has been the increased community knowledge of the meaning of democracy. This can be seen from the Village Representative Councils in the villages. The atmosphere of the KDP meetings has been absorbed in each forum held by the Village Representative Council so that the democracy in process in these meetings is incredibly dynamic. . . . One example is the Pademawu subdistrict Village Representative Council "Working Together" forum which has been formed, where the members are from the Village Representative Councils in the villages. This forum functions to unify the perceptions on *perdas* [district regulations] that are implemented at the village level. They meet for hours and hours until nighttime without even getting a little tired! . . . Apart from that, at the community level . . . since KDP, the community has gained more knowledge of how to reach consensus in decision making, while still having their own desires.

—SUBDISTRICT HEAD, PADEMAWU, PAMEKASAN

I have watched the village administration and the Village Representative Council learn from KDP over the past year. The Council was elected last year in this subdistrict and in most villages it truly represented each of the hamlets in the village. The members in most villages were not the village head's cronies but instead were ordinary villagers for once, and in some villages they even held parties to celebrate the election results. . . . I watched as the members of the Village Representative Council and village administration battled it out in KDP forums. If the village head tried to dominate the process, members of the Village Representative Council would stand up and point this out, quoting back program rules. . . . This worked both ways, though, where, for example, in one village I saw the village head and other members of the administration stand up and do the same thing when the Village Representative Council dominated the process. So they are learning from each other and the program.

—KDP SUBDISTRICT FACILITATOR, PASEAN, PAMEKASAN

The community's democratic maturity following KDP is manifest in the forums found in the Village Representative Council that follow the KDP pattern. . . . They are more mature in dealing with differences of opinion between Village Representative Council members as well as with the village head in conflict resolution. . . . Usually the problem relates to land boundaries; it often happens in Padellegan village. In order to solve the problem, the Village Representative Council and the village head sit together to mediate between the two disputing land owners. Then the two land owners are truly satisfied with all the resulting decisions.

—HEAD OF THE KDP FINANCIAL MANAGEMENT UNIT, PASEAN, PAMEKASAN

There is some evidence that KDP is contributing to changes in relations between different arms of the state at the village level. Moreover, there has been an impact on the expectations of villagers. We also found examples of KDP changing norms of solving problems between villagers:

Through KDP, villagers are learning to accept difference of opinion in a more mature and peaceful fashion, compared with previously. These skills are being transferred to negotiations in other village meetings and negotiations between the Village Representative Council and government. There was also a case where there was a land dispute. The Village Representative Council organized a meeting between the warring parties and the final resolution was accepted without protest, violence, or further tension. Normally, people in the community hate to lose face in a public forum, causing community tension, and won't interact on the street.

—KDP SUBDISTRICT FACILITATOR, PASEAN, PAMEKASAN

Indeed, the community has benefited indirectly from the critical discussions about public policy, evaluations, monitoring, and proposal formulation as well as the technical side of construction. The concept of learning by doing is the key to success:

Before it [KDP], I never knew that there were so many clever people in the village . . . perhaps before KDP villagers' potential had never been utilized, so their capabilities had never been evident.

—SAVING AND LOANS GROUP HEAD, JENANGAN, JENANGAN, PONOROGO

As for positive effects, I think it [KDP] can increase the community's outlook, from one of ignorance to one of knowing. The community can learn how to lobby other delegations so their proposals succeed.

—SECRETARY OF THE KDP VILLAGE PROJECT IMPLEMENTATION TEAM
AND TEACHER, WATES, SLAHUNG, PAMEKASAN

This is not to say that KDP is changing norms in all places or that it is not susceptible to elite capture or the strength of village-level norms pertaining to patronage; rather, where there are signs of change, it is generally positive and managing to some extent to build cohesion and nonviolent procedures for the negotiation of problems.

The Impact on Conflict Outcomes

We have seen the impact of KDP on a number of variables that, we have argued, help determine the local environment that makes conflict more or less likely, that help dictate its nature when it does arise, and that help shape local capacity to manage it in more or less violent ways. But demonstrating a causal link between KDP and changes in local conflict environments goes only part of the way toward showing a link between the program and local conflict management capacity. We must also test the second part of the hypothesis: that changes in these environmental variables help shape the outcomes of conflicts.

Establishing this link empirically is difficult, and we are acutely aware of the limitations of the strategy we invoked. Part of our strategy sought to use the newspaper dataset on reported incidents of conflict to look for correlations between reductions in violence levels and improvements in group relations and behavioral or normative changes. We found no such clear correlation: subdistricts reporting larger improvements in the variables explored in this chapter did not see larger reductions in levels of violent conflict than those where indirect impacts were not as great. Does this disprove the hypotheses that improvements in group relations, increases in participation and decision making, and changing attitudes toward problem-solving and conflict resolution can limit the occurrence and escalation of conflict?

In the remainder of this chapter we turn to case analysis and lessons from theory to understand better the ways in which local structure and norms may affect conflict incidence and outcome. We argue that one of the reasons for the lack of correlation between changes in the variables measured in the survey and changes in levels of conflict is that conflict is explained, in part, by extralocal factors. This limits the effectiveness of local approaches to limiting violent conflict *when implemented alone,* that is, without complementary approaches to get at larger drivers of conflict. Yet, we argue, local factors do often matter in determining the likelihood of whether small-scale, everyday conflicts escalate into larger ones. We also argue that, over time, approaches to strengthening the social fabric of local communities can make it more likely for conflicts to arise in the first place.

Extralocal Factors and the Incidence of Violent Conflict

It is unsurprising that we do not, at an aggregate level, find a link between changes in these variables and levels of conflict over time. One important reason is that local conflict cannot be explained entirely by local factors. Changes at the local level may increase conflict management capacity, but local capacity can be overwhelmed by large-scale problems. It is clear that many of Indonesia's larger conflicts—in Poso, in Maluku, in Aceh before the peace agreement—have as much to do with elite interests (at various levels) as they do with local cohesion and forms of decision making. This was also evident in some of the cases already discussed and in others we collected. Two cases, one in East Java, the other in NTT, illustrate this point.

The Mining Company in Ponorogo

Sari Gunning State Enterprise, a company owned by the Ponorogo district regional government, carries out limestone mining on government land in Sampung village. Formally, Sari Gunung is responsible to the Ponorogo district government. On a day-to-day basis, however, it has the authority to make technical decisions.

> This is a regional government enterprise, so profits are not prioritized. In fact it has more of a social function. Every year we must make a contribution to local revenue. . . . I don't know the history of it, but this is government-owned land. . . . Because it belongs to district government, we do not have obligations to the village or the subdistrict. We've already provided funds to the district government. As to how much of these funds are allocated here, that's up to them. If it's just about helping out, when, for example, the village or the subdistrict has an event and then asks for a contribution from [Sari Gunung], well, we give it. . . . But if special funds are being sought because we carry out mining here, there aren't any, because that's the local government's responsibility.
> —DIRECTOR, SARI GUNUNG STATE ENTERPRISE, SAMPUNG, SAMPUNG

Because the state enterprise makes payments to the district government, company officials argue that they have no responsibility to the local peoples in the areas where they are situated and that any such responsibility falls instead to the district government. In the 1980s, *grosok* (limestone mining refuse) began to destroy several sections of road in the hamlets to the west of Sampung's main road. After a series of complaints throughout the 1980s, drains were finally built to carry the grosok away. But the residents did not know who had built the drains because they were not consulted in the design. The drains only shifted the refuse problem to a different hamlet farther down the hill.

> At my place it was just the same. The waste from the market would come into the house. When it rained the grosok mixed with gravel would be affected by rainwater. Well, that mixed with market waste and came into my house. Now it's like a ditch.
>
> —VILLAGER, SAMPUNG, SAMPUNG, PONOROGO

The matter soon became contentious and, over time, the number of actors in the conflict grew, as did its complexity. It influenced the allocation of development funds and increased tensions between the different hamlets in the village.

> There used to be aid, but it was given to other hamlets. The reason they gave was that the community here could not take care of the environment, so it did not deserve to obtain aid. . . . At this thanksgiving event many commented about the aid. The community in the region over there [the other hamlets] said all sorts of things about the community here, especially my family, because the biggest amount of grosok had piled up in front of my house but I just left it alone. Initially I just stayed quiet; I let them say whatever they wanted. After many people had commented I said every year when it rains the grosok is always carried down by the water. Not only mud, but also grosok, is carried by the water. My house happens to be the lowest. So the grosok and mud pile up in front of my house. There used indeed to be voluntary labor. But after a while no one wanted to do it anymore, they were exhausted. The grosok increased, and one person could no longer clean it up, it needed many. The village or subdistrict authorities alone wouldn't be capable of overcoming this matter. If you don't believe me, tell the local government people to come here. If they can manage to clean it up, I'll drink their urine!
>
> —VILLAGER, SAMPUNG, SAMPUNG, PONOROGO

In December 2002 the rains were so heavy that the drains could not handle the volume of refuse; they backed up, and the refuse blocked off the main road and peoples' front yards. The villagers had reported these problems several times in the past to the village administration, which said it had inadequate resources to fix the problem. The complaints were also being ignored by both the district administration and the state enterprise, each claiming that the other had jurisdiction and responsibility for dealing with the problem. The following month youths from the area most seriously affected by the problem blocked off the drains as a means of protest and of reducing the impacts of the refuse on their living environment. This shifted the problem back up to the main road in the center of the village. An agreement was made between hamlets not to clean up the main road as a means of drawing the attention of the district and other authorities. The problem remains unresolved, and, at the time the research was conducted, the Village Representative Council was trying to negotiate with the company on behalf of the villagers affected by the problem.

Who Owns the Mbondei Land? Tradition and Mediation in Western Flores

Like many of the villages throughout Manggarai, Tanah Rata is in the midst of a controversial land dispute. At the center of the dispute is the Mbondei land, a fifty-hectare expanse that was originally clan land administered by the Motu Poso ethnic group. The land's status is now unclear. The dispute involves the Kisol Seminary, Himastan (a community group of farmers), two smaller groups of villagers, and the original clan owners. The numerous attempts to resolve the dispute have been fruitless, and the possibility of bloodshed remains.

In 1967 the Motu Poso clan's landowners transferred the rights to the Mbondei land to the Kisol Seminary so that it could use the land to herd its cattle. Because most customary practices involving the transfer of land in Flores are based on oral agreement, there was no written documentation that could be used to clarify whether the Kisol Seminary was given ownership or simply usage rights. Conflicting versions of events from the surviving witnesses were of little help in determining the status of the land. In the resulting confusion and contestation, provocative actions could lead to conflict.

By mid-2002 tensions had begun to surface. On a fresh June morning in Tanah Rata, about 140 members of Himastan arrived at Mbondei and began dividing the land among themselves for the cultivation of crops. Not only was it time to draw attention to the injustice of seeing someone else occupy and claim the land of their ancestors; they could also see the benefits of the extra money that the cropland would bring them. By the end of the year, after encouragement from Himastan, two other groups of villagers from Tanah Rata decided to also lay claim to parts of the land. The once-quiet grazing pastures of Mbondei were suddenly a hive of activity, with people cutting down trees and cultivating crops on a daily basis.

Not only was the Kisol Seminary shocked and angered by Himastan's actions; the original landowners were also outraged. In response to Himastan's actions, the government (the village, the subdistrict, and finally the district) stepped in, as did the adat elders and church representatives. In general, these institutions agreed: according to the government and the adat institution, Himastan and the two village groups had not only violated adat law, but they had also violated government regulations by cultivating the Mbondei land. Even so, confusion about who had jurisdiction to address the problem made things worse.

The adat functionaries requested that the cultivators sign a statement declaring that they would cease activities on the disputed land, but the head of Himastan refused, saying: "We don't need to write a statement and we will continue to work. We will ignore the warning from the village head and the adat functionaries." The subdistrict government then decided to get involved, drafting and distributing a warning letter prohibiting the cultivators from working the land. The government held several meetings with the disputing parties, with no success. Finally, the cultivators signed a statement declaring that they would cease their activities on the land. Yet just as the case looked as if it were coming to an end, the cultivators withdrew their statement and went back to working the land. Tensions rose once again. The subdistrict government had reached a dead end, as had the numerous other mediators who had made efforts to resolve the case. There was little more they could do except hand the case over to the district government. Still, the resolution strategy is unclear. The conflict is currently in the hands of the district government and, with tensions mounting, one wrong move from any of the parties could result in bloodshed.

Power, Complexity, and the Limits of Local Conflict Management Capacity

In the case related to the Sari Gunung mining company, the sheer number of actors involved and the fact that a powerful company with links to state interests was one of them meant that local attempts to solve the problem were unsuccessful. The complexity of the problem, the lack of resources, and lack of clear responsibility and cohesion between different levels of government (and the company) were the driving factors. In such a case, it is unlikely that local capacity would provide the means to resolve the issue, although the local Village Representative Council made a valiant attempt. In the land case in Manggarai, the host of different parties involved in conflict resolution also led to a level of complexity that meant that local efforts at resolution were ineffective.

For many such conflicts, incidents such as this, powerful interests with broad reach are at play. It is not surprising that, in such cases, local conflict management capacity is in some ways irrelevant. Indeed, the village in Ponorogo was one of the strongest in our sample in terms of local conflict management capacity. This should serve as an important warning to those who see community-driven development projects such as KDP as *the* answer to problems of local conflict. Such projects need to be accompanied by complementary strategies that focus on power relations and incentives at higher levels.

Local Factors and the Likelihood of Conflict Incidence and Escalation

It is too easy, however, to write off the importance of local factors in limiting violence and wider outbreaks of conflict. Extralocal factors do matter; the extent to which violent conflict occurs at the local level is dependent on both exogenous and endogenous factors. Exogenous variables may include national economic policy, population flows, and centralized security institutions. Such forces can and do overwhelm local communities. Large shocks can lead to both high levels of social tension and violent conflict. But external macro forces only explain in part why some conflicts take violent form. Social tensions exist in many places yet only lead to violent conflict in some. Similarly, external forces of the same type and scale impact matters in different ways in different places.

Our case studies show that in environments such as East Java and NTT, which are characterized by frequent low-intensity conflicts, local factors related to both social structure and dominant norms of power and decision making matter vis-à-vis the likelihood that relatively simple local disputes will arise and whether they escalate into more complex and protracted conflicts.[31] One of the reasons cases such as the land conflict in Manggarai get so complex and involve so many actors is that they are allowed to escalate. Comparative analysis of our conflict cases shows that major conflicts often have their roots in smaller-scale everyday forms of conflict. Using a modified version of the process-tracing methodology (George and Bennett 2005), we traced the chronologies of sixty-eight cases of local conflict with the aim of establishing why conflicts ended up the way they did (violent or not, escalated or not), and the pathways they took to get there. We broke each conflict up into a series of chronological parts; at any given moment, an existing conflict might (a) stay at the same level of intensity, (b) escalate, or (c) be resolved, either temporarily or permanently, through negotiation or outside mediation. Breaking down conflicts into smaller parts allowed us to analyze the factors that led to outcome (a), (b), or (c).[32]

We found that three realms of variables helped shape the pathways along which conflicts traveled and helped determine outcomes.[33] The first realm centers on the actions of mediators, leaders, or officials in conflict resolution and the extent to which they possess the necessary legitimacy, willingness, and capacity to both make and enforce decisions (see Chapter 5). It is not surprising that our analysis found an inverse relationship between the *efficacy of intermediaries* at local level and the likelihood of conflict escalation. Direct conflict management interventions, such as strengthening the legitimacy and capacity of local mediators and providing incentives such that they are willing to address conflict issues, can limit the likelihood that a given conflict will turn violent.

Second, the comparative case analysis highlighted the extent to which the structure of inter- and intragroup relations and the relationship between society and the state affected conflict patterns. In conjunction with the efficacy of intermediaries, two additional realms of variables relating to what we have called the local conflict environment mattered in terms of influencing the likelihood of conflicts' escalating and turning violent. One of these centers on various elements of the *rules of the game*—the laws and norms that shape the immediate context in which disputants, their representatives, or external mediators engage one another. Conflicts are less likely to escalate and turn violent when people have a collective sense of what behavior is acceptable and how a particular dispute should be decided (and by whom). When the rules system that is applicable to a particular action or behavior is hazy or disputed, or where multiple sets of (coherent or incoherent) norms exist, people may be more likely to engage in provocative and ultimately conflictual behavior (Ross 1993; Rothchild 1997). In our sample, this was particularly true of conflicts about land, where different kinship groups had different rules and understandings of how land should be allocated. The largest conflict in our newspaper dataset—resulting in fifteen deaths—was of such a nature.

The final realm focuses on the norms and politics pertaining to inter-group (us-them) relations—or what we call the *dynamics of difference*—and the ways and means by which differences are constructed and are able to be mobilized, reimagined, and exploited for strategic advantage. Where boundaries between groups are marked, with little opportunity for cross-group interaction, conflicts were more likely to take place. When they did occur, they also escalated more easily, largely because the appeals to group interests were used as a basis for mobilization.[34]

These contextual variables are important at multiple levels. Anderson (1991), for example, has shown in his work on nationalism how identity formation and transformation are conditional on demographic, political, economic, cultural, policy, and legislative environments at multiple units of analysis. Likewise, the rules that structure human exchange exist at multiple levels. Laws can be passed by legislatures at the national, provincial, and district levels; subdistrict and village heads also shape local rule systems; and civil society exists at multiple levels and has an impact at each. The relative youth of Indonesia as a postcolonial nation and the correspondingly short time for national legislation to have developed into everyday and effective norms in remote and still traditional areas have meant that (locally derived) traditional laws and customs continue to frame everyday life.

Thus, a key finding was that local social and political structures matter in important ways. Our research strategy sought to isolate the importance of local factors by comparing cases concerning similar issues but with different outcomes within subdistricts and districts, so as to control for extralocal factors.[35] On a case-by-case basis, local factors played a large role in determining both the pathways conflicts would take and their eventual outcomes. Even most of the conflicts that overwhelmed communities (for example, the land case in Manggarai) had their roots in *local* issues; all the evidence points to the fact that they would not have escalated in the way they did and hence become unmanageable at the local level if they had been dealt with early on. Further, if local rule systems had been less incompatible or group boundaries less marked, it is unlikely the conflict would have escalated in the way it did. Improving the number and quality of intergroup interactions in most cases makes group identities less divisive, and it makes it harder for elites to mobilize community members on the basis of narrowly particularistic senses of "us" and "them."[36] Increasing access to decision making is also likely to make local rule systems more cohesive. Decision making that encourages access by all sections of the population is less likely to result in outcomes that provoke conflict, because (a) when people are involved in processes that they deem equitable and legitimate, they are less likely to dispute their outcomes, and (b) institutionalizing open discussion can help parties find common ground, much of which only becomes clear through the very process of discussion itself.[37]

Strategies for Improving Conflict Management Capacity: Enhancing the Demand Side of Good Governance

If both local and extralocal factors matter, a key policy question becomes, Which should be prioritized? Should strategies to limit violent conflict in Indonesia and elsewhere focus on trying to affect local conflict environments, or should they concentrate on national factors (such as correcting inequitable and unclear means of land distribution or strengthening weak justice and security sector institutions)? From our research it appears that both are necessary. There are real limits to what locally focused approaches can achieve. In particular, in cases involving the military or large private companies, often in collaboration with local or national government, local capacity becomes largely irrelevant. This is true for many of the massive conflicts about land and natural resources that occur throughout the archipelago.

Yet, at the same time, there does appear to be an important role for local approaches. In the medium-to-long run, stimulating demand for reform from the bottom up through participatory sphere institutions may be the best way of changing the institutional structures that allow conflict to flourish (Cornwall and Coelho 2007). Lessons from around the world show that exclusively top-down or technocratic approaches to "improving justice systems" or "building government capacity" often fail, primarily because they do not affect the incentives at play or take adequate account of the identities, values, and systems of meaning in which such incentives are embedded.[38] More recent and alternative approaches such as KDP seek to correct these shortcomings by incrementally building the demand for and capacity of local governments. They do so by simultaneously increasing the "capacity to engage" (Gibson and Woolcock 2008)—that is, the civic skills and public confidence—of everyday citizens and by establishing new procedures and precedents for positive engagement between citizens and their state.

Generally KDP has had a positive impact . . . it has trained and educated the villagers in musyawarah and *mufakat* [discussion aimed at reaching an agreement] and the right procedures for reaching an agreement. KDP has taught the villagers how to discuss issues and come to a democratic agreement based on deliberation and consensus. It has also taught people to value other people's opinions.

—FORMER SECTION HEAD OF COMMUNITY EMPOWERMENT BOARD IN
THE DISTRICT GOVERNMENT, RUTENG, MANGGARAI

Such approaches invariably take time, and in building up the demand side it is also important to work directly with governments to help strengthen the corresponding supply side. Such efforts may not yield outcomes that emerge in a linear or predictable manner, making their design, implementation, and assessment especially problematic for agencies that strongly prefer more standardized "blueprint" responses (Evans 2004; Woolcock 2009). Yet in such places as contemporary Indonesia, a key strategy for facilitating change at higher levels is itself stimulating demand from below. It is vital to build, consolidate, and refine such approaches, not only for making services work in poor communities but, more fundamentally, for making democracy work in volatile settings in the midst of multiple economic, social, and political transitions, the unsettling vicissitudes of which are likely to be a feature of life in Indonesia (and elsewhere) for decades to come.

Summary

Local conflict in Indonesia is largely a product of weak institutions. Chapter 5 assessed whether KDP had a direct impact on strengthening conflict management institutions by introducing people (facilitators) and spaces (decision-making forums). The research found that, in general, direct impacts are minimal, but in places where effective local conflict management institutions do not exist, KDP forums and facilitators at times play a role.

Whereas the direct impacts of KDP on conflict management are small, the program has notable and positive indirect impacts on the local institutional environment in the areas in which it operates, particularly when real participation manages to circumvent the power and hegemony of incumbent elites. By changing relations between groups as well as those between citizens and the state, the project affects local conflict environments, that is, the structures and norms that make conflict more or less likely to arise and to escalate. The program is helping improve intergroup and state-society relations and so helping make project areas more resistant to violent conflict.

We found that, across a range of identity cleavages, KDP had helped contribute to improvements in intergroup relations. Ethnic, religious, and class relations in NTT have improved since the program was introduced, and these changes are greater in program areas than in comparison areas. There is also some evidence that relations between those affiliated with competing martial arts groups have improved in East Java. Further, improvements in group relations grow larger over time. Villages that have taken part in KDP for four years show, in general, greater improvements than those that have taken part for shorter periods. The program provides a space for different groups to come together to collectively discuss their needs and priorities, something that is increasingly rare, especially at the intervillage level. Moreover, the program facilitates group interaction by improving transportation networks.

Also, KDP appears to be effectively reengineering the relationship between citizens and the state at the local level. It brings a set of rules and norms concerning, among other things, who should participate in decision making, the criteria that should be used for resource allocation, and the checks and balances that should be in place to control local power. In this sense, projects such as KDP are inherently political: they value one system of social order more than another, and they introduce resources (financial and human) to change incentives so that it is more likely that this form of social order will materialize (and routinize itself). The evidence shows that the program is helping democratize village life. Marginalized groups, in particular, women, are far more likely to take part in KDP meetings than in other village government meetings, and increased participation in KDP also appears to be spilling over into other domains of village life. Forty-two percent of villagers in matched areas that had not had KDP reported that more marginalized groups were coming to village meetings, compared to 62 percent in KDP areas. Seventy-five percent of villagers in four-year KDP villages reported that more groups came to village meetings than in the past. Decision making in village meetings has also become more democratic, and this effect is greater in KDP areas than in the matched comparison sites.

Villagers also report that problem solving has improved and conflict resolution has become more democratic since the program's arrival. The key informant survey shows similar reported rates of improvement for KDP and non-KDP areas. The qualitative fieldwork, however, shows clear links between the program and such normative changes, with KDP (when it functions well) creating a positive precedent, in the process helping stimulate demand for changes in the ways in which local decision making and conflict resolution operate.

We find no direct correlation between the levels of indirect change and reduced levels of conflict. This, we argue, is partly because of the importance of extralocal factors in determining conflict levels; it is also because it will take time for the democratization impacts of KDP to lead to increased conflict management capacity. However, analysis of the cases shows that local factors do matter significantly, especially in determining whether a conflict is likely to escalate to a level at which communities can no longer deal with it. The cases also suggest that the democratization of Indonesian village life and the strengthening of intergroup relations will make communities more resistant to conflict in the medium to long term and that demand-side approaches are a necessary complement to strategies that address the supply of good governance.

The research shows that KDP alone does not create these profound changes. Rather, when it works well, and in environments favorable to change, it catalyzes existing processes of social and political transformation. Indonesia, at present, is in the middle of a complex and contested transition from authoritarian state to democracy and from being an extremely centralized state to one where powers are held and resources are managed in provinces and districts. The research shows broadly positive changes from Indonesia's transition at the local level. Village-level decision making is becoming more democratic. Villagers are participating to a greater extent in local political life, and, increasingly, they are holding their leaders to account. Norms of leadership and dispute resolution are changing. The program is a vital resource that reformers at the local level can use to legitimize their position and actions. Indeed, the indirect impacts of KDP on conflict management are greater in higher-capacity areas, places where an alignment of people and processes combines to encourage progressive social and political change. Programs such as KDP do not operate in a vacuum. The success or failure of programs that aim to promote local-level democratization in a post-authoritarian environment should be measured not solely by the observable impacts of the program but by whether they effectively support *existing* processes of change. An exploration of the influence of these contextual factors on the impact and efficacy of KDP is the concern of Chapter 7.

CHAPTER 7

How Contexts Shape Project Performance and Conflict Trajectories

Thus far we have examined the different impacts, positive and negative, direct and indirect, that KDP has on local conflict and its management. We have found that KDP triggers conflicts and interacts with existing tensions, but that these do not become violent. The program has little direct impact on either conflict levels or conflict management; its forums and facilitators are not often used for disputes unrelated to the program. It does, however, indirectly affect conflict environments and, in so doing, helps improve medium- to long-term conflict management capacity.

These are aggregate findings representing general trends across the different research areas. The general results, however, mask tremendous variation between different areas. For example, although KDP triggers low-level conflict in many areas in which it operates, in some villages it does not. Similarly, KDP facilitators and forums are rarely used for resolving conflicts that are not related to the program, but in some villages they are. Across the forty-one villages studied, the program was found to lead to positive normative and behavioral changes and improved relations between different identity groups, yet in some villages these effects were negligible. Why? This chapter seeks to provide a basis for explaining variation in KDP's impact on local conflict. The focus is on understanding interactions between types of disputes, the efficacy of program implementation, and levels of local and district capacity.

Explaining Variation

In this chapter we outline the extent of variation between areas where KDP is implemented for each of the dimensions of impact discussed in previous chapters. We have not yet examined how the various factors in the program's differential impacts on conflict management capacity interact with different levels of preexisting capacity. Understanding such interactions and the impact of context is important for projects such as KDP, which aim to do "small development" on a large scale. How can projects be designed that allow for local discretion in implementation yet take account of differences in local capacity? In what kinds of areas can such projects have an impact on local conflict and its management? How, and to what extent, does the way in which KDP operates affect its impacts? We examine reasons for variation by looking primarily at three variables: capacity at the district level, capacity at the village level, and program functionality.

That KDP varies in its impacts is not surprising for a number of reasons, some relating to the characteristics of Indonesian villages, others to the nature of the program itself. First, the villages in which we conducted research are vastly different. The differences between a village in a prosperous part of Ponorogo, East Java, and one in a remote corner of Manggarai, Flores, is about as large as could be imagined in Indonesia. Even within a given region, socioeconomic and informal institutional structures can vary greatly between villages in, say, Madura and those in Sikka, Flores. Distinct cultures exist at the local level as well. In such diverse climates, it is not surprising that the impacts of KDP differ from area to area. Indeed, our research design was explicitly set up to maximize contextual variation.

Second, local capacity also varies enormously. *Capacity* is an oft-used but ambiguous, abstract, and contested term because it is normatively loaded. It has a number of dimensions and it can be measured at different levels. Debates rage as to its most important determinants; different people emphasize, among other things, education and skills, access to financial resources, institutional quality, collective action, and social capital or cohesion.[1] There is debate about the extent to which capacity is an individual or collective attribute, with differential emphases on the agency and opportunity structures that help shape the freedoms that people have (Alsop and Heinsohn 2005). For some, it is a development input: local capacity is necessary to produce development outcomes such as economic growth; for others, it is a development outcome in itself (witness the explosion of capacity-building programs by development agencies of all types).[2] It is beyond the scope of this chapter to provide a detailed overview or critique of "capacity" as used in the development studies literature; for our present purposes, it is sufficient to note that different forms of local capacity clearly have the potential to affect the way KDP functions in different areas and the project's resulting impacts on local conflict and conflict management. In the analysis below, we consider what we regard as the two defining elements of local capacity— problem solving and collective action—at the district and the village levels. Given the extent to which KDP relies on local actors, it is not surprising that it functions in different ways in areas with different preexisting levels of capacity.

Third, the structure of KDP itself arguably contributes to variation in performance between areas. The program deliberately devolves decision making to the local level. Strict program rules determine, for example, meeting requirements, decision-making processes, disbursal of funds, and so on, but tremendous discretion exists at the local level for program staff and participants. Indeed, as we have already noted, KDP is a conscious attempt to use development projects as mechanisms to help villagers prioritize and resolve self-identified development problems (Guggenheim 2006). It is thus not surprising that program performance and impacts vary considerably at the local level.[3]

The three variables that we examine warrant a little explanation. We define *capacity* as the ability to engage in collective action and to solve shared problems.[4] We derived measures of capacity at the district and village levels.[5] We did so for the former by conducting interviews at the provincial level with government officials and with representatives of international and national NGOs, regional development experts, academics, and KDP staff. At the village level, the researchers ranked the villages where they conducted research about problem solving and collective action. Vignettes were used to ensure comparability across districts and provinces.[6] Villages were then categorized as having high, medium, or low capacity. Given that each of these is in a district with either high or low capacity, a given village will thus be of one of six different types—a low-capacity village in a high-capacity district, a medium-capacity village in a low-capacity district, a high-capacity village in a high-capacity district, and so on. We used this ranking of villages to tease out differences in the impacts of KDP between areas with different levels and kinds of capacity; it also allowed us to determine for a given dimension of impact whether the district or the village context matters more.

Second, we sought to see how program functionality affected program impact. In spite of vigilant oversight, KDP does not always function as intended. Sometimes elites control the program; sometimes a facilitator or program participant runs off with the money. Both of these situations obviously result in less than optimal program performance. But how does this affect the program's impact on conflict? For each dimension of impact, we examined the extent to which and the ways in which program functionality matters.[7]

KDP-Triggered Conflict and Local Context

In Chapter 4 we argued that KDP forums can trigger three common forms of conflict—in-built, malfunction, and interaction conflict—which seldom become violent. Among our survey informants, 46 percent in East Java and 19 percent in NTT reported that village-level forums triggered conflicts, whereas at the subdistrict level, reported rates were higher: 85 percent and 57 percent, respectively. But almost no respondents said that these conflicts turned violent.

The Effect of Local Capacity on KDP-Triggered Conflict

The Impact of District Capacity

Survey respondents in the districts with high conflict management capacity (Ponorogo and Sikka) were far more likely to report that KDP triggered conflict than those in the low-capacity districts (Pamekasan and Manggarai). This was particularly true for KDP meetings held at the village level, which triggered more conflict than did meetings at the subdistrict level. The difference was most marked in East Java (see figure 7.1). A clear difference between Pamekasan (low-capacity) and Ponorogo (high-capacity) districts was apparent. In NTT there was less variation between high- and low-capacity districts, and the higher reported rate in Sikka was a function of one subdistrict, namely, Paga.[8] This fits with reports of particular implementation problems in Paga:

> Delinquent loans have become a big problem, proving to hamper the performance of KDP and making it difficult for the program to reach its target, namely, improving the livelihood of the poor. According to me, it is a result of poor coordination at the district level. From a different perspective, the KDP process in the first year was weakly executed,

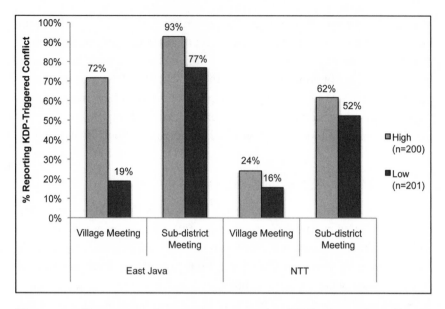

Figure 7.1   Percentage of respondents reporting KDP-triggered conflict, by district capacity.

Source: Key informant survey (KDP program sites only).

perhaps because it used a new pattern . . . a pattern for empowering the grassroots community. Everyone was shocked, most of all the beneficiaries. They were still infected with the ways of the previous period whereby infringements were considered normal. . . . Other weaknesses at the village level included poor management. Just imagine, our village heads are trying to manage just Rp. 10 million [US$1,000] in village aid and the administration half kills them. Then all of a sudden they are faced with tens or even hundreds of millions of rupiah. They are just so confused, even though they are being helped by a facilitator.

—SUBDISTRICT HEAD, PAGA, SIKKA

When the responses across both the provinces and the two levels of meetings types are combined, 63 percent of informants in the two high-capacity districts reported that a KDP forum had triggered conflict, compared to 44 percent in the low-capacity districts.

Why would conflict be more likely in districts with high capacity? Would we not think that KDP would be more likely to trigger disputes in areas lacking the capacity to deal with problems?

Two factors explain the higher reported rates in high-capacity districts. First, in some of the lower-capacity areas (in particular, Pamekasan, East Java), elites consciously prevented conflict from arising or from being reported if it did by not allowing KDP to operate as it is meant to. In the fieldwork we found examples of funds being distributed in equal proportions among villages without the required competition; KDP participants were not socialized properly, so elites faced little dissent when they captured the program. This conflict avoidance, although it limited tensions in the short run, could provide a basis for future conflict. The survey does not capture the subsequent effects of conflict avoidance strategies, but the qualitative fieldwork showed some of the risks.[9] As we discussed in Chapter 4, preventing competition can lead to other forms of conflict in the future or to the problems reemerging in other forms of grievances. Interaction conflict is more likely. Indeed, the lower level of reported KDP-related conflict in the low-capacity areas appears to be in part an indication of the program not working as intended.

The second pertinent factor concerns respondents' perceptions of what constitutes conflict. The fieldwork found than an important precondition for communities to effectively manage conflict is for them to first identify it. In areas where local capacity is greater—that is, where people are generally more able to deal with conflicts as they arise—there was a greater recognition of the problems. The presence of grievances that are expressed rather than repressed and are more frequently reported is not necessarily a negative thing; they may be more quickly resolved than those that fester below the surface and thus an indicator of an emerging public space within which to voice discontent. As implied above, we can consider high reported rates of *nonviolent* KDP-related conflict as a positive sign of good program operation.

The Impact of Village Capacity

The picture changes somewhat if village-level capacity is factored in. While KDP-triggered conflict is more likely (according to the respondents) in high-capacity districts, it is less frequently reported in high-capacity villages across all forms of district capacity (see figure 7.2). Subdistrict-level conflicts are more frequently reported than those at the village level; the former are captured in the district capacity measures, but village-level conflicts are not. It is not surprising that village capacity has little impact on the levels

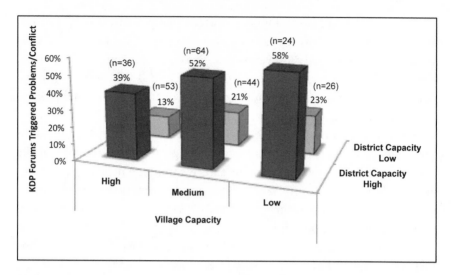

Figure 7.2   Relation of local capacity to whether KDP forums triggered problems/conflicts.

Source: Key informant survey (KDP program sites only).

of conflict at the subdistrict intervillage meetings.[10] When KDP-triggered conflict at the village level does occur, the data from the survey respondents demonstrates that it is more likely in the low-capacity villages across all levels of district capacity. More people reported that KDP triggered conflict in low- and medium-capacity villages (40 and 39 percent, respectively) than the high-capacity villages (24 percent).

Furthermore, when village-level KDP-triggered conflict occurs in districts that have high conflict management capacity, it most often occurs in low-capacity villages. In other words, district and village-level capacity appear to work in opposite directions when it comes to the likelihood that the program will trigger conflicts. As figure 7.2 shows, low-capacity villages in high-capacity districts are most likely to report that village-level KDP meetings triggered conflict (58 percent of respondents) across all regions. At the same time, the low-capacity villages in the low-capacity districts report the most KDP-triggered conflict within these districts (23 percent of respondents compared to 13 percent in high-capacity villages).

How do we explain this? In line with previous discussions and findings, this demonstrates that district-level capacity contributes to villagers' knowledge of their rights and KDP processes and the likelihood that they will recognize, respond to, and seek solutions for problems. But these problems are more likely in low-capacity villages, where people are less likely to understand the program (also adding to tensions), and where the likelihood that they have the capacity to manage the more difficult problems is lower. All these factors account for the interesting findings of opposing forces. District-level capacity appears to be more important than village capacity; the differences between high- and low-capacity districts are greater across all village capacity types than are the differences between villages within each district capacity type. This suggests that districts and villages interact with KDP in different ways. We discuss this further below.

Forms of KDP-Triggered Conflict and Forum and Facilitator Use

We have outlined the three different types of KDP-related conflict: in-built conflict (which relates to competition at various stages in the project cycle), program malfunction conflict (a product of not following project processes and rules as intended), and interaction conflicts (disputes indirectly caused by the program's interaction with existing tensions or power structures). Using evidence from the key informant survey, the following discussion demonstrates that local capacity (at the village or district level) has little effect on the extent to which KDP forums are used to address in-built conflict—they are used in all cases. It also has little effect on the likelihood that KDP processes will successfully resolve either in-built or malfunction conflicts when they are used. Yet local capacity does appear to have an impact on the likelihood that KDP processes (forums and facilitators) are used to address malfunction conflicts. As with the findings discussed above, district- and village-level capacity work in opposite directions. This time, it is the districts with lower conflict management capacity that are more likely to use the forums.

Forums

Local capacity has little effect on the use of KDP forums for in-built conflict. Rates of forum use for this type of conflict are high across areas with differing capacity; 79 percent of survey informants in both high- and low-capacity districts said that KDP forums were used to address in-built conflicts. At the village level, rates are also similar, the sole outlier being high-capacity villages in high-capacity districts, where use of forums is lower.[11] This could suggest either that high-capacity villages are more accustomed to dealing with the type of minor in-built problems generated by KDP and hence do not consider them conflicts or that they resolve such problems before they reach the forums or through other means. Evidence from the qualitative fieldwork and from other survey results suggests the former. One of the impacts of the program is that KDP-type processes and the social changes they bring about become more widely accepted. As we discuss below, these shifts are likely to be greater in high-capacity areas, which tend to be more receptive to change.

In contrast, local capacity appears to contribute to variations in reported levels of forum use for program malfunction conflict. In low-capacity districts, the use of KDP forums for addressing such conflicts is higher: 45 percent of informants said forums were used for this type of conflict in low-capacity districts in both provinces, and 23 percent reported the same for high-capacity districts. The one exception is the use of forums in high-capacity villages; here, the rates are similar across high- and low-capacity districts, suggesting that village capacity compensates for lack of district capacity and that forums are recognized as a means of resolving problems when district conflict management capacity in general is low (see figure 7.3).

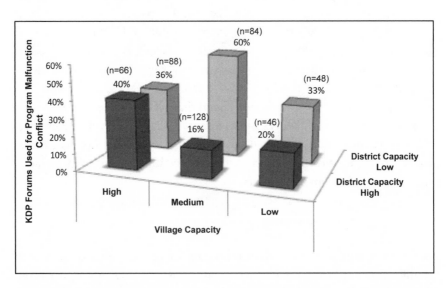

Figure 7.3   Relation of local capacity to use of KDP forums to resolve program malfunction conflict.

Source: Key informant survey (KDP program sites only).

Facilitators

Program facilitators are also more likely to be used to successfully address KDP problems in low-capacity districts than in high-capacity ones.[12] Sixty-four percent of respondents in the former said that they were successfully used; 43 percent in the latter said the same. Again, in the former, people resort to program mechanisms to seek to resolve problems. As before, we found that village-level capacity works in the opposite direction. High-capacity villages in low-capacity districts, where knowledge of the program is better but where ability to manage problems is lacking, were the most likely to use facilitators (68 percent); low-capacity villages in high-capacity districts were the least likely (33 percent).

In general, the higher reported rate of use of forums and facilitators in low-capacity areas is not surprising. The measure in the survey conflates two things: the incidence of conflict of a given type and the use of the forum to deal with it. Levels of more serious program malfunction conflict (which previous chapters have demonstrated is more problematic than other forms of project-related conflict) could be more frequent in districts with less ability to manage conflict. In all development programs, program malfunction conflicts are more likely to occur when socialization has been poor or where local elites have been resistant to sharing local decision-making responsibilities (see Chapter 4)—all frequent findings in the fieldwork in low-capacity districts. It may also be the case, however, that reported rates are higher because in low-capacity areas people have fewer avenues for redress than do higher-capacity areas. The fieldwork shows that both hypotheses have some explanatory power.

The Success of Forums and Facilitators in Managing KDP-Triggered Conflict

Reported rates of KDP-triggered conflict are higher in high-capacity districts. Conflicts related to in-built competition are equally likely to be addressed in KDP forums in high- and low-capacity districts. Conflicts related to malfunctions in the program are more likely to be addressed in forums in areas with little conflict management capacity and also successfully addressed in these areas by facilitators. But when KDP forums are used, regardless of the type of KDP problem or conflict, they are highly successful across areas with varying capacity. Where in-built conflicts are addressed in KDP forums, they are slightly more likely to be resolved in high-capacity districts than in low-capacity ones, but the difference is small, and resolution rates are uniformly high (98 percent versus 93 percent). Conversely, low-capacity districts report higher rates of resolution for malfunction conflicts (86 percent versus 71 percent). Despite these differences, all areas show extremely high levels of success. There are no clear patterns when we factor in village capacity, but the fieldwork in these areas demonstrated that in villages with lower conflict management capacity, the likelihood that facilitators or forums would actually be successful was also dependent on the extent to which they integrated informal leaders and mechanisms into the resolution process.[13]

The data thus show that variation between regions is greater in terms of the levels of use of forums and facilitators for addressing different types of problems than in terms of successful resolution. Levels of success, though they vary, are still high when we aggregate responses at the district level. But we need to consider the cause and seriousness of the problems in lower-capacity areas in order to account for the 30 percent (in high-capacity districts) and 14 percent (in low-capacity districts) of respondents who did not consider the program malfunction conflicts to be successfully resolved through KDP. The key informant survey data presented in Chapter 4 outline the way KDP forums and facilitators were often unable to resolve corruption cases or those in which the facilitator was the source of the problem at the village or subdistrict level.

Given that many respondents claimed that conflicts are successfully resolved once they are brought to KDP forums or facilitators, attention must focus on why people in some areas chose to bring malfunction conflicts to forums and why KDP facilitators get involved outside forums, whereas they do not do so in other areas. Gaining a better understanding of the criteria used by actors in different places to decide when a particular forum is appropriate or whether a facilitator should get involved helps in determining why there are different levels of use.

There are several reasons for this. The results support the conclusion that communities or elites within them assess the likelihood of successful resolution of a given type of problem through a particular dispute resolution forum or mechanism before opting for its use.[14] Both the qualitative fieldwork and other empirical research concerning dispute resolution in villages indicate that this kind of selection process occurs. Community leaders tend only to become involved in disputes that they feel they can ably resolve based on their experience or that will improve their standing within the community (World Bank 2008; McLaughlin and Perdana 2009).

Local norms also matter. In understanding how local capacity matters in different ways for in-built and malfunction problems and different ways of addressing them (in forums and by facilitators), it is instructive to distinguish between uses that are perceived as normal and those that are (or could be) considered "extra-ordinary" and "extra-ordinary plus." For example, the discussion of in-built tensions in KDP forums is considered by both program staff and participants as usual and normal, whereas their deployment for particularly sensitive intra-KDP problems (such as allegations of corruption or misappropriation of project funds by the village head or program staff) can be considered extra-ordinary.[15] The use of KDP personnel and mechanisms to address non-KDP problems (for example, disputes about property boundaries and problems generated by other development projects), on the other hand, can be seen as extra-ordinary-plus.

When survey respondents were asked why in-built problems were resolved in KDP forums, the two most popular responses were that there was no other place (East Java) or because it was the appropriate place (NTT). This did not vary across areas with differing local capacities. In contrast, the use of forums for complex malfunction conflicts (except those that involve unintentional problems of omission), such as those relating to corruption and the active intervention of facilitators in conflicts outside of KDP forums, are more unusual. Local capacity at both levels appears to influence the processes by which people identify and select KDP forums or facilitators to deal with such problems. These extra-ordinary uses are more common in low-capacity areas for a couple of reasons. First, the need is greater; levels of program malfunction conflict tend to be higher. Second, few other avenues exist for dealing with these problems; other actors, such as local government, may be less likely to intervene—indeed, in many cases they are implicated in the conflict. As we discuss below, the different interaction of local capacity with normal and extra-ordinary-plus uses of KDP forums and facilitators also helps explain their greater use for nonprogram conflicts in low-capacity areas.

Program Functionality and KDP-Triggered Conflict

Variation in the extent to which KDP functions as intended did not affect aggregate levels of KDP conflict in our research areas. Yet the ways in which the program functioned did affect the *types* of KDP-related conflict that were most likely to emerge. It is not surprising that more serious forms of conflict (related to program malfunctions and interaction with existing tensions) were more likely in areas where KDP did not work well. The quality of program functionality is thus of great importance, because where it is low, the forms of program-related conflict that erupt are far more likely to have negative consequences than the kinds that emerge where KDP works as intended, where conflict can often have positive impacts.

In Chapter 4 we demonstrated that three types of conflict are associated with participatory development projects such as KDP. The impacts of each form tend to be different. Conflict related to competition—a consequence of the principles of open decision making with insufficient resources available for all ideas and proposals to be funded—was, we argued, generally a positive phenomenon. As we saw in Chapter 6, it is by such competition that some of the cognitive and behavioral changes that can help improve conflict management capacity in the long run are generated. Rather, it was a lack of opportunity for open competition or competition without a level playing field that was more likely to lead to prolonged tensions or destructive conflict.

This was the case in Jenangan subdistrict in Ponorogo. As in Pademawu subdistrict in Pamekasan, it was decided (against program rules) that in the first year of KDP only five villages would be eligible for the program, the criteria being those which had been funded as part of a previous (different) development project. This caused villagers to protest the lack of competition in the first year, especially when they learned more about KDP rules in later years.[16]

Disputes related to competition were thus more likely in areas where the program functioned well. Where the program was not allowed to function as intended (with program rules subverted or money misappropriated) disputes of this type were less common. The incidence of micro-conflicts related to the competition embedded in the KDP system is, we have argued, a direct sign of good program functioning and an indirect indicator of positive spillover. Although this kind of development-related conflict is more common in cases where KDP works well, conflicts of this sort (directly or indirectly) in most cases have a net positive effect.

In contrast, program malfunction conflict, in which problems of omission (such as poor socialization and implementation) or problems of commission (such as corruption) lead to disputes, and interaction disputes—when projects interact with preexisting local tensions, power structures, and conflicts—tend to have negative impacts. Program dysfunctionality is at the root of both forms of conflict. As we explored in depth in Chapter 4, these conflicts tend to have negative impacts, both in terms of the seriousness of conflict that emerges and the difficulty of solving such problems.

Figure 7.4 shows schematically the different forms of project-related conflicts that are likely to occur in places where program functionality is good and where it is poor.

The Direct Impacts of KDP on Conflict Management Capacity and Local Context

Program forums and facilitators are infrequently used to deal with conflicts unrelated to the program. Thirteen percent of survey respondents in East Java and 20 percent in NTT said that non-KDP problems were addressed in KDP forums. Facilitators almost never address non-KDP conflicts outside of the forums.[17] (Because facilitator use for nonprogram conflicts is so low, we are unable to disaggregate by capacity level.)

		FORM OF IMPACT	
		Direct	*Indirect*
PROGRAM FUNCTIONALITY	*Good (+)*	Ia. Direct In-built competition	Ib. Indirect In-built competition
	Poor (–)	II. Program Malfunction	III. Interaction Conflict

Figure 7.4   Types of KDP-related conflict and program functionality

Use and Success of KDP Forums for Non-KDP Conflicts

Local capacity appears to influence whether KDP processes are utilized for extra-ordinary uses. As we discussed above, use of KDP forums for program malfunction issues is higher in low-capacity areas, with district capacity exerting a larger influence than village-level capacity because higher levels of the administrative hierarchy are required to address the more serious problems. A similar pattern is observable for extra-ordinary-plus uses, namely, addressing nonprogram conflicts in KDP forums. The most common such disputes relate to other development projects. In East Java, 36 percent of respondents who reported that KDP forums were used for non-KDP issues, and 58 percent in NTT, said they were used for conflicts related to development projects. Other kinds of conflict addressed included disputes between villagers, problems with thieves, and conflicts with other villages.

When the data are disaggregated at the district level, we see that low-capacity areas are consistently more likely to utilize KDP forums for non-KDP problems or conflicts, and the conflicts are also more likely to be successfully addressed there. The use of these forums is two and a half times more likely in low-capacity districts than in high-capacity ones (see table 7.1).

Closer examination of the data shows what is driving this difference. Whereas the use of KDP forums for addressing problems with other development projects was similar across districts with different capacities, nondevelopment issues (other conflicts within and between villages) increased the use of forums for non-KDP issues in the low-capacity districts.

This hints at the reason why such usage of KDP forums is greater in lower-capacity districts: in these areas, fewer institutions exist for effectively dealing with conflict. This finding is supported by the qualitative data

TABLE 7.1   LOCAL CAPACITY AND USE OF KDP FORUMS FOR NON-KDP CONFLICTS

District Capacity	Use (%)	Success (%)
High (n=118)	8.5	84.6
Low (n=110)	20.9	92.9

Source: Key informant survey (KDP program sites only).

presented in previous chapters. Indeed, in the low-capacity subdistricts, the main cited reasons for successful use of KDP forums related to a combination of appropriateness and necessity: the KDP forums and processes were viewed as being good for problem solving (in Lamba Leda subdistrict), as were the skills of the subdistrict facilitators (in Ruteng); more prosaically, in Cibal the lack of other options was cited. This is an important finding, especially when thinking about applying KDP-type development projects in high-conflict areas where capacity is low. It suggests that where the program works well and has a good reputation, and in areas where conflict mediation capacity is otherwise limited, KDP may be able to play a role in addressing certain kinds of conflict. In contrast to the findings for conflicts arising from program malfunctions, village capacity has little effect on the likelihood that conflicts unrelated to KDP will be addressed in program forums.[18]

The Different Impacts of District and Village Capacity

Table 7.2 summarizes the impacts of capacity at different levels on the variables discussed above. A number of points are clear. First, district capacity matters more than village capacity in determining program impacts. Second, for most variables, impacts are greater in low-capacity districts. Third, in many cases, district and village capacity work in opposite directions.

From these results it is clear that district capacity is more important in determining the effects of KDP than is capacity at the village level. The table shows that for five of the nine variables, village capacity had no or negligible effect, compared to only two variables for district capacity. Further, the difference in impact between low- and high-capacity districts is generally higher than the difference between low- and high-capacity villages.[19] This all suggests that KDP's effect on numerous dimensions of conflict and its management varies more between districts than between villages with different levels of capacity. In understanding why this is so, it is necessary to consider why greater effects are observed in low-capacity districts.

Program forums and facilitators are used more often for different forms of conflict (both those related and unrelated to KDP) and (as table 7.2 shows) are more successful in low-capacity districts.[20] The evidence points to the fact that forums and facilitators are used most where they are needed when problems arise. For problems unrelated to the program, the reasons

TABLE 7.2   IMPACTS OF DISTRICT AND VILLAGE CAPACITY ON CHANGE VARIABLES

	Form of capacity	
Variable	District capacity	Village capacity
Conflict level		
Level of KDP-triggered conflict	High capacity, larger impact	Low capacity, larger impact
Level of use of KDP mechanisms		
In-built conflict	No pattern or effect	No pattern or effect
Program malfunction conflict	Low capacity, larger impact	High capacity, larger impact[a]
Non-KDP conflict	Low capacity, larger impact	No pattern or effect
Facilitators using outside forums	Low capacity, larger impact	High capacity, larger impact
Level of success when KDP mechanisms are used		
In-built conflict	No pattern or effect	No pattern or effect
Program malfunction conflict	Low capacity, larger impact	No pattern or effect
Non-KDP conflict	Low capacity, larger impact	No pattern or effect
Success of facilitators	Low capacity, larger impact	High capacity, larger impact

[a] Only in high-capacity districts.

are clear: in areas with low capacity, fewer effective institutions and mechanisms exist to deal with problems and conflicts (as we saw in the examples provided in Chapter 4).

It is not surprising that, for these types of conflict, district capacity matters more than village capacity. The newspaper data showed that levels and forms of conflict tend to vary more at the district level than at the provincial, subdistrict, or village level.[21] Conflict is concentrated in particular districts and not in others. The reasons for this are cultural and structural (Barron and Sharpe 2005), with both factors being shaped by the existing institutions in an area. Many important institutions, formal and informal, at the district level contribute to resolving larger-scale conflicts. As we noted above, the district now has tremendous policymaking discretion, far more so than at lower levels or at the provincial level (McCarthy 2004).[22] Local elites also tend to be most powerful and cohesive in district capitals (Barron, Nathan, and Welsh 2005).

The research also shows that most problems that occur at the village level can be addressed effectively if the scale of the problem is limited to the village. It is only the larger problems and conflicts—such as those between parties from different villages—that tend to escalate, in large part because of a lack of effective intervillage mediation mechanisms. Institutions and actors at the district level structure village-level norms pertaining to government administration and decision making. There is less variation in demand for new mediating institutions between villages in districts with similar levels of capacity than between villages in districts with differing capacity. For problems related to KDP, use of forums and facilitators is also greater in low-capacity areas. This, as we argued above, relates to the increased likelihood of program malfunction conflicts in districts with low capacity and the nature of the problems, which require higher levels of authority and intervention for resolution.

Village-level capacity, however, is not irrelevant. Indeed, the data show that whereas district-level capacity largely determines the need for KDP forums and facilitators to aid in conflict resolution, village capacity has an impact on the likelihood that they will be used, given a certain level of need. Some capacity is required at the village level in order for KDP mechanisms to be used in nonsimple ways, such as dealing with program malfunction conflict. Local leaders in low-capacity villages may be less supportive of the use of institutions that they do not fully control for problem resolution.

Indeed, in places such as Pamekasan, a low-capacity district in East Java, many village elites saw KDP as a threat to their authority and hence undermined its use. Only in villages with higher capacity (such as Padellegan or Sumedangan) was the program able to operate effectively, with the community involved in the planning process. As one member of Golkar (the governing party under Suharto) in Pamekasan put it, "In my opinion, the KDP process is the only program that involves the community. From the planning process to the implementation, each component is involved from the beginning. This is different from P3DT [Infrastructure Development Program for Less-Developed Villages], where the community is not involved in the processes."

The evidence suggests that local capacity does matter in determining the use of KDP for different types of problems and conflicts. Use depends in large part on the need, and this in turn depends on the presence or absence of existing institutions. Yet even in areas where need is great, a minimal level of capacity is required in order for the program to fill the gap. Thus, while local capacity may be more important in determining usage, attention should still focus on building village-level capacity.

Program Functionality and the Direct Impacts of KDP

Programs forums and facilitators are far less likely to be used to address conflicts not related to KDP in areas where the program is not functioning well. The use of such resources for non–project-related conflict resolution is rare and ad hoc. They were most likely to be used for this purpose when either facilitators or other program staff took the initiative to intervene in such disputes or where the parties to the conflict or the community more broadly took the dispute to KDP staff or meetings. For a number of reasons, both scenarios are much less likely in places where KDP is not implemented well.

First, KDP facilitators and staff are much less likely to agree to use the program's forums for conflict resolution when program performance is poor. In such cases, they may (rationally) feel that the program is already overwhelmed by internal problems and hence be reluctant to take on extra tasks that are not prescribed within the project's operational guidelines. In general, poor program implementation is the result of weak performance by local facilitators and staff. We found, time and again, that the best facilitators were those who exercised autonomy and creativity to deal with the numerous issues that arise during the project cycle. The best facilitators know how to apply the spirit of KDP rules rather than just blindly implementing the letter of the law; they are able to ascertain when extra-ordinary and nonprescribed uses of KDP mechanisms, such as dealing with nonprogram disputes, are suitable. Weaker facilitators are less likely to be able or willing to exercise such discretion. As a result, they may be less keen on using the KDP forums for conflict resolution, even in lower-capacity areas where there may be a real need and demand for it.

Second, we found that people were less likely to take problems to KDP forums or staff when they did not trust their local facilitators. As we discussed in Chapter 4, mediators must have both institutional and personal legitimacy if they are to be effective. Where the public views either the program or particular staff as tainted, they are much less likely to bring non-project-related problems to project forums. In places such as Lamba Leda in Manggarai, where a subdistrict facilitator ran off with US$9,000, trust in KDP diminished quickly. It is hardly surprising that villagers do not trust the program or see it as an appropriate avenue for dealing with nonproject problems when KDP staff have proved themselves incapable of administering the project in a fair and impartial way.[23]

Related to the second reason is the third: people tend to bring their problems to venues where they feel resolution is most likely. This explains the high success rate of KDP forums and facilitators for all types of problems that are brought to them. In areas where project performance is poor, it is unsurprising that people feel that resolution of a given problem is not likely. They are less likely to bring the problem forward in the first place.

The program is unlikely to have any positive direct effects on the resolution of local conflicts if the program does not function as intended, and this is true in high- and low-capacity areas. If KDP forums or facilitators are to be used for conflict resolution, a first-order task is thus ensuring that the program functions well.

Indirect Impacts and Local Context

Whereas the direct impacts of KDP on conflict management tend to be more noticeable in low-capacity districts, the opposite holds for indirect impacts. In Chapter 6 we examined the effect of KDP on three dimensions of social change: group relations, behavioral change, and normative change. The evidence shows that local capacity is not particularly important in determining changes in relations between groups. For most dimensions of behavioral and normative change, however, impacts are more noticeable in high-capacity areas. This suggests that although KDP stimulates processes of positive change, it does not cause them. Rather, the program is a catalyst that has a multiplier effect on processes of social change; where these are already under way, indirect program impacts are likely to be greater.

Group Relations

The survey results and qualitative fieldwork indicate that KDP strengthens relations between different identity groups. Where a given identity cleavage such as ethnicity, religion, class, or political affiliation is salient, KDP contributes to improved relations. The data from Chapter 6 note on average a 17 percent greater likelihood of improved group relations in program sites compared to comparison locations. The survey data show little correlation, however, between the preexisting capacity in an area and the observed extent of change in group relations. There is considerable variation, yet no patterns emerge. For example, improvements in relations between the rich and poor are greater in high-capacity districts for both program and comparison sites, most likely because of trends in democratization across the board. At the same time, the survey data show greater change in relations between religious groups in low-capacity districts. With regard to ethnicity in NTT, high-capacity districts in KDP sites report little change; in comparison sites the opposite is true, with low-capacity areas experiencing greater change. Similarly, there are no clear trends when we factor in village capacity.[24]

That local capacity has little effect on group relations is at first surprising. One might think that the presence of capacity as we measured it—that is, where problem solving and collective action are strong—would be reflected in positive changes in group relations. Yet two reasons present themselves as to why this might not be the case. First, the survey question is measuring *change* in group relations over a given period rather than the strength of intergroup relations at a given point. Presumably, capacity is to a large extent endogenous, that is, deeply embedded in local social structures and cultural practices, and as such is hard to change. Thus in high-capacity areas, group relations may have been strong from the outset, and thus reported rates of change in group relations may be smaller than in areas where such capacity did not exist in the first place.

Second, in order for there to be a change in a given type of group relation (ethnic, religious, and so on), there needs to be a relevant initial cleavage of that type. In Chapter 6 we discussed changes in ethnic and religious relations only in Flores; these cleavages are not important markers of identity in East Java. Variation in the presence of a given cleavage exists not only between provinces but between districts and, indeed, between villages in the same district. Some of our villages in Flores, for example, have more prominent ethnic cleavages than others; in East Java, the rich-poor divide is greater in some locations than others. There is no clear correlation between variation in the presence and strength of identity cleavages and local capacity.

As Anderson (1991) and others have reasoned, identity formulation and transformation are contingent on demographic, political, economic,

cultural, policy, and legislative environments at multiple levels and grievances concerning changes in these environments.[25] Across the cases, we
found three major factors relevant to the construction, maintenance, and
salience of group difference: (a) history as institutional legacy and consolidation, (b) history as the invocation and re-imagining of the group's
biographical narrative, and (c) appeals to present interests and future
aspirations to sustain group size and vibrancy.[26] Local capacity will matter
in shaping these factors. For example, in an area with a history of collective
problem solving, it is more unlikely that leaders will appeal to narrow interests that emphasize the difference between one group and another. These
factors are relevant, but demographic factors such as the heterogeneity of a
given population are equally so. The variation between districts and villages
in the degree of change in group relations is explained more by the different
demographic characteristics and the different histories of our research
locations than by capacity itself.

Behavioral Change

Whereas the data show no clear link between preexisting local
capacity and changes in group relations, the same is not true for behavioral
changes. Earlier, we examined two dimensions of behavioral change: participation and decision making. Disaggregated at the district level, levels of
participation improved to a greater extent in low-capacity areas. With
respect to decision making, in contrast, greater improvements were noted in
high-capacity districts.

In Chapter 6 we showed that villages which have participated in KDP
showed greater increases in the number of groups coming to non-KDP
village meetings than did those that had not been in the program, and that
increasing numbers of groups came as the program stayed in an area for
longer periods of time. If we compare program and matched comparison
sites, it seems that the impact is concentrated heavily in low-capacity
districts (see figure 7.5). The rates of positive change were almost the same
for program and comparison areas in high-capacity districts, but positive
change was 25 percent more likely to be reported in villages in low-capacity
districts that have been in KDP than in those that have not.[27]

In contrast, the impact of the program on local decision making appears
to be larger in high-capacity districts. Survey respondents were asked
whether decision making had become more democratic since KDP had

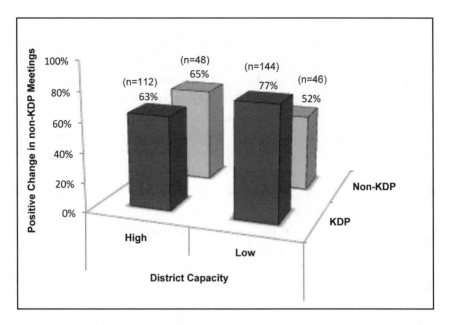

Figure 7.5   Local capacity and positive change in participation in non-KDP meetings.

Source: Key informant survey (KDP program and comparison sites).

arrived (or for an equivalent amount of time for comparison locations). Improvements in democratic decision making were greater in KDP areas than in non-KDP areas. Figure 7.6 shows that in KDP areas, decision making is likely to have become more democratic in high-capacity districts. Further, in low-capacity districts, village capacity is important: only 35 percent of informants living in low-capacity villages in low-capacity districts noted positive change, compared to 72 percent of respondents in high-capacity villages in low-capacity districts. This suggests that a certain level of local capacity is necessary for decision making to become more democratic, but that when this capacity exists, KDP is able to complement it.

If we compare program and comparison areas, it is clear that, at least at the margin, KDP can help make decision making more democratic in low-capacity areas. As figure 7.7 shows, in low-capacity districts, 24 percent more people in KDP districts reported that decision making is becoming more democratic than in non-KDP areas. Among KDP locations, residents in low-capacity districts are 16 percent more likely to report improvements in decision making than their counterparts in high-capacity locations.

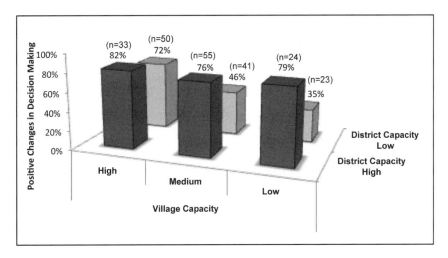

Figure 7.6   Local capacity and positive changes in decision making.

Source: Key informant survey (KDP programs sites).

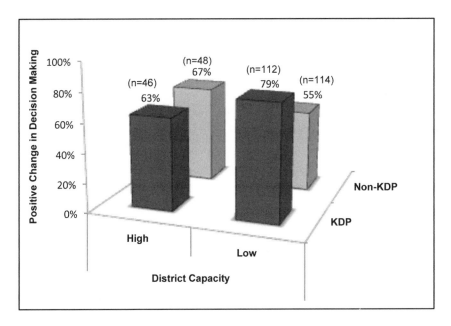

Figure 7.7   Local capacity and positive change in decision making, KDP sites and comparison sites.

Source: Key informant survey (KDP program and comparison sites).

Thus local capacity has differential effects on the likelihood that more groups will participate in village meetings and on the probability that decision making will become more democratic. This can be explained by the different levels of discretion and control that local elites have over the two variables. The qualitative fieldwork showed that in the low-capacity districts (Pamekasan and Manggarai), local elites tended to protect more closely their monopoly on the exercise of political power. This was also true at the village level. In low-capacity areas, elites tend to prefer participation to be limited to a closed group of people. Decision making also tends to be more authoritarian. In high-capacity villages, however, the villages had developed the strength to break free of district-wide cultures of patronage, as was the case in Padellegan and Sumedangan villages in the low-capacity district of Pamekasan. The program is running quite smoothly in these areas, with higher levels of participation by women, fewer complaints of lack of transparency or information, and better competition than in the other research villages in the district.

It is relatively easy for elites to control decision-making processes in meetings. Given their dominant role in village life, they can fairly readily hijack the agenda and dictate the direction of meetings. It is thus not surprising that it is only in areas with higher capacity (at the district and village level) that KDP has an effect. In these areas elites tend to be more open to having inclusive decision-making processes, and thus the program is allowed to function as intended.

In contrast, local elites have much less control over participation in meetings. The research showed that the primary factor driving low attendance in village meetings was that people simply were not invited. A separate study found that distributing formal invitations to KDP meetings more widely increased participation in KDP accountability meetings by 35 percent and non-elite attendance by 80 percent (Olken 2007). If KDP facilitators perform well, therefore, it is relatively easy to improve participation in meetings, at least compared to changing decision-making patterns within them. The behavior of elites thus matters less in determining patterns of participation than methods of decision making which ensure that marginalized groups actually secure a serious role in decisions affecting their welfare (see Gibson and Woolcock 2008).

Why would increases in the participation of marginalized groups be greater in low-capacity areas? Two major reasons emerged from the qualitative fieldwork. First, the starting point is lower: fewer groups tend to participate in village-level decision making, hence there is more room for improvement; improvements in participation are notable to a greater extent in program and nonprogram low-capacity areas. Second, KDP compensates to some extent for the lack of capacity in low-capacity areas. In high-capacity areas, processes of political and social change have already altered the nature of participation in village-level meetings. In low-capacity areas, where this has not occurred, KDP—when it functions well—can help stimulate broad-based participation.

Changes in Norms

We measured two dimensions of normative change: village problem-solving and village conflict resolution. Figures 7.8 and 7.9 show that for both, capacity matters. Levels of improvement consistently are considerably higher in high-capacity districts. A similar but less marked pattern is visible at the village level: improvements in villages in KDP are greater in high-capacity ones than in medium- and low-capacity ones. But the effects of village capacity are almost entirely confined to those in low-capacity districts.

The picture becomes clearer when we compare KDP locations with the matched comparison sites. As figures 7.10 and 7.11 demonstrate, only in

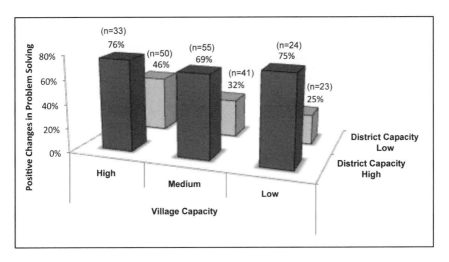

Figure 7.8   Local capacity and positive changes in problem solving.

Source: Key informant survey (KDP program sites only).

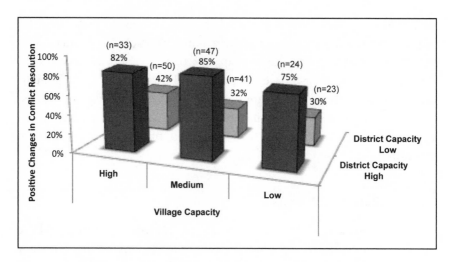

Figure 7.9   Local capacity and positive changes in conflict resolution.

Source: Key informant survey (KDP program sites only).

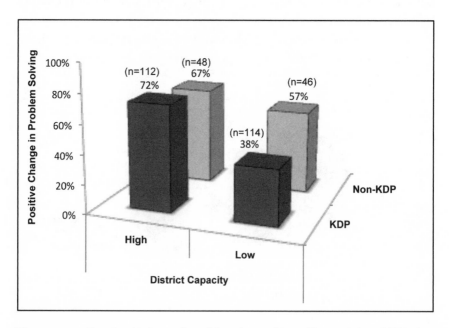

Figure 7.10   Local capacity and positive change in problem solving, KDP sites and comparison sites.

Source: Key informant survey (KDP program and comparison sites).

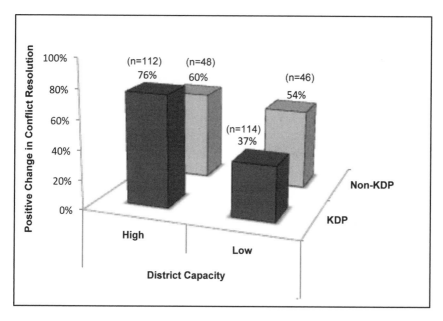

Figure 7.11   Local capacity and positive change in conflict resolution.
Source: Key informant survey (KDP program and comparison sites).

high-capacity areas does KDP appear to be having an impact with respect to creating positive changes in problem-solving capacities. Indeed, in low-capacity districts, reported improvements in the indicators of change in norms are *lower* in KDP areas than in non-KDP ones.

Why might this be? One explanation is that KDP's resources fuel existing tensions between village elites and that in low-capacity environments, program participants, processes, and facilitators are unable to stem these tensions, frustrating villagers and leading them to report falling levels of problem-solving capacity. Alternatively, it may be that newly empowered KDP participants in low-capacity villages are both presenting fresh challenges to prevailing power structures and expecting more of their leaders, in the process eliciting resistance from village elites; this manifests itself as heightened tensions and thus perceptions that problem-solving capacity is falling. It is hard to distinguish empirically between the relative merits of these possibilities, but both find support elsewhere in our data (as reported in Chapters 4 and 6, respectively). Either way, these findings should not be interpreted as arguments for *not* introducing KDP-type development projects into environments of moderate conflict (or low capacity); rather, they should be read as (a) a serious caution against the belief that community-driven development projects, merely by virtue of being participatory, will help foster better conflict resolution skills and (b) evidence for the importance of understanding local social structures and the ways development projects interact with them, in order to assess overall project efficacy.

This evidence clearly indicates that KDP's ability to bring about positive changes in norms of decision making is contingent on existing capacity, thus further strengthening the conclusion that the program can tap into existing processes of change but is less able to generate that momentum single-handedly.

Program Functionality and Indirect KDP Impacts

The program is unlikely to have positive indirect impacts on conflict management in areas where program performance is poor. Whenever there are significant levels of elite capture of KDP processes, corruption of the program, or excessive intervention by external actors, the effectiveness of KDP as a stand-alone program is reduced, as is its potential for spilling over into enhanced conflict resolution, institutional strengthening, and democratization.

We have discussed the way in which program malfunction conflicts could be caused by either problems of omission (poor socialization, weak implementation) or problems of commission (deviations from program rules, corruption). Both forms of program dysfunctionality affect the likelihood that the program will have positive indirect spillovers. Poor socialization limits the impacts of KDP on group relations and on behavioral and normative change. The reasons for this, not surprisingly, are that it is impossible for villagers to engage in new routines of behavior (such as taking up new opportunities for participation and changing the way collective decision making should take place) if they are not properly told that these new opportunities exist and if they do not see practical examples of them. The New Order state sent out very clear signals about the role that ordinary villagers should play in economic development—namely, that of passive beneficiaries rather than active participants. Strong hierarchical structures limited the chances for villagers to substantively engage in decision making outside a clearly bounded realm of local activities where *gotong royong* (collective action) was encouraged (see Rao 2008). In the program and the comparison villages in our study, we found that the discourse of participation that accompanied the fall of Suharto and the electoral democratization of Indonesia was strong but did not always translate into changes in behavior. Norms are sticky; changes in patterns of behavior normally lag behind changes in rule systems (North 1990; Ellickson 1991). Many Indonesian villages remain quasi-feudal, with strong expectations as to who can appropriately participate in different realms of village life.

Much of KDP's power lies in its capacity to provide a readily visible example of how local decision making can be done differently. Where people do not receive a clear signal that KDP really is different, the program will not have any impact on modes of participation or decision making. Without a strong and active public information campaign, it is unlikely that the program will change existing norms. The indirect impacts of KDP do not come naturally and automatically; they require ongoing efforts from program facilitators and staff to show that the new discourse can actually translate into doing things differently (and better) at the village level. Such efforts are the very essence of democratization.

If problems of omission limit the indirect impacts of KDP, problems of commission are likely to have a bigger effect. Impacts are limited when elites capture the project; clearly in such cases there are fewer opportunities for participation by ordinary villagers, and hence changes in participation and decision making are less likely. Likewise, where there are inadequate opportunities for real participation, group relations are less likely to improve because KDP forums may not be places where people from different (conflicting) identity groups can come together for joint decision making. Poor targeting, which can stem from biases in decision-making processes, will likely reduce the incentive for active involvement by groups that lose out, making improvements in participation and group relations less likely. Said one KDP group in Manggarai: "The KDP funds were meant to help the poor, but it was the rich people who received them. This is because they are revolving funds and they weren't prepared to take the chance of funds not being repaid. The poor people were afraid."

Corruption is also likely to have a significantly negative effect on degrees of indirect impact. We cannot state strongly enough that KDP's impact comes largely from the precedent it sets in visible and visceral ways. In villages where KDP was working well, meetings really were open to all, and decision-making processes were fully democratic, indirect spillover effects on broader village decision making were observed. When people see this in action, almost without exception they embrace it and push for these changes in other aspects of village life. But in cases were nothing seems to have changed, for example, where project money was stolen, cynicism only increases. This, in turn, neuters opportunities for noticeable social and political change, because significant reform is always predicated not only on demand from the bottom but also the belief that such reform is attainable (Appadurai 2004).

Summary

Although it is important to recognize the institutional imperatives for statements regarding the aggregate impact of development projects—at the end of the day, governments need to know why they should invest finite resources in particular strategies to reduce poverty—it is also important to "look beyond averages" (Ravallion 2001) and explore the sources of variation in project performance.[28] Such variation is inevitably associated with development initiatives, especially those with a strong social participatory component, since such initiatives rely not on a single homogenous technology (for example, textbooks or immunization) but the far more heterogeneous skills and motivation of people, individually and collectively. Understanding this variation in the performance of social development projects is vital not only for presenting an honest and accurate account of project impact but also for identifying key organizational features (in KDP's case, the forums and facilitators) and contextual junctures (district and village capacities) in the project's life cycle that may help managers and participants alike improve the project's overall quality.

Figure 7.12 summarizes the results reported in this chapter and, indeed, many of the key findings of the study as a whole.[29] It shows how both the strength and direction of each form of impact (direct and indirect) of KDP on conflict management is contingent on program functioning and the contexts in which it works. Each of the boxes is filled in with a relative impact score: the minus sign (–) denotes a negative program effect, the plus sign (+) denotes a positive effect, and a zero (o) demonstrates no impact. For both negatives and positives, the number of plus or minus signs demonstrates the strength of impact (hence +++ shows a greater positive impact than +).

A number of key messages emerge. First, and most broadly, it is hard to discern a pure impact on local conflict; that is, KDP's programmatic impact

	Type of Impact	Context Capacity			
		Low		High	
		Program Functionality		Program Functionality	
		Low	High	Low	High
Direct	Forums (places)	– –	+ +	– *	o
	Facilitators (people)	o	o	o	o
Indirect	Group Relations	o	+ +	+	+ + +
	Behavioral (participation)	o	+ + +	o	+
	Behavioral (decision making)	o	+	+	+ + +
	Normative	o	+	o	+ + +

Figure 7.12 The impacts of KDP on conflict management in different environments.

* Though we noted higher rates of KDP-triggered conflict in high-capacity areas, such conflict is much less likely to escalate or turn violent. Hence negative impacts are greater in low-capacity areas, where program functionality is poor.

is inseparable from the nature of the social context and the extent to which it is effectively implemented. In low-capacity environments where KDP is poorly implemented (as a result of, say, inadequate socialization of participants or weak enforcement of program rules), it can exacerbate local conflict by providing a new resource over which elites compete. A well-implemented program in a low-capacity environment can, however, produce positive development outcomes and enhance conflict management capacity.

Second, capacity operates at multiple levels and can work in multiple— sometimes opposing—directions, depending on the form of impact we are assessing. The use and success of KDP mechanisms for addressing conflicts stemming from the program, for example, varies considerably depending on specific interactions between implementation effectiveness and district and village capacity, with district capacity often playing the primary role. Where conflict stems from KDP malfunction, for example, lower district capacity increases the use of KDP forums and facilitators, whereas forums have little strength in lower-capacity villages. Conversely, local capacity has little effect on the use of KDP forums for in-built issues.

Third, whether KDP is working well is more important than the context in determining the level and direction of impact (although, of course, the two are often related). Where program functionality is poor, hardly any positive spillover effects are observed, and only marginal positive impacts on group relations and on decision making. In low- and high-capacity areas, getting the program working greatly enhances the positive impacts the program can have on both conflict management and development outcomes.

Fourth, and related, where the program does not work as intended, not only are positive effects limited, but there is also a chance that the program will have negative impacts. As we have discussed, KDP forums can trigger conflicts or exacerbate existing ones when program functionality is poor. Given that this is more likely to be the case in low-capacity areas, particular attention and resources should be directed toward improving KDP performance in areas with low capacity.

Fifth, the impacts of KDP on constructive conflict management are primarily indirect. Program forums and facilitators are rarely called on to address non-KDP problems except as a last resort; for the most part, the program generates positive impacts indirectly by changing group relations (bringing diverse groups together), enhancing negotiation skills (the capacities of marginalized groups to engage in public debate), and altering perceptions and expectations (enhancing these groups' "capacity to aspire" [Appadurai 2004] and the new standards they require of public officials and local leaders). There is nonetheless important variation in these outcomes. Local capacity at the village or the district level seems to have little effect on whether KDP forums are used to address in-built conflict and little effect on the likelihood that KDP processes will successfully resolve either in-built or malfunction conflicts when they are used. Yet local capacity does appear to have an impact on the likelihood that program forums or facilitators will be used to address KDP malfunction conflicts.

Sixth, KDP does not displace existing forums for local dispute resolution; in high-capacity environments it can serve as a valuable complement, strengthening already well-functioning institutions, while in low-capacity environments it can provide a positive alternative to or substitute for absent, captured, or dysfunctional forums. The marginal impacts of the program when it functions well are higher in low-capacity areas because KDP forums must take on a wider range of tasks, although a minimal level of capacity is needed to provide a basic foundation on which to build. On the other hand, indirect impacts are greater in high-capacity areas, where KDP can enhance and act as a catalyst to existing processes of political and social change.

PART III

Applications, Implications, Invocations

CHAPTER 8

Contesting Development
Policies and Projects as if Social Theory Mattered

This book has focused on the local-level dynamics of social change and conflict that are part of the larger processes of development. These dynamics are accentuated by, and can often be most clearly observed by studying, initiatives such as development projects that explicitly seek to intensify the scale and pace of those processes, often for targeted groups (such as the poor). In this sense, development is "history in a hurry." This book has explored these processes through an examination of the conflict-development nexus in Indonesia, in particular, via a detailed examination of the Kecamatan Development Program, a project designed largely on the basis of social theory and research. KDP's overall effectiveness, however, is less a product of applied social theory per se than a careful matching of a pair of development goals—providing resources to vulnerable groups during and after an economic crisis, and building local-level governance institutions—with a solution (KDP) based on an appropriate *combination* of principles and evidence from different social scientific disciplines. We contend that the design, implementation, and assessment of development projects of all kinds would benefit from access to broader stocks of accumulated knowledge in the social sciences, not only the forms that happen to be located within economics, the field's dominant social scientific discipline. Put most simply, diversity of ideas and inputs is as important for generating high-quality context-specific development policies and projects as it is in other fields of collective human endeavor (see Page 2007). Harnessing such diversity is even more important for development problems, such as the reform of local governance and legal institutions, for which there is no single (technical) answer.

The program is a product of, among other things, many strands of theory from across the social sciences. From economics comes the notion of taking incentives seriously; competition is used to elicit and select high-quality proposals, and to overcome pervasive information asymmetries between the knowledge of villagers and program officials regarding local development priorities. But it is also infused, unlike most large-scale development projects, with an explicit dose of social theory and research. From anthropology it takes the importance of context, providing general administrative procedures and principles that can nonetheless be adapted to idiosyncratic local circumstances. From political science comes its emphasis on the centrality of clear and enforceable rules for ensuring program coherence, managing conflicting interests, and mitigating some of the inequities of power among different stakeholders. And sociology contributes the recognition that both progressive social change (for example, successfully empowering women, the poor, and other marginalized groups) and program failure (such as corruption) are likely to generate conflict, which in turn requires constructive, legitimate, and accessible mechanisms for redress. Our analysis has shown not only how all of these component elements come together in KDP but also how they inform and complement each other.

How might development policy and practice in other countries (and within Indonesia) be different if ideas from social theory and research had greater influence? Ideas and evidence are, of course, only two of the many factors that come to shape the content and efficacy of policy in any country, and the very diversity of social theory itself means that there is hardly a single policy message or modality of inquiry to call upon.[1] But to the extent that ideas frame the contours of what is thinkable, say-able, and do-able in any field of endeavor and in turn shape the criteria against which knowledge claims are assessed, we believe that there is merit in outlining some of the major themes and distinctive knowledge claims to which social theory points. The argument for taking social theory more seriously in development policy is, at a minimum, simply pragmatic—it has the potential to inform better strategy and practice with respect to existing agendas. At best, however, it can help us reimagine development assistance and engage more constructively, justly, and equitably with deeply complex issues such as governance, building the rule of law, and managing conflict that are now central to the development agenda but that are qualitatively different—as development problems—from roads, hyperinflation, and epidemics.[2] That is to say, they are different from the *types* of problems (important as they are) and *types* of responses (as effective as some of them have been) that have dominated our conceptions of how to think about development problems and solutions in general, and around which most of the organizational apparatus in international development has been assembled in the past sixty years.

Although KDP has inevitably drawn criticism and should continue to welcome constructive feedback, by any administrative, political, or economic criteria it is hard to argue that it has not been spectacularly successful.[3] At the Government of Indonesia's request, it has grown from a pilot operation to a fully national (and government-funded) program, a reflection of its broad popularity. It has mobilized and dispersed huge sums of money in a relatively short timeframe, generating high positive economic rates of return in its own right (and greater than those of many comparable projects) with a minimum amount of corruption. Within the World Bank it is regarded as a flagship project that has regularly featured in high-profile international gatherings.[4] And, as we hope we have shown in this book, it is also successful when assessed against a different set of criteria, metrics we think are vital but too often ignored: its capacity to manage conflict, to facilitate local democratic processes of deliberation, and to empower otherwise marginalized groups.

The program is a relatively rare embodiment of four factors: (a) good prior research to better ascertain the problems, the options, and the contexts into which any of them would be delivered; (b) a willingness and ability on the part of the project's leadership team to pragmatically combine diverse strands of theory and evidence and to give them sustained traction within large bureaucratic structures (both the Indonesian government and the World Bank); (c) a deep commitment to incorporating effective feedback and learning mechanisms, especially during its early implementation and scale-up phases but continuing to this day in the form of major investments in evaluations of all kinds—monitoring mechanisms, supervision missions, and long-term process studies—the better to promote operational refinements and to understand in real time how the contexts (at multiple levels) in which it operates are evolving; and (d) good fortune—coming to organizational fruition at a time of critical importance (that is, in the midst of a major economic crisis) and when the policy response, for political reasons, needed to be both very different from past responses and credible. At least the first three of these conditions might be more generally replicable elsewhere. To the extent that the ideas and evidence from economics are more than abundantly represented in contemporary development debates, building upon our earlier analysis in this chapter we consider some of the ideas and evidence that the noneconomic social sciences could (and should) contribute to the design, implementation, and assessment of development interventions.

Development as Problem Solving

Before outlining some of these themes, however, it bears repeating that, at the end of the day, KDP lives because it works.[5] That is, its traction and credibility with Indonesian government officials, villagers, and World Bank senior management is a product not of compelling social theory per se but of its capacity to move large amounts of money, to function in difficult and diverse environments, to remain relatively free of corruption and violence, and to provide resources that meet local demands via allocation mechanisms that villagers seem to value (particularly their involvement in decision making). If it could not do any of these things—if it could only absorb and disburse small sums of money, could only function in selected settings, were plagued with administrative problems, encountered wide-spread resistance from villagers, or could not contain the tensions which it triggered—no amount of deft salesmanship or tight conceptual reasoning on the part of its architects would give it a chance of success.

But projects are not born successful (or unsuccessful); they become so over time and for many different reasons in different places. Although KDP's initial success begat further expansion in a virtuous cycle of learning, adaptation, and refinement, and therein vindicated (ex post) the decisions of its architects to base a policy response to a major economic and political crisis on social research, this book has shown that contextual and broader institutional factors—that is, factors beyond the content and scope of KDP—have a major bearing on the results. Even if we believe that the program's "local average treatment effect" (Imbens and Angrist 1994) is net positive, the standard deviation is not only large but is a product of factors beyond its technical content. These include variations in context effects at multiple levels (from the village to the district to the region—what we might collectively call, following Briggs [2008], "civic capacity") and wide varia-tion (actual and potential) in the effectiveness of implementation, not least because extensive face-to-face interaction between different people (facili-tators and villagers) is so central to KDP's delivery mechanism.[6] It is almost impossible, therefore, to identify a pure KDP effect and thus make broader claims about its likely efficacy in other countries.[7] This does not mean that the program should not have to formally document its efficacy and compete for resources in a portfolio that includes other worthy (but easier to assess) projects; it does mean that the tone and terms of debate surrounding project design and evaluation have to change. The use of mixed methods and diverse forms of social scientific theory are required in order to engage sensibly in these debates.

We contend that, beyond the methodological challenges, much of the lack of success that is too often associated with development projects more broadly stems from a fundamental mismatch between the type of problem encountered (as articulated by development experts) and the type of solutions invoked in response to it. In the worst instances, development agencies become peddlers of solutions, possessing hammers (because they "work") and thus seeing nails, rather than co-producers (with governments, firms, and citizens) of problem-solving mechanisms (cf. Rondinelli 1993)— that is, ways of jointly crafting responses to policy problems that obtain a coherent alignment between types of problems (correctly specified) and responses that are technically sound, politically supportable, and administratively implementable. This matters because it is often not apparent, especially to outsiders, exactly what the problems are (beyond broad categories), what the crafting of particular solutions might entail, and what obstacles (observed and unobserved) might stand in the way of their realization. Social theory can be useful in the first instance in helping us recognize this fact; it can be useful in the second instance to the extent that a better alignment of problem and solution does, indeed, yield better policy outcomes and that social theory can constructively provide a basis for obtaining this alignment. The program can be said to represent one instance of such an alignment, and there are many others.

To put in motion more of these virtuous cycles, however, requires that senior managers be attuned to the way powerful organizational imperatives constantly assert themselves in ways that short-circuit the problem-solving process, inherently favoring standard, uniform responses no matter the idiosyncrasies of the issue at hand. It requires a deft capacity to distinguish between problems that map onto a known response package (such as roads, hyperinflation, and epidemics) and those (such as governance) that do not but that command—whether by ethical imperative or client-citizen demand— a response nonetheless. The organizational imperatives of high-modern bureaucracies will always favor the former over the latter; the former is known, predictable, manageable, amenable to hard science and rigorous assessment, though it may only amount to a small fraction of the underlying development problem in the context in question. Responding effectively to these challenges thus also requires recognizing that insights from other disciplines, rather than automatic deferment to economics, might have something important to offer.

The Disciplinary Monopoly and Its Discontents

Many different theoretical perspectives from across the social sciences are represented in the range of approaches adopted by the development community at large, but it remains the case that, for the most part, economic theory, economic assumptions, and economists rule. This is true in most large development agencies, but it is especially so in the World Bank, where the dominance is such that a "disciplinary monopoly" (Rao and Woolcock 2007)—with all the attendant inefficiencies that economists usually associate with monopolies—prevails. Economics is clearly central to understanding and responding to many key problems in development, and our general argument should not be read as one that is unappreciative of that discipline's vital role. And in certain respects, especially as it pertains to understanding nonrational aspects of human behavior, modern economics appears more open to the insights of other disciplines. If a major tenet of economic theory, however, is the importance of harnessing comparative advantage, it is only right and proper that the ideas and skills of those who specialize in areas now deemed central to development are consulted. To the extent that the development community now broadly agrees that history, space, context, institutions, and governance matter for development, it should not be a radical claim to argue that it should be actively seeking the inputs of the disciplines—history, geography, anthropology, sociology, and political science, respectively—that have long specialized in precisely these issues.[8] Too often, regrettably, the monopoly prevails, and the opportunity to incorporate the valuable insights from these disciplines is lost.

Economics dominates contemporary development policy and practice for two major reasons. The first is that it provides large and influential organizations with the kinds of analyses to which they can most readily respond.[9] Despite frequent protestations to the contrary (such as concessions that one size doesn't fit all, there are no silver bullets, and that context matters), large organizations fundamentally want universal solutions to development problems, as the pervasive language of celebrating (and searching for new) "best practices" and "tool kits" attests. The logic and career incentives within large organizations predispose them to favor big projects that generate high impacts in short timeframes; that is the gravitational pull that the logic exerts (especially during crises), even when individual innovators manage to steer it (temporarily) in another direction. To borrow from Scott (1998), economics derives its political power from its capacity to help high-modern development bureaucracies "see" the diversity, contradictions, and complexity of the world in terms those bureaucracies can understand and process (Ferguson 1990; Mitchell 2002); put another way, it renders complexity "legible" via measurement and simplifying assumptions so that the administrative infrastructure of policies and projects—log frames, Excel spreadsheets, appraisal documents, completion reports, impact assessments, presentations to senior directors, and advocacy at international conferences—can be satisfied. For all its apparent sophistication and rigor, the paradox (and beauty) of economics is that it provides simple answers.

Moreover, most fads in development—from microfinance to property rights to community-driven development to conditional cash transfers—are driven by a craving for a technical solution that works independent of context and can be rapidly replicated elsewhere and scaled up. For all the good they have done in raising the profile of global poverty, the Millennium Development Goals—the putative commitment by the international community to helping developing countries reach broad human welfare targets by 2015—both reflect and intensify such imperatives, as does the current methodological focus on randomization as the gold standard against which knowledge claims regarding project efficacy should be made. From this standpoint, economics is not wrong, but, rather, is a willing intellectual enabler and arbiter of society-wide policy responses to prevailing social problems, providing a rigorous and useful evidence base on which to interpret, respond to, and assess these problems. Economics dominates policymaking in industrial countries, but it is even more dominant in developing countries, where the problems are more numerous and complicated but where the connection between enacted policies and actual responses in the world—the will and the way, as Briggs (2008, 11) puts it—is often tenuous at best. Put differently, the policy challenge in developing countries is not simply determining what the policies might be but also constructing (often from scratch) the mechanisms to enact them (World Bank 2003). Fads, though, are all about simple, clean policies, not complex, messy implementation mechanisms on which their efficacy—as this study has shown—ultimately turns.

We should stress again that for certain development problems economics provides a set of analytical approaches that is exactly what is needed; if the issue is hyperinflation, trade, growth, national poverty measures, or calculating the welfare effects of subsidies, then economics has a clear comparative advantage and should rightly be expected to take the lead. Our concern is that there are many other issues—especially those pertaining to history, space, local contexts, and institutional change—for which the combined influence of bureaucratic imperatives and the monopoly of economics yield ways of thinking and doing in development that become part of the problem, and against which a range of intellectual inputs needs to be championed as one means of redress. For these types of issues, the assumed dominance of economics manifests itself in an expectation that new contributions or insights must constantly demonstrate their "value added"—that is, in such discussions the working assumption is that economic orthodoxy is basically fine and just needs a little tweaking.[10] Many social scientists, however, feel that their contributions to development debates amount to far more than "just the last five percent tacked onto the end of the regression equation to sop up the little bit of variance that somehow neoclassical theory missed" (Mark Granovetter, quoted in Swedberg 1990, 107). Indeed, for such issues, we submit, historians, geographers, anthropologists, sociologists, and political scientists have enormous positive contributions to make. In economists' terms, such disciplines are not only complements; with regard to certain issues, they can be eminently superior substitutes.

The second major reason why economics dominates, however, is that potentially countervailing alternatives tend to be articulated in ways that are either not all that alternative (putting merely a social gloss on an otherwise orthodox interpretation of problems and solutions) or, when genuinely alternative, offer only critique or a call for radical abolishment of the prevailing development institutions. Put another way, if there is an absence of more regular input from the other social sciences into development policies and projects, it is not entirely due to the disciplinary monopoly; it is also in part a product of the reluctance of those disciplines to move beyond critique and more clearly and compellingly articulate how, why, and by whom things might be done better. There may be good reasons for this reluctance—for example, a concern, not unfounded, that careful, nuanced research findings will be distorted by the imperatives of high-modern bureaucracies into simplistic responses that risk doing more harm than good—but there is also an argument for at least trying to articulate what alternative renderings of problems and solutions might look like.[11] Too often, social scientists are solely critics of development and the international aid agencies, known more for what they are against (neoliberalism, the Washington consensus) than what they are for. Inside development agencies, social scientists too often capitulate to organizational imperatives, offering, for example, indexes for nonmeasurable (but important) entities, social risk factors to explain conflict, or social best practices as responses to poverty. Such contributions not only fail to do justice to the rich storehouse of ideas in the social sciences, but, more pragmatically, allow the monopoly to continue, safely unchallenged for want of compelling, supportable alternatives. If the worst thing in policy debates is not to be wrong but to be ignored, then many contributions from the noneconomic social sciences are, to borrow a famous phrase from the physicist Wolfgang Pauli, "not even wrong" because they, too, often reside in a world far removed from the corridors of power where key development decisions are made and policies are determined. Or, when they are inside such corridors, they are articulated in ways that too often demonstrate not their value added but their capitulation to orthodoxy or organizational imperatives, becoming pale imitations of their fullest expression.

Good contests, we have argued, are central to institution-building, and they are also central to refining and improving ideas in development. Every academic seminar is conducted within the terms of well-known rules that permit, even encourage, an honest tussle of views; through this messy process, ideas and evidence in the most exacting disciplines are refined, and scholarship advances. Analogously, most contemporary debates in development theory and policy are, unfortunately, more accurately characterized as bad contests: highly inequitable interactions between parties with vastly different power, resources, and frames of reference, with neither side really taking the other seriously. In the spirit of seeking more equitable and informed contests over ideas in development, we next spell out a view of the issues that social theory brings to the table and the ways in which these ideas can more constructively engage with those of economists.

Social Theory and Development Policy

As we have seen, KDP's theoretical foundations draw on sources from across the social sciences. It is the significant and explicit contribution of social theory to the program's design, implementation, and assessment, however, that distinguishes KDP from many other large-scale development projects.[12] As we have also seen, social theory holds that conflict emanates from change to prevailing social structures, political configurations, and institutional arrangements, whether that change stems from positive events (local democratization, the empowerment of marginalized groups) or negative ones (economic collapse, corruption). Below, we spell out more precisely the mechanisms that underpin such outcomes, but it is also important to recognize that social theory has significant contributions to make to several other issues that are of direct relevance to development policy and projects. When future alignments of people and events make it possible for social theory to contribute once again to such efforts, it may be helpful to have to hand an overview of what these contributions might entail. The summary of issues and mechanisms we provide below is neither exhaustive nor a substitute for a comprehensive development strategy, but rather should be seen as complementary input into the broader array of intellectual sources on which any such strategy, wittingly or unwittingly, draws.

Before proceeding further, we should freely concede that social theory itself is far from a unified field of scholarship. Several graduate courses would be needed to cover everything from rational choice theory (essentially economic assumptions applied to social life) and feminism to poststructuralism (variants on postmodernism and critical theory, which asserts the primacy of political power manifest in discourse as the basis of knowledge claims) and symbolic interactionism (understanding the processes by which actors learn to assume their various roles in society). Not all of these are equally useful as a basis for thinking about development policy, and among those that could be called on for this purpose, certain pairings would offer diametrically opposing perspectives and claims (but then, so would certain combinations of economic theory). Nevertheless, on this broad canvas lie particular strands of social theory that are of direct and constructive significance for issues that are currently at the heart of the development enterprise; indeed, they first emerged in response to the unfolding of development itself, during the "great transformations" (Polanyi 1944) put in motion in the late eighteenth and nineteenth centuries and whose effects continue to reverberate.

With these clarifications and caveats in mind, social theory's contribution to development policy and practice can be inferred at two basic levels. The first level concerns the broad paradigmatic ways in which the development process itself is (or can be) understood; we consider two specific manifestations and the course of action to which they give rise. The second level speaks to more pragmatic policy issues, of which we address five. Let us take each of these levels in turn.

The Big Picture: Development Paradigms

The first level focuses on the historical direction (or more formally, the teleology) of development and the mechanisms underpinning the nature and extent of the accompanying changes. This may sound somewhat esoteric, but it is of enormous practical and political consequence. To see why, consider that the development enterprise was founded and predicated on two key assumptions, both of which—at least during their high moment of influence in the period from the late 1940s to the early 1970s—drew strong support along the ideological and disciplinary spectrum.

The first assumption, with its intellectual origins and enduring legacy in modernization theory, is that the experience of today's rich countries during their period of transition from poor, feudal, agrarian economies to rich, services-based, democratic nation-states is the historical norm, the path down which today's poor countries will and should travel, sooner or later.[13] From anthropology to economics, from Smith to Marx, the notion that development was essentially a unidirectional process was used to justify everything from colonialism (bringing civilization, commerce, and Christianity to backward nations) and big-push industrialization to communism (for Marxists, the ultimate end point of history beyond capitalism and socialism), structural adjustment (in Latin America), and shock therapy (in Eastern Europe). From this perspective, development is thus a process of economic, political, social, and administrative convergence; put crudely, Swaziland's prospects will be best enhanced if it seeks to emulate Switzerland. The peak of modernization theory's influence was the period during which much of today's international aid architecture was laid down, with subsequent efforts at reform amounting to little more than refinements of existing institutional arrangements.

The second key assumption is that the technical knowledge that underpins the development process is, for the most part, known (or at least knowable) and shareable, and thus those who possess such knowledge (that is, development experts) can and should be dispatched to offer their advice and instructions to those lacking such knowledge, lest the wheel be unnecessarily reinvented. Efficiency, expediency, and moral urgency thus demand that "lessons learned" and "best practices" be disseminated as broadly and rapidly as possible; political will and money are the only serious binding constraints to reducing global poverty. If the destination is known, if the path to get there is or is thought to be clearly mapped, if the tools to navigate it are available and shareable, and if there is money or power to be gained along the way, then you have a very powerful combination of means, motive, and opportunity to create an enterprise called development.

Before going further, let us make clear that these two assumptions are not entirely wrong—history clearly matters, certain forms of development knowledge can be known and should be shared, modernity is a historical fact, and certain aspects of globalization do have homogenizing effects. In most quarters of academic social science, however, modernization theory has long since been discredited and abandoned, whether as a statement of the means or the ends of development. Few now believe that history's arrow leads inexorably to either Western capitalism or Eastern socialism (or, indeed, that history even has an arrow), that Western legal, political, or economic systems are morally superior, or that the West constitutes a coherent administrative or cultural template for others. But in rightly discarding many of the unsavory and untenable aspects of modernization theory, we should not lose sight of modernization as a real historical process, one that has wrought— and continues to bring about—fundamental changes to social, political, economic, and administrative life around the world (see table 8.1). These range from traditional approaches that have literally been in place for thousands of years (such as kinship systems as a basis of risk management) to high-technology mechanisms (banking via cellular telephones). The political salience of different social identities, the nature and extent of interactions between different business and interest groups, intra-household relations, how people make sense of what happens to them (for example, why they get sick and what remedies they should take)—all of these are fundamentally altered as modernity is encountered.

In recognizing modernization but rejecting modernization theory, some contemporary social theorists now speak of an emerging "multiple modernities" paradigm (see Woolcock 2009a and the references therein), one grounded in a historical appreciation of the different times, places, and ways—some of them long antedating "the West"—in which modern institutions and sensibilities emerged and continue to emerge today.[14] The multiple modernities paradigm remains a work in progress, and should it mature into

TABLE 8.1   TRANSITIONS IN MODERN INSTITUTIONS

	Pre-modern	High Modern	Post-modern
Economy	Agricultural, small-scale, informal	Corporations; low-cost, arm's-length transactions	~Zero transaction costs, product differentiation, immaterial value added
Politics	Fractured, personalistic	Nation-state, democratic	More local *and* more global
Administration	Patronage-based	Civil service: merit recruitment, impersonal application of rules, hierarchical	Reinventing Government or New Public Management; increased civic engagement
Society	Kith and clan, familism	Allegiance to nation-state over all else	Global and local allegiances, virtual networks

Source: Adapted from Pritchett (2007).

a coherent theoretical framework for development, it is nonetheless unlikely ever to enjoy the broad ideological and intellectual support of its predecessors. But that need not be a bad thing; a feature of this emerging paradigm is likely to be precisely that it does not provide simple, uniform answers to complex problems but rather articulates, among other things, the analytical contours of that class of development problems for which there is *inherently* no answer ex ante, only one that emerges through a process of (more or less equitable) contestation, deliberation, and dialogue. For such problems the solution is "good struggles" (Adler, Sage, and Woolcock 2009); the wheel must be reinvented each time, even if the end result is something that happens to look a lot like its counterpart elsewhere. If the content and legitimacy of a new institution have been forged by an equitable (if messy and time-consuming) process of contestation, it is a qualitatively different entity than the seemingly similar best practice institutional form borrowed (or enforced) from outside. From a multiple modernities perspective, in matters pertaining to institutional change, governance reform, and building the rule of law, institutional isomorphism (DiMaggio and Powell 1983)—or the wholesale transplanting of institutional blueprints from one country context to another—is bad theory, bad history, and bad practice.[15] And to reiterate: though individual actors disavow the merits of (or their individual participation in) institutional isomorphism, the *core logic* of the international development apparatus is fundamentally predisposed to perpetuate it. This does not mean that large development agencies cannot or should not be engaged in the matters pertaining to institutional change; the very existence of such initiatives as KDP indicates that they can and (where countries explicitly seek their support) should. It does mean, however, that if such agencies are to engage more systematically in these matters, a very different body of knowledge will need to be drawn upon, and very different modalities of engagement will need to be conceived and enacted.

Following this approach, Swaziland's development objective should be to become not Switzerland but a more prosperous and equitable version of itself. That might not seem a grand claim on the face of it, but if the international development agencies took it seriously it would amount to nothing less than a paradigm shift in the way they conceive of themselves and the modalities by which they engage their counterparts.[16] If the changes wrought by modernization are of first-order significance for understanding the vicissitudes of efforts to enhance the quality of governance and basic service delivery, to improve legal codes and judicial systems, to facilitate exchange and resolve conflict, then so is the lens through which we endeavor to make sense of them. If that lens reveals a landscape in which all roads lead to the same basic destination, it justifies and legitimates one course of action; if through a different lens one sees instead rivers meandering at varying speeds in different ways at different times, it leads to a quite different course of action (or set of actions), most especially with respect to whether and how one seeks to alter the pace, direction, or modality of change. As the old saying goes, a way of seeing is always a way of not seeing, and in contemporary international development policy the map laid out on the decision-making table displays mostly converging roads, not meandering rivers.

The Smaller Picture: Five Substantive Issues

Beyond broad paradigmatic changes, development policy carried out as if social theory mattered would be attuned at a more pragmatic level to several substantive themes. Social theory has already had some traction in development policy debates in recent years in the areas of culture, networks, and exclusion,[17] but to these we add the following five themes, all of them readily apparent in our analysis of KDP and the conflict-development nexus in Indonesia.

Nonlinear Trajectories of Change

A consistent lesson of social and political theory for development policy is that institutional change is rarely a linear process. As in evolutionary biology and intellectual paradigm shifts, institutional change is more accurately characterized by punctuated equilibriums—long periods of stasis that give way relatively suddenly (triggered by exogenous forces or the accumulation of endogenous pressures) to a new alignment of prevailing interests and ideas (see Woolcock 2009c). Ideas themselves can play a key role in bringing about change, as Hunt (2007) so powerfully demonstrates with respect to the emergence of human rights in the eighteenth century: within fifty years, societies such as France and Great Britain that were routinely practicing judicial torture and expanding their slave trade produced the Declaration of the Rights of Man and the Citizen.

But this was not accomplished without serious (often brutal) resistance from powerful groups with strong vested interests in the status quo. Indeed, as Hunt (2007) also points out, a century and half passed between the extraordinary documents of the French and American Revolutions and the appearance of the Universal Declaration of Human Rights in 1948. In matters pertaining to the enfranchisement of women and minority groups or the inclusion of marginalized communities in everyday economic and social life, the trajectory of change is more likely to be a J curve—things get worse before they get better. Moreover, the depth and length of the J curve is often impossible to discern ex ante; human rights campaigners often embark on such risky ventures knowing full well the likely costs to themselves, their families, and their careers and that change may not occur in their lifetime. Played out across countries and regions, especially those that are ethnically diverse, broad processes of democratization and economic development can thus be expected to generate considerable levels of conflict, with a high likelihood that contention will become violent. Development projects that are targeted at the poor and at disadvantaged groups or areas are especially susceptible. And precisely because the trajectories of change are likely to be punctuated equilibriums (at best) or J curves (most likely), especially when policies and projects seeking to bring this about are diligently implemented, very different analytical tools are needed to design and assess them.[18] The importance of this only increases when the trajectories of change are not merely nonlinear—after all, a J curve has a mathematical functional form which, if known in advance, could, in principle, be incorporated into an orthodox econometric assessment of project impact—but inherently highly irregular, as we saw with Hunt's (2007) history of the episodic "invention" of human rights, and thus exhibiting a trajectory that is likely to be both idiosyncratic and only apparent in hindsight.

Rules Systems

A key reason why social change is usually nonlinear or irregular is that rules systems, in different domains and at different levels, shift in various ways at different times for different groups. Every group that has ever existed has had to articulate rules that define, among many other things, membership status and jurisdiction (who is "us" and who is "them"), mechanisms for collective action, economic exchange and reproduction, sanctions for violating the rules, and procedures to follow in the event of ambiguity. For most groups for most of history, these rules have been expressed as norms (customary law), their exact content, application, and enforcement presided over by community elders. As we noted above, modernization fundamentally transforms and often overwhelms such systems and of necessity (via improved transportation and communication) brings different—sometimes competing or deeply antagonistic—normative orders into contact with one another. Our analysis of KDP shows that it offers a potential bridging mechanism for different rules systems—in short, it offers what we might call "meta-rules" (Barron, Smith, and Woolcock 2004), or rules that make it possible for other rules systems to engage peacefully with one another.

If the importance of understanding the rules of the game is another development cliché about which there is broad agreement, social theory offers an entry point for unpacking the various ways and means by which rules systems are constituted. As Briggs (2008, 22) rightly stresses, social theory points beyond the narrower (if more technical) analyses of game theory—"how the players play particular games"—to "why those games, and not others, arise in the first place, why some players, and not others, get to play, how rules of engagement shift . . . and how players acquire the resources—both tangible and intangible—with which to play." Constructively managing the vicissitudes of the dynamics of contention entails engaging with prevailing rules systems, in all their different forms, in these terms.

Rules systems encompass not only informal norms but their selective codification into and interaction with formal bodies of law presided over by legal professionals such as judges and lawyers. Religions (individually and as a category) may be another form of rules system, exerting a powerful influence on (indeed, deeply constituting) peoples' identities and cosmologies, offering potentially alternative renderings of justice and how it should be obtained. A defining feature of modernity is the incremental (if no less contentious) process by which these diffuse rules systems (legal pluralism) cohere into or become bound by a more unified, overarching, and formal rule of law, even as an assortment of normative orders remains the enduring social context in which any such system is necessarily embedded (Granovetter 1985). To again invoke Scott (1998), high-modern bureaucracies, however, "see" only (or "see" more clearly) the formal rules systems, believing these to be the most important and most transferable determinant of development, failing to recognize that such systems are not only the products of an idiosyncratic historical process in any given country but are inseparable from the informal ("unseen" or "unobservable") normative orders in which they are located (Sage and Woolcock 2006, 2008).

Social Relations

Arguing for a focus on social relations as a basis for understanding economic outcomes goes at least as far back as Adam Smith (see Muller 1993), but for our purposes it should direct our attention to three key subissues.[19] First, following (among others) Emirbayer (1997), Tilly (1998), and Rao and Walton (2004), it should help us understand how groups are defined (by themselves and others), the social mechanisms by which boundaries between groups are created, sustained, and transgressed, and how these shift during periods of economic and political transformation. It is in and through groups that identities are formed, and a defining feature of modernity is that it simultaneously fractures individual identity into multiple (sometimes competing) strands—home/work, citizen/subject, sacred/profane, private/public—and requires individuals (and, by extension, communities) to manage these different claims on their time, resources, and loyalty (Gellner

1988). As Polanyi (1944) famously argued, "the great transformation" unleashed by the industrial revolution—and whose workings continue to unfold today—rendered separate what had previously been unified.

Second, humans are relentlessly status-oriented beings, constantly assessing their preferences, aspirations, and strategies on the basis of their place in a hierarchy within various identity groups and broader communities in which their lives are embedded. Recent work in experimental economics has confirmed a long-standing tenet of sociology and social psychology, namely, that individual choices and values are heavily influenced by the particular reference groups one believes most salient and the perceived legitimacy and permeability of the boundaries separating these groups (Haslam 2004). The direst circumstances of poverty, for example, in which all sense of hope or expectation for escaping it appears to be lost, can itself undermine "capacities to aspire" (Appadurai 2004) and thereby contribute to the persistence of inequality traps. Similarly, membership in a stigmatized group (such as a low caste in India) can, all other things being equal, contribute to low performance on standardized tests (Hoff and Pandey 2006). These results and others like them, such as the influential work of William Julius Wilson (see Wilson 2009) help explain why, when aggregate poverty numbers fall, particular social groups—African Americans in the United States, Aborigines in Australia, scheduled castes in India, the Roma in eastern Europe—tend to remain mired at the bottom of the distribution.

Third, many key services such as health, education, and social work are *necessarily* delivered in and through social relationships such as those between doctor and patient, teacher and student, or counselor and client. There is no shortchanging the fact that schooling, for example, whether it is conducted privately, by the state, or by parents at home, essentially takes human interaction over the course of six hours per day, two hundred days per year, for twelve years in order to produce a young adult socialized and educated sufficiently to take his or her place in our modern economy and society. Making development programs work is key to enhancing the welfare of the poor (World Bank 2003), but—as the interactions between villagers and KDP facilitators in our analysis demonstrates—responding effectively, especially where ethically sensitive matters such as conflict and the management of competing interests are involved, will entail paying serious attention to the relational aspects of program implementation (Pritchett and Woolcock 2004), rather than just technical issues such as the pricing of those services or administrative issues such as procurement procedures, important as these are.

Capacity Building

In development policy and practice there is wide agreement about the importance of building capacity, usually interpreted to mean upgrading the technical skills of civil servants, program managers, and front-line project staff.[20] Our findings suggest that, in matters pertaining to empowerment, local governance reform, and conflict management, enhancing the "capacity to engage" from below is as important as improving analytical and technical skills. Our analysis of KDP shows that if social norms and elite politics combine to exclude marginalized groups, arguments leveraged by such groups within KDP's deliberative spaces succeed to the extent that they are able to dilute the influence of elites and, at times, replace a normative, power-politics logic of bargaining with reason-based argumentation. In other words, the force of the better argument, often one based in social justice, sometimes won the day (even if elites eventually prevailed).[21] Similarly, if marginalized groups succeeded (even fleetingly) in substituting reason-based argumentation as the accepted procedure for decision making within deliberative spaces, it was generally because they supplemented these arguments with the understated power of their obstinacy, dogged persistence being a defining quality of mobilization tactics. In other words, the moral authority of these arguments became powerful in part because the marginalized groups that leveraged them were willing and able to participate in forum after forum after forum. This persistence and refusal to have one's voice ignored is not typically associated with deliberation, yet it played no small part in the efforts of marginalized groups to disrupt the very mechanisms of durable inequality that had perhaps silenced them in the first place.

Building the capacity to engage is also important because, through it— and by virtue of the fact that KDP forums were set up to privilege a type of countervailing power that may be endemic to deliberative contestation— marginalized groups acquired a capacity to engage with governing elites by formulating and leveraging rights-based validity claims in public settings. Within these settings, the social legitimacy of their claims gave them a comparative advantage over the elites. Thus, the concept of deliberative contestation speaks to the fact that, although deliberative settings are shaped by quite palpable power differentials, such settings can be made to privilege rights-based claims-making as the favored currency of exchange between participants.[22] Carefully cultivated spaces, incentives, and resources play a decisive role; where they operate effectively, marginalized groups may be better equipped for public decision making.

One implication is that promoting deliberative contestation within participatory democracy may require a new breed of bureaucrats with qualities, skills, and orientations that are fundamentally distinct from those we associate with representative democracy. If a class of rule-upholding, Weberian bureaucrats is an indispensable component of functioning representative democratic institutions, something like a "Habermasian bureaucrat" may be requisite for the functioning of participatory democracy, especially in countries just embarking on democratic forms of governance.[23] According to our data, in order to effectively introduce deliberative spaces that remain open to the influence of marginalized groups, facilitators required not only local knowledge (or *metis;* see Scott 1998) but a capacity to adjust to some local norms and resist others. *How* they did their job in the highly diverse social and cultural contexts of our research areas (and of Indonesia more broadly) was, in other words, highly discretionary and transaction-intensive (Pritchett and Woolcock 2004). The micro-relations between them and participants, and the introduction of spaces, incentives, and resources that marginalized groups can use to modify them, involve fundamentally dynamic processes and interactions, the facilitation of which is more an art than a science. As custodians of deliberation, facilitators faced the daunting task of upholding the general but radical principle of creating openness in decision making for the most marginalized groups in village life. The competencies and sources of identity that they required to go about this work differentiate them in important ways from the impartial and consistent archetype of the bureaucrat that Weber had in mind. Focusing analytical attention on these differences is a promising area for future research concerning deliberative development and democracy.

State-Society Relations

The final theme on which there is broad policy consensus (concerning ends, if not means) in the development community is the importance of "good governance." Although ideological debates continue in certain quarters regarding the primacy of states or markets as the appropriate engines of economic development, most practitioners and policy makers have long since arrived at the pragmatic conclusion that "better is better"[24]—that is, that economic growth, poverty reduction, and responsive institutions will occur to the extent that a country possesses good governments, profitable firms, and an active civil society. The larger and enduring problem, however, is that no one really knows how to put such a process in motion, least of all from scratch or where institutions of all kinds lie devastated in the aftermath of violent conflict or autocracy.

Social theory is not alone in struggling with these issues, and it makes no claims to having the answer, but neither is it silent. One important realm of scholarly inquiry explores the nature and extent of relations between states and their societies (Migdal 2001). The policy challenge arising from this line of work focuses on the plausible and supportable routes one takes to enhance the quality of government. For scholars such as Tendler (1997), good government in northeastern Brazil is a product not only of a vibrant civil society but also of frequent personnel exchanges between governments and civil society organizations. From this standpoint, external development projects, especially those offering high salaries and prestige, potentially threaten to disrupt this mutually beneficial process by siphoning off the most talented staff and bypassing the regulatory oversight mechanisms of the state (Tendler 2000). In post-Suharto Indonesia, however, as we have seen, this option was not really viable: consolidating proto-democratic processes required a different approach, given that the remaining autocratic state apparatus was in disarray, the economy was spiraling ever downward, and nascent civil society organizations were struggling to emerge after decades of brutal suppression. The program was, in effect, a wager that using an initially parallel mechanism of resource provision—that is, one that temporarily bypassed the weakest levels of the government—founded on accountability, transparency, and responsiveness could set strong precedents that would, over time, generate powerful externalities for the rest of local government while enhancing the capacity of citizens to be directly involved in that process (Guggenheim 2006).

With the benefit of hindsight, that wager has been won: KDP is now a national program fully owned and operated by the Indonesian government. Yet the point is not that KDP is *the* solution to the local governance problem but rather that careful analysis of the prevailing political economy and cultural context produced an innovative response to this specific manifestation of the general problem of good governance. In this sense, the program was an "interim institution" (Adler, Sage, and Woolcock 2009), an organizational halfway house founded on the realities of the prevailing political economy and cultural context, envisioned not as an end in itself but as a means to the larger goal of building the democratic state in Indonesia. At the outset it was not at all obvious that it would succeed, and, indeed, the results of the pilot phase were less than impressive, but through ongoing adaptation and refinement it *became* successful.

One might also characterize KDP as a "learning organization" (Senge 2006), a program deeply committed to research, feedback, and appraisal of all kinds, a platform on which a host of related governance initiatives (for example, women's empowerment and local justice) could be developed, tested, and scaled up. These mechanisms, as we have shown, are also vital to ensuring that the program manages early and effectively the conflicts to which it inevitably (and by design) gives rise. Properly understanding the efficacy of projects such as KDP, however, requires a focus not only on internal organizational features, impressive as these are, but also on the structures of the multiple contexts in which it operates. As our analysis has shown, the quality of the broader civic capacity (Briggs 2008) at the village and regional levels can both facilitate and undermine the effectiveness of development projects. In the best of circumstances, learning organizations work in a synergistic partnership with high-capacity environments to generate equitable institutional reform. These factors are the key to understanding whether and how development projects work, but seeing them in proper focus requires carefully incorporating insights from across the social sciences.

Conclusion

Growing awareness of the pervasiveness and consequences—at the local, regional, and global levels—of violent conflict in developing countries creates strong imperatives to identify programmatic solutions and to expand or replicate putative success stories and best practices. Owing to the high international profile that KDP now rightly enjoys, the pressures are considerable to portray it and CDD projects more generally as solutions to violent conflict. The results of this study suggest a more measured response. At an aggregate level, we find little evidence that the program, in and of itself, reduces levels of violent conflict. Rather, we find that at the community level, KDP, unlike many other development projects, is largely successful at resolving the conflicts it generates. Moreover, its indirect impacts on group relations, civic skills, and norms of cooperation, though significant, depend heavily on how well the project is implemented and the characteristics of the broader institutional context (specifically, the capacity of local governance mechanisms) in which it operates.

In short, KDP and CDD projects more generally do not constitute a silver bullet for local conflict. At worst, they can inflame existing tensions and thereby become part of the problem; at best, they can be *part of* a solution when they complement ongoing governance reform processes. As such, projects such as KDP should be regarded as components of, not substitutes for, coherent development strategies for enhancing local conflict mediation capacities and improving the transparency, accountability, and inclusiveness of decision making regarding development resources.

Much remains to be done to explore the ways and means by which development projects shape the dynamics of social and political change at the local level. As a basic first requirement for project design, our findings highlight the central importance of having accessible and effective feedback mechanisms in place, both for improving project performance and for addressing the distributional conflicts that even (or especially) successful projects generate. As is true elsewhere in life, an ounce of prevention is better than a pound of cure; pay now or pay later. The second key issue for project designers and evaluators is the challenge of taking seriously the impact of context. Much lip service is given to such development bromides as "one size doesn't fit all," but it is much rarer to see explicit attention given to crafting projects that are at once large enough to achieve broad impact and able to adapt themselves to the idiosyncrasies of particular settings.

Moreover, the prevailing imperatives of large development agencies for neat metrics of project performance, and the corresponding skill sets they tend to require and reward, makes it difficult to assess the efficacy of CDD projects such as KDP, whose mechanisms (participation, inclusion) and outcomes (empowerment, capacity for collective action) are inherently hard to define and measure and consist of many interacting parts. Taking context seriously should mean that the perspectives and methodologies best suited to engaging with and responding to it are given their due.

Indonesia is undergoing a momentous triple transition in its political, social, and economic life. Power relations are in flux, identities are being renegotiated, and institutions are being transformed. Changes in incentives and in the role of formal and informal institutions at various levels have altered the ways in which individuals and groups relate to each other and the nature and extent of their relation to the state. This is the contested and uncertain arena into which development programs such as KDP, which aim to promote progressive social change and more accountable government, enter. Change is invariably slow and uneven, and the mechanisms by which it occurs are diffuse and complex. Yet our research suggests that KDP contributes in important ways to making local democracy work. Significant lessons can be learned from the program regarding ways to design and promote constructive development transitions in Indonesia and beyond. Not least among these is the importance of calling on the full repertoire of social scientific knowledge to inform the design, implementation, and evaluation of development projects and to thereby craft policy responses that more appropriately match the particular types of problems now being confronted. Chief among these is the ubiquitous challenge of institution-building, a problem whose resolution lies less in the minds of technocrats than in the spaces wherein equitable contests between contending ideas, ideals, and interests can be waged.

Additional Methodological and Empirical Details

In recent years the development community has taken welcome, if belated, steps to improve the quality and frequency of evaluations, the better to improve the evidence base on which policy and project decisions are made.[1] There are still powerful incentives against making evaluation a routine element of the project cycle (Pritchett 2002), but progress of sorts has been made in terms of improving the rigor of the techniques used to identify the impact of project interventions net of other contending factors.[2] These advances, however, have largely been made in areas where the intervention itself is relatively standardized (for example, textbooks, cash transfers, and infant immunizations) and where project objectives (improving test scores, lowering infant mortality rates) are clear and readily measurable. In such cases, calls have been extended to adopt the standards and techniques of biomedical research, where the canonical protocol requires (among other things) random assignment to treatment and control groups. "Just as randomized trials revolutionized medicine in the twentieth century," argue Duflo and Kremer (2005, 228), "they have the potential to revolutionize social policy during the twenty-first."

While entirely sympathetic to the need for more and better evaluation, the approach taken in this study stems from the conviction that participatory development projects such as KDP present qualitatively distinct evaluation challenges, in that the intervention itself is a variable (not a constant, like a tax cut or a pill).[3] Adapting to the idiosyncrasies of the context within which the project is operating is, by design, a major feature of CDD projects, even as the objectives—enhancing empowerment, participation, collective action, and conflict management—are inherently hard to define and measure. The core evaluation challenge remains one of disentangling project effects from selection and context effects (Baker 2000), but the inherent complexity of trying to assess the efficacy of a large participatory project on local conflict—which is a product of numerous simultaneously interacting variables—means that a correspondingly eclectic (though no less rigorous) methodology must be employed (Mosse, Farrington, and Rew 1998). Put another way, the standards and goals remain the same, but the means used to realize them, on both ethical and methodological grounds, must be those best suited to the distinctive challenges that the problem presents.

In order to answer the range of research questions and investigate the complex causal chains of events, we designed a mixed-method assessment strategy that incorporates qualitative and quantitative components in a complementary and mutually reinforcing way.

Qualitative Methods

The distinctive empirical contributions of qualitative methods stem from their comparative advantage with respect to assessing the complexities surrounding context-specific subject matter and the various processes shaping their historical evolution. As such, qualitative approaches are best suited to assessing the dynamics and trajectories of local-level conflict because these phenomena are difficult to quantify or reduce to static numbers and are intricately tied to (and embedded in) local context. Moreover, since the dynamics of (local) conflict are far from exhaustively researched, qualitative methods helped the research team remain open to unexpected findings, allowing us to inductively generate theory about causal processes and sources of variation.

The study is especially concerned with process, an area that, for two major reasons, can be more comprehensively addressed by qualitative exploration. First, qualitative approaches are needed to identify the key mechanisms that trigger, sustain, or resolve conflict. To this end, the research team conducted seven months of qualitative ethnographic fieldwork to develop case studies of the ways different actors negotiate different types of conflicts in different settings. Using a modified version of the

process-tracing method (George and Bennett 2005), researchers investigated conflict pathways, seeking to understand the discrete stages in the
evolution of conflicts. By doing this, researchers were better able to identify
the factors that transform underlying social tensions into different
outcomes (namely, violence or peace).[4] Second, as an evaluation of KDP,
the study sought to dissect the various components of and processes of the
program, the better to understand how each interacts with conflict and the
attempts by various actors to manage it. The identification of positive and
negative areas of KDP influence is information that project managers
can use to improve the program's effectiveness. For both areas, in short,
qualitative methods are critical to understanding the mechanisms by which
and the conditions under which particular variables become salient, and the
importance of local contexts.

Types of Qualitative Data Collected

A team of twelve researchers and supervisors conducted qualitative
quasi-anthropological fieldwork in forty-one villages (see research areas and
sampling strategy below) over the course of seven months. When in the
villages, the researchers had a number of tasks.

First, they developed case studies (sixty-eight in all) of the ways
villagers, facilitators, and local leaders negotiate or fail to negotiate different
types of conflicts in different settings. Some of these cases were violent;
some were not. Collectively, they covered a wide range of dispute types,
including conflicts about land and natural resources (from large-scale inter-
ethnic conflicts to smaller private conflicts over the inheritance of land),
cases of vigilante justice (actions against thieves and witch doctors, for
example), gang fights, political disputes (such as those over local elections
and administrative boundaries), conflict over development resources, and
domestic and sexual violence. Throughout the study, these case studies are
used for illustration, as well as for comparative analysis.

Second, the researchers collected information about fourteen topic
areas ranging from the functions of local government to local socioeconomic conditions to the role of traditional and religious leaders in order to
allow for cross-village comparison. The general data helped illuminate the
cases we followed, gave us a broader picture of the "conflict map" of the
research sites, and allowed us to test the generality of the hypotheses that
emerged from the conflict pathway case studies.[5]

Qualitative Data Collection Tools

Researchers used four qualitative instruments—in-depth key informant interviews, focus group discussions (FGDs), informal interviews, and participant observation. The in-depth interviews accounted for the majority of researchers' field time and the greater part of the data we report in this study. In all, the research team conducted more than eight hundred in-depth interviews. They used an open approach, in which they were given a range of topics to cover but were free to choose which to address in a particular interview; similarly, they were given a list of guiding questions but were free to adapt them in order to get at the information needed. All the field staff were given extensive training in research ethics—especially important when addressing sensitive issues such as conflict, in which respondents may well be implicated as victims or perpetrators—and specific strategies for both conducting these interviews and writing them up afterwards in a manner that would facilitate coherent data management (more than ten thousand pages of text were generated by the researchers) and subsequent analysis.[6]

The focus group discussions had three purposes. First, they gathered information about specific conflicts from groups that might be hard to access in other settings. These groups included the marginalized (such as poor women), as well as those that one might have difficulty reaching individually (for example, victims of domestic abuse). Second, FGDs were used to collect background information about the villages being studied, including data about community life, groups and networks in the village, and economic conditions. Third, FGDs were used to gather diverse perspectives on conflict and, more broadly, security. Women, in particular, often have different perspectives than authority figures on the major problems and issues in a village and how they are being addressed. In all, more than one hundred FGDs were conducted.

For in-depth interviews and FGDs, researchers followed specific guidelines regarding the sampling of respondents. A cross-section of the population was covered, balancing authority figures and ordinary villagers, men and women. Researchers interviewed members of a variety of organizations, professions, and village groups. For the conflict cases, researchers used snowball sampling to identify experts on a particular case, including those involved and observers.

The study used informal interviews and participant observation for two main purposes: first, to gather key unspoken information from the way people act, their relationships, and so on; and second, to gather spoken information that people provided in more informal settings. These techniques further help establish relationships, build trust, and pave the way for formal in-depth interviews, all of which take substantial time. Unlike the other tools used, they involve no formal sampling of respondents. Rather, anyone the researchers met, and everyone they saw, became a potential source of information. These techniques were especially useful, though, at getting information from marginalized and silenced groups. For example, in some cases women were uncomfortable being formally interviewed but were happy to talk when the researchers were helping them in the house.[7]

Quantitative Methods

The major contributions of quantitative methods revolve around establishing a defensible basis for generality and causality, a task that is difficult for the qualitative work because of its relatively small samples and the deliberately nonrandom selection of research sites and respondents. At the broadest level, the research design used a quantitative sampling frame to capture the major dimensions of heterogeneity within the population and increase the reliability of results (discussed below). Because we were looking for common patterns of project impact, our qualitative findings would be strengthened if they held up in a variety of settings. Thus we chose two very *different* provinces and both high- and low-capacity districts for fieldwork and then tracked *similar* conflicts in matched KDP and non-KDP subdistricts. We used qualitative investigation to verify the accuracy of matches identified using quantitative techniques, to ensure that they reflected realities on the ground. Put more formally, qualitative methods can help compensate for a key weakness of quantitative matching techniques, namely, that they can match only on the basis of observable variables such as age, income, and plot size. It is well known, however, that unobserved and sometimes unobservable factors such as motivation and political connections influence project placement and participation; therefore, the deployment of qualitative approaches helped us "observe the unobservables," thereby generating a more accurate empirical match between the KDP and non-KDP settings.

Types of Quantitative Data Collected

Where the qualitative data were susceptible to the subjectivity of the researchers who collected it, we used less context-based methods to elicit numerical data. We used four main sources of quantitative data and other secondary data: a focused key informant survey, a very large but less focused key informant survey (PODES), a nationwide household survey (GDS), and a new dataset consisting of local newspaper reports of conflict and violence.[8]

Quantitative Data Collection Instruments

Key Informant Survey

In the third phase of the qualitative work, the research team administered surveys to a range of key informants at the subdistrict and village levels. The survey gathered comparable responses to perception questions relating to the outcomes and processes of KDP and to broader dimensions of social change in the same locations as the qualitative research. The questionnaires focused largely on the role of KDP in the locality, the extent to which it was used to solve problems related to KDP and those that were not, and the extent to which spillover effects could be determined. A shorter survey was implemented in non-KDP sites. In all, the survey was implemented in twenty-eight program sites and twelve matched comparison villages. These villages vary along a number of dimensions: years of participation in KDP, governance and problem-solving capacity, and the functioning of the program. The data gave us information not only about program effects (comparing program and matched comparison sites) but also allowed us to test a number of explanations for variation *within* KDP sites. The surveys were administered to three informants at the subdistrict level and eight at the village level, thus giving a sample of 352 respondents (subdistrict respondents were not interviewed in matched nonprogram locations).[9]

PODES

The Village Potential series (PODES) is a long-standing survey administered by the Indonesian government's Bureau of Statistics that collects data at the lowest administrative tier of local government. It gathers detailed information about a range of characteristics from infrastructure to village finance for the more than sixty-nine thousand villages and neighborhoods in Indonesia. The 2003 PODES was fielded at the end of 2002 as part of the 2003 Agricultural Census and included, for the first time, a section on politics, conflict, and crime. We used the PODES data to map out the incidence of conflict and violence across Indonesia and to test a range of basic hypotheses about factors correlated with higher levels of conflict (Barron, Kaiser, and Pradhan 2009). The data have limitations; the only respondents interviewed were village heads, who tend to underreport conflict in their villages and have a vested interest in presenting a picture of peace and harmony in order to access development funding. Nevertheless, the data help provide a glimpse of the general patterns of conflict and violence in Indonesia around the time our research was conducted.

Governance and Decentralization Survey

A second large-n dataset is the World Bank's Governance and Decentralization Survey (GDS), the first (baseline) iteration of which was conducted in 2002. The GDS is part of the Indonesian Decentralization Empirical Analysis (IDEA) project, which was conducted by the World Bank together with the Centre of Public Policy Studies at Gadjah Mada University. The survey aims to ascertain the effects and impacts of the rapid decentralization that took place in Indonesia in 2001 on a number of factors ranging from the performance of local governments, to service delivery, to the functioning of the justice system. The initial (baseline) enumeration took place in 150 (that is, almost half) of Indonesia's districts in 2001. As part of the follow-up survey, a module on conflict and problem solving was inserted into the survey and the sample was extended. The GDS provide a rich data source on levels of conflict (as reported at the household level) and data on a range of other institutional and governance factors that can be regressed against conflict and violence levels. The formulation of this module was based in part on the emerging hypotheses from the qualitative fieldwork, newspaper analysis, and the results of the PODES survey. Methodological insights from the latter also affected the survey design itself. (Results are outlined in McLaughlin and Perdana 2009.)

Newspaper Data Collection

In order to assess patterns and forms of conflict, and variations between areas, we needed to create a conflict map showing levels of conflict across geographic areas. Satisfactory data did not exist to allow for this. As Barron, Kaiser, and Pradhan (2009) note, household and key informant surveys are weak at accurately measuring conflict. Formal government statistics are also poor.[10] Because of this, we decided to create a dataset of all reported conflicts in the research areas (and surrounding districts) for the 2001–2003 period using three local news sources for each area. This allowed us to broadly map conflict in our research locations, to estimate aggregate levels of violence, to characterize the incidents (by conflict type, actors involved, impacts, and so on), and to identify how representative our qualitative case studies were. Analysis of the newspaper data, and an outline of the methodology, is presented in Barron and Sharpe (2005, 2008).

Other Secondary Data

Other secondary data utilized for the study include police records and data from health care providers, primary documents found in villages (such as written adat laws), and KDP project documentation (for example, complaints and how they are handled). An extensive review of the literature concerning development, conflict, Indonesia, and our specific research areas was conducted. In addition, background papers about a number of issues relating to KDP, local conflict, and the research areas were written throughout the study.

Integration of Methods

The research design used an iterative strategy to integrate qualitative and quantitative methods, establishing an ongoing dialogue between the two approaches. Examining the subject matter from multiple angles, we used triangulation to verify that our research findings reflected accurately the relation between KDP and local conflict. As such, each item makes a distinct contribution to capturing the larger truths that our research seeks to uncover (see figure 3.1).

Preliminary research on the field sites (including collection of government statistics, relevant academic writings, and a rapid review of newspaper articles) was conducted before the intensive qualitative fieldwork began and informed the design and implementation strategies for the qualitative and quantitative work that followed. This initial work began the process of mapping the spatial distribution and characteristics of conflict in order to help with the sampling of districts and subdistrict sites, and it provided input into the development of the research hypotheses, the questions, and the data collection instruments. Once under way, the in-depth qualitative research identified the right kinds of questions (and their wording) for inclusion in the more general quantitative surveys. Note that the quantitative instruments were designed and developed while the qualitative work was being conducted; their design thus reflected the ongoing findings of— and methodological lessons learned from—the qualitative fieldwork. In return, the quantitative fieldwork provided a test of the generality of the hypotheses emerging from qualitative investigation. Analysis of the newspaper and other secondary data sources also helped us estimate aggregate levels and impact of violent conflict in our research areas.

Many of the subjects for which we wanted to collect specific survey data mirrored the general data categories that the qualitative researchers used. This was deliberate: looking at a problem from more than one methodological angle gives us increased confidence that what we are finding is accurate and that the inevitable, though variable, bias built into any research method is not unduly distorting findings. In short, if we get the same answers to the same questions twice using different methods and taking different approaches, we can be reasonably confident that the answers are as reliable and objective as possible.

Sampling

One of the most important aspects of the research design is the use of a quantitative sampling frame to select the sites for qualitative investigation. As indicated above, accounting for heterogeneity within the population gives us greater confidence that our research findings do not turn on the particular (perhaps idiosyncratic) characteristics of our research sites.

Variation at the Provincial Level

Our objective was to pick two very different provinces in which to work: as we sought common patterns of project impact, our assumption was that the findings would be strengthened if they held up in different settings. We focused on a range of variables to help determine the nature of a province, including population size and density, ethnic homogeneity, religious homogeneity and dominant religious group, and level of provincial development, including quality of and ease of access to public services and infrastructure.

We excluded provinces with the highest and lowest levels of conflict. Because KDP operates at the subdistrict level and below, any positive externalities it may produce are likely to be directed at managing conflicts that exist at those levels. Given the nature of conflict in many high-conflict provinces, where cleavages exist on a provincial or at least district level, if we had selected such provinces we would have biased our research against observing any project impact. Moreover, in areas of high conflict, where levels of violence are significantly affected by external actors and exogenous factors (such as military action), it would be much harder to separate the potential impact of a local-level project from all the other causal variables in the research site.

Variation at the District Level

In each province, we selected one district with a high capacity to manage conflict and one with a low capacity. We selected these after extensive consultation at the provincial level with international and local NGOs, government officials, regional development experts, research institutes and religious institutes, universities, and KDP staff. Choosing such districts allowed us to defend our claims regarding the nature and extent of KDP's impacts on local conflict resolution by showing that they take place irrespective of whether the broader environment is conducive to conflict resolution.[11] We were fully aware of the inherent limitations of seeking to assess capacity in this manner, but in the end there was a broad and deep consensus among our informants as to which regions had high capacity and which had low capacity (as we defined it).

Subdistrict Matching

For the first two phases of qualitative fieldwork, we chose two subdistricts within each of the research districts—a KDP site and a non-KDP site—that were as similar as possible. The former, our program sites, had already had been in KDP for three years; the latter, our matched comparison sites, had not yet taken part in the program. If one selects similar comparison sites, one controls as much as possible for nonprogram effects that may stem from socioeconomic, institutional, or other differences. For reasons outlined above, we used mixed methods to identify these matches. We first used the propensity score matching technique to select similar KDP and non-KDP sites on the basis of pre-intervention characteristics.[12] The actual propensity score was derived using explanatory variables from the PODES 1996 dataset that could serve as proxies for the subdistrict's level of economic development prior to the advent of KDP. Among the PODES variables used were population, access to markets, department stores, health and education resources, income, and perceptions of poverty level, each of which was used to assign the program.[13] These are observable variables. To control for unobservable variables such as motivation, cohesion, leadership, and political connections, other factors that we believe played a role in program placement, we used the propensity score to select three statistically comparable non-KDP (comparison) subdistricts and then asked our field research team to identify which of these was the most appropriate match for the subdistricts participating in KDP. They did this by conducting qualitative interviews at the district level with government officials and other experts to choose among the identified pairs and incorporate other sources of difference or similarity.[14] This generated the overall sample frame shown in figure A1.

The third phase of qualitative research extended to an additional two subdistricts in each research district. We did this to verify that KDP's performance in the research sites was representative and to include new program sites to replace areas where KDP was not working as intended.[15] We selected additional subdistricts that had received the program for at least three years, had passed a minimum threshold of KDP performance acceptability relating to transparency and accountability, and were different from the other KDP sites we were studying in terms of culture, geography, and demographics. We added two KDP subdistricts in each research district: Slahung and Jenangan in Ponorogo; Pasaen and Pademawu in Pamekasan; Talibura and Paga in Sikka; and Cibal and Ruteng in Manggarai.

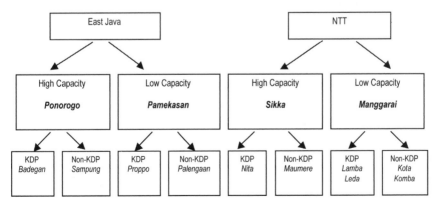

Figure A1   Overview of site selection

Case and Village Selection

We determined specific qualitative research locations by conflict rather than by village. Our initial maps of major social tensions (constructed in Phase 1 of the research) helped us select the following primary cases in each subdistrict to investigate in non-KDP sites (Phase 2A) and matched KDP sites (Phase 2B).

Cases One and Two: Similar Cases, Different Outcomes (within the Same Subdistrict)

Within each subdistrict, we selected two cases of conflict that were similar but that had different outcomes: one violent, one peaceful. We evaluated similarity by type and scale of conflict, underlying tensions, and types of actors involved. By doing so we gained a better idea of the factors that result in violence or peace.

Case Three: Similar Cases in Two Subdistricts (KDP and Non-KDP)

A conflict in the non-KDP subdistrict was matched with a similar case in the KDP subdistrict. We used the same similarity criteria noted above but compared cases in different subdistricts within the same district. Not only were the conflicts similar in type and scale, but so, too, were the general characteristics of the villages chosen.

Cases Four and Five: Peaceful Resolution in a Violent Area, a Violent Case in a Peaceful Area

In these cases we used a qualitative version of a difference-in-difference strategy, identifying instances of peaceful conflict resolution in otherwise relatively high-conflict villages and instances of escalated conflict in otherwise relatively peaceful villages.[16] This yielded insights into local mechanisms related to peace and conflict that were as independent as possible of the broader institutional environment (thereby replicating at the local level the broader selection strategy adopted at the district level). We compared similar cases in KDP and non-KDP locations matched by pre-intervention characteristics in order to evaluate possible program impacts. Moreover, we selected similar villages and cases with similar conflict dynamics.

Case Six: KDP-Related Matters

For the research in the sites participating in the program (Phase 2B), we also chose KDP-related cases of conflict or conflict mediation. These included examples of KDP directly or indirectly causing conflict and cases where we had preliminary evidence that KDP had been used to help resolve conflict. In Phase 3, we encouraged the research team to find more KDP-related cases, as well as those related to other development programs. Table A1 summarizes the comparative analysis strategy.

Analytical Tools

Assessing Local Capacity: Use of Vignettes

Developing measures of local capacity is difficult because capacity is an abstract concept and is difficult to define without reference to concrete

TABLE A1 OVERVIEW OF UNITS OF ANALYSIS AND PRIMARY DATA SOURCES

Analysis type	Form or unit of analysis	Sources	Variables compared[a]	Sample
1	Comparison of pathways	Conflict case studies	O, M	68
2	Comparison of villages	Fieldwork and demographic data, key informant survey	C C, M	41 41[b]
3	Comparison of subdistricts	Fieldwork and demographic data, key informant survey, newspaper dataset	C C, M O	16 12[c] 208[d]

[a] Types of variables: C = contexts; O = outcomes; M = mechanisms.
[b] In some places we use the key informant survey data only from areas using the program (twelve subdistricts and thirty villages). In other places we use data from both program sites and matched non-KDP comparison sites (forty-one villages).
[c] The key informant survey was not conducted at the subdistrict level in control sites.
[d] We used data from PODES for 2001, updated by data from the electoral commission (KPU) from 2003, for a full list of subdistricts. Since then some subdistricts have split. However, we code new subdistricts as still remaining within previous boundaries, as of 2003.

examples. It is also difficult to develop a capacity metric because conceptions of what constitutes capacity and what to measure it against vary across places, people, and cultures. We sought to use anchoring vignettes to try to develop a common metric and hence to allow for comparison across areas.[17] As shown in box A1, the anchoring vignettes method attempts to measure the comparability of responses by getting a better understanding of how respondents comprehend the question posed to them.

BOX A1   POLITICAL VOICE IN MEXICO AND CHINA

In an attempt to understand "political efficacy" across countries, the following question was asked in both China and Mexico:

> How much say do you have in getting the government to address issues that interest you?
>   (1) No say, (2) Little say, (3) Some say, (4) A lot of say, (5) Unlimited say

It is interesting that respondents in Mexico reported having substantially less political voice than those in China. For example, more than 50 percent of Mexican citizens reported having no say in government, whereas less than 30 percent of Chinese citizens replied that they had no say in government. Given the strikingly different political situations of the two countries, these responses suggest a potential problem with the survey question or how it is understood. There are a number of reasons why Mexican and Chinese citizens may have very different perceptions of what "having a say" in government means. Additional questions can be used to anchor their perceptions of what they understand. For example:

> [Moses] lacks clean drinking water. He would like to change this, but he can't vote, and feels that no one in the government cares about this issue. So he suffers in silence, hoping something will be done in the future. How much say does [Moses] have in getting the government to address issues that interest him?

This allows respondents to be broken into categories based on their understanding of Moses' rights. With additional vignettes, respondents can be placed on a spectrum of understanding of political efficacy that allows responses about their own political voice to be interpreted more accurately.

Source: Adapted from King and Wand (2007).

This methodology was developed primarily for survey use. We used the method in a somewhat different way. Researchers were asked to categorize the capacity of the different villages they had worked in along two dimensions: problem solving and capacity for collective action. Collective action was defined as the positive act of coming together to create or address something; problem solving could relate to either formal or informal responses to a given problem. We developed a series of vignettes that researchers used to categorize the villages by deciding which vignette best described the situation in a given village (box A2).

BOX A2   ANCHORING VIGNETTES USED TO ASSESS CAPACITIES FOR PROBLEM SOLVING AND COLLECTIVE ACTION

Which of these scenarios best characterizes life in your village?

Problem solving

1. X had a disagreement with Y. Though it was initially a small argument, X and Y have called on their respective groups to intimidate the other person and seek retribution. As a result, tension increased in their village, as more people became involved. There is no person or group that is willing to assert their authority to solve the problem, and no one trusts the formal legal system to settle the issue. The problem continues to grow.

2. X had a disagreement with Y. Though it was initially a small argument, X and Y have called on their respective groups to intimidate the other person and seek retribution. As a result, tension increased in their village, as more people became involved. Authority figures try to step in if the problem becomes violent, but there is very little that they can do to solve the problem. The problem does not grow, but continues to fester.

3. X had a disagreement with Y. They took their problem to the village head, who was able to provide a solution. Though they both agreed to a solution when they were in the meeting, X does not carry through with his part of the agreement. He plans on taking the issue to another authority figure or even to court for another solution that will be closer to his goals.

4. X had a disagreement with Y. They are able to reach a solution with the assistance of the tokoh masyarakat/village head. He is able to resolve the problem. Though both Y and X are still upset, they will abide by the agreement because it is important to uphold the rules of the community.

Capacity for collective action

1. The main road in village M was severely damaged in a recent flood. Though everyone in the village needs the road to be repaired as soon as possible, there are many disagreements about the building process. X is losing a great deal of money from the road damage, but she does not feel she has enough power within the village to help craft a solution. Most community members want the road repaired, but are afraid to get involved because it will cause more trouble than the gains it might bring. The road remains unrepaired.

2. The main road in village M was severely damaged in a recent flood. Though everyone in the village needs the road to be repaired as soon as possible, disagreements about the building process have developed. There was initial support for plans to rebuild the road: materials were purchased, and many people planned to help with construction. Now, some of the materials have been stolen and community members are less willing to assist, as they no longer think that the project will succeed. X is very angry since he made a contribution, but it was wasted, and now there is little that he can do.

3. The main road in village M was severely damaged in a recent flood. Everyone in the village agreed that the road needed to be repaired as soon as possible, and they were able to work together to fix it, despite many problems along the way. Some of the money and materials for the road were stolen, so the road is not as good as it could have been. Many people are angry that some of their money was stolen, and they are worried that the road will soon wash out again.

4. The main road in village M was severely damaged in a recent flood. Everyone in the village agreed that the road needed to be repaired as soon as possible, and they were able to work together to fix it. Most of the villagers were involved in some part of the rebuilding process, and the community as a whole is satisfied with quality of the road. There were, of course, some disagreements along the way, but they were able to be resolved in a way that kept most people content.

The vignettes were developed using an iterative process with the help of the researchers. Drafts were written on the basis of a review of case studies and village demographics forms. The drafts were then checked by a number of researchers and revised to more accurately reflect village situations that would be applicable across research locations. The final vignettes were sent to all researchers, who used them to rank the villages where they conducted research. After villages were ranked, some of the rankings were checked by groups of researchers to see if the rankings (and vignettes) were accurate.

The two dimensions of capacity were aggregated to provide an overall indicator for the village. This indicator was adapted from a five-point scale to a three-point one (high, medium, and low) based on the overall distribution of villages (see table A2). These categories, in turn, were used for further analysis of conflict dynamics.

TABLE A2   VILLAGE-LEVEL CAPACITY

Phase	District	Subdistrict	Village	Problem solving	Collective action	Score	Ranking
3[a]	Manggarai	Cibal	Pagal	4.00	4.00	4.00	High
3	Manggarai	Ruteng	Wae Belang	4.00	4.00	4.00	High
3	Pamekasan	Pasaen	Sana Daya	4.00	4.00	4.00	High
3	Ponorogo	Jenangan	Kemiri	4.00	4.00	4.00	High
3	Sikka	Paga	Loke	4.00	4.00	4.00	High
3	Manggarai	Ruteng	Cumbi	4.00	3.50	3.75	High
3	Pamekasan	Pademawu	Padellegan	3.50	4.00	3.75	High
3	Pamekasan	Pademawu	Sumedangan	3.50	4.00	3.75	High
3	Sikka	Talibura	Wereng	3.50	4.00	3.75	High
3	Sikka	Talibura	Nebe	3.50	4.00	3.75	High
3	Manggarai	Cibal	Lande	3.00	4.00	3.50	Medium
2A	Manggarai	Kota Komba	Watu Nggene	3.33	3.67	3.50	Medium
2B	Pamekasan	Proppo	Tattangoh	3.33	3.67	3.50	Medium
2A	Sikka	Maumare	Watugong	3.33	3.67	3.50	Medium
2B	Pamekasan	Proppo	Maper	3.67	3.00	3.33	Medium
2B	Ponorogo	Badegan	Biting	3.00	3.33	3.17	Medium
2B	Sikka	Nita	Nita	3.00	3.33	3.17	Medium
2B	Manggarai	Lamba Leda	Satar Punda	3.00	3.00	3.00	Medium
2B	Pamekasan	Proppo	Proppo	3.67	2.33	3.00	Medium
2B	Ponorogo	Badegan	Dayakan	2.67	3.33	3.00	Medium
3	Ponorogo	Slahung	Wates	3.00	3.00	3.00	Medium
3	Ponorogo	Slahung	Slahung	3.50	2.50	3.00	Medium
2A	Sikka	Maumere	Koting A	2.67	3.33	3.00	Medium

(Continued)

TABLE A2   CONTINUED

Phase	District	Subdistrict	Village	Problem-solving	Collective action	Score	Ranking
3	Sikka	Paga	Paga	2.00	4.00	3.00	Medium
2A	Manggarlli	Kota Komba	Golo Meni	2.33	3.33	2.83	Medium
2A	Manggarai	Kota Komba	Tanah Rata	2.33	3.33	2.83	Medium
2B	Sikka	Nita	Bloro	3.33	2.33	2.83	Medium
2B	Manggarai	Lamba Leda	Galo Mangu	2.67	3.00	2.83	Medium
2A	Pamekasan	Palengaan	Palengaan Laok	2.67	3.00	2.83	Medium
2A	Ponorogo	Sampung	Pagerukir	2.00	3.67	2.83	Medium
3	Pamekasan	Pasaen	Tlontohraja	2.00	3.50	2.75	Low
2B	Ponorogo	Badegan	Badegan	2.33	3.00	2.67	Low
2B	Manggarai	Lamba Leda	Tengku Leda	2.67	2.33	2.50	Low
2A	Sikka	Maumere	Nele Wutung	2.33	2.33	2.33	Low
3	Ponorogo	Jenangan	Panjeng	2.50	2.00	2.25	Low
2A	Pamekasan	Palengaan	Palengaan Daya	2.67	1.67	2.17	Low
2B	Sikka	Nita	Magepanda	2.67	1.67	2.17	Low
2A	Pamekasan	Palengaan	Banyupelle	2.67	1.33	2.00	Low
2B	Pamekasan	Proppo	Panagguan	2.33	1.33	1.83	Low
2A	Ponorogo	Sampung	Gelangkulon	1.67	2.00	1.83	Low
2A	Ponorogo	Sampung	Sampung	2.00	1.00	1.50	Low

[a] Note: We dropped locations with four years' participation because the number of observations was too small.

Classifying Conflict Outcomes

A key part of our strategy was comparative analysis of cases of conflict. Examining seemingly similar cases, involving like issues and in similar structural environments but with different outcomes, can help illuminate the particular factors that led to given conflict outcomes. We therefore sought to categorize the seriousness and impacts of each of the sixty-eight case studies. We used two variables: the extent to which a conflict had violent impacts and the extent to which resolution was successful and lasting. Each conflict was coded along these two dimensions on a scale of one to three:

Impacts

1. Deaths (one or more)
2. Serious damage (injuries, property damage, kidnapping, rape, serious intimidation)
3. Limited or no damage (impacts were indirect and small or were absent)

Resolution

1. Long-term
2. Short-term
3. None

Each of the cases of conflict will fit into one of the nine boxes in the grid shown in figure A2. Those in the top left box are most serious; they have had the highest impact and appear to have the greatest chance of continuing or reigniting in the future. At the opposite extreme, cases that belong in the bottom right box are those with limited or no damage and deep and lasting resolution.

VIOLENCE IMPACTS

		Deaths	Serious Damage	Limited or No Damage
	None			
DURABILITY OF RESOLUTION	**Short-term**			
	Long-term			

Figure A2   Seriousness of conflicts

Patterns of Conflict in KDP and Non-KDP Areas

Creating the Dataset

In order to assess patterns of conflict in program and nonprogram areas, we merged the data in the KDP and Community Conflict Negotiation (KDP and CCN) dataset with information about which subdistricts had participated in the program and for how long. The dataset contains information about conflicts in East Java and NTT for a three-year period. We used the resulting dataset to examine the program's impact on conflict outcomes in two ways: first, we looked to see if there was an impact on violent conflict due to a subdistrict having ever received KDP; second, we disaggregated the data to see if there were different effects on the number of violent conflicts as locations spent more years in the program.

For both types of analysis, we broke the observations out by year, as shown in table A3.

We combined all of this information, creating a new dataset that contained the number of years in KDP for each of the three years of available data. That means that each location appears three times in our dataset. For example, for two different villages—Village A, which started in the second year of KDP 1, and Village B, which started in the first year of KDP 2—observations would be as depicted in table A4.

Together, these two villages would provide six observations in the data. Counting this way, rather than just looking at the total data in a given year, allows us to be more precise in looking for KDP effects and eliminates (or at least minimizes) any bias that might result from counting conflicts that took place in a particular location before the arrival of KDP.

TABLE A3   OVERVIEW OF KDP AND CONFLICT DATA

Year of KDP implementation	Possible number of years in KDP	Year of conflict data
1999–2000	0, 1, 2	2001
2001–2002	0, 2, 3	2002
2003–2004	0, 1, 2, 3, 4	2003

TABLE A4   OVERVIEW OF COMPARATIVE KDP DATA IN DIFFERENT VILLAGES

Location	Number of years in KDP	Conflict variables	Location	Number of years in KDP	Conflict variables
Village A	0	2001 data	Village B	0	2001 data
Village A	1	2002 data	Village B	0	2002 data
Village A	2	2003 data	Village B	1	2003 data

The Impact of Exposure to KDP

In order to look at the impact of exposure to the program, we separated nonprogram locations from program sites. Based on the examples of Villages A and B above, we would have had three observations of places that never were in KDP (Village A in 2001, Village B in 2001, and Village B in 2002) and three of sites that had been in the program (Village A in 2002, Village A in 2003, and Village B in 2003). Once the data were broken down in this way, we looked at the differences in impact on violent conflict, in particular conflicts that resulted in deaths, injuries, or property damage. Because we would expect KDP to be effective in preventing conflict, not in reducing the number of deaths or injuries, we counted cases that contained violence, not the number of people affected.

Impacts of KDP over Time

We expect the impact of KDP to increase over time, improving as people gain familiarity with the procedures, trust the process, see its benefits, and adapt it to their own needs. To try to evaluate the impacts over time, we broke the village observations down by the number of years that they had been in the program. Again, drawing from the example above, the data would be broken down as outlined in table A5.

With the data disaggregated in this way, we conducted the same analysis regarding violent conflict, deaths, injuries, and property damage. This allowed us to look for trends over time. Again, we used the number of cases in our analysis, rather than the number of people affected or the amount of total property damage. (Further details of the cases are presented in Barron, Diprose, and Woolcock 2007a.)

TABLE A5   OVERVIEW OF KDP IMPACT DATA OVER TIME

Years in KDP	Data
0	Village A, 2001
	Village B, 2001
	Village B, 2002
1	Village A, 2002
	Village B, 2003
2	Village A, 2003

A Final Word: Conflict of Interest?

All the authors and researchers involved in the study are or have been employed by the World Bank; as such, we are "inside evaluators." Given that the results of the study are likely to be used as a basis for future program design, critics could perhaps argue that the team faced additional pressure to come up with results that justify an already given course of action.[18] In response, we can say that we were conscious of the inherent tensions in this arrangement from the outset and took all possible steps to control at all times for real or perceived conflicts of interest. External peer reviewers were involved at all stages of the research design and data evaluation, and they provided extensive comments on the final draft of the analysis. A module in the training program for the field research team attempted to address these issues explicitly.

We also note that the conflict of interest issue does not necessarily go away if evaluations are outsourced to ostensibly independent third parties such as consulting firms or academics. We argue that exactly the same pressures identified above accrue to evaluators who work for external agencies. In any event, we present our findings with the hope that they will be interpreted and assessed with the same constructive skepticism, scrutiny, and engagement with which all empirical research should be treated.[19]

Notes

Chapter 1. Institutional Change, Development Projects, and Local Conflict Dynamics

1. We recognize the distinction between development as a historical-political process and development as a geo-strategic humanitarian project. The English language does not make this distinction very well, but we hope the particular form to which we are referring is clear from the context.

2. On trends in global poverty between 1980 and 2005, see Ravallion and Chen (2007), who find a steady relative decline in poverty but note stagnation in terms of absolute poverty levels. The South Asia and East Asia regions have shown unprecedented rates of decline in absolute and relative poverty during this time period. On the economic, health, and geographical inequalities of the development process, see (among others) Pritchett (1997), Milanovic (2005), Szreter (1997), and World Bank (2005b). For now, we focus only on poverty narrowly defined (that is, by consumption measures); as we discuss in subsequent chapters, environmental degradation, social exclusion, and cultural loss, which have accompanied the development process, contribute in no small measure to the dynamics driving the local-level conflicts that we describe.

3. For a related stylistic point of departure, see Morris (1963), who proposed in his delightful book *The Road to Huddersfield: A Journey to Five Continents* (a global review of selected World Bank projects in the early 1960s) that the otherwise unremarkable town of Huddersfield in the northwest of England was a model for developing countries because it was here—in a place with no particular geographical, political, or demographic advantages—that the technological innovations in textile production that gave rise to the Industrial Revolution were born in the early nineteenth century. Likewise, today's developing countries, Morris argued, needed to work with what they had to try to spark their own endogenous processes of innovation

and growth. For our purposes (though not Morris's), it is telling that Huddersfield was also rent by civic unrest during the Industrial Revolution—Luddites repeatedly attacked factories and burned mills they feared would ruin the basis of their livelihoods and thus lead to starvation, actions that in turn once provoked the government to send in a thousand soldiers to restore order (see Sale 1996).

4. It is one of the many ironies of development that a project initially approved by a dictator seeking to bypass corrupt regional government officials (Suharto sought to ensure that a greater proportion of development resources actually made it from Jakarta to villagers) evolved into a nationwide initiative based on, and seeking to instill, democratic principles. From the outset, KDP was part of a broader strategic "wager [that reform in Indonesia would] succeed in moving away from the development authoritarianism of the New Order government toward a model built on representative institutions" (Guggenheim 2006, 138).

5. An urban version of KDP, the Urban Poverty Project, was launched soon afterward, but it is not a focus of our study. Further details about the origins, structure, and evolution of KDP are discussed in later chapters.

6. The phenomenon of *silat* violence is discussed briefly in Chapter 3. See also Wilson (2002).

7. Lembaga Ketahanan Masyarakat Desa (LKMD) is translated more literally as the Village Community Resilience Council and is referred to in some academic writing as such (see, e.g., Antlov 2003a; Aspinall and Fealy 2003). According to Kato (1989, 94), the "LKMD is construed as a village cabinet whose main function is to assist the *desa* [village] head in carrying out development planning and efforts." For the benefit of readers unfamiliar with Indonesian village governance, we translate it as the Village Development Council. The LKMD became the LKD (Lembaga Kemasyarakatan Desa, or Village Social Council) in some places following the implementation of regional autonomy.

8. See Szreter (1997) for a historical discussion of the disruption, deprivation, disease, and death that accompany the growth process.

9. As of mid-2008, official United Nations assessments stated that Indonesia was on track to meet all eight MDGs. Some, however, such as eradicating extreme poverty and hunger, will require policy changes if they are to be met (MDG Monitor 2008).

10. Chapters 3 and 5 address the specifics of the incidence, forms, and spatial and temporal distribution in more detail.

11. Varshney (2002), Brass (2003), and Wilkinson (2004) differ with respect to the relative contributions of civic, elite-driven, and electoral processes to ethnic violence, but there is little dispute about the prevalence of conflict itself. For a literary perspective on the multiple tensions accompanying modernization in South Asia, see Mishra (2006).

12. Critics from the right (e.g., Clark 2008) dismiss Polanyi as an enemy of free markets, an ahistorical romantic erroneously imagining a tranquil pre-capitalist past. Irrespective of his personal politics, Polanyi, along with many others (see Chapter 8), made important insights into the dynamics that drive these processes and the conflicts to which they give rise.

13. See, among others, Fukuyama (1999) on the "disruptions" that accompany such change, and, of course, the seminal work of North (1990, 2005; North, Wallis, and Weingast 2009).

14. This thesis is, perhaps not surprisingly, a source of scholarly contention; we discuss the origins and contours of these debates and their implications for development policy in Chapter 8.

15. Helpman (2004b); Easterly (2001b) more accurately calls it an elusive quest.

16. To give the recent Commission on Growth its due, important conclusions of the final report (Commission on Growth and Development 2008) include a call to experiment with different policy innovations in different contexts, to focus on the institutional underpinnings of the growth process, and to recognize the key role played by the state. In a similar vein, see also Rajan and Zingales (2004).

17. For a while, spectacular growth in Indonesia under Suharto actually *prevented* institutional reform by consolidating elite power and appeasing rival groups, but this proved unsustainable, as it has elsewhere (see World Bank 2005b, 126–28).

18. Heifetz (1994) makes the important distinction between technical and adaptive policy problems, going so far as to argue that "the single most common source of leadership failure . . . in politics, community life, business or the nonprofit sector . . . is that people, especially those in positions of authority, treat adaptive challenges like technical problems" (Heifetz and Linksy 2002, 14). So understood, the challenge of institution-building and managing institutional change is an example of an adaptive problem. We refine this distinction in Chapter 8.

19. This phrasing and the deeper argument on which it rests come from Pritchett and Woolcock (2004).

20. We draw on selected aspects of social theory, which in its fullest expression says many things about a vast range of issues (see, e.g., Alexander 2006). If it cannot be said to have the parsimony or unified coherence of economic theory, neither should it be regarded as inherently antithetical to economic theory (indeed, certain strands of it—such as rational choice theory—are direct extensions of economic theory). We argue, however, that it does nonetheless have distinctive contributions to make to practical development issues. KDP is one such manifestation.

21. Good overviews of this period include Schwartz (1999), Kingsbury (2002), Friend (2005), Vickers (2005), and Sidel (2006).

22. See Bebbington et al. (2006) for a discussion of the processes that shaped efforts to raise the status and profile of social development activities within the World Bank during the Wolfensohn presidency (and the limits thereof). The concept of "high modern" bureaucracies, of which the World Bank is one manifestation, comes from Scott (1998). In this study we are also concerned with the transformation of the post–New Order Indonesian state, because KDP was (and remains) a project of the Indonesian government.

23. Varshney, Tadjoeddin and Panggabean (2008) estimate that 10,700 people died between 1990 and 2003, with most of the deaths occurring between 1998 and 2001. Their figure excludes deaths from the conflict in Aceh, where local government

authorities estimate that thirty-three thousand people died over the course of thirty years of fighting (Aspinall 2009).

24. It has nonetheless allowed for greater ethno-religious segregation in some of Indonesia's most diverse districts, strengthening group boundaries and potentially providing new avenues for conflict (Diprose 2008, 2009b).

25. Reflecting at least the current scholarly consensus, Hoff (2003, 205), in a major review article, concludes that institutions form no less than "a key determinant of the wealth and poverty of nations."

26. Throughout the book, we refer to the program as KDP rather than the PNPM, since that was its name during the period when we studied it.

27. The most recent survey of the literature is contained in Mansuri and Rao (forthcoming). Cornwall and Coelho (2007) also provide a set of case studies of participatory institution-building and the gaps between policy and practice. The program, including its social impacts, has received more attention than most World Bank CDD projects. See, e.g., Woodhouse (2005), Olken (2007), McLaughlin, Satu, and Hoppe (2007), Voss (2008), Barron, Humphreys et al. (2009), and Morel, Watanabe, and Wrobel (2009). We draw on these studies throughout the book. Li (2007) provides a critical review of some of the literature that evaluates KDP.

28. More extensive documentation of the methodology employed in this study and the specific challenges it endeavored to address is provided in Chapter 3 and in the appendix.

29. For example, the presence or absence of reported conflict may or may not accurately reflect the extent of underlying tensions—military dictatorships may be able to suppress dissent, whereas frequent open expressions of it may be common in democracies. Political elites and the police will have strong incentives to underreport conflict (lest it reflect poorly on their capacity to maintain order), and cultural norms can strongly influence what is deemed an acceptable expression of conflict (such as domestic violence).

30. For a related argument, see also the important work of Briggs (2008), who argues that "civic capacity cannot determine all the 'cards' that a local community will get to play, but that capacity shapes, quite directly, how well the cards get played" (18).

Chapter 2. The Conflict-Development Nexus Revisited

1. Conflict, to use Coser's classic definition (1956, 8), is the "struggle over values and claims to scarce status, power, and resources, a struggle in which the aims of opponents are to neutralize, injure or eliminate rivals." If status, power, and resources are scare—as, inevitably, they are, given that they are, in part, relational constructs—it would seem that conflict is inevitable. For an interesting discussion of contrasting views of the inevitability of conflict, see Bjorkqvist (1997).

2. From the UNHCR and IDMC Web sites (see World Bank forthcoming).

3. The term *primordialism* was coined by the sociologist Edward Shills (1957) and popularized by the anthropologist Clifford Geertz (1963). Conceptions of cultures as

the embodiment of primordial sentiments flow from the work of, among others, Ruth Benedict (1934) and Margaret Mead (1958).

4. Related accounts of cultural motivations for conflict have circulated in the popular press; see, e.g., Kaplan (1997). Among economists, the early work of Easterly and Levine (1997) made similar claims with respect to Africa (though these authors and others extending this line of research—for example, Rodrik 1999—now make stronger links between growth collapses and the role of institutions).

5. Varshney (2007) notes that although the original essentialists have now been discredited, neo-essentialist arguments focusing on the role of emotions (e.g., Petersen 2002) have recently emerged, and they offer an important future research program concerning the causes of violence.

6. McAdam, Tarrow, and Tilly (2001), in the context of their summary of contemporary collective action theory, point out the difference between structural and rationalist explanations for episodes of contention. Structural analyses look at the interests of collectivities (communities, classes) and examine both individual and group relations. Rational analyses, in contrast, use the individual as the unit of analysis, focusing on the incentives for individuals to join rebel groups and use them as vehicles for the pursuit of their interests (Collier et al. 2003). Weinstein (2007) usefully combines both types of explanation, showing how incentives shape rebel combatants' behavior in times of war and how these nonetheless are shaped in turn by structural issues such as sources of finance and recruitment patterns.

7. Jha (2007) uses a similar argument to explain long-standing historical variation in Hindu-Muslim conflicts in the port cities of western India.

8. The exception is the Uppsala/PRIO dataset commissioned by the Human Security Report for 2002–3. Their standard dataset, which involves counting conflicts involving the state, was expanded to include data on violence between nonstate actors (with a minimum threshold of twenty-five battle-related deaths in one year). With the new data it was found that nonstate conflicts were far more frequent in 2002 and 2003 than state-based conflicts (see Human Security Centre 2005).

9. Collier (2007, 2009) provides a summary. This work has raised much controversy. Some have critiqued their dichotomization of greed and grievance as divergent explanations for war (Murshed and Tadjoeddin 2007), and others have pointed to weaknesses in the methodological approach (Suhrke, Villanger, and Woodward 2005). Others have investigated particular claims and come up with different results. Fearon (2005), for example, questions Collier and Hoeffler's findings concerning the role of primary commodity exports in causing war, arguing that if the sampling frame is changed, even in a minor way, and missing data are included, the results are undermined.

10. A new project of PRIO, the Armed Conflict Location and Events Data (ACLED), now records conflict event incidence by geographic location *within* states, allowing for more nuanced analyses. See Raleigh and Hegre (2009) and Hegre, Ostby, and Raleigh (2009).

11. See, e.g., Justino (2004), Murshed and Gates (2005), Do and Iyer (2007). Kalyvas (2008) provides an overview and critique.

12. Such approaches gained attention in the 1980s with the rise of structural adjustment, in which aid was provided in exchange for policy reforms aimed at reducing borrowing countries' fiscal imbalances. Although structural adjustment has fallen by the wayside, conditionality is still a major tool of development agencies. The Development Policy Loans of the World Bank and the Millennium Challenge Corporation in the United States, for example, both provide resources in exchange for policy reforms. The European Union has followed a similar approach in using EU membership as bait for policy reforms (Knaus and Cox 2005).

13. Disarmament, demobilization, and reintegration (or DDR) programs have become standard elements of international assistance to countries emerging from war. A number of frameworks for DDR, most notably the UN Integrated DDR Standards (United Nations 2006) and the Stockholm Initiative on DDR (Ministry for Foreign Affairs 2006), have been developed that reflect decades of best practice and lessons learned.

14. The focus on democratization as a peace-building initiative has attracted criticism from some quarters. Such efforts have been driven by the "democratic civil peace thesis" (Cramer 2006), which rests on the assumption that democracies are more peaceable than other polities. Snyder (2000) and Paris (2004), among others, warn of the risks of rapid democratization in postwar situations.

15. Search for Common Ground was founded in 1982, International Alert in 1985, and the International Crisis Group in 1995.

16. These include the World Bank's Conflict Analysis Framework (World Bank 2005a), the U.K. Department for International Development's Strategic Conflict Assessments (DFID 2002), and USAID's Conflict Assessments (USAID 2004).

17. See International Rivers Network/Witness for Peace (1996). "Press release: NGOs Demand World Bank Investigation Into 1980s Massacres at Guatemalan Dam Report Reveals 376 Murdered After Resisting Eviction." 9 May. Available at http://internationalrivers.org/en/latin-america/mesoamerica/chixoy-dam-guatemala.

18. International Rivers Network (2004). "Press Backgrounder: Controversial Lao Dam Not Suitable for World Bank Support." 8 September. Available at http://www.edf.org/documents/4139_NT2_backgrounder.pdf.

19. This was an underlying theme of the classic work of Polanyi (1944), Moore (1967), and Skocpol (1979), who studied longer-run development trajectories and the social revolutions that accompanied them, but even among the more recent East Asian tigers (such as South Korea), rapid development and serious conflict went hand in hand (see Kim 1997). We return to this theme in more detail below and in Chapter 8.

20. We are indebted to James Copestake of the University of Bath for bringing this apt phrase to our attention.

21. Caffentzis and Federici (2001) provide a long list of examples of violent resistance to structural adjustment programs (SAPs). A few examples will suffice. In Algeria in October 1998, two hundred people were killed in rioting about price increases and unemployment in the wake of a new SAP. In Bolivia in April 2000, protests against plans by the Bolivian government to privatize water supplies resulted in seven deaths. In Niger in February 1990, between three and fourteen students were

killed by police after protesting against reductions in education funding mandated by a SAP. For a broader historical narrative of efforts by groups across the interior of Southeast Asia to resist modernization and incorporation by the state, see Scott (2009).

22. Alison des Forges (1994, 37) has argued that all foreign aid agencies accepted the continuation of the ethnic identity cards, even as it became clear that they were being used to target Tutsis.

23. Okumu (2003, 130) notes that NGOs frequently lose around 30 percent of their budgets in this way.

24. The legal anthropology literature has contributed greatly to showing how communities navigate such changes and maintain order. Moore (2004) presents a useful overview of the classic readings in this field. See Merry (1992) for a review of changing local dispute resolution mechanisms.

25. Muggah's (2009c) edited volume is one recent exception.

26. In some places, KDP uses preexisting forums though, in many cases, the legitimacy and use of these forums had eroded during the New Order era, when there were few opportunities for genuine participation in local decision making by villagers.

27. Village facilitators (FDs) are selected by vote within the villages they represent; almost all live within those villages and thus inevitably play the role of insiders. In contrast, subdistrict facilitators (FKs) are outsiders, in that they are appointed by the project bureaucracy and almost always are placed in areas that they are not from.

28. They are also obviously shaped by such contexts; see Mosse (2005a, 2005b).

29. This is the causal chain outlined in the UN Human Development Report (UNDP 2002) and implicit in the work of Varshney (2002). We are testing this at the micro level.

30. As Scott (1998) and others have shown, local knowledge (metis) provides a rich (but not always adequate) set of resources on which villagers call as they attempt to solve the problems they face. The New Order state, in its attempts to standardize structures of local government, eroded the role of traditional and community leaders (*tokoh masyarakat*). In creating a formal role for such leaders, KDP could allow for the incorporation of local knowledge into program and nonprogram problem solving and also help create the synergy between civil society and the state necessary for effective development in general (Woolcock 1998) and conflict management in particular.

31. Stewart (2005) argues that violence begets violence and that it is one of the most salient predictors of further violence and conflict escalation. This, of course, makes de-escalating conflicts more difficult.

32. The research found numerous examples of areas where violence is the norm for solving certain kinds of problems. Studies in other parts of Indonesia have demonstrated the pervasiveness and impacts of vigilante justice killings (see Welsh 2008; Varshney 2008; Colombijn 2002, 2005; Abidin 2005).

33. This is particularly true for transaction-intensive programs such as KDP, where local actors have a certain degree of autonomy in decision making. See Pritchett and Woolcock (2004) and Whiteside, Woolcock, and Briggs (2005).

34. Although we treat elite involvement as endogenous to the program, in reality it will in part be a function of exogenous factors (such as whether a community is

accustomed to having high levels of elite involvement in decision making) as well as the ability of the program to manage or change this factor.

35. For a fuller discussion of the way we understand and define *capacity*, see the discussion below. Our approach was influenced by that used during a previous World Bank study on local level institutions study (see Evers 2000).

Chapter 3. Methods, Contexts, and Project Characteristics

1. There are now a number of excellent overviews of comparative case methods. These include Ragin (1987), Geddes (2003), George and Bennett (2005), and Gerring (2007).

2. See the appendix for a summary of the way the cases were chosen.

3. The results of PODES and GDS are summarized, respectively, in Barron, Kaiser and Pradhan (2009) and in McLaughlin and Perdana (2009).

4. See McAdam, Tarrow, and Tilly (2001) for methodological and analytical insights into breaking down larger events into smaller episodes for analysis.

5. See Barron and Madden (2004), Tajima (2004, 2009), and Smith (2005).

6. Researchers were given training in ethical issues associated with carrying out qualitative research on conflict (which is highly sensitive, and itself potentially conflict-inducing).

7. At the time of the research, East Java alone had thirty-seven districts and municipalities.

8. The assumption that local capacity matters in determining the outcomes of development and conflict may seem an obvious one, especially given the extent to which scholars and practitioners have increasingly emphasized the importance of governance, often at the subnational level, in recent years. Yet there is still a tendency in much research on conflict to focus solely on the degree and types of underlying problems as the determinants of levels and outcomes of conflict, rather than the endogenous ability of communities to deal with it. Chapter 7 provides details of interaction effects between KDP and the capacity existent in the prevailing institutional environment.

9. See Barron and Sharpe (2008) for a fuller explanation of the newspaper methodology.

10. See the appendix for a full list of research subdistricts and villages.

11. Subdistricts were selected using propensity score matching techniques (see the appendix for details) and in-field interviews, in order to match on both observable factors (variables that could serve as proxies for the subdistrict level of economic development, such as population size, access to markets, hospitals, department stores, health and education resources, main source of income, perception of poverty levels) and unobservable factors (social cohesion, motivation, leadership quality). This process generated project recipient sites and matched comparison sites that were as statistically (and qualitatively) identical as possible; the other two program recipient locations in each district were picked to maximize diversity in local conditions and KDP performance.

12. In three of the four matched comparison locations, KDP began to operate in the year after the qualitative research was finished and before the survey implementation; thus the areas were no longer pure "control" locations. As such, for some of the comparative analysis in later chapters, we disaggregate analysis by the number of years an area had participated in KDP, rather than simply comparing KDP and matched comparison locations.

13. More details about local-level sampling (including maps of the research districts) are contained later in this chapter and in the appendix.

14. Groups can have ascriptive identities (race, language, clan, caste, and so on) or broader, more affiliative identities (village, political party, economic group, and so on). Horowitz (2000, 55–57) argues that identity groupings fall within a birth-choice continuum where ethnicity is likely to be associated with an ascribed categorization based on birth, whereas other affiliative identities involve choices of group members. We use the term *affiliation* to denote chosen identity group membership.

15. Beatty's (2009) account of life in Banyuwangi provides useful insights into how this tension is playing out at the village level.

16. The districts belonging to the horseshoe area include all of those on the island of Madura (Bangkalan, Sampang, Pamekasan, and Sumenep), as well as Banyuwangi, Situbondo, Pasuruan, Jember, Probolinggo, Lumajang, and Bondowoso on the Javanese mainland.

17. For example, the legend of Prince Sagoro describes his struggle to defeat two giant snakes coming from the ocean. With the aid of the Muslim cleric Kyai Poleng, Prince Sagoro finally succeeded, and the snakes turned into a pair of spears. Prince Sagoro is traditionally considered to be the first occupant of Madura and the pair of spears to be Madura's first weapons.

18. Police records in Pamekasan document 202 incidents of carok in the five years between 1990 and 1994. Of these cases, 40.6 percent of participants were uneducated or had never attended school, 53.1 percent had SD (primary school) educations, and 6.3 percent had SLTP (junior high school) education. Not one carok actor described in these data had studied at an Islamic boarding school (Wiyata 2002, 51).

19. This area includes Batu Marmar, Pasean, Waru, and parts of Pegantenan and Pakong subdistricts.

20. This area is made up of Propo, Palengaan, and parts of Pegantenan and Pamekasan subdistricts.

21. This area includes Pademawu, Tlanakan, Pamekasan, and parts of Galis and Larangan subdistricts.

22. Bajingan are people involved in organized crime networks, that is, local mafia-like figures. This term is usually translated as "thug," but in Madura bajingan often act as part of an informal security network and have leadership and problem-solving qualities. *Bajingan* is used in the singular as well as the plural.

23. Geertz classifies Javanese society into the categories abangan, santri, and priyayi. Priyayi are the Javanese elites connected with the ancient Javanese aristocracy

who adhere to the practices of the traditional Hindu and Javanese faith and who use the high Javanese language. The santri are the members of the community originally associated with seafaring merchants who adhere to the teachings of Islam. The abangan are associated with the Javanese peasant farmers who have a diverse spirituality, often continuing to practice their traditional rituals as well as those encouraged by Islam (see Geertz 1987). These categories are ideal types, with many shades of gray in between (see, e.g., Fauzanafi 2002).

24. Ponorogo's style of reyog is famous for its masked performers, in particular, those who perform using the *singabarong,* a large tiger mask with peacock feathers on the top. Simatupang (2002) argues there are a multitude of local versions of the performance and interpretations of its meaning. These include the possibility that they satirically criticize the spread of Islam in Java following the demise of the Majapahit kingdom, present broader forms of antiestablishment protest in historical and contemporary times, or communicate Islamic teachings. Fauzanafi (2002, 64–67) argues that initially the tiger-masked character of Singabarong symbolized the weakening rule of the Majapahit kingdom and in particular King Brawijaya V (Majapahit), whose dominating wife encouraged him to embrace Islam. Male dancers dressed like women mocked the Majapahit armed forces by portraying them as sick chickens. In contrast, the spirited and free dance of the Pujang Ganong character symbolized Ki Ageng Kutu (a Ponorogo chief who did not support conversion to Islam), ridiculing Singabarong and defeating him. Later interpretations of the dance changed after Ki Ageng Kutu was killed in the battle with Bethara Katong and his supporters, who proselytized for Islam. The dance was later interpreted to mean that the Singabarong character represented Ki Ageng Kutu and the ridiculing dance of Pujang Ganong represented Bethara Katong, who defeated him (Fauzanafi 2002, 64–67).

25. The highlands include Ngrayun, Sooko, Pulung, and Ngebel subdistricts. The lowlands include Slahung, Bungkal, Sambit, Sawoo, Mlarak, Siman, Jetis, Balong, Kauman, Jambon, Badegan, Sampung, Sukorejo, Ponorogo, Babadan, and Jenangan subdistricts.

26. In 2002 Ponorogo also sent a higher number of female migrant workers overseas than any other district in East Java.

27. Another term used to describe the kejawen, both in anthropological studies and by the community, is *abangan.*

28. The reyog community is now a part of the Insan Taqwq Ilahi (INTI), an informal organization started by Golkar (the New Order government party) in the 1980s.

29. According to many people we interviewed, he should not have been chosen as district head that year because the district legislature that appointed him was politically dominated by the Indonesian Democratic Party of Struggle (PDI-P) and already had a preferred candidate from within their party. Since 2004, district heads throughout Indonesia have been popularly elected.

30. Only in West Kalimantan, Central Sulawesi, Maluku, North Maluku, and Papua was the percentage of other ethnicities (that is, ethnic groups other than the seventeen largest) greater (Suryadinata, Arifin, and Ananta 2003).

31. At the time the research began, we had limited information with which to make this claim. The International Crisis Group's (2002) report on violence in Flores argued that it provides a useful lens to examine larger issues in Indonesia. Some papers by local academics and seminarians had highlighted problems with conflict (see, e.g., Lawang 1996; Tule 2000; Muda and Satu 2001). Prior (2003) provides a useful summary of the (mainly Indonesian) sources and argues that land conflicts in Flores have yet to be comprehensively understood (31). As our research proceeded, we were able to get a better sense of the degree of violence in the province.

32. The term *major outbreak* is relative; some individual cases of conflict in Flores have had significant impacts. One case encountered during the research in Lamba Leda subdistrict (in Manggarai district) resulted in eight deaths and damage to eighty houses. In another case, the police shot dead seven people in Ruteng, the capital of Manggarai.

33. Although all the selected subdistricts still fall within the borders of Manggarai district, we use the old boundaries for district-level analysis.

34. See the discussion in Barron and Sharpe (2005).

35. Interview conducted by Patrick Barron with Oscar Maggdelini, a local historian and an expert on adat law, Maumere, Sikka, November 2002. Although Catholicism did not enter Manggarai until the first missionaries arrived in the 1912–18 period, Sikka has been Catholic since the sixteenth or seventeenth century, when the religion was brought in by the Portuguese from the easternmost part of Flores (the island of Solor).

36. Over the course of the research, the district was connected to a mobile phone network, and then it opened its first Internet café.

37. Participatory sphere institutions are new institutions that provide spaces for decision making with regard to public policy and have a semiautonomous existence outside the institutions of formal politics, the bureaucracy, and everyday associational life. They are spaces of contestation into which heterogeneous participants bring diverse interpretations of participation and democracy and divergent agendas (Cornwall and Coelho 2007, 1–2).

Chapter 4. When Do Development Projects Generate Conflict?

1. Throughout the study, respondents were asked about "community problems/conflicts." We used both terms to ensure that informants defined conflict widely to include small-scale disputes and nonviolent clashes. In this study we use the terms *problems* and *conflicts* interchangeably. For the full definitions used in the study, see Barron et al. (2004, 11–14).

2. For East Java, n = 132; for NTT, n = 134. We explore reasons for variation between areas in greater depth in Chapter 7.

3. For East Java, n = 80; for NTT, n = 82.

4. Following on from this research, a mixed-methods study of development and conflict was conducted by the Department of International Development at the University of Oxford. Based on a survey of 2,200 people across three "post-conflict"

districts in Indonesia and three in Sri Lanka, it found that the perceived likelihood of voicing grievances with development programs by taking some kind of action (grievance-driven action, or GDA) was lowest in the districts experiencing higher levels of violent conflict in both countries. Levels of development-related disputes were lower where large-scale political conflict had recently taken place and was in early phases of de-escalation such as in parts of Batticaloa in Sri Lanka and North Aceh in Indonesia. This finding was based on a comparison with districts in both countries where (a) conflict had not escalated into widespread collective violence but tensions and smaller-scale localized violence existed (such as Puttalam in Sri Lanka) or where (b) a once-violent conflict environment had de-escalated to such an extent that peace had taken hold and re-escalation was unlikely (for example, Poso, Indonesia—see Brown and Diprose [2009] on the strength of the peace in Poso). In the lower-conflict areas the levels of grievances with development programs were roughly similar to those in higher-conflict environments, but in these "safer" places people were far more likely to take part in GDA. Most variation was found at the subdistrict level in Indonesia and the equivalent DS division level in Sri Lanka. The level of perceived grievances and consequent GDA was related to the context in which the program was operating, that is, whether the civic space for voicing and taking action concerning grievances was limited (or not) by existing hegemonic power structures or concerns for physical safety, as well as the number of programs present and the kinds of resources they offered. Grievance-driven action was more likely to take place in the more peaceful areas, indicating as much the presence of a healthy space for "voice" and action by citizens (either existing in the region itself or through that provided by the program) as their having knowledge of or being able to identify problems with implementation. In all places, very little GDA resulted in violence. In the most peaceful conflict-affected district in Indonesia at the time the research was conducted, Poso, KDP was perceived to have one of the highest levels of GDA among all programs captured in the survey (see Diprose and Rianom 2010; Diprose, Abdul Cader, and Thalayasingam 2010).

5. See Gibson and Woolcock (2008). Fung and Wright (2003) make similar arguments in a different context.

6. In East Java, 95 percent said there was no violence, and 5 percent did not know. In NTT, 92 percent said there was no violence, 4 percent reported violence, and 4 percent did not know. In East Java, n = 60; in NTT, n = 26.

7. In East Java, 91 percent said there was no violence, 2 percent reported violence, and 7 percent did not know. In NTT, 91 percent said there was no violence, 4 percent reported violence, and 4 percent said they did not know. For East Java, n = 68; for NTT, n = 47.

8. Interviews with editors and journalists in both provinces determined that most incidents of serious violence would be reported in local newspapers (Barron and Sharpe 2005, 2008).

9. The one case of KDP-related violence was a result of corruption (see box 4.4).

10. The conflict may be violent or nonviolent. The forces that help initiate a conflict may not be the same as those that make it escalate or turn violent. In the

analysis of each of the KDP conflict types (below), we explore these issues in more depth.

11. Roads and other types of small-scale infrastructure make up the majority of funded proposals. For the first year of KDP-II, for example, KDP resources went to the following main subproject activities: roads (48 percent), savings and loans (10 percent), clean water (10 percent), education (6 percent), irrigation (6 percent), bridges (5 percent), other economic activities (4 percent), other infrastructure (4 percent), sanitation (2 percent), health (2 percent), markets (1 percent), and electricity (0.4 percent) (Government of Indonesia 2004).

12. Mahmud (2007) reports a similar result from efforts to reform the health system in Bangladesh. Existing vertical social cleavages ultimately mapped on to the groups who participated and had adequate influence in what were meant to be participatory institutions for social change. Poorer men and women, the ultimate beneficiaries of the health services, were reduced to silence; the existing power hierarchies prevailed.

13. For East Java, n = 132; for NTT, n = 134.

14. In Jenangan subdistrict, Ponorogo, a number of informants made this claim: the head of the Saving and Loans Group in Jenangan village; a teacher and former member of the Village Development Council in Kemiri village; and the treasurer of the Saving and Loans Group, the village head, the Krajan hamlet head assistant, and a female community figure, all in Panjeng village. The only case we found where tensions did spill over related to tensions surrounding the building of a kiosk in Badegan village, Ponorogo. See the case study "Caught Between a Rock and a Hard Place: The Dilemma for KDP Facilitators in the Kucur Tourism Market Case" (Anggraini 2003).

15. In villages where participatory mechanisms were more foreign to the inhabitants or where socialization was poor, tensions continued to rise.

16. The decision as to which subdistricts should be rewarded with a fourth year of KDP assistance is made by the Regional Management Unit (RMU) in consultation with the district-level consultants. Across Indonesia, forty-eight subdistricts received a fourth year of KDP-I.

17. A subset of this type of tension could result from what might be called rational resistance on the part of participants, which could take two forms: (a) villagers fully understand KDP's rules and procedures and appear to comply with the outcomes of its competitive bidding mechanisms and inclusion requirements, but they nonetheless use the occasions and resources provided by KDP to express, actively or passively—à la "weapons of the weak" (Scott 1985)—their more general dissatisfaction with external development interventions and the changes they require, or (b) villagers fully understand project rules but do not follow them because to do so would lead them into direct conflict with powerful local elites. (Thanks to David Mosse for reminding us of this point.)

18. This name derives from the fact that the saving and loans scheme was used to grow red onions. Another group was called Bawang Putih (White Garlic).

19. Indeed, corruption is a common problem within KDP, as it is with other development programs. A study of corruption in KDP road projects that looked at the

effect of various "interventions" such as increased probability of auditing found that in control locations—that is, locations without any extra audits—29 percent of funds were lost to corruption (Olken 2007). This figure is high, although we should note that this was 29 percent of micro-project funds and not of the project's budget. This figure still is probably lower than that for projects without participatory mechanisms (Guggenheim 2006). For example, Mallaby (2004) notes that a similar level (approximately 30 percent) of World Bank loans in Indonesia, most of which were of a top-down nature, were corrupted in the years leading to the financial crisis. That corruption rises to the surface in KDP can be seen as a positive sign, however, as it means that, at least in principle, redress can be pursued, and this may have deterrent effects in the future.

20. This was clear in research conducted on the 2004 local legislative elections in East Java, NTT, Maluku, and Bali (Barron, Nathan, and Welsh 2005).

21. For a cross-national analysis of the use of cultural symbolism as a mechanism for the maintenance of power, see Wolf (1999).

22. See Barron, Smith, and Woolcock (2004) for a discussion of how incoherence and incompatibilities with respect to "the rules of the game" affect the likelihood of conflict.

23. As noted in table 4.2, 78.2 percent of survey respondents in Proppo reported that elites played a disproportionately large role in decision making in KDP. For other development projects, the figure was 100 percent.

24. For East Java, n = 119; for NTT, n = 130.

25. In East Java, 92 percent reported use at the village level, and 95 percent reported use at the subdistrict level (n = 99 and n = 20, respectively). In NTT, 97 percent reported use at the village level, and 95 percent reported use at the subdistrict level (n = 111 and n = 19, respectively).

26. For East Java, n = 119; for NTT, n = 129.

27. Across the two provinces, 65 percent of informants at the subdistrict level said forums were used to deal with problems concerning KDP staff or facilitators, compared to 12 percent at the village level. For corruption, the figures are 35 percent (subdistrict level) and 6 percent (village level). For the village level, n = 99; for the subdistrict level, n = 20.

28. Wong (2003, 17) argues that it "was much more difficult [for the complaints handling unit of KDP] to resolve cases related to the misuse of funds and corruption than those involving procedural violations."

29. These figures are averaged across problems relating to corruption and to facilitation.

30. See Barron, Clark, and Mawardi (2004, 49–51) for a fuller analysis and breakdown of the survey data.

31. As noted above, the newspaper conflict datasets (see Barron and Sharpe 2008) provide evidence.

32. For East Java, n = 132; for NTT, n = 134. In East Java, all of the problems solved by KDP facilitators were related to KDP. In NTT, three informants said that the problems solved by KDP facilitators were not related to the project.

33. Most of the responses of "others" refer to formal and informal leaders who are not KDP staff. For example, thirty-five respondents (twenty-five in East Java, ten in NTT) mentioned the village head and village officials, and twenty-eight (twenty-two in East Java, six in NTT) mentioned community leaders. In terms of others who were directly related to KDP, twenty-three respondents mentioned the subdistrict-level KDP team (ten in East Java, twelve in NTT) and four (all in East Java) mentioned the provincial-level KDP team.

34. See further discussion and breakdowns of the survey data in Barron, Clark, and Mawardi (2004, 64–66).

35. It does seem, however, that the government's program of rice for the poor (formerly OPK, now relaunched as Raskin) is particularly prone to corruption; see Olken (2006).

36. Data are from the Complaints Handling Unit of the KDP National Management Consultants, Jakarta.

37. See Barron and Diprose (2006) for the cases and some analysis.

38. This case and all the others referred to in the paper are available online at www.conflictanddevelopment.org.

39. See the analysis above and the material discussed in Chapter 7.

Chapter 5. Can Development Projects Be Part of a Solution?

1. We conducted the newspaper survey in our four research districts plus their neighboring districts. We therefore collected data about three clusters of districts: the Ponorogo cluster (Ponorogo plus Madiun and Magetan), the Pamekasan cluster (Pamekasan plus the three neighboring districts on the island of Madura), and the Flores cluster (all districts on the island of Flores). Over the course of the research, two of the five Florenese districts split, making a total of seven districts on the island. For coding purposes, however, we use the old district boundaries.

2. Again, we used a wide definition of *conflict* that includes relatively minor disputes. We did so in order that we could compare conflicts over similar issues that had different outcomes; see the discussion in Chapters 1 and the appendix.

3. Other impacts of violent conflict, such as property damage and injuries, also varied considerably by district and did not always correlate with death levels. See Barron and Sharpe (2005).

4. The big exception is communal land conflicts in Manggarai. These conflicts are between groups and have much larger impacts each time they occur.

5. Clark (2004) gathers together many of the case studies relating to land conflicts that were followed in the research.

6. We matched the conflict data by year to whether a subdistrict had been in KDP in the previous year. We lagged that data in order to ensure that the full project cycle had finished—a necessary step if we assume that KDP only has a significant impact over a full program cycle. To illustrate, take, for example, a subdistrict that received project aid in cycle 2 (2001–2002) and cycle 3 (2003–4) but not in cycle 1 (1999–2000). The conflicts recorded in years 2 and 3 of our conflict data (2002 and

2003) would be included in the KDP total. Those that took place in the first year (2001) were recorded in the non-KDP total because the program had not yet operated in that subdistrict at that time. Thus one particular subdistrict will contribute toward both the KDP and the non-KDP totals unless it was in the program for at least three years. If a subdistrict was in KDP for three years, it would contribute three years' worth of data to the KDP sum; if was in the program for two years, it would contribute two years' worth of data to the KDP total and one to the non-KDP total; and so on. But once a subdistrict was in the program, all subsequent years were counted in the KDP total because we assume that the program's effects will hold after the program finishes. If, for example, a subdistrict was in KDP in years 1 and 2 but not in year 3, we would still count all three years of conflict data in the KDP total. Doing the analysis this way allows us to factor in conflicts that took place before the program arrived in an area. If we simply compared KDP and non-KDP areas, these conflicts would bias the comparison. See appendix.

7. In East Java, the difference between KDP and non-KDP areas is not significant; in NTT it is significant at the 10 percent level.

8. The data should be interpreted carefully. The bar for "One year," for example, includes only data about conflicts that took place in subdistricts during the first year the program was there; the bar for "Two years" includes only data for subdistricts in their second year of the program. Again, the data are lagged; as such, a subdistrict that was in KDP for three years would contribute one year's worth of data to the "One year" bar (for 2001), one year's data to the "Two years" bar (2002), and one year's data to the "Three years" bar (2003). Because the "Zero years" bar includes three years' data for places that did not participate in the program, two years for those that were in it for one year, and so on, the sample size is larger, even in NTT, where most places have now participated in the program.

9. See discussion in Chapters 6 and 7.

10. A long list of poor subdistricts was prepared using data from the SUSENAS survey to assign KDP. This list was cross-checked locally. This process allowed for local knowledge of the incidence of poverty to be factored in. But at the same time, it did mean that in places political calculations helped determine the list.

11. A number of researchers and theorists have identified absolute poverty as a source of conflict. Burton (1990), for example, argues that violent conflict is a result of the denial of basic absolute needs. Addison (1998) has used the African experience to hypothesize that slow growth is a predictor of violent unrest. Galtung (1969) argues that where underlying structural inequality exists, "positive peace" is unattainable. William Easterly (1999, 2001a, 2001b) has used empirical evidence from Africa to demonstrate that poverty, when combined with inequality, can lead to violence.

12. In a comparison of conflict dynamics in Indonesia and Nigeria, for example, Diprose (2008, 2009a, 2011) finds that despite similar multiethnic and religious contexts, national and local sociopolitical and institutional histories, and similar resource bases, more people fell into poorer household asset wealth deciles in the peaceful districts than in the neighboring conflict-affected districts.

13. Take, for example, the separatist conflict in Aceh. Peace talks between the separatists and the Indonesian government took place in Japan and Finland. Reasons for this included attempts by the separatists (GAM) to internationalize the conflict and their mistrust of the Indonesian government. Indeed, given that GAM representatives at earlier talks were promptly arrested upon returning to Aceh, their concerns may have been sensible.

14. The UN estimates that there were 2,794 deaths from collective violence between 1990 and 2003 in North Maluku (Varshney, Tadjoeddin, and Panggabean 2008, 383).

15. This is based on field visits in January 2002.

16. For East Java, n = 119; for NTT, n = 130.

17. Sample sizes, however, are small: for East Java, n = 20; for NTT, n = 19.

18. Note the small sample size. Only respondents who had said that KDP forums were used for addressing non-KDP problems or conflicts (thirty-three in NTT and twenty-four in East Java) answered this question.

19. For East Java, n = 24; for NTT, n = 33.

20. As noted above, 84 percent of informants in East Java, and 72 percent in NTT reported that KDP-related conflicts or problems dealt with in KDP forums were successfully resolved.

21. For more about who is seen as legitimate for addressing which types of conflict, see the two provincial reports: Diprose (2004) and Satu and Barron (2005). The Governance and Decentralization survey finds that across Indonesia, the main actors in dispute resolution are village officials (generally village heads), informal leaders, and the police. Different types of disputes in different areas, however, tend to go to different mediators (McLaughlin and Perdana 2009).

22. The introduction of the Village Representative Council (Badan Perwakilan Desa, or BPD), an elected body that holds the village head accountable, has changed the unipolar system of power in village life (see Antlov 2001). The results, though generally positive, show that many latent conflicts are often made more explicit, when dissenting villagers have a new and legitimate institution through which to voice their grievances. Yet there are few effective mechanisms for dealing with inter-institution conflict at the village governmental level.

23. When averaged across the two provinces, n = 67.

24. This is not to say that outside intervention has not been important. Indeed, policies of the central state, especially during the New Order era, did much to shape local institutional environments. In particular, Law 5/1979 went a long way toward homogenizing village structures across Indonesia. However, outside interventions have had little effect in determining *difference* in local institutional structures.

25. This does not hold at the village level (see Chapter 7).

26. This results not only in a reluctance to discuss contentious issues in KDP forums; we also found examples in the field of KDP officials pushing for economic production funds to be allocated to those who were already reasonably well-off, knowing that they were more likely to be repaid (Ghewa 2003). Creating an environment that strikes a balance between having clear rules (and sanctions for

breaking them) but that allows for altruistic deviance by KDP staff is a major challenge.

27. We are grateful to Sentot Satria for discussions on this point. More formally, see Barron, Clark, and Daud (2005), which outlines the extent to which KDP was in many places the only local development project operating in Aceh.

28. Their involvement in these activities within forums is covered above.

29. In East Java, 40 percent said facilitators did not solve problems outside of forums, with 8 percent saying they did not know (n=132). In NTT, 38 percent said facilitators did not solve problems outside of forums, with 2 percent saying they did not know (n=134). Note that these figures refer to KDP facilitator *success* and not *use*. Informants were asked whether "conflicts or community problems [were] *resolved* or *partially resolved* by a KDP facilitator." Thus these figures do not include use that was unsuccessful.

30. Across all types of problems (KDP and non-KDP), subdistrict facilitators and village facilitators were the most likely KDP staff to be involved in dealing with conflicts outside of KDP forums. This is unsurprising given their proximity to the communities they serve and their facilitation mandate.

31. The rate at which KDP facilitators addressed non-KDP conflicts may be higher than these results suggest. Respondents who answered that facilitators did address problems outside the forums were only asked whether the problem or conflict was related to KDP. Respondents were not given an option of answering that facilitators addressed both KDP and non-KDP conflicts. Hence, where facilitators addressed both types of conflicts, this may not have been noted.

32. This section draws heavily on the discussion of the "efficacy of intermediaries" in Barron, Smith, and Woolcock (2004, 30–32).

33. This information is from a former village facilitator in Sumedangan, Pademawu, Pamekasan.

34. This is also a good reason why there should never be only one facilitator assigned to a conflict region. There should be at least two facilitators (at each level), so that if one is perceived as biased, the other can be used.

35. On the importance of culture and symbols for addressing public goods, such as the maintenance of peace, see Rao (2008).

Chapter 6. Indirect Effects of Development Projects on Local Conflict Dynamics

1. We should note how we are defining our nonprogram (matched comparison) locations. Three of four subdistricts are not pure nonprogram controls. Whereas these places had not participated in KDP when the qualitative fieldwork was conducted, by the time the second round of the key informant survey was conducted (February 2005), they had participated in one cycle of KDP. (The one exception was Sampung subdistrict in Ponorogo, East Java, which had not participated in the program.) This was unfortunate but unavoidable given the program's scale. By the time the research concluded, almost all poor areas had taken part in the program. In NTT, the only

areas that had not done so by late 2004 were rich or urban areas. As such, it was impossible to find pure matches for our treatment sites. Nevertheless, we can still use these areas as control locations for a number of reasons. First, we hypothesize that the program's effects are cumulative over time; hence by disaggregating by the number of years a location participated in KDP, we can get a sense of the program's impact over time. (Indeed, the analysis below shows that, in general, this hypothesis holds true.) Disaggregating by years of KDP participation also evens up the sample sizes. Second, we argue that one cycle alone of KDP is insufficient to have any real impact on social relations and structures. Given the slow speed at which norms change, we cannot expect real changes in the first year. When we selected our treatment areas, we chose only places that had taken part in KDP for two years or more. As such, the matched comparison site data do help us to discern program impact.

2. Varshney is but one of a number of scholars who have started to draw attention back to how state-society relations and systems of social order help in determining the propensity of individuals or groups to take violent action and the mechanisms by which they do so (see King 2004).

3. These figures are taken from analysis of the KDP and CCN newspaper dataset.

4. Indeed, the causality works both ways. Groups that emphasize narrow identities are probably more likely to conflict with neighboring groups, because the emphasis on the particularity of a given identity increases the extent to which neighboring groups are seen as different. In turn, emphasizing difference can be a strategy to mobilize a group for conflict, often for political or economic reasons (see Barron, Smith, and Woolcock 2004, 21–29).

5. These are outlined in greater detail in Diprose (2004).

6. Nahdlatul Unama (NU) is one of the largest Islamic mass organizations in Indonesia. It has thirty-five million members and represents an important segment of the progressive modernist Islamic movement (see Hefner 2000 for a discussion).

7. Muslims are generally referred to as *ata nggobhe mite*, whereas Catholics are *ata serani*. The former literally means "to wear a black hat"; the latter has its roots in the word *Kristiani* (Christian). Local terms for other religions have yet to be developed.

8. Such electoral patterns are certainly not unique to Flores. See the articles in Erb and Sulistiyanto (2009).

9. This is very different than evidence from elsewhere. Barron and Madden (2004) show, in the case of Lampung, how drunken clashes often develop into larger clashes and how they lead to worsened relations between groups. There is evidence that this also takes place in other areas such as West Kalimantan (Parry 2005).

10. These changes are actually a combination of legislative or political action and broader transnational processes of change (such as globalization and modernization). Of the many legal tools used to these ends, Law 5/79, on village governance, was probably the most important (see Antlov 2001; Evers 2000).

11. The kecamatan is only an arm of the district government apparatus, with no autonomous authority or decision-making power.

12. Take, for example, the case of Cibal subdistrict, Manggarai. According to data obtained in the field, twenty-three small roads in seventeen villages (of twenty-seven in total) were funded during the four years when KDP was operational. In the same period, informants knew of only one other project, P2JD (Proyek Peningkatan Jalan Desa, or Village Road Upgrading Project) that focused on local infrastructure. The government project improved roads in only three villages in the subdistrict.

13. In East Java, 79 percent of the population is Javanese and 18 percent Madurese. No other group makes up more than 1 percent of the provincial population (see Suryadinata, Arifin, and Ananta 2003).

14. Twenty-six percent said relations had improved a lot, 32 percent said they had improved a bit, and 37 percent noted no change. Three percent reported a worsening of relations, and 3 percent said they did not know if there had been any change (n=115).

15. Informants in treatment sites (that is, villages that were two-, three-, and four-year participants in KDP) were asked about changes since the program came to the area. For informants in control sites (that is, zero- and one-year participants), the time period in question was derived by taking the rounded mean number of years of KDP presence in the research locations in that district. Thus, in Pamekasan, informants were asked for changes in the past three years; in the other three districts, they were asked for changes in the past two years.

16. This is taken from the KDP and CCN dataset. Of violent conflicts in 2001, 31 percent had an ethnic basis (22 of 71); 19 percent did in 2002 (16 of 83), and 11 percent did in 2003 (8 of 73).

17. Not surprisingly, in our religiously homogenous East Javanese locations, informants said either that KDP had not made any difference or they did not know whether it had.

18. For one-year villages, n=47; for other villages, n=115.

19. An important critique of community-driven development projects such as KDP is that they set up structures that are parallel to the state and, in doing so, undermine it (see Tendler 2000). This raises vital policy questions. In the Indonesian context, when KDP was designed in 1997, it deliberately bypassed the state because (a) the system of patronage and corruption that characterized the Indonesian state prevented the delivery of services to the local level, and (b) it was felt that it would be easier to reform the state from the outside—for example, by creating visible examples of processes that worked, and hence demand for similar structures within the state—than by tackling state corruption directly (see Guggenheim 2006). Now that Indonesia is further along its path of democratic transition, questions arise as to how and to what extent projects like KDP should link in to formal state structures. The transformation of KDP into the National Community Empowerment Program (PNPM) is a conscious attempt to increase the involvement of government ministries.

20. This is the hypothesis that informs the 2002 UNDP Human Development Report (UNDP 2002).

21. See, e.g., Polanyi (1944), Moore (1967), Skocpol (1979), Goldstone (1991), and Bates (2000).

22. See International Crisis Group (2003, 2005), McCarthy (2004), Cribb (2005), and van Klinken (2007).

23. Note that a movement has developed to limit the degree of autonomy that can be exercised at the local level. Law 32/2004 dilutes some devolution measures (e.g., BPDs will now be appointed rather than elected), while strengthening others (such as provisions for the direct election of bupati). It is still unclear how changes to the role of the BPD will play out or even whether these changes will be fully implemented.

24. In many (usually private) realms of village life, women play a key role. In particular, it is common for women to be in control of household economics, looking after money and outgoing expenses. Thanks to Michael Dove for this point.

25. If we count one-year villages as comparison sites, then the proportions of respondents reporting more groups coming to village meetings are 52 percent (comparison locations) and 61 percent (project locations).

26. Similar accounts were provided by a religious community figure in Wates, Ponorogo, and in an interview with a development coordinator in Slahung, Ponorogo. This supports other evidence from KDP supervision missions. See Guggenheim (2006) for a good example from Sulawesi.

27. Informants in KDP areas were asked whether decision making had become more democratic after the program had arrived. For the comparison areas, we calculated the mean number of years that KDP had been in operation in the research subdistrict in each district. Informants were asked for changes over this period.

28. See the discussion in Chapter 5 about the different qualities that interveners need.

29. This is also true in other provinces; see World Bank (2004) and Stephens (2003).

30. Regarding both questions, for project areas, n = 226; for matched comparison areas, n = 96.

31. One of the reasons we concentrated on local factors in the study was that most studies, at least in Indonesia, have tended to prioritize extralocal (often national) explanations of conflict in Indonesia (see Bertrand 2004 and much of the literature concerning institutional transitions).

32. For a justification of breaking larger events down into smaller episodes for analysis, see McAdam, Tarrow, and Tilly (2001).

33. We outline this model in much greater depth in Barron, Smith, and Woolcock (2005). The two provincial papers—Diprose (2004) on East Java and Satu and Barron (2005) on NTT—apply these frameworks to much of the case material.

34. This was particularly true in Manggarai (see the more detailed discussion in Barron, Smith, and Woolcock 2005). On the ways in which culture can provide a basis for group mobilization by leaders seeking to consolidate or expand their power, see also Wolf (1964, 1969, 1999) and Brass (1991).

35. See the appendix for a fuller discussion of how case studies were selected and local factors were disaggregated from extralocal ones.

36. It is important to reiterate that such interactions need to be institutionalized.

37. In the short run, of course, opening up local decision making can increase tensions and conflict, as elites lose their monopoly. We saw in Chapter 4 that their resistance to democratization can make conflict more likely. The literature has also shown the extent to which transitions to democracy can see surges in levels of conflict (Gurr 2001; Haggard and Kaufman 1995; Snyder 2000). This was all too evident in Indonesia, which saw a massive upsurge in violence in the years immediately following the fall of Suharto (Varshney, Tadjoeddin, and Panggabean 2008).

38. On the limits of past approaches to judicial reform in developing countries and the (more hopeful) prospects of current initiatives, see Carothers (2006) and Sage and Woolcock (2008).

Chapter 7. How Contexts Shape Project Performance and Conflict Trajectories

1. On approaches to understanding capacity building and their implications for development policy, see McNeil and Woolcock (2004). See also Eade (1997).

2. Fukuyama (2004) makes the case for conceptualizing development as capacity building. He argues that "the problem of capacity destruction cannot be fixed unless donors make a clear choice that capacity-building is their *primary* objective, rather than the services that the capacity is meant to provide" (55; emphasis in original).

3. On the importance of discretionary and face-to-face decision making for explaining development failure (and, concomitantly, as a key ingredient in making services work), see Pritchett and Woolcock (2004).

4. The approach of understanding local capacity as the ability to solve collective problems was also at the heart of the Local Level Institutions study, which preceded KDP and provided the empirical base on which much of it was designed (Guggenheim 2006).

5. In the Indonesian context, the district is extremely important because, with decentralization, tremendous resource allocation and policymaking discretion exists at this level. The quality of local government helps determine both the ways in which development programs are implemented and the likelihood of violent conflict. The village level is also important because decentralization has helped open up village-level politics.

6. See the appendix for the methodology and the ranking. Anchoring vignettes (see King et al. 2004) are short, familiar anecdotes that are presented to villagers in different settings; the vignettes are drawn from everyday life and include examples of, say, strong, moderate, and weak program performance. The responses to these vignettes can be used to ensure greater compatibility and comparability between questions asked in different contexts.

7. We do not have a quantitative measure of program performance similar to the one for capacity. At face value, it is hard to conceive of reliable indicators that would be truly independent of local context effects. For example, one could use data about the presence or absence of corruption, but the measured presence of corruption could actually be a sign of good program operation if the corruption was caught through the

program and then effectively addressed. For our present purposes, we can only make binary distinctions between "strong" and "weak" program performance on the basis of evidence drawn from our case studies, which document instances of program malfunction; for future work, we would recommend incorporating common anchoring vignettes as a way of qualitatively assessing (and then quantitatively validating) comparative measures of program performance.

8. In Paga, 47 percent of informants reported that KDP village forums triggered conflict. Across the five other subdistricts in Flores, the shares of those giving this response were between 10 percent (Cibal and Talibura) and 21 percent (Lamba Leda).

9. The survey does not capture the seriousness of conflicts in terms of the numbers of people involved, scale of the impact, or the length of time it took to resolve the dispute.

10. Very similar proportions of informants—70 percent in high-capacity villages, 71 percent in medium-capacity villages, and 72 percent in low-capacity villages— reported that KDP triggered conflict in subdistrict meetings. This is not surprising, given that a subdistrict is likely made up of many villages with different capacity and that the villages under study were not selected to be representative of the subdistrict in which they lie.

11. The reported level is 58 percent compared to a range of 73 percent to 89 percent for the other village/district capacity combination types.

12. The survey question refers to the "successful" use of KDP facilitators "outside of KDP forums." We thus do not have quantitative information about when they are used unsuccessfully or about their role inside forums.

13. For in-built conflicts, however, the success rate is lower in areas with low capacity at both the village and the district levels (78 percent) than in any other village-district capacity combination (which range from 93 percent to 100 percent). Sample sizes are too low for malfunction conflicts to be disaggregated for both village and district capacity levels.

14. Ellikson (1991, 240–64) uses the concept of "controller-selecting rules" to account for this phenomenon.

15. Just as one might be reluctant to go to the police with allegations of police corruption, so, too, might one expect villagers to be unlikely to use KDP forums to raise concerns pertaining to the inappropriate actions of local power holders.

16. Protesters were a subdistrict head of PMD, Jengangan, Ponorogo and a saving and loans group head, Jenangan, Jenangan, Ponorogo. This is a program malfunction conflict, in that the intended KDP rules and procedures were not applied.

17. In NTT, 4 percent of informants said they did; none in East Java agreed.

18. The reported rates of forum use for non-KDP problems are 13 percent in high-capacity villages, 15 percent in medium-capacity villages, and 15 percent in low-capacity villages. Sample sizes are 77, 104, and 47, respectively.

19. The gap in reported rates of KDP-triggered conflict is 31 percent between low- and high-capacity districts, compared with 16 percent between low- and

high-capacity villages. Other differences are use for program malfunction conflicts (21 percent in districts, 10 percent in villages), use for non-KDP conflicts (12 percent in districts, 2 percent in villages), facilitator use (21 percent in districts, 13 percent in villages), and successful use for malfunction conflicts (15 percent in districts, 11 percent in villages). The sole exception is for successful use of forums for non-KDP conflicts. In this case, village capacity matters more than district capacity: there is a 16 percent gap between high- and low-capacity villages in successful use, compared with an 8 percent gap at the district level.

20. The one exception is for in-built KDP conflict where district capacity has little effect. This, as we argued above, is because this is a normal and routine use for KDP.

21. This supports other evidence that shows Indonesian conflict to be geographically concentrated in a small number of districts (Varshney et al. 2008; Varshney 2008).

22. There have been moves to roll back decentralization, with some fearing it has gone too far.

23. In Lamba Leda a number of informants still felt that KDP forums were good for problem solving. This shows the extent to which community members are able to distinguish the actions of particular individuals within the program (such as the subdistrict facilitator) from the worth of the program overall. Informants told us that the project bureaucracy's following up on the case had restored people's faith in KDP, although they were frustrated that at the time of the interviews (February 2005) there had not yet been a conviction because the case was stuck in the provincial court in West Timor.

24. The full results are given in the summary of the key informant survey; see Barron, Clark, and Mawardi (2004).

25. On this subject, see also the work of Eric Wolf (1964, 1999) who has shown how structures and power relations shape cultures.

26. See the discussion of the "dynamics of difference" in Barron, Smith, and Woolcock (2004, 21–29) and in Diprose (2004).

27. As for many of the direct impact measures, although low-capacity districts are more likely to report more groups coming to meetings, village capacity works in the opposite direction, with high-capacity villages more likely to report improvements than are medium- or low-capacity ones (76 percent versus 68 percent and 66 percent, respectively).

28. Ravallion's (2001) arguments pertain to understanding the relation between economic growth and poverty reduction, but the general principle that documenting and exploring sources of variation—or unpacking standard deviations, not simply reporting mean impacts—yields important insights is equally relevant to understanding the efficacy of projects.

29. We have split behavioral change into two dimensions: participation and decision making. The reason is that context has a different effect on each. The program is likely to have a greater impact on levels of participation in low-capacity areas. Conversely, impacts on decision making are greater in high-capacity areas.

Chapter 8. Contesting Development

1. Indeed, for some social theorists (see Escobar 1995), the very notion of development, let alone the practice of it, is so infused with Western conceptions of progress, capitalism ("neoliberalism"), and domination that it should be abandoned entirely in favor of a post-development discourse. We do not engage such debates in this book; we simply assert that bilateral and multilateral agreements between elected governments regarding development assistance activities of various kinds, though not without problems, nonetheless remain eminently defensible as a basis on which to conduct international relations. From that premise, and an underlying belief that certain forms of progress (from war to peace, from destitution to sufficiency, from repression to opportunity) are both desirable and possible, we are immediately cast into all the familiar problems of development and associated modalities (and politics) of engagement, to which we think social theory can make many important substantive contributions. We maintain that, beyond merely trying to improve existing mechanisms of development assistance (though that would be an important contribution in its own right), social theory, taken seriously, has the potential to inform—and, crucially, to be informed by—new ways of conceiving problems and enacting constructive responses.

2. Responding effectively to the challenges of improving physical infrastructure, lowering inflation, and reducing mortality also requires no small measure of social input.

3. We recognize the formal critiques of KDP (for example, that it is merely "neo-liberalism" with a "social" face—Li 2007) and the points they are trying to raise, but we think they give inadequate attention to the genuinely unique features of KDP within the World Bank portfolio (and international development efforts more generally). Often, as we discuss below, such responses seem more committed to offering yet more criticism than to providing constructive, supportable alternatives.

4. One example is the Scaling Up Poverty Reduction Conference held in Shanghai in May 2004 to spotlight the projects deemed to be helping developing countries make the fastest progress toward attaining the Millennium Development Goals. Even if this is a classic high modern bureaucratic response—fret about failure to meet general targets, identify projects from particular countries that "work," then argue that those projects can and should be replicated elsewhere—for present purposes we simply note that KDP, for all its idiosyncrasies and unusual intellectual moorings, is held in high regard in most quarters of the World Bank.

5. This expression is adapted from Briggs (2008), who persuasively demonstrates that democracy works at the local level to the extent that it provides mechanisms not only for contestation and deliberation but also for problem solving.

6. See also the important work of other scholars (such as Sampson, Morenhoff, and Earls 1999) who have referred to this general concept as "collective efficacy."

7. Olken (2006, 2007) has shown that specific *aspects* of KDP can be modified such that impacts on selected outcome variables can be more formally identified.

8. On the importance of history for understanding development, see (most recently) Lewis (2009) and Woolcock, Szreter, and Rao (forthcoming); on the lack of

geographers as authors of and advisors to the World Development Report 2009 on economic geography, see Rigg et al. (2009); on the potential contributions of anthropology to development, see (among many others) Gardner and Lewis (1996) and Rao and Walton (2004); on sociology, see Evans (2004) and Portes (2006); on political science see Tendler (1997), Grindle (1997), and Corbridge et al. (2005), among many others. It is perhaps no coincidence that the Indonesian team was among the first in the World Bank to appoint a senior governance advisor with a Ph.D. in political science.

9. On the historical rise to prominence of economics over law as the dominant profession within public policy, see Markoff and Montecinos (1993). In Morris's (1963) instructive review of World Bank projects in the early 1960s, for example, economists play a relatively minor role compared to engineers, accountants, lawyers, and politicians in determining the content, placement, and effectiveness of projects, most of which were concerned with large-scale infrastructure.

10. Or "color," as a colleague once pejoratively put it.

11. In this sense, novelists (and artists more generally) sometimes provide quite different renderings of development problems, experiences, and responses from those presented in scholarly tomes or policy reports (see Lewis, Rodgers, and Woolcock 2008). These renderings can be usefully understood in their own right and as an important medium wherein popular understandings of development process (for better or worse) are forged.

12. The particular confluence of events and processes that enabled social theory to play the central role in the design of KDP is outlined in Guggenheim (2006). On the broader analytical underpinnings of the World Bank's governance work in Indonesia, see Guggenheim (2008). We recognize that many small-scale development interventions overseen by NGOs are designed (implicitly, if not explicitly) on the basis of social theory.

13. See Martinussen (1997, chapter 5). Moore (1997) provides a masterful account of the ways in which all entities (disciples, ideologies) that were signatories to modernization theory systematically undervalued the enduring role and importance of social relations.

14. That some of these early modernities struggled or failed to sustain themselves—or underwent significant change as a result of domestic, demographic, environmental, and external pressures—is itself an interesting issue of scholarly inquiry with direct significance for development policy today.

15. For a related argument, see Evans (2004). See also Carothers (2006) and Sage and Woolcock (2008) on the legacies of the law and development movement of the 1970s and the legal reform movement of the late 1980s and early 1990s, both of which explicitly sought to import Western legal systems and precepts into developing and transitional countries.

16. Echoes of this approach can actually be seen in the Paris Declaration on Aid Effectiveness (signed in March 2005 by ministers, senior officials, and heads of agencies from more than one hundred developed and developing countries), a document whose significance is underappreciated by the broader development

community. The declaration is available at http://www.oecd.org/dataoecd/11/41/34428351.pdf.

17. See Woolcock (2009b) and the references therein. For a more general discussion of "usable social theory," see Rueschemeyer (2009).

18. This applies not only to empowerment initiatives but also to evaluations of all development projects, very few of which explicitly specify the shape of the impact trajectory that can be expected (whether on the basis of theory, experience, or empirical evidence). Absent such a specification, the default assumption (readily on display in introductory project evaluation courses) is that impact trajectories are monotonically linear and increasing. But on closer inspection this is a very hard assumption to accept, leaving evaluators open to routinely drawing false conclusions about project efficacy, even when a "gold standard" randomization protocol has been used as part of the assessment exercise (Woolcock 2009c).

19. This section draws on Woolcock (2009c).

20. This section draws on Gibson and Woolcock (2008).

21. This echoes Baiocchi's observation that deliberation may take place not only under the aegis of rationality and problem solving and with the goal of reforming government but also that of empowerment of the poor and social justice (Baiocchi 2001, 55–56).

22. For similar examples from Cambodian labor reform initiatives, see Adler, Sage, and Woolcock (2009).

23. Jürgen Habermas is one of the leading social theorists of deliberative democracy (see, among many other seminal contributions, Habermas 1984). For a broader treatment of this issue, see Fung and Wright (2003).

24. We thank Lant Pritchett for this deft encapsulation.

Appendix

1. The full methodological details underpinning this study are outlined in Barron, Diprose, Smith, et al. (2004).

2. There are strong incentives against conducting evaluations. These include (a) the political and career stakes, which are such that the risk of finding out that a project does not work persistently trumps the value of any design lessons that could be learned by subjecting a project to a stringent evaluation, and (b) the chance that the size of the portfolio one manages continues to be more prestigious than the demonstrated impact that one's projects might achieve (and which may only be realized long after the manager has moved on—for example, in the case of education).

3. The important work of Olken (2006, 2007), which complements our study, shows that innovative quantitative evaluation techniques can be adapted to assess the efficacy of particular programmatic aspects of participatory projects such as KDP, but this type of research is only possible because of deep engagement with the particularities of Indonesian village life (that is, prior and simultaneous qualitative work makes possible the more public stand-alone quantitative findings). See also Alatas (2005), Voss (2008), and Barron, Humphreys et al. (2009).

4. We also recognized, of course, that the trajectory of many conflicts includes periods of stagnation when the conflict became mired (whether by design or default on the part of participants or third-party negotiators) and was thus neither escalating nor diminishing. On these dynamics, see Barron, Smith, and Woolcock (2004).

5. Full analysis of the qualitative data is given in the two provincial reports: Diprose (2004) and Satu and Barron (2005). Other papers from the study also draw heavily on the qualitative findings (e.g., Gibson and Woolcock 2008). A volume of case studies on land conflict collected during the study is Clark (2004).

6. The training manuals (Barron, Diprose, and Smith 2004) are available online at www.conflictanddevelopment.org.

7. The field researchers often lived in the spare rooms of the houses of such interviewees during their time in the villages, since there were no hotels nearby. The researchers were in villages for several days, and these living arrangements afforded them a unique opportunity to engage in quite detailed and personal conversation in a safe space (often the kitchen, in the case of female informants) with those who would otherwise be very hard to reach. It also meant that they had multiple occasions on which to cross-check the reliability and validity of both respondents' statements and their own observations.

8. To be precise, we designed and fielded the key informant survey, compiled the newspaper dataset, contributed one module to the GDS survey but did not participate in the fielding, and borrowed data generated by the government's PODES survey.

9. See below for a full breakdown of respondents.

10. As noted by Varshney, Tadjoeddin, and Panggabean (2008), the New Order did not publish any figures about the impacts (death, injuries, other destruction) of conflicts. A number of different ministries and departments have launched programs that aim to assess the potential for conflict. Kesbang (within the Ministry of Home Affairs) and the Centre for Religious Harmony (within the Religious Affairs Department) have started such programs, with the Coordinating Ministry of Politics and Security coordinating the information. These programs are still at embryonic stages, however, and do not provide comparable information across different geographic areas (see UNDP 2004, especially Technical Annex A, "Knowledge Management for Conflict Risks, Impact and Needs Assessment"). Police data are also weak, and analysis is hampered by the lack of common definitions and categories.

11. Ideally, we would have used statistical data about the incidence of conflict to help make these selections, but such evidence did not exist in Indonesia at the time.

12. This is a statistical technique used to identify otherwise comparable treatment and nontreatment groups on the basis of the probability of being selected. See Rosenbaum and Rubin (1983, 1985) or, for a general introduction, Baker (2000).

13. Our thanks go to Vivi Alatas for doing the propensity score matching.

14. We learned through this selection process that ensuring the accuracy of propensity score matches involves a substantial amount of field investigation.

15. Where the program was not working properly, KDP impacts were clearly difficult to find. In order to compensate, we purposively extended the sample into subdistricts where the program was functioning properly. In effect, this means that

our research investigates KDP impacts *conditional on KDP functioning relatively well*, and not KDP program impacts more generally, although, as we discuss, there is considerable variation in KDP performance and functionality throughout our sample.

16. "Peaceful" resolution of conflict is a relative concept that includes "less violent" and "nonviolent but not harmonious" resolution. In Indonesia, as elsewhere, peaceful resolution at times means suppression of a particular incident, with the underlying conflict continuing to fester below the surface. See the discussion below.

17. King et al. (2004) provide a detailed discussion of the underlying principles and rationale. For additional application of anchoring vignettes to development issues, see Das and Hammer (2005).

18. One of the initial reasons the study was launched was to help determine how the KDP model could be modified to work better in areas with high levels of conflict. The result has been the design of a World Bank and Indonesian government program, the Support for Poor and Disadvantaged Areas project.

19. In order to facilitate cross-checking of our findings, our data are available in various levels of aggregation on the project's Web site: www.conflictanddevelopment.org.

Glossary

Acronyms

ADR	Alternative dispute resolution
APBDes	Village budget (*Anggaran Pendapatan dan Belanja Desa*)
CCN	Community conflict negotiation
CDD	Community-driven development
CRDP	Community Reintegration and Development Project (Rwanda)
FGD	Focus group discussion
GAM	Free Aceh Movement (*Gerakan Aceh Merdeka*), an organization previously seeking Acehnese independence
GDS	Governance and Decentralization Survey
IDPs	Internally displaced people
IDT	Presidential Instruction for Underdeveloped Areas
MDGs	Millennium Development Goals
NGOs	Nongovernmental Organizations
NTT	Nusa Tenggara Timur (East Nusa Tenggara), Indonesia
OPK	Special Market Operation (a rice subsidy program)
PAN	National Mandate Party (*Partai Amanat Nasional*)
PKB	National Awakening Party (*Partai Kebangkitan Bangsa*)
PODES	Village Potential Statistics (*Potensi Desa*)
PPP	United Development Party (*Partai Persatuan Pembangunan*)
SPADA	Support for Poor and Disadvantaged Areas project, Indonesia
SUSENAS	Indonesian Socioeconomic Survey

Indonesian Jurisdictional Levels

Kabupaten	District
Kecamatan	Subdistrict
Desa	Village
Dusun	Hamlet
RT/RW	Neighborhood/collection of neighborhoods

Institutions

BPD	Village Representative Council (*Badan Perwakilan Desa*)
BPS	Bureau of Statistics (*Badan Pusat Statistik*)
Dolog	Government warehouses for foodstuffs
DPRD II	District Legislative Council
Itwilkab	District Inspectorate (*Inspektorat Wilayah Kabupaten*)
Kesbang	National Security and Emergency Agency (*Kesbang Linmas*)
KPU	National Electoral Commission
LKD	Village Social Council/Village Development Council (*Lembaga Kemasyarakatan Indonesia*) under regional autonomy, previously the LKMD
LKMD	Village Community Resilience Council under the Suharto government but translated in text as Village Development Council to convey the substance of the council as a development decision-making board (*Lembaga Ketahanan Masyarakat Desa*). This became the LKD with regional autonomy.
LMD	Village Deliberation Council (*Lembaga Musyawarah Desa*)
Menko Polkam	Coordinating Ministry of Politics and Security
Muspika	Forum of district representatives from all security and government agencies
PKK	Family Welfare Organization (*Pemberdayaan Kesejahteraan Keluarga*)
PMD	Community Development Agency within the Ministry of Home Affairs (*Pemberdayaan Masyarakat Desa*)
P2JD	Village Road Upgrading Project (*Proyek Peningkatan Jalan Desa*)

Government Positions

Camat	Subdistrict head
Bupati	District head
Kepala Desa	Village head
Klebun	Village head (Madura)
Lurah	Village head in urban areas

KDP Positions and Institutions

KDP	Kecamatan Development Program
KDP-I	First phase of KDP
KDP-II	Second phase of KDP
KDP-III	Third phase of KDP
FD	Village facilitator (*Fasilitator Desa*)
FK	Subdistrict facilitator (*Fasilitator Kecamatan*)
KMKab	District management consultant (*Konsultan Manajemen Kabupaten*)
KSP	Saving and loan groups (*Kelompok Simpan Pinjam*)
MAD	Subdistrict Development Forum (*Musyawarah Antar Desa*), also known as the intervillage forum and as UDKP
MD	Village meeting (*Musyawarah Desa*)
Musyawarah Desa	Village meeting, also known as *Musbangdes* (Village Development Forum, or *Musyawarah Pembangunan Desa*)
Musdes	See *Musyawarah Desa*, above.
Penggalian Gaggasan	Brainstorming session (hamlet KDP meeting), also known as *Musbungdus* (*Musyawarah Pembangunan Dusun*, Hamlet Development Forum)
PjOK	Subdistrict-level development coordinator
PTO	Operations Technical Guidelines
RAB	Draft budget
RMU	Regional Management Unit
TPK	Project Implementation Team (*Tim Pelaksana Kegiatan*)
TTD	Village technical staff (*Tim Teknis Desa*)
UDKP	Subdistrict Development Forum (*Unit Daerah Kerja Pembangunan*), also known as MAD
UEP	Productive economic enterprises (*Unit Economi Produktif*)
UPK	Financial management unit at the subdistrict level (*Unit Pengelola Kegiatan*)

Other Terms

Abangan	Non-Muslims or Muslims influenced by traditional mystical beliefs (Java)
Adat	Traditional or customary (as in *hukum adat*, traditional law)
Bajingan	Mafia-like criminal groups (Madura)
Belis	Bride price
Bima	System of governance (Manggarai)
Campursari	Javanese dance performance to pentatonic music (Java)
Carok	Duels over honor or for justice, usually carried out with sickles (Madura)
Engkel-engkelan	To be locked in argument (Java)

Gotong royong	Mutual cooperation
Kampung	Residential area or hamlet
Kedaluan	Traditional subdistricts (Manggarai)
Kejawen	Syncretic Islam (Java)
Kelompok	Group
Kerja bakti	Community service (Java)
Ketua	Head (as in head of)
Kota	Town, city
Kyai	A Muslim cleric or teacher
Musyawarah	Meeting where decisions are made based on deliberation and consensus
Nyikep	Custom of carrying weapons (Madura)
Orang miskin	Poor people
Pajak Bumi dan Bangunan	Land and building tax
Pemekaran	Division of administrative areas
Preman	Thugs
Priyayi	Bureaucrats and gatekeepers of morality (Java)
Raskin	Rice for the Poor (*Beras Miskin*)
Reformasi	The reform era
Rp.	Indonesian currency (*Rupiah*)
Rumah Aspirasi	House of Aspiration (proposed district-level forum)
Santri	Orthodox Muslims (Java)
Silat	Martial arts groups
Suku	Ethnic group
Tim Sukses	Success teams
Tokoh Masyarakat	Respected community figure or elder

References

Abidin, Zainal. 2005. *Penghakiman Massa: Studi Psikologi Sosial Tentang Kekerasan Kolektif Terhadap Orang-Orang Yang Dipersepsi Sebagai Pelaku Kejahatan.* Jakarta: Gramedia.

Addison, Tony. 1998. *Rebuilding Post-Conflict Africa: Reconstruction and Reform.* Helsinki: WIDER/United Nations University.

Adler, Daniel, Caroline Sage, and Michael Woolcock. 2009. Interim Institutions and the Development Process: Opening Spaces for Reform in Cambodia and Indonesia. Working Paper no. 86. Brooks World Poverty Institute, University of Manchester.

Alatas, Vivi. 2005. Economic Analysis of KDP Infrastructure. Mimeo, World Bank Office, Jakarta.

Alexander, Jeffrey C. 2006. *The Civil Sphere.* New York: Oxford University Press.

Alsop, Ruth, and Nina Heinsohn. 2005. Measuring Empowerment in Practice: Structuring Analysis and Framing Indicators. Policy Research Working Paper no. 3510. World Bank, Washington, D.C.

Anderson, Benedict. 1991. *Imagined Communities: Reflections on the Origins and Spread of Nationalism.* Rev. ed. London: Verso.

Anderson, Mary B. 1999. *Do No Harm: How Aid Can Support Peace—Or War.* Boulder: Rienner.

Anggraini, Novia Cici. 2003. Caught Between a Rock and a Hard Place: The Dilemma for KDP Facilitators in the Kucur Tourism Market Case. Mimeo, World Bank Office, Jakarta

———. 2004. The Village Representative Board (BPD) in Kecamatan Badegan and Sampung, Kabupaten Ponorogo. Mimeo, World Bank Office, Jakarta.

Anggraini, Novia Cici, and Imron Rasyid. 2004. KDP Implementation and Dreams of Social Change. Mimeo, World Bank Office, Jakarta.

Antlov, Hans. 2001. Village Governance and Local Politics in Indonesia. Paper presented at session on Decentralization and Democratization in Southeast Asia at SOAS, London, 6–9 September.

———. 2003a. "Not Enough Politics! Power, Participation and the New Democratic Polity in Indonesia." In *Local Power and Politics in Indonesia: Decentralisation and Democratisation*, ed. Edward Aspinall and Greg Fealy. Singapore: Institute of Southeast Asian Studies, 72–86.

———. 2003b. "Village Government and Rural Development in Indonesia: The New Democratic Framework." *Bulletin of Indonesian Economic Studies* 39(2): 193–214.

Appadurai, Arjun. 2004. "The Capacity to Aspire: Culture and the Terms of Recognition." In *Culture and Public Action*, ed. Vijayendra Rao and Michael Walton. Palo Alto: Stanford University Press, 59–84.

Ashari, Luthfi. 2003. Power Sharing Between the Kyai, Bajingan and the Village Head. Mimeo, World Bank Office, Jakarta.

———. 2005. The Dynamics of District Governance: Forums, Budgetary Processes and Transparency: Case Studies of Bangkalan and Poso Districts. Indonesian Social Development Paper no. 1. World Bank, Jakarta.

Aspinall, Edward. 2009. *Islam and Nation: Separatist Rebellion in Aceh, Indonesia*. Stanford: Stanford University Press.

Aspinall, Edward, and Greg Fealy, eds. 2003. *Local Power and Politics in Indonesia: Decentralisation and Democratisation*. Singapore: Institute of Southeast Asian Studies.

Ayres, Robert L. 1998. *Crime and Violence as Development Issues in Latin America and the Caribbean*. Washington, D.C.: World Bank.

Baare, Anton. 2004. Policing and Local Level Conflict Management in Resource Constrained Environments: Case Studies in Kabupaten Sikka (NTT) and Kabupaten Ponorogo (East Java), Indonesia. Mimeo, NCG/World Bank, Jakarta.

Badan Pusat Statistik. 2000. *Indonesia Census Data—2000*. Jakarta: Badan Pusat Statistik.

———. 2002a. *Jawa Timur Dalam Anka*. Jawa Timur: Badan Pusat Statistik.

———. 2002b. *Kabupaten Ponorogo Dalam Anka 2001*. Ponorogo: Badan Pusat Statistik.

———. 2002c. *Nusa Tenggara Timur Dalam Anka*. Nusa Tenggara Timur: Badan Pusat Statistik.

Baiocchi, Gianpaolo. 2001. "Participation, Activism, and Politics: The Porto Alegre Experiment and Deliberative Democratic Theory." *Politics and Society* 29(1): 43–72.

Baker, Judy. 2000. *Evaluating the Impact of Development Projects on Poverty: A Handbook for Practitioners*. Washington, D.C.: World Bank.

Barnawi, Saifullah. 2003. KDP Under the Hegemony of the Klebun: A General Picture of the Implementation of KDP in Kec. Proppo, Pamekasan. Mimeo, World Bank Office, Jakarta.

Barron, Patrick, Samuel Clark, and Muslahuddin Daud. 2005. *Conflict and Recovery in Aceh: An Assessment of Conflict Dynamics and Options for Support to the Peace Process*. Jakarta: World Bank.

Barron, Patrick, Samuel Clark, and Ambar Mawardi. 2004. The Links Between
    KDP and Local Conflict: Results from a Key Informant Survey in East Java and
    NTT. Rev. version. Mimeo, World Bank Office, Jakarta.
Barron, Patrick, and Rachael Diprose. 2006. Nine Cases of Development and Conflict
    in Indonesia. Mimeo, World Bank Office, Jakarta.
Barron, Patrick, Rachael Diprose, David Madden, Claire Q. Smith, and Michael
    Woolcock. 2004. Do Participatory Development Projects Help Villagers Manage
    Local Level Conflicts? A Mixed Methods Approach to Assessing the Kecamatan
    Development Project, Indonesia. Conflict Prevention and Reconstruction
    Working Paper no. 9. Rev. ed. Social Development Department, World Bank,
    Washington, D.C.
Barron, Patrick, Rachael Diprose, and Claire Q. Smith. 2004. *Field Research Guides:
    KDP and Community Conflict Negotiation Study*. Jakarta: World Bank.
    www.conflictanddevelopment.org.
Barron, Patrick, Rachael Diprose, Claire Q. Smith, Katherine Whiteside, and
    Michael Woolcock. 2004. Applying Mixed Methods Research to
    Community-Driven Development Projects and Local Conflict Mediation:
    A Case Study from Indonesia. Mimeo, World Bank Office, Jakarta. www.
    conflictanddevelopment.org.
Barron, Patrick, Rachael Diprose, and Michael Woolcock. 2007a. Local Conflict and
    Community Development in Indonesia: Assessing the Impact of the Kecamatan
    Development Program. Indonesian Social Development Paper no. 10. World
    Bank, Jakarta.
————. 2007b. Local Conflict and Development Projects in Indonesia: Part of the
    Problem or Part of a Solution? Policy Research Working Paper no. 4212. World
    Bank, Washington, D.C.
Barron, Patrick, Macartan Humphreys, Laura Paler, and Jeremy Weinstein. 2009a.
    Community-Based Reintegration in Aceh: Assessing the Impacts of BRA-KDP.
    Indonesian Social Development Paper no. 12. World Bank, Jakarta.
Barron, Patrick, Sana Jaffrey, Blair Palmer, and Ashutosh Varshney. 2009b.
    Understanding Violent Conflict in Indonesia: A Mixed Methods Approach.
    Social Development Paper no. 117. World Bank, Washington, D.C.
Barron, Patrick, Kai Kaiser, and Menno Pradhan. 2009. "Understanding Variations in
    Local Conflict: Evidence and Implications from Indonesia." *World Development*
    37(3): 698–713.
Barron, Patrick, and David Madden. 2004. Violence and Conflict Resolution in
    Non-Conflict Regions: The Case of Lampung, Indonesia. Indonesian Social
    Development Paper no. 2. World Bank, Jakarta.
Barron, Patrick, Melina Nathan, and Bridget Welsh. 2005. Consolidating Indonesia's
    Democracy: Conflict, Institutions and the "Local" in the 2004 Legislative
    Elections. Conflict Prevention and Reconstruction Working Paper no. 31. Social
    Development Department, World Bank, Washington, D.C.
Barron, Patrick, and Joanne Sharpe. 2005. Counting Conflicts: Using Newspaper
    Reports to Understand Violence in Indonesia. Conflict Prevention and

Reconstruction Paper no. 25. Social Development Department, World Bank, Washington, D.C.

———. 2008. "Local Conflict in Post-Suharto Indonesia: Understanding Variations in Violence Levels and Forms Through Local Newspapers." *Journal of East Asian Studies* 8(3): 395–424.

Barron, Patrick, Claire Q. Smith, and Michael Woolcock. 2004. Understanding Local Level Conflict in Developing Countries: Theory, Evidence and Implications from Indonesia. Conflict Prevention and Reconstruction Paper no. 19. Social Development Department, World Bank, Washington, D.C.

Bates, Robert H. 2000. *Prosperity and Violence: The Political Economy of Development.* New York: Norton.

———. 2008. "State Failure." *Annual Review of Political Science* 11:1–14.

Bayly, Christopher. 2004. *The Birth of the Modern World, 1780–1914: Global Connections and Comparisons.* Oxford: Blackwell.

Beatty, Andrew. 2009. *A Shadow Falls: In the Heart of Java.* London: Faber.

Bebbington, Anthony, Michael Woolcock, Scott Guggenheim, and Elizabeth Olson, eds. 2006. *The Search for Empowerment: Social Capital as Idea and Practice at the World Bank.* Bloomfield, Conn.: Kumarian.

Benedict, Ruth. 1934. *Patterns of Culture.* Boston: Houghton Mifflin.

Bertrand, Jacques. 2004. *Nationalism and Ethnic Violence in Indonesia.* Cambridge: Cambridge University Press.

Bjork, Christopher. 2003. "Local Responses to Decentralization Policy in Indonesia." *Comparative Education Review* 47(2) (May): 184–216.

Bjorkqvist, Kaj. 1997. "The Inevitability of Conflict, but Not of Violence: Theoretical Considerations on Conflict and Aggression." In *Cultural Variation in Conflict Resolution: Alternatives to Violence,* ed. Douglas P. Fry and Kaj Bjorkqvist. Mahwah, N.J.: Erlbaum.

Blanning, Tim. 2007. *The Pursuit of Glory: The Five Revolutions That Made Modern Europe, 1648–1815.* New York: Viking.

Bowen, John R. 2003. *Islam, Law and Equality in Indonesia: An Anthropology of Public Reasoning.* New York: Cambridge University Press.

Brass, Paul R. 1991. *Ethnicity and Nationalism.* New Delhi: Sage.

———. 1997. *Theft of an Idol: Text and Context in the Representation of Collective Violence.* Princeton: Princeton University Press.

———. 2003. *The Production of Hindu-Muslim Violence in Contemporary India.* Seattle: University of Washington Press.

Briggs, Xavier de Souza. 2008. *Democracy as Problem Solving: Civic Capacity in Communities Across the Globe.* Cambridge: MIT Press.

Brown, Graham K., and Rachael Diprose. 2009. "Bare Chested Politics in Central Sulawesi: Local Elections in a Post-Conflict Region." In *Deepening Democracy in Indonesia? Direct Elections for Local Leaders (Pilkada),* ed. M. Erb and P. Sulistiyanto. Singapore: ISEAS, 352–73.

Burton, John W. 1990. *Conflict: Resolution and Prevention.* New York: St Martin's.

Caffentzis, George, and Silvia Federici. 2001. "A Brief History of Resistance to Structural Adjustment." In *Democratizing the Global Economy*, ed. Kevin Danaher. Monroe, Me.: Common Courage.

Carothers, Thomas, ed. 2006. *Promoting the Rule of Law Abroad: In Search of Knowledge*. Washington, D.C.: Carnegie Endowment for International Peace.

Caufield, Catherine. 1998. *Masters of Illusion: The World Bank and the Poverty of Nations*. New York: Pan.

Cernea, Michael M., and Scott E. Guggenheim. 1993. *Anthropological Approaches to Resettlement: Policy, Practice and Theory*. Boulder: Westview.

Chauvet, Lisa, Paul Collier, and Håvard Hegre. 2008. The Security Challenge in Conflict-Prone Countries. Conflicts Challenge Paper. Copenhagen Consensus Centre. Web edition. http://www.humansecuritygateway.info/documents/ CP_Collier_securitychallengeinconflictpronecountries.pdf (accessed June 2008).

Chopra, Jarat, and Tanya Hohe. 2004. "Participatory Intervention." *Global Governance* 10:289–305.

Chretien, Jean-Pierre. 2003. *The Great Lakes of Africa: Two Thousand Years of History*. New York: Zone.

Clark, Gregory. 2008. "Reconsiderations: 'The Great Transformation' by Karl Polanyi." *New York Sun,* 4 June. http://www.nysun.com/arts/reconsiderations -the-great-transformation-by-karl/79250/ (accessed 27 May 2010).

Clark, Samuel, ed. 2004. More Than Just Ownership: Ten Land and Natural Resource Conflict Case Studies from East Java and NTT. Indonesian Social Development Paper no. 4. World Bank, Jakarta.

Cliffe, Sarah, Scott Guggenheim, and Markus Kostner. 2003. Community-Driven Reconstruction as an Instrument in War-to-Peace Transitions. Conflict Prevention and Reconstruction Working Paper no. 7. Social Development Department, World Bank, Washington, D.C.

Coehlo, Vera Schattan P. 2007. "Brazilian Health Councils: Including the Excluded?" In *Spaces for Change? The Politics of Citizen Participation in New Democratic Arenas,* ed. Andrea Cornwall and Vera Schattan P. Coelho. London: Zed, 33–54.

Colletta, Nat J., and Michelle L. Cullen. 2000. *Violent Conflict and the Transformation of Social Capital: Lessons from Cambodia, Rwanda, Guatemala and Somalia*. Washington, D.C.: World Bank.

Collier, Paul. 1999. "On the Economic Consequences of Civil War." *Oxford Economic Papers* 50(4): 168–83.

———. 2007. *The Bottom Billion: Why the Poorest Countries Are Failing and What Can Be Done About It*. Oxford: Oxford University Press.

———. 2009. *Wars, Guns, and Votes: Democracy in Dangerous Places*. New York: Harpers.

Collier, Paul, Lani Elliot, Håvard Hegre, Anke Hoeffler, Marta Reynal-Qeurol, and Nicholas Sambanis. 2003. *Breaking the Conflict Trap: Civil War and Development Policy*. New York: Oxford University Press.

Collier, Paul, and Anke Hoeffler. 2002. "On the Incidence of Civil War in Africa." *Journal of Conflict Resolution* 46(1): 13–28.

Collier, Paul, Anke Hoeffler, and Mans Soderbom. 2008. "Post-Conflict Risks."
    Journal of Peace Research 45(4): 461–78.
Collier, Paul, and Nicholas Sambanis. 2005. *Understanding Civil War: Evidence and
    Analysis—Africa*. Washington, D.C.: World Bank.
Colombijn, Freek. 2002. "Maling, Maling! The Lynching of Petty Criminals." In
    Roots of Violence in Indonesia: Contemporary Violence in Historical Perspective, ed.
    Freek Colombijn and J. Thomas Lindblad. Leiden: KITLV.
———. 2005. "A Cultural Practice of Violence in Indonesia: Lessons from History."
    In *Violent Internal Conflicts in Asia Pacific: Histories, Political Economies and
    Policies*, ed. Dewi Fortuna Anwar, Helene Bouvier, Glenn Smith, and Roger Tol.
    Jakarta: KITLV/Buku Obor.
Commission on Growth and Development. 2008. *The Growth Report: Strategies for
    Sustained Growth and Inclusive Development*. Washington, D.C.: World Bank.
Corbridge, Stuart, Glyn Williams, Manoj Srivastava, and Rene Veron. 2005. *Seeing the
    State: Governance and Governmentality in India*. New York: Cambridge
    University Press.
Cornwall, Andrea. 2002. "Making Spaces, Changing Places: Situating Participation
    in Development," Sussex: Institute of Development Studies Working Paper No. 173.
Cornwall, Andrea, and Vera Schattan P. Coelho. 2007. "Spaces for Change? The
    Politics of Participation in New Democratic Arenas." In *Spaces for Change? The
    Politics of Citizen Participation in New Democratic Arenas*, ed. Andrea Cornwall
    and Vera Schattan P. Coelho. London: Zed, 1–30.
———, eds. 2004. "New Democratic Spaces?" *IDS Bulletin* 35(2): 1-10.
Coser, Lewis. 1956. *The Functions of Social Conflict*. New York: Free Press.
Cramer, Christopher. 2006. *Civil War Is Not a Stupid Thing: Accounting for Violence in
    Developing Countries*. London: Hurst.
Cramer, Christopher, and John Weeks. 2002. "Macroeconomic Stabilization
    and Structural Adjustment." In *The Prevention of Humanitarian Emergencies*,
    ed. E. Wayne Nafzinger and Raimo Wayrnyen. Basingstoke: Palgrave/
    UN WIDER.
Cribb, Robert. 2005. "Legal Pluralism, Decentralization and the Roots of Violence in
    Indonesia." In *Violent Internal Conflicts in Asia Pacific: Histories, Political
    Economies and Policies*, ed. Dewi Fortuna Anwar, Helene Bouvier, Glenn Smith,
    and Roger Tol. Jakarta: KITLV/Buku Obor.
Cutura, Josephina. 2003. Women in Village Governance and Problem-Solving: The
    Case of Sikka, Flores. Mimeo, World Bank Office, Jakarta.
Das, Jishnu, and Jeffrey Hammer. 2005. "Which Doctor? Combining Vignettes and
    Item Response to Measure Clinical Competence." *Journal of Development
    Economics* 78(2): 348–83.
De Jonge, H. 1998. *Madura dalam Empat Zaman: Pedagang, Perkembangan Ekonomi
    dan Islam*. Suatu Studi Antropologi Ekonomi. Jakarta: Gramedia.
"Democracy in South-East Asia: The Indonesian Surprise." 2009. *Economist*, 2 April.
Department for International Development. 2002. *Conducting Conflict Assessments:
    Guidance Notes*. London: Department for International Development.

des Forges, Alison. 1994. *Leave None to Tell the Story: Genocide in Rwanda*. New York: Human Rights Watch.

Didakus, Stanis. 2004. Civic Interaction and Identity Groups in Sikka. Mimeo, World Bank Office, Jakarta.

DiMaggio, Paul, and Walter W. Powell. 1983. "The Iron Cage Revisited: Institutional Isomorphism and Collective Rationality in Organizational Fields." *American Sociological Review* 48 (April): 137–60.

Diprose, Rachael. 2004. Conflict Pathways in Indonesia: Conflict, Violence and Development in East Java. Mimeo, World Bank Office, Jakarta.

———. 2008. "Passing on the Challenges or Prescribing Better Management of Diversity? Decentralization, Power-Sharing, and Conflict Dynamics in Central Sulawesi, Indonesia." *Conflict, Security, and Development* 8(4): 393–425.

———. 2009a. "Decentralisation, Horizontal Inequalities and Conflict Management in Indonesia." *Ethnopolitics* 8(1): 107–34.

———. 2009b. Profiteers, Religious Warriors, or Homeland Defenders? Understanding Conflict Mobilisation Processes Through the Case of Central Sulawesi, Indonesia. Paper presented to the conference Mobilisation for Political Violence: What Do We Know? Oxford, 17–18 March 2009, Department of International Development, University of Oxford.

———. 2011. Sub-national Variations in Communal Violence: A Comparison of Peace and Conflict Dynamics in Indonesia (Central Sulawesi Province) and Nigeria (Kaduna State). DPhil diss., University of Oxford.

Diprose, Rachael, Azra Abdul Cader, and Prashan Thalayasingam. 2010. Development Effectiveness, Inequalities and Conflict in Sri Lanka: Understanding Aid, Voice and Action in Local Conflict-Affected Environments. CRISE Working Paper, Department of International Development, University of Oxford.

Diprose, Rachael, and Ariyanti Rianom. 2010. Development Effectiveness, Inequalities and Conflict in Indonesia: Understanding Aid, Voice and Action in Local Conflict-Affected Environments. CRISE Working Paper, Department of International Development, University of Oxford.

Diprose, Rachael, and Ukoha Ukiwo. 2008. A Comparison of Communal Conflict Dynamics in Indonesia and Nigeria. CRISE Working Paper no. 49. Department of International Development, University of Oxford.

Do, Quy-Toan, and Lakshmi Iyer. 2007. Poverty, Social Divisions, and Conflict in Nepal. Policy Research Working Paper 4228. World Bank, Washington, D.C.

Dominguez, Andrea. 2008. "The High Cost of Violence in Central America." http://www.comunidadesegura.org/?q=en/STORY-High-Cost-of-Violence-in -Central-America.

Duffield, Mark. 2001. *Global Governance and the New Wars: The Merging of Security and Development*. London: Zed.

Duflo, Esther, and Michael Kremer. 2005. "Use of Randomization in the Evaluation of Development Effectiveness." In *Evaluating Development Effectiveness*, ed. George Pitman, Osvaldo Feinstein, and Gregory Ingram. New Brunswick: Transaction, 205–31.

Eade, Deborah. 1997. *Capacity-Building: An Approach to People-Centred Development*. Oxford, U.K.: Oxfam.

Easterly, William. 1999. "Life During Growth." *Journal of Economic Growth* 4(3): 239–75.

———. 2001a. "Can Institutions Resolve Ethnic Conflict?" *Economic Development and Cultural Change* 49(4): 687–706.

———. 2001b. *The Elusive Quest for Growth: Economists' Adventures and Misadventures in the Tropics*. Cambridge: MIT Press.

Easterly, William, and Ross Levine. 1997. "Africa's Growth Tragedy: Policies and Ethnic Divisions." *Quarterly Journal of Economics* 112 (November): 1203–50.

Easterly, William, Jozef Ritzen, and Michael Woolcock. 2006. "Social Cohesion, Institutions, and Growth." *Economics and Politics* 18(2): 103–20.

Ellickson, Robert C. 1991. *Order Without Law: How Neighbors Settle Disputes*. Cambridge: Harvard University Press.

Emirbayer, Mustafa. 1997. "Manifesto for a Relational Sociology." *American Journal of Sociology* 103(2): 281–317.

Erb, Maribeth. 1999. *The Manggaraians: A Guide to Traditional Lifestyles*. Singapore: Times.

Erb, Maribeth, and Priyambudi Sulistiyanto, eds. 2009. *Deepening Democracy in Indonesia? Direct Elections for Local Leaders (Pilkada)*. Singapore: Institute of Southeast Asian Studies.

Eriksen, Thomas Hylland. 1993. *Ethnicity and Nationalism: Anthropological Perspective*. London: Pluto.

Escobar, Arturo. 1995. *Encountering Development: The Making and Unmaking of the Third World*. Princeton: Princeton University Press.

Evans, Peter. 2004. "Development as Institutional Change: The Pitfalls of Monocropping and the Potentials of Deliberation." *Studies in Comparative International Development* 38(4): 30–52.

Evers, Pieter. 2000. Resourceful Villagers, Powerless Communities: Rural Village Governance in Indonesia. Mimeo, World Bank Office, Jakarta.

Fauzanafi, Muhammad Zamzam. 2002. Reog: Sebuah Ritus Pemranataan (Konstruksi Tradisi dalam Pertunjukan Reog Ponorogo). PhD diss., Universitas Gadjah Mada, Yogyakarta.

Fearon, James. 2005. "Primary Commodity Exports and Civil War." *Journal of Conflict Resolution* 49(4): 493–507.

Fearon, James, and David Laitin. 2003. "Ethnicity, Insurgency and Civil War." *American Political Science Review* 97:75–90.

Ferguson, James. 1990. *The Anti-Politics Machine: Development, Depoliticisation and Bureaucratic Power in Lesotho*. Cambridge: Cambridge University Press.

Fogel, Robert. 2004. *The Escape from Hunger and Premature Death, 1700–2100: Europe, America and the Third World*. New York: Cambridge University Press.

Forman, Shepard, and Stewart Patrick, eds. 2000. *Good Intentions: Pledges of Aid for Postconflict Recovery*. Boulder: Reinner.

Fox, Fiona. 2001. "New Humanitarianism: Does It Provide a Moral Banner for the 21st Century?" *Disasters* 25(4): 275–89.

Friend, Theodore. 2005. *Indonesian Destinies*. Cambridge: Harvard University Press.

Fukuyama, Francis. 1999. *The Great Disruption: Human Nature and the Reconstitution of Social Order*. New York: Free Press.

———. 2004. *State Building: Governance and World Order in the Twenty-First Century*. London: Profile.

Fung, Archon, and Erik Wright. 2003. *Deepening Democracy: Institutional Innovations in Empowered Participatory Governance*. London: Verso.

Galtung, Johan. 1969. "Violence, Peace, and Peace Research." *Journal of Peace Research* 6(3): 167–91.

Gardner, Katy, and David Lewis. 1996. *Anthropology, Development and the Post-Modern Challenge*. London: Blackwell.

Gaventa, John. 1980. *Power and Powerlessness*. Urbana: University of Illinois Press.

———. 2005. *Claiming Citizenship: Rights, Participation and Accountability*. London: Zed.

Geddes, Barbara. 2003. *Paradigms and Sand Castles: Theory Building and Research Design in Comparative Politics*. Ann Arbor: University of Michigan Press.

Geertz, Clifford. 1963. "The Integrative Revolution: Primordial Sentiments and Civil Politics in the New States." In *The Interpretation of Cultures*, ed. Clifford Geertz. New York: Free Press, 255–310.

———. 1976. *The Religion of Java*. Chicago: University of Chicago Press.

———. 1983. *Local Knowledge: Further Essays in Interpretative Anthropology*. New York: Basic.

———. 1987. *Abangan, Santri, Priyayi*. Jakarta: Pustaka Jaya.

Gellner, Ernest. 1988. *Plough, Sword and Book: The Structure of Human History*. Chicago: University of Chicago Press.

Geneva Declaration Secretariat. 2008. *Global Burden of Armed Violence*. Geneva: Geneva Declaration Secretariat.

George, Alexander, and Andrew Bennett. 2005. *Case Studies and Theory Development in the Social Sciences*. Cambridge: MIT Press.

Gerring, John. 2007. *Case Study Research: Principles and Practices*. New York: Cambridge University Press.

Ghani, Ashraf, and Clare Lockhart. 2008. *Fixing Failed States: A Framework for Rebuilding a Fractured World*. New York: Oxford University Press.

Ghewa, Yohanes. 2003. The Role of KDP in Kabupaten Manggarai. Mimeo, World Bank Office, Jakarta.

Gibson, Christopher, and Michael Woolcock. 2008. "Empowerment, Deliberative Development and Local Level Politics in Indonesia: Participatory Projects as a Source of Countervailing Power." *Studies in Comparative International Development* 43(2): 151–80.

Goldstone, Jack. 1991. *Revolution and Rebellion in the Early Modern World*. Berkeley: University of California Press.

Goody, Jack. 2001. "How Ethnic Is Ethnic Cleansing?" *New Left Review* 7 (January–February): 5–15.

Gourevitch, Philip. 1999. *We Wish to Inform You That Tomorrow We Will Be Killed With Our Families: Stories from Rwanda.* New York: Farrar, Straus, and Giroux.

Government of Indonesia. 2002. "Kecamatan Development Program: KDP in Conflict Areas." Jakarta: Ministry of Home Affairs, Community Development Agency, and National Management Consultants.

————. 2004. "Kecamatan Development Program Phase II Results." Jakarta: Ministry of Home Affairs, Directorate General of Rural and Community Empowerment, KDP National Secretariat, and National Management Consultants.

Granovetter, Mark. 1985. "Economic Action and Social Structure: A Theory of Embeddedness." *American Journal of Sociology* 91:481–510.

Grimes, Charles E., Tom Therik, Barbara Dix Grimes, and Max Jacob. 1997. *A Guide to the Peoples and Languages of Nusa Tenggara.* Kupang: Artha Wacana Press/ Alfa Omega Foundation.

Grindle, Merilee. 1997. *Getting Good Government: Capacity Building in the Public Sectors of Developing Countries.* Cambridge: Harvard University Press.

Guggenheim, Scott. 2006. "The Kecamatan Development Program, Indonesia." In *The Search for Empowerment: Social Capital as Idea and Practice at the World Bank,* ed. Anthony Bebbington, Michael Woolcock, Scott Guggenheim, and Elisabeth Olson. Bloomfield, Conn.: Kumarian, 111–44.

————. 2008. Goodbye to All That: Reflections on Governance at the Grassroots. Presentation to the Third Gathering of the Field Based Governance Group, Istanbul, Turkey.

Gurr, Ted. 2000. *People Versus States: Minorities at Risk in the New Century.* Washington, D.C.: United States Institute of Peace Press.

————. 2001. *Peace and Conflict 2001: A Global Survey of Armed Conflicts, Self-Determination Movements, and Democracy.* College Park: Center for International Development and Conflict Management, University of Maryland.

Gurr, Ted R., Monty G. Marshall, and Deepa Khosla. 2001. "Peace and Conflict 2001: A Global Survey of Armed Conflicts, Self-Determination Movements, and Democracy." College Park, Md.: University of Maryland Center for International Development and Conflict Management.

Habermas, Jürgen. 1984. *The Theory of Communicative Action.* Vol. 1. Trans. Thomas McCarthy. Boston: Beacon.

Haggard, Stephan, and Robert R. Kaufman. 1995. *The Political Economy of Democratic Transitions.* Princeton: Princeton University Press.

Haggard, Stephan, Andrew MacIntyre, and Lydia Tiede. 2008. "The Rule of Law and Economic Development." *Annual Review of Political Science* 11:205–34.

Harbom, Lotta, and Peter Wallensteen. 2007. "Armed Conflict, 1989–2006." *Journal of Peace Research* 44(5): 623–34.

————. 2008. "Patterns of Major Armed Conflict, 1998–2007." In *SIPRI Yearbook 2008.* Oxford: Oxford University Press. http://www.sipri.org/ yearbook/2008/02/02A.

Haslam, S. Alexander. 2004. *Psychology in Organizations: The Social Identity Approach.* 2d ed. New York: Sage.

Hedman, Eva-Lotta E., ed. 2008. *Conflict, Violence, and Displacement in Indonesia.* Ithaca: Southeast Asia Program, Cornell University.

Hefner, Robert W. 2000. *Civil Islam: Muslims and Democratization in Indonesia.* Princeton: Princeton University Press.

Hegre, Håvard, Tanja Elingsen, Scott Gates, and Nils Petter Gleditsch. 2001. "Towards a Democratic Civil Peace? Democracy, Political Change, and Civil War, 1816–1992." *American Political Science Review* 95(1): 33–41.

Hegre, Håvard, Gudrun Ostby, and Clionadh Raleigh. 2009. "Poverty and Civil War Events: A Disaggregated Study of Liberia." *Journal of Conflict Resolution* 53(4): 598–623.

Heifetz, Ronald. 1994. *Leadership Without Easy Answers.* Cambridge: Harvard University Press.

Heifetz, Ronald, and Marty Linksy. 2002. *Leadership on the Line: Staying Alive Through the Dangers of Leading.* Boston: Harvard Business School Press.

Helpman, Elhanan. 2004. *The Mystery of Economic Growth.* Cambridge: Harvard University Press.

Hewitt, J. Joseph. 2008. *Peace and Conflict 2008.* Boulder: Paradigm.

Hobsbawm, Eric. 1998. *On History.* London: Abacus.

Hoeffler, Anke, and Marta Reynal-Querol. 2003. *Measuring the Costs of Conflict.* Washington, D.C.: World Bank.

Hoff, Karla. 2003. "Paths of Institutional Development: A View from Economic History." *World Bank Research Observer* 18(2): 205–26.

Hoff, Karla, and Priyanka Pandey. 2006. "Discrimination, Social Identity and Durable Inequalities." *American Economic Review* 96(2): 206–11.

Horowitz, Donald. 2000. *Ethnic Groups in Conflict.* 2d ed. Berkeley: University of California Press.

Human Security Centre. 2005. *Human Security Report 2005: War and Peace in the 21st Century.* New York: Oxford University Press.

Humphreys, Macartan, and Jeremy Weinstein. 2007. "Demobilization and Reintegration." *Journal of Conflict Resolution* 51(4): 531–67.

Hunt, Lynn. 2007. *Inventing Human Rights: A History.* New York: Norton.

Huntington, Samuel. 1993. "The Clash of Civilizations?" *Foreign Affairs* 72(3): 22–49.

Ignatieff, Michael. 1994. *Blood and Belonging: Journeys into the New Nationalism.* London: Viking.

Imbens, Guido, and Joshua Angrist. 1994. "Identification and Estimation of the Local Average Treatment Effect" *Econometrica* 61(2): 467–76.

International Crisis Group. 2002. "Tensions on Flores: Local Symptoms of National Problems" Indonesia Briefing. International Crisis Group, Jakarta/Brussels.

International Crisis Group. 2003. "Indonesia: Managing Decentralization and Conflict in Indonesia." Report no. 44. International Crisis Group, Jakarta.

———. 2005. "Decentralisation and Conflict in Indonesia: The Mamasa Case." Asia Briefing 37. International Crisis Group, Singapore.

Jha, Saumitra. 2007. "Maintaining Peace Across Ethnic Lines: New Lessons from the Past." *Economics of Peace and Security Journal* 2(2): 89–93.

Justino, Patricia. 2004. "Redistribution, Inequality and Political Conflict." HiCN Working Paper no. 5. Institute of Development Studies, Univeristy of Sussex, Brighton.

Kaldor, Mary. 2006. *New and Old Wars: Organized Violence in a Global Era*. 2d ed. Cambridge: Polity.

Kalyvas, Stathis N. 2006. *The Logic of Violence in Civil War*. New York: Cambridge University Press.

———. 2008. "Promises and Pitfalls of an Emerging Research Program: The Microdynamics of Civil War." In *Order, Conflict, and Violence*, ed. Stathis N. Kalyvas, Ian Shapiro, and Tarek Masoud. Cambridge: Cambridge University Press.

Kalyvas, Stathis N., and Matthew Adam Kocher. 2007. "How Free Is 'Free Riding' in Civil Wars? Violence, Insurgency, and the Collective Action Problem." *World Politics* 59(2): 177–216.

Kaplan, Robert D. 1997. *The Ends of the Earth: From Togo to Turkmenistan, from Iran to Cambodia: A Journey to the Frontiers of Anarchy*. New York: Vintage.

Kato, Tsuyoshi. 1989. "Different Fields, Similar Locusts: Adat Communities and the Village Law of 1979 in Indonesia." *Indonesia* 47 (April): 89–114.

KDP National Secretariat and National Management Consultants. 2003. *Indonesia: Kecamatan Development Program*. December 2003, Jakarta.

Kim, Eun Mee. 1997. *Big Business, Strong State: Collusion and Conflict in South Korean Development, 1960–1990*. Albany: SUNY Press.

King, Charles. 2004. "The Micropolitics of Social Violence." *World Politics* 56(3): 431–55.

King, Gary, Christopher J. L. Murray, Joshua A. Salomon, and Ajay Tandon. 2004. "Enhancing the Validity and Cross-Cultural Comparability of Survey Research." *American Political Science Review* 98(1): 191–207.

King, Gary, and Jonathan Wand. 2007. "Comparing Incomparable Survey Responses: Evaluating and Selecting Anchoring Vignettes." *Political Analysis* 15(1): 46–66.

Kingma, Kees. 2001. *Demobilisation and Reintegration of Ex-Combatants in Post-War and Transition Countries*. Eschborn: Deutsche Gesellschaft für Technische Zusammernarbeit.

Kingsbury, Damien. 2002. *The Politics of Indonesia*. 2d ed. New York: Oxford University Press.

Knaus, Gerald, and Marcus Cox. 2005. "The 'Helsinki Moment' in Southeastern Europe." *Journal of Democracy* 16(1): 39–53.

Kraay, Aart. 2006. "When Is Growth Pro-Poor? Evidence from a Panel of Countries." *Journal of Development Economics* 80(1): 198–227.

Krugman, Paul. 2000. *The Return of Depression Economics*. New York: Norton.

Kuntowijoyo. 2002. *Perubahan Sosial dalam Masyarakat Agraris: Madura, 1850–1940*. Yogyakarta: Mata Bangsa.

Lawang, M. Z. R. 1996. *Konflik Tanah di Manggarai, Flores Barat—Pendekatan Sosiologik*. Jakarta: Penerbit Universitas Indonesia.

Leader, Nicholas. 2000. The Politics of Principle: The Principles of Humanitarian Action in Practice. HPG Report no. 2. Overseas Development Institute, London.

Leftwich, Adrian. 2007. The Political Approach to Institutional Formation, Maintenance and Change: A Literature Review Essay, Discussion Paper Series no. 14. Research Programme Consortium for Institutions for Pro-Poor Growth, University of Manchester and University of York.

Lewis, David. 2009. "International Development and the 'Perpetual Present': Anthropological Approaches to the Re-Historicization of Policy." *European Journal of Development Research* 21(1): 32–46.

Lewis, David, and David Mosse, eds. 2006. *Development Brokers and Translators: The Ethnography of Aid and Agencies*. Bloomfield, Conn.: Kumarian.

Lewis, David, Dennis Rodgers, and Michael Woolcock. 2008. "The Fiction of Development: Literary Representation as a Source of Authoritative Knowledge." *Journal of Development Studies* 44(2): 198–216.

Li, Tanya Murray. 2007. *The Will to Improve: Governmentality, Development, and the Practice of Politics*. Durham: Duke University Press.

Liddle, William. 1999. "Indonesia's Unexpected Failure of Leadership." In *Politics of Post-Suharto Indonesia*, ed. Adam Schwartz and Jonathan Paris. New York: Council on Foreign Relations, 16–39.

Lijphart, Arend. 1977. *Democracy in Plural Societies*. New Haven: Yale University Press.

———. 2008. *Thinking About Democracy: Power Sharing and Majority Rule in Theory and Practice*. London: Routledge.

Lukes, Steven. 1974. *Power: A Radical View*. London: Macmillan.

MacRae, Joanna, and Anthony Zwi. 1994. "Famine, Complex Emergencies and International Policy in Africa: An Overview." In *War and Hunger: Rethinking International Responses to Complex Emergencies*, ed. Joanna MacRae and Anthony Zwi. London: Zed.

Mahmud, Simeen. 2007. "Spaces for Participation in Health Systems in Rural Bangladesh: The Experience of Stakeholder Community Groups." In *Spaces for Change? The Politics of Citizen Participation in New Democratic Arenas*, ed. Andrea Cornwall and Vera Schattan P. Coelho. London: Zed, 55–75.

Mahur, Agus. 2003. Land Conflicts and the Mechanisms Used to Resolve Them in Kabupaten Manggarai. Mimeo, World Bank Office, Jakarta.

Mallaby, Sebastian. 2004. *The World's Banker: A Story of Failed States, Financial Crises, and the Wealth and Poverty of Nations*. New York: Penguin.

Mansuri, Ghazala, and Vijayendra Rao. 2004. "Community Based (and Driven) Development: A Critical Review." *World Bank Research Observer* 19(1): 1–39.

———. 2011. *Localizing Development: Does Participation Work?* Washington, D.C.: World Bank.

Markoff, John, and Veronica Montecinos. 1993. "The Ubiquitous Rise of Economists." *Journal of Public Policy* 13(1): 37–68.

Martinussen, John. 1997. *Society, State and Market: A Guide to Competing Theories of Development*. London: Zed.

McAdam, Doug, Sidney Tarrow, and Charles Tilly. 2001. *Dynamics of Contention*. New York: Cambridge University Press.

McCarthy, John. 2004. "Changing to Gray: Decentralization and the Emergence of Volatile Socio-Legal Configurations in Central Kalimantan, Indonesia." *World Development* 32(7): 1199–1223.

McLaughlin, Karrie, and Ari Perdana. 2009. Conflict and Dispute Resolution in Indonesia: Information from the 2006 Governance and Decentralization Survey. Indonesian Social Development Paper no. 16. World Bank, Jakarta.

McLaughlin, Karrie, Adam Satu, and Michael Hoppe. 2007. *Kecamatan Development Program Qualitative Impact Evaluation.* Jakarta: World Bank.

McNeil, Mary, and Michael Woolcock. 2004. Capacity Enhancement and Social Development: Building on Local Context and Process. World Bank Institute Working Paper no. 37245. World Bank, Washington, D.C.

MDG Monitor. 2008. "Tracking the Millennium Development Goals: Indonesia." 28 August. www.mdgmonitor.org/factsheets_00.cfm?c=IDN.

Mead, Margaret. 1958. "Cultural Determinants of Behavior." In *Behavior and Evolution,* ed. A. Roe and G. Simpson. New Haven: Yale University Press, 480–96.

Medicins Sans Frontiers. 1994. "Breaking the Cycle: Calls for Action in the Rwandese Refugee Camps." 10 November. www.doctorswithoutborders.org/publications/reports/before1999/breaking_1994.cfm.

Meliala, Adrianus, ed. 2005. Evaluation of the Police Role in the 2004 General Elections. Partnership for Governance Reform in Indonesia, Jakarta.

Merry, Sally Engle. 1992. "Anthropology, Law, and Transnational Processes." *Annual Review of Anthropology* 21:357–79.

Mietzner, Marcus. 2008. *Military Politics, Islam and the State in Indonesia: From Turbulent Transition to Democratic Consolidation.* Singapore: ISEAS.

Migdal, Joel S. 2001. *State in Society: Studying How States and Societies Transform and Constitute One Another.* New York: Cambridge University Press.

Milanovic, Branko. 2005. *Worlds Apart: Measuring International and Global Inequality.* Princeton: Princeton University Press.

Mills, C. Wright. 1959. *The Sociological Imagination.* New York: Oxford University Press.

Ministry for Foreign Affairs. 2006. *Stockholm Initiative on Disarmament Demobilisation Reintegration: Final Report.* Stockholm: Ministry of Foreign Affairs. http://www.regeringen.se/sb/d/4890.

Mishra, Pankaj. 2006. *The Temptations of the West: How to Be Modern in India, Pakistan and Beyond.* London: Picador.

Mitchell, Timothy. 2002. *Rule of Experts: Egypt, Techno-Politics, Modernity.* Berkeley: University of California Press.

Mohanty, Ranjita. 2007. "Gendered Subjects, the State and Participatory Spaces: The Politics of Domesticating Participation in Rural India." In *Spaces for Change? The Politics of Citizen Participation in New Democratic Arenas,* ed. Andrea Cornwall and Vera Schattan P. Coelho. London: Zed, 76–94.

Moore, Barrington. 1967. *Social Origins of Dictatorship and Democracy: Lord and Peasant in the Making of the Modern World.* Boston: Beacon.

Moore, Mick. 1997. "Societies, Polities and Capitalists in Developing Countries: A Literature Survey." *Journal of Development Studies* 33(3): 287–363.

Moore, Sally Falk, ed. 2004. *Law and Anthropology: A Reader*. Waltham, Mass.: Blackwell.

Morel, Adrian, Makiko Watanabe, and Rob Wrobel. 2009. Delivering Assistance to Conflict-Affected Communities: The BRA-KDP Program in Aceh. Indonesian Social Development Paper no. 13. World Bank, Jakarta.

Morishita, Akiko. 2005. Today's Local Politics in Indonesia, 1998–2004: Who Controls the Political and Economic Interests in Kalimantan? Paper presented at the University of Indonesia 4th International Symposium of Journal Anthropologi Indonesia, Depok, 12–15 July.

Morris, James. 1963. *The Road to Huddersfield: A Journey to Five Continents*. New York: Pantheon.

Moser, Caroline O. N. 2006. Reducing Urban Violence in Developing Countries. Policy Brief 2006–1. Brookings Institute, Washington, D.C.

Moser, Caroline O. N., and Cathy McIlwaine. 2006. "Latin American Urban Violence as a Development Concern: Towards a Framework for Violence Reduction." *World Development* 34(1): 89–112.

Mosse, David. 2005a. *Cultivating Development: An Ethnography of Aid Policy and Practice*. London: Pluto.

———. 2005b. "Global Governance and the Ethnography of International Aid." In *The Aid Effect: Giving and Governing in International Development*, ed. David Mosse and David Lewis. London: Pluto, 1–36.

Mosse, David, and David Lewis, eds. 2005. *The Aid Effect: Giving and Governing in International Development* London: Pluto.

Mosse, David, John Farrington , and Alan Rew. 1998. *Development as Process: Concepts and Methods for Working with Complexity*. London: Routledge.

Muggah, Robert. 2009a. "Introduction: The Emperor's Clothes." In *Security and Post-Conflict Reconstruction: Dealing with Fighters in the Aftermath of War*, ed. Robert Muggah. London: Routledge, 1–29.

———. 2009b. "Securing the Peace: Post-Conflict Security Promotion." In *Small Arms Survey Yearbook 2009: Shadows of War*. Cambridge: Cambridge University Press, 219–48.

———, ed. 2009c. *Security and Post-Conflict Reconstruction: Dealing with Fighters in the Aftermath of War*. London: Routledge.

Muldavin, Joshua. 2006. "In Rural China, a Time Bomb Is Ticking." *International Herald Tribune*, 1 January. http://www.iht.com/articles/2006/01/01/opinion/edmuldavin.php.

Muller, Jerry Z. 1993. *Adam Smith in His Time and Ours: Designing the Decent Society*. New York: Free Press.

Muna, Riefqi. 2004. "Security Reform: Reform of the Security Sector Is Fundamental for Achieving a Democratic Indonesia." *Inside Indonesia* 77 (January–March): n.p. http://www.insideindonesia.org/edition-77/security-reform.

Murshed, Syed Mansoob, and Scott Gates. 2005. "Spatial-Horizontal Inequality and the Maoist Insurgency in Nepal." *Review of Development Economics* 9(1): 121–34.

Murshed, Syed Mansoob, and Mohammad Zulfan Tadjoeddin. 2007. Reappraising the Greed and Grievance Explanations for Violent Internal Conflict. MICROCON Research Working Paper no. 2. MICROCON, Brighton, U.K.

North, Douglass. 1990. *Institutions, Institutional Change and Economic Performance*. New York: Cambridge University Press.

———. 2005. *Understanding the Process of Economic Change*. Princeton: Princeton University Press.

North, Douglass, John J. Wallis, and Barry R. Weingast. 2009. *Violence and Social Orders: A Conceptual Framework for Interpreting Recorded Human History*. New York: Cambridge University Press.

Nyheim, David, Manuela Leonhardt, and Cynthia Gaigals. 2001. Development in Conflict: A Seven-Step Tool for Planners. FEWER/International Alert/ Saferworld, London.

Okumu, Wafula. 2003. "Humanitarian International NGOs and African Conflicts." *Peacekeeping* 10(1): 120–37.

Olken, Benjamin. 2006. "Corruption and the Cost of Redistribution." *Journal of Public Economics* 90(4–5): 853–70.

———. 2007. "Monitoring Corruption: Evidence from a Field Experiment in Indonesia." *Journal of Political Economy* 115(2): 200–49.

Page, Scott E. 2007. *The Difference: How the Power of Diversity Creates Better Groups, Firms, Schools, and Societies*. Princeton: Princeton University Press.

Paris, Roland. 2004. *At War's End: Building Peace After Civil Conflict*. Cambridge: Cambridge University Press.

Parry, Richard Lloyd. 2005. *In the Time of Madness*. London: Cape.

Perry, Elizabeth L., and Mark Seldon. 2003. *Chinese Society: Change, Conflict and Resistance*. 2d ed. London: Routledge.

Petersen, Roger D. 2002. *Understanding Ethnic Violence: Fear, Hatred, and Resentment in Twentieth-Century Eastern Europe*. New York: Cambridge University Press.

Polanyi, Karl. 1944. *The Great Transformation*. Boston: Beacon.

Ponorogo Manunggal Terate Cooperative. n.d. *Compilation of Materials from the S. H. Terate Martial Arts School*. Ponorogo: Ponorogo Manunggal Terate Cooperative.

Portes, Alejandro. 2006. "Institutions and Development: A Conceptual Reanalysis." *Population and Development Review* 32(2): 233–62.

Poser, Daniel N. 2005. *Institutions and Ethnic Politics in Africa*. New York: Cambridge University Press.

Prendergast, John. 1996. *Frontline Diplomacy: Humanitarian Aid and Conflict in Africa*. Boulder: Reinner.

Prior, John. 2003. The Church and Land Disputes: Sobering Thoughts from Flores. Mimeo, Chandraditya Research Center for the Study of Religion and Culture, Maumere, Indonesia.

———. 2004. "Land, Church and State: Forestry Business Packaged in Ecological Concerns in Flores." *Inside Indonesia* 78 (April–June): n.p. http://www .insideindonesia.org/index.php/component/content/243?task=view.

Pritchett, Lant. 1997. "Divergence, Big Time." *Journal of Economic Perspectives* 11(3): 3–17.

———. 2002. "It Pays to Be Ignorant: A Simple Political Economy of Program Evaluation." *Journal of Policy Reform* 5(4): 251–69.

———. 2007. W(h)ither the Flailing State? Coping with Failed Administrative Modernism. Mimeo, Kennedy School of Government, Harvard University.

Pritchett, Lant, and Michael Woolcock. 2004. "Solutions When *the* Solution Is the Problem: Arraying the Disarray in Development." *World Development* 32(2): 191–212.

Probo, Endro. 2003a. On KDP in Pamekasan. Mimeo, World Bank Office, Jakarta.

———. 2003b. The Phenomenon of the Martial Arts Schools in Kabupaten Ponorogo. Mimeo, World Bank Office, Jakarta.

Ragin, Charles C. 1987. *The Comparative Method: Moving Beyond Qualitative and Quantitative Strategies*. Berkeley: University of California Press.

Rajan, Raghuram G., and Luigi Zingales. 2004. *Saving Capitalism from the Capitalists: Unleashing the Power of Financial Markets to Create Wealth and Spread Opportunity*. Princeton: Princeton University Press.

Raleigh, Clionadh, and Håvard Hegre. 2009. "Population Size, Concentration and Civil War: A Geographically Disaggregated Analysis." *Political Geography* 28(4): 224–38.

Rao, Vijayendra. 2008. "Symbolic Public Goods and the Coordination of Public Action: A Comparison of Local Development in India and Indonesia." In *The Contested Commons: Conversations Between Economists and Anthropologists*, ed. Pranab Bardhan and Isha Ray. New York: Wiley-Blackwell, 168–86.

Rao, Vijayendra, and Michael Walton, eds. 2004. *Culture and Public Action*. Palo Alto: Stanford University Press.

Rao, Vijayendra, and Michael Woolcock. 2007. "The Disciplinary Monopoly in Development Research at the World Bank." *Global Governance* 13(4): 479–84.

Rasyid, Imron. 2004. KDP Implementation and Its Spillover Effects on the Lives of the Villager in Ponorogo. Mimeo, World Bank Office, Jakarta.

Ravallion, Martin. 2001. "Growth, Inequality and Poverty: Looking Beyond Averages." *World Development* 29(11): 1803–15.

Ravallion, Martin, and Shaohua Chen. 2007. "Absolute Poverty Measures for the Developing World, 1981–2004." *Proceedings of the National Academy of Science* 104(43): 16757–62.

Restrepo, Jorge, Brodie Ferguson, Jukliana M. Zúñiga, and Adriana Villamarin. 2008. Estimating Lost Product Due to Violent Deaths in 2004. Unpublished background paper for the Small Arms Survey. Small Arms Survey/CERAC, Geneva.

Rieff, David. 2002. "Humanitarianism in Crisis." *Foreign Affairs* 81(6): 111–21.

———. 2003. *A Bed for the Night: Humanitarianism in Crisis*. New York: Simon and Schuster.

Rieffel, Lex. 2004. "Indonesia's Quiet Revolution." *Foreign Affairs* 83(5): 98–110.

Rigg, Jonathan, Anthony Bebbington, Katherine V. Goff, Deborah F. Bryceson, Jytte Agergaard, Niels Fold, and Cecilia Tacoli. 2009. "The World Development

Report 2009 'Reshapes Economic Geography': Geographical Reflections." *Transactions of the Institute for British Geographers* 34:128–36.

Rist, Gilbert. 1997. *A History of Development: From Colonial Origins to Global Faith.* London: Zed.

Rodrik, Dani. 1999. "Where Did All the Growth Go? External Shocks, Social Conflict and Growth Collapses." *Journal of Economic Growth* 4(4): 385–412.

Rondinelli, Dennis. 1993. *Development Projects as Policy Experiments: An Adaptive Approach to Development Administration.* 2d ed. New York: Routledge.

Rosenbaum, Paul R., and Donald B. Rubin. 1983. "The Central Role of the Propensity Score in Observational Studies for Causal Effects." *Biometrika* (70): 41–55.

———. 1985. "Constructing a Control Group Using Multivariate Matched Sampling Methods That Incorporate the Propensity." *American Statistician* (39): 33–38.

Ross, Marc. 1993. *The Culture of Conflict: Interpretations and Interests in Comparative Perspective.* New Haven: Yale University Press.

Rothchild, Donald. 1997. *Managing Ethnic Conflict in Africa: Pressures and Incentives for Cooperation.* Washington, D.C.: Brookings Institution Press.

Roy, Beth. 1994. *Some Trouble with Cows: Making Sense of Social Conflict.* Berkeley: University of California Press.

Rueschemeyer, Dietrich. 2009. *Useable Social Theory.* Princeton: Princeton University Press.

Sage, Caroline, and Michael Woolcock, eds. 2006. *Law, Equity, and Development.* Amsterdam: Martinus Nijhoff; Washington, D.C.: World Bank.

———. 2008. "Breaking Legal Inequality Traps: New Approaches to Local Level Judicial Reform in Low Income Countries." In *Inclusive States: Social Policy and Structural Inequalities*, ed. Anis Dani and Arjan de Han. Washington, D.C.: World Bank, 369–93.

Sale, Kirkpatrick. 1996. *Rebels Against the Future: The Luddites and Their War on the Industrial Revolution.* New York: Perseus.

Sampson, Robert, John Morenhoff, and Fenton Earls. 1999. "Beyond Social Capital: Spatial Dynamics of Collective Efficacy for Children." *American Sociological Review* 64(5): 633–60.

Satu, Adam, and Patrick Barron. 2005. Understanding Local Conflict Pathways in Flores. Mimeo, World Bank Office, Jakarta.

Sayogyo. 1994. "Pembangunan Daerah dan Masyarakat di NTT Dalam Sekilat Sorotan Kritis." In *Kemiskinan dan Pembangunan di Propinsi Nusa Tenggara Timur,* ed. Sayogyo. Jakarta: Yayasan Obor Indonesia.

Schwartz, Adam. 1999. *A Nation in Waiting: Indonesia's Search for Stability.* 2d ed. Boulder: Westview.

Scott, James C. 1985. *Weapons of the Weak: Everyday Forms of Peasant Resistance.* New Haven: Yale University Press.

———. 1998. *Seeing Like a State: How Certain Schemes to Improve the Human Condition Have Failed.* New Haven: Yale University Press.

————. 2009. *The Art of Not Being Governed: An Anarchist History of Upland Southeast Asia*. New Haven: Yale University Press.

Sen, Amartya. 2006. *Identity and Violence: The Illusion of Destiny*. New York: Norton.

Senge, Peter M. 2006. *The Fifth Discipline: The Art and Practice of the Learning Organization*. Rev. ed. New York: Doubleday.

Shils, Edward. 1957. "Primordial, Personal, Sacred and Civil Ties." *British Journal of Sociology* 7:113–45.

Sidel, John T. 2006. *Riots, Pogroms, Jihad: Religious Violence in Indonesia*. Ithaca: Cornell University Press.

Simatupang, G. R. Lono Lastoro. 2002. Play and Display: An Ethnographic Study of Reyog Ponorogo in East Java, Indonesia. PhD diss., University of Sydney.

Singer, J. David, and Paul Diehl, eds. 1990. *Measuring the Correlates of War*. Ann Arbor: University of Michigan Press.

Skocpol, Theda. 1979. *States and Social Revolutions: A Comparative Analysis of France, Russia and China*. Cambridge: Cambridge University Press.

SMERU. 2004. *Peta Kemiskinan Indonesia 2000 (Poverty Map of Indonesia 2000)*. CD-Rom. www.smeru.or.id.

Smith, Claire Q. 2005. The Roots of Violence and Prospects for Reconciliation: A Case Study of Ethnic Conflict in Central Kalimantan, Indonesia. Conflict Prevention and Reconstruction Paper no. 23. World Bank, Washington, D.C.

Snyder, Jack. 2000. *From Voting to Violence: Democratization and Nationalist Conflict*. New York: Norton.

Stephens, Matthew. 2003. "Local-level Dispute Resolution in Post-Reformasi Indonesia: Lessons from the Philippines." *Australian Journal of Asian Law* 5(3): 213–59.

Stewart, Frances. 2005. Policies Towards Horizontal Inequalities in Post-Conflict Reconstruction. CRISE Working Paper no. 7. CRISE, Department of International Development, Oxford University.

————, ed. 2008. *Horizontal Inequalities and Conflict: Understanding Group Violence in Multiethnic Societies*. London: Palgrave.

Stockton, Nicholas. 1998. "In Defense of Humanitarianism." *Disasters* 22(4): 352–60.

Suhrke, Astri, Espen Villanger, and Susan L. Woodward. 2005. Economic Aid to Post-Conflict Countries: A Methodological Critique of Collier and Hoeffler. CMI Working Papers no. 2005:4. Chr. Michelson Institute, Bergen, Norway.

Suryadinata, Leo, Evi Nurvidya Arifin, and Ariss Ananta. 2003. *Indonesia's Population: Ethnicity and Religion in a Changing Political Landscape*. Singapore: Institute of Southeast Asian Studies.

Swedberg, Richard. 1990. *Economics and Sociology: Redefining Their Boundaries; Conversations with Economists and Sociologists*. Princeton: Princeton University Press.

Szreter, Simon. 1997. "Economic Growth, Disruption, Deprivation, Disease and Death: On the Importance of the Politics of Public Health for Development." *Population and Development Review* 23(4): 693–728.

Tadjoeddin, Mohammad Zulfan. 2002. Anatomy of Social Violence in the Context of Transition: The Case of Indonesia. UNSFIR Working Paper 02/01. UNSFIR, Jakarta.

Tadjoeddin, Mohammad Zulfan, and Syed Mansoob Murshed. 2007. "Socio-Economic Determinants of Everyday Violence in Indonesia: An Empirical Investigation of Javanese Districts, 1994–2003." *Journal of Peace Research* 44(6): 689–709.

Tadjoeddin, Mohammad Zulfan, Widjajanti I. Suharyo, and Satish Mishra. 2001. "Regional Disparity and Vertical Conflict in Indonesia." *Journal of the Asia Pacific Economy* 6(3): 283–304.

Tajima, Yuhki. 2004. Mobilizing for Violence: The Escalation and Limitation of Identity Conflicts; The Case of Lampung, Indonesia. Indonesian Social Development Paper no. 3. World Bank, Jakarta.

———. 2008. "Explaining Ethnic Violence in Indonesia: Demilitarizing Domestic Security." *Journal of East Asian Studies* 8(3): 451–72.

———. 2009. Order and Violence in Authoritarian Breakdowns: How Institutions Explain Communal Violence in Indonesia. PhD diss., Harvard University.

Tendler, Judith. 1997. *Good Government in the Tropics*. Baltimore: Johns Hopkins University Press.

———. 2000. "Why Are Social Funds so Popular?" In *Local Dynamics in an Era of Globalization*, ed. Shahid Yusuf, Weiping Wu, and Simon Evenett. New York: Oxford University Press, 114–29.

Terry, Fiona. 2002. *Condemned to Repeat? The Paradox of Humanitarian Action*. Ithaca: Cornell University Press.

Tilly, Charles. 1998. *Durable Inequality*. Berkeley: University of California Press.

Tirman, John. 2003. "The New Humanitarianism: How Military Intervention Became the Norm." *Boston Review*, December 2003–January 2004.

Toda, Dami. 1999. *Manggarai Mencari Pencerahan Historiografi*. Ende, Indonesia: Nusa Indah.

Toft, Monica Duffy. 2005. *The Geography of Ethnic Violence: Identity, Interests and the Indivisibility of Territory*. Princeton: Princeton University Press.

Tule, Philipus. 2000. "Religious Conflicts and a Culture of Tolerance: Paving the Way for Reconciliation in Indonesia." *Antropologi Indonesia* 63 (Sept.–Dec.): 92–108.

Unger, Jonathan. 2002. *The Transformation of Rural China*. New York: Sharpe.

United Nations. 2006. *Integrated Disarmament, Demobilization and Reintegration Standards*. http://www.unddr.org/iddrs/index.php.

United Nations Development Programme. 2002. *United Nations Human Development Report 2002: Deepening Democracy in a Fragmented World*. Oxford: Oxford University Press; New York: UNDP.

———. 2004. Indonesia: Decentralized Conflict Sensitive Planning and Development: An Assessment and Project Formulation Report. Mimeo, UNDP, Jakarta.

United States Agency for International Development. 2004. *Conducting a Conflict Assessment: A Framework for Strategy and Program Development*. Washington, D.C.: Office of Conflict Management and Mitigation, USAID.

Uvin, Peter. 1998. *Aiding Violence: The Development Enterprise in Rwanda*. West Hartford, Conn.: Kumarian.

———. 2002. "The Development/Peacebuilding Nexus: A Typology and History of Changing Paradigms." *Journal of Peacebuilding and Development* 1(1): 5–24.

van Klinken, Gerry. 2007. *Communal Violence and Democratization in Indonesia: Small Town Wars*. London: Routledge.

Varshney, Ashutosh. 2002. *Ethnic Conflict and Civic Life: Hindus and Muslims in India*. New Haven: Yale University Press.

———. 2007. "Ethnicity and Ethnic Conflict." In *The Oxford Handbook of Comparative Politics*, ed. Charles Boix and Susan C. Stokes. Oxford: Oxford University Press, 274–96.

———. 2008. "Analyzing Collective Violence in Indonesia: An Overview." *Journal of East Asian Studies* 8(3): 341–59.

Varshney, Ashutosh, Mohammad Zulfan Tadjoeddin, and Rizal Panggabean. 2008. "Creating Datasets in Information-Poor Environments: Patterns of Collective Violence in Indonesia, 1990–2003." *Journal of East Asian Studies* 8(3): 361–94.

Verheijen, J. A. J. 1991. *Manggarai dan Wujud Tertinggi*. Jakarta: LIPI.

Vickers, Adrian. 2005. *A History of Modern Indonesia*. New York: Cambridge University Press.

von Lieres, Bettina. 2007. "Citizen Participation in South Africa: Land Struggles and HIV/AIDS Activism." In *Spaces for Change? The Politics of Citizen Participation in New Democratic Arenas*, ed., Andrea Cornwall and Vera Schattan P. Coelho. London: Zed, 226–39.

von Lieres, Bettina, and David Kahane. 2007. "Inclusion and Representation in Democratic Deliberations: Lessons from Canada's Romanow Commission." In *Spaces for Change? The Politics of Citizen Participation in New Democratic Arenas*, ed. Andrea Cornwall and Vera Schattan P. Coelho. London: Zed, 131–53.

Voss, John. 2008. *Impact Evaluation of the Second Phase of the Kecamatan Development Program in Indonesia*. Jakarta: World Bank.

Waiselfisz, Julio Jacobo. 2008. *Mapa da Violencia: Os Jovens da America Latina: 2008*. Brasilia: Institute Sangari.

Wallensteen, Peter, and Margaerta Sollenburg. 1998. "Armed Conflict and Regional Conflict Complexes: 1989–1997." *Journal of Peace Research* 35(5): 621–34.

Weinstein, Jeremy M. 2007. *Inside Rebellion: The Politics of Insurgent Violence*. New York: Cambridge University Press.

Welsh, Bridget. 2003. Street Justice: Vigilantism in West Java. Paper prepared for the Workshop on Contentious Politics, Columbia University, February.

———. 2008. "Local and National: Keroyakan Mobbing in Indonesia." *Journal of East Asian Studies* 8(3): 473–504.

Whiteside, Katherine, Michael Woolcock, and Xavier Briggs. 2005. Assessing the Impact of Social Development Projects: Integrating the Science of Evaluation and the Art of Practice. Mimeo, World Bank, Washington, D.C.

Wilkinson, Steven I. (2004). *Votes and Violence: Electoral Competition and Ethnic Riots in India*. Cambridge: Cambridge University Press.

Williams, John J. 2007. "Social Change and Community Participation: The Case of Health Facilities Boards in the Western Cape of Africa." In *Spaces for Change? The Politics of Citizen Participation in New Democratic Arenas*, ed. Andrea Cornwall and Vera Schattan P. Coelho. London: Zed, 95–113.

Williamson, John. 1989. "What Washington Means by Policy Reform." In *Latin American Adjustment: How Much Has Happened?* ed. John Williamson. Washington, D.C.: Institute for International Economics, 7–24.

———. 1994. *The Political Economy of Policy Reform*. Washington, D.C.: Institute for International Economics.

Wilson, Ian Douglas. 2002. The Politics of Inner Power: The Practice of Pencak Silat in West Java. PhD diss., Murdoch University, Perth.

Wilson, William Julius. 2009. *More Than Just Race: Being Black and Poor in the Inner City*. New York: Norton.

Wiyata, A. Latief. 2002. *Carok: Konflik Kekerasan dan Harga Diri Orang Madura*. Yogyakarta: LKiS.

Wolf, Eric. 1964. *Anthropology*. Englewood Cliffs: Prentice-Hall.

———. 1969. *Peasant Wars of the Twentieth Century*. New York: Harper and Row.

———. 1999. *Envisioning Power: Ideologies of Dominance and Crisis*. Berkeley: University of California Press.

Wong, Susan. 2003. Indonesia's Kecamatan Development Program: Building a Monitoring and Evaluation System for a Large-Scale Community-Driven Development Program. Discussion Paper, Environment and Social Development Unit, East Asia and Pacific Region, World Bank, Washington, D.C.

Woodhouse, Andrea. 2005. Village Corruption in Indonesia: Fighting Corruption in the World Bank's Kecamatan Development Program. Indonesian Social Development Paper no. 6. World Bank, Jakarta.

Woolcock, Michael. 1998. "Social Capital and Economic Development: Toward a Theoretical Synthesis and Policy Framework." *Theory and Society* 27(2): 151–208.

———. 2009a. "The Next Ten Years in Development Studies: From Modernization to Multiple Modernities, in Theory and Practice." *European Journal of Development Research* 21(1): 4–9.

———. 2009b. "Toward an Economic Sociology of Chronic Poverty: Enhancing the Rigor and Relevance of Social Theory." In *Poverty Dynamics: Interdisciplinary Perspectives*, ed. Tony Addison, David Hulme, and Ravi Kanbur. New York: Oxford University Press, 348–68.

———. 2009c. "Toward a Plurality of Methods in Project Evaluation: A Contextualised Approach to Understanding Impact Trajectories and Efficacy." *Journal of Development Effectiveness* 1(1): 1–14.

Woolcock, Michael, Simon Szreter, and Vijayendra Rao. Forthcoming. "How and Why Does History Matter for Development Policy?" *Journal of Development Studies*.

World Bank. 1998. Post-Conflict Reconstruction Precis no. 189. Operations Evaluation Department, World Bank, Washington, D.C.

———. 2002. Back to Office Report: KDP Supervision Mission and Assessment of Social Service Delivery. Mimeo, World Bank Office, Jakarta.

———. 2003. *World Development Report 2004: Making Services Work for Poor People.* New York: Oxford University Press.

———. 2004. *Village Justice in Indonesia: Case Studies on Access to Justice, Village Democracy and Governance.* Jakarta: World Bank.

———. 2005a. *Conflict Analysis Framework.* Washington, D.C.: World Bank.

———. 2005b. *World Development Report 2006: Equity and Development.* New York: Oxford University Press.

———. 2008. *Forging the Middle Ground: Engaging Non-State Justice in Indonesia.* Jakarta: World Bank.

———. 2009. Issue Note: Effective Poverty Reduction in Fragile and Conflict Affected Countries: Lessons and Suggestions. Mimeo.

World Commission on Dams. 2000. *Dams and Development: A New Framework for Decision-Making.* Cape Town: World Commission on Dams.

Zoellick, Robert B. 2008. "Fragile States: Securing Development." Speech given to the Institute for Strategic Studies, Geneva, 12 September.

Index